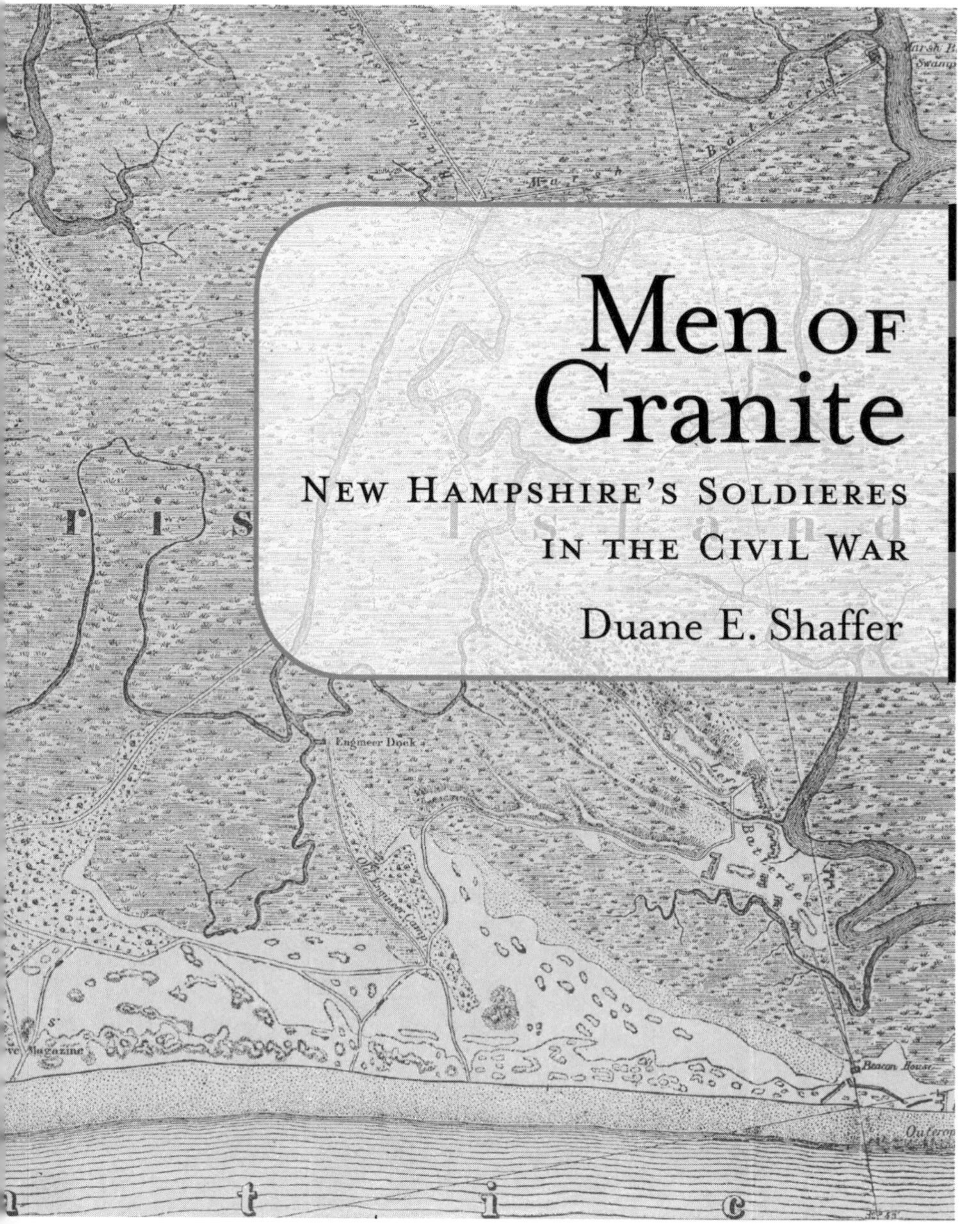

Men of Granite

New Hampshire's Soldieres in the Civil War

Duane E. Shaffer

The University of South Carolina Press

© 2008 University of South Carolina

Published by the University of South Carolina Press
Columbia, South Carolina 29208

www.sc.edu/uscpress

Manufactured in the United States of America

17 16 15 14 13 12 11 10 09 08   10 9 8 7 6 5 4 3 2 1

Library of Congress Cataloging-in-Publication Data

Shaffer, Duane E., 1954–
  Men of granite : New Hampshire's soldiers in the Civil War / Duane E. Shaffer.
    p. cm.
  Includes bibliographical references and index.
  ISBN 978-1-57003-751-1 (cloth : alk. paper)
  1. New Hampshire—History—Civil War, 1861–1865. 2. New Hampshire—History—
Civil War, 1861–1865—Regimental histories. 3. United States—History—Civil War,
1861–1865—Regimental histories. 4. United States—History—Civil War, 1861–1865—
Campaigns. I. Title.
  E520.4.S53 2008
  973.7'42—dc22

                                                                        2008013979

This book was printed on Glatfelter Natures, a recycled paper with 30 percent
postconsumer waste content.

Dedicated to my historical woman,
Holly, dear loving helpmate,
I love you more.

CONTENTS

ILLUSTRATIONS

Maps

PREFACE

It was my good fortune after graduate school that I was able to live for a short time in Gettysburg, Pennsylvania. I had become a historian, my love of history coming from my father, a navy veteran and an engineer. We lived in Pittsburgh, and every year he took the family on vacation to all of his favorite spots, which were always historic places like Harrisburg, Hershey, Gettysburg, and Valley Forge, Pennsylvania. At Gettysburg, I asked my father many specific questions about the American Civil War. He was able to answer all of them to my satisfaction except one: Why?

This question has perplexed Americans and historians for generations, resulting in a plethora of books and magazines searching for the reasons such a catastrophe befell America. This book is not an attempt to explain why the Civil War happened or to describe it in its entirety. The current volume focuses on the stories of the New Hampshire soldiers themselves so that we can better appreciate their part in the greater struggle. The book is, I hope, as balanced an account as possible of the role of New Hampshire in the Civil War. The story is told through the experiences of the common soldier, whose companions were lice-infested clothes, weevil-ridden hardtack, and numbing fear.

Like so many families during the war, my great-grandfather's family who lived in Frederick, Maryland, was torn in two, not because of vague ideological notions but because issues like unionism and state's rights were of critical and very real importance to them. From the beginning of the war, the soldiers from New Hampshire fought to preserve the Union, the reason most often given in the soldiers' letters as to why they joined the army. Becoming a volunteer soldier meant leaving farms or factories for a horrifying experience for which they had no preparation. Wives, friends, parents, and siblings from Dixville to Derry had to say good-bye to husbands, fathers, sons, brothers, and friends, knowing that they might not return home. The only links to their loved ones were occasional letters from the front, newspapers, and casualty lists at the post office.

New Hampshire's sons served in the war in about the same ratios as the sons of the mid-Atlantic states and the Midwest. The 1860 census counted 326,064 people in New Hampshire; Published figures of men who served vary from 32,000 to 37,000. Using the average of these two numbers, 35,000, approximately 11 percent of the New Hampshire population went off to war. During the war, the state raised seventeen regiments of infantry, two cavalry regiments, three artillery batteries, and three companies of sharpshooters and sent men to the navy, marines, and other organizations. Like many of the Northern states, because of an antiquated militia system, New Hampshire was unprepared for war. Part of New Hampshire's fascinating story is how quickly it was able to muster regiments and put them into the field.

New Hampshire's casualties were also proportionate to the other northern states. About forty-eight hundred men died, and another five thousand were wounded, which roughly accounts for 25 percent of the men who served. New Hampshire soldiers fought in most of the large battles, including the sanguinary clashes at Second Bull Run, Antietam, and Gettysburg, which all produced long casualty lists of the Granite Staters. The sorrows of war were visited upon the hearths of the rich and poor alike. Small towns, however, such as, Raymond, Epping, and New Durham suffered—at war's end twenty-five to thirty percent of its sons were gone.

From 1985, the first time I came to New Hampshire, whose nickname is the Granite State, I wanted to write a book about the state's role in the American Civil War; just like the larger states, New Hampshire has its share of stories, heroes, and deserters. Until 2004, I crisscrossed the state several times giving presentations to local historical societies and gathering valuable information along the way, and that year I decided it was time for me to get started on a book. The first step was sending out two hundred surveys to the state's libraries, historical societies, and other institutions inquiring if they had any primary source material in their collections on their town's role in the war. Richard Winslow, my friend and historical advisor, correctly predicted that 25 percent of the surveys would be returned and that perhaps half would have useful information. I spent the next two years researching that information and the sources at the New Hampshire Historical Society as well as the state's colleges and universities. Two file cabinets of information later, I began the overwhelming work of deciding what to use. The stack of my note cards for cataloging became over eight inches thick. In 2001, with my outline at my side, I began writing; two years later I finished this book. The first chapter of *Men of Granite* examines New Hampshire's place in the American historical experience of the first half of the nineteenth century. The remaining chapters are a chronological treatment of the war told mainly through primary sources.

Statistical information regarding individual soldiers may be found in the rosters of the New Hampshire regimental histories available in public and academic libraries in New Hampshire. Readers seeking more information about New Hampshire's colonels can consult either the specific regimental history or *Colonels in Blue: The New England States* by Roger D. Hunt.

My interest in New Hampshire's role in the Civil War is ongoing, so I invite and encourage you to write to me at duaneshaffer@earthlink.net with any comments, questions, or stories you may have about the soldiers from New Hampshire. New sources, including letters and diaries, are out there to be discovered. I hope that they will also be published, thereby increasing our understanding of New Hampshire's role in the American Civil War.

ACKNOWLEDGMENTS

When the library surveys began trickling in from across the state of New Hampshire, I knew that the task ahead of me was not going to be a singular effort but one involving many people. Several people figured prominently in the production of this book, and I would like to recognize them for their time, help, and guidance.

This book could never have seen the light of day without the help of my wonderful wife, Holly. She was a steadfast influence as well as my chief research assistant, transcriber, reader, detective, and critic. "Condense, Duane, condense" was her constant refrain when I would stray too far from the topic.

Naval historian Richard Winslow of Portsmouth, New Hampshire, read the text for historical accuracy. Dick, a tireless researcher, is also an author and a longtime friend, who, although he is constantly busy, will always take the time to help with historic research. The Reverend Roland Kimball of Newmarket, New Hampshire, edited the text for punctuation and grammar and added many helpful comments. He taught me a new appreciation for the punctuation keys on the right side of the keyboard.

David Smolen from the New Hampshire Historical Society Library was instrumental in providing access to the large number of manuscripts. He was very patient with all our questions, and because of us, he has memorized the exact location of the George F. Towle and Daniel Eldredge collections. Bill Ross from the University of New Hampshire gave good advice on the use of the manuscripts of the Douglas and Helena Milne Special Collections. I hope he likes the sections on Louis Bell and the Fourth New Hampshire.

Research assistant Lindsey Fogg and her amazing typing skills were very helpful in the production of the bibliography. Technical assistant Ashley Fogg helped me with some rather difficult computer problems. Jeremy Fogg deserves special mention for his help in procuring many of the historical photographs in this book.

Other individuals who contributed to this work are: David Arends, Nathalie Ball, Russell Bastedo, Mrs. Kendall Chase, Lydia Frink, Sarah Hartwell, Cornella Jenness, Cynthia Allard Mendez, Barbara Myers, Veda O'Neill, Jim Perkins, Chris Pratt, Bob Randall, Fred Soucy, Matthew Thomas, Ed Wentworth, Madelyn Williamson, and Roberta Wingerson.

Special acknowledgement is here given to Ken Leidner and the New Hampshire Veterans Association. The NHVA generously gave its permission to use the majority of the photographs in the book. Ken is the undisputed leader in the field of conservation and preservation of New Hampshire's history and priceless heritage.

Thanks are owed to the following libraries and institutions for placing their resources at my disposal: Alton Historical Society, Boscawen Historical Society, Bowdoin College Library, Chesterfield Historical Society, Civil War Roundtable of the New Hampshire Library, Concord Public Library, Curtis Library, Dartmouth Library, Dover Public Library, Francestown Historical Society, Harvey-Mitchell Memorial Library, Laconia Public Library, Langdon Public Library, Moultonborough Public Library, New Durham Public Library, New Hampshire Antiquarian Society, New Hampshire Historical Society, New Hampshire State Library, Newington Historical Society, Newmarket Public Library, Ossipee Historical Society, Peterborough Historical Society, Rochester Public Library, and the Strawbery Banke Library.

I would like to thank my mother, Louise Shaffer, for buying me a book every time we went downtown.

Finally, I would like to thank my feline writing assistants: my beloved WeeGee and Wimsey, who are waiting for me at the Rainbow Bridge, and Harriet and Buzzy, who helped me pass the seemingly endless hours of writing, editing, and footnoting.

MEN OF GRANITE

Introduction

The men from New Hampshire who would fight and die in the coming War of Rebellion were born in a time of sweeping social, political, and technological changes. New Hampshire historian James Duane Squires articulates the effect of these transformations on the people of New Hampshire in the nineteenth century: "It is one of the persistent illusions of every generation that the changes in the pattern of daily living which it witnesses are the most extreme in history. This conviction was held by New Hampshire folk in the first half of the nineteenth century. . . . When the century dawned, men lived, traveled and communicated with each other in a way that would have been entirely comprehensible by Julius Caesar. Sixty years later the pattern had been so changed that no man living before the nineteenth century could have understood it."[1]

In the early to mid–nineteenth century, New Hampshire residents farmed and worked in manufacturing. Subsistence farming had been a way of life since the state was settled in the early 1600s. Farmers lived on $10 a year. By 1850 the sons of those farmers needed $100 a year to survive. The thirty thousand farms in the state were mostly self-sufficient and produced such basic crops as potatoes, wheat, and corn.[2]

Although New Hampshire farmers had been cultivating the sandy and rocky land for one hundred thirty years, the majority of the state was still heavily wooded. The state produced large supplies of apples, grapes, and even ice for export. The average New Hampshire farmer had an apple orchard that could yield as much income as all the rest of assets combined. He made his living not only by farming crops but also by livestock and dairy farming.[3]

The Industrial Revolution, which had already swept through Europe, was slowly making its way into New Hampshire and with it came the inevitable division of labor. With the increase of immigration from 1820 to 1850, urbanization of the towns and cities of New Hampshire began to accelerate. The effect of industrialization on New Hampshire was that "the steam engine, the harnessing of electricity, the introduction of coal gas, and new kinds of oil, the putting into practical use of countless new types of machines and mechanical contrivances—all resulted in changes in the social order unprecedented in human history."[4]

Before the Civil War, New Hampshire was considered one of the most educated and progressive regions of the country. The state's seacoast and shining granite mountains covered with verdant pine whispered great promise for the small state. New Hampshire's lands had been overfarmed and depleted, but the rise of her logging industry and mills allowed the state to gradually enter the industrial age. Changes also occurred with the once-grand tradition of the state militia. The militia system had been abandoned because of overlegislation, thereby making the state woefully unprepared for the great collision that was to come.

After the American Revolution, slavery was no longer an economically viable system in New Hampshire. The northern slave owners freed their slaves or sold them south, thus spreading the dark stain of slavery into other regions of the young country. The population of the state jumped from 82,000 during the time of the American Revolution to nearly 200,000 in 1800 when only eight slaves were recorded in the entire state. In 1840 only one slave was listed, and she lived in Hollis.[5]

Moral objection against slavery was first recorded in the state of New Hampshire in 1796 when the Joseph Whipple, customs collector, in Portsmouth, replied to a letter from President George Washington, who was requesting the return of a runaway female slave. In a letter Whipple stated that returning the slave was impossible because the sentiments of the public were too strong.

The antislavery movement began in Boston in 1831 when William Lloyd Garrison founded the antislavery newspaper the *Liberator.* Individuals with strong moral convictions against slavery began spreading the word in New Hampshire as well,[6] and several newspapers followed the *Liberator,* including the *Herald of Freedom* in 1838, edited by Nathaniel Peabody Rogers of Plymouth, New Hampshire.

The early abolitionist movement in New Hampshire met with extreme resistance. In 1835 in the town of Canaan, New Hampshire abolitionists established a school for both black and white students in an integrated environment. On August 10, 1835, the townspeople opposed to having such a school in their midst gathered ninety-five yoke of oxen, uprooted the school, and tried to haul it to the edge of town. The chains broke. Men were sent to the nearby Shaker community of Enfield for bigger chains. They succeeded in moving the school to the edge of the town square but no farther. The heat was overpowering so the effort was postponed for a month. When the work parties resumed, the building was hauled to a swamp at the edge of the town.[7]

An outspoken advocate of abolition in New Hampshire was Stephen Symonds Foster of Canterbury, who began orating on the abolition issue in 1841 in the middle of church services at the Old North Church in Concord. Claiming the right to be heard, Foster exhorted against the evils of slavery. He was physically ejected from several churches and was imprisoned ten to twelve times in New Hampshire and Massachusetts. Nathaniel Rogers and the poet John Greenleaf Whittier, who was a Quaker, began to emulate his example.[8]

The Underground Railroad maintained houses in Canaan, Canterbury, Concord, and Milford, New Hampshire, and operated alongside unofficial houses such as those in Epping and Exeter. Of the thirty-two hundred operators nationwide in the Underground Railroad system, at least eighty are identified as clergymen in the northern states. The homes of Sawyer and Moses Cartland served as stations in the Underground Railroad. Moses Sawyer, a Quaker who with his friend Thomas Folsom ran a safe house in Epping for runaway slaves, made the acquaintance of Whittier.[9] Frederick Douglass wrote his autobiography while staying at the Moses Sawyer home in Weare, New Hampshire. In 1842 Douglass stimulated awareness of the slavery issue by speaking in towns and cities throughout New Hampshire and again in 1944 spoke throughout New Hampshire but found the state "less receptive to the message than Massachusetts and found resistance to borrowing or renting halls."[10]

In 1844 the crisis with the annexation of Texas to the United States propelled the antislavery movement to the national stage. The chief opponent of President John Tyler's proposal to add Texas was Representative John Parker Hale of Dover, New Hampshire. Hale, a Federalist who left his party to become a Democrat, wrote to prominent citizens and politicians in the state that annexing Texas would encourage the spread of slavery. Franklin Pierce, the recognized head of the Democratic Party in New Hampshire who later became the fourteenth U.S. president, immediately opposed him.

Hale's bold resistance inspired Whittier to pen the poem "New Hampshire 1845."

> God Bless New Hampshire-from her Granite Peaks,
> once more the voice of Stark and Langdon speaks.
> The long-bound vassal of the exulting South,
> for very shame her self-forged chain has broken.
> Torn the black seal of slavery from her mouth
> and in the clear tones of her old times spoken.[11]

Because of Hale's agitation on the Texas issue, Pierce pressured the party into dropping him from the Democratic ticket in the next election. Trying to consolidate the Democratic Party, Pierce made speeches throughout southern New Hampshire, stating, "We must throw overboard Mr. Hale or we will lose favor with Southern men." Pierce was prepared to condemn Hale in order to keep a steady supply of Southern cotton flowing to New Hampshire's growing textile

JOHN PARKER HALE. *Born in 1806, Hale was a lawyer and congressman from Dover, New Hampshire. One of the abolitionist movement's earliest leaders, he opposed the annexation of Texas in 1845 and was the Free-Soil Party candidate for president in 1852. Photograph courtesy of Russell Bastedo and N.H. Division of Historical Resources*

mills. Amos Tuck of Exeter said he would resign the party if the party expelled Hale.[12] President Tyler annexed Texas on March 1, 1845, which, with the provocative actions of the following administration under James Knox Polk, made war between the United States and Mexico a certainty.[13]

New Hampshire's role in the war with Mexico was minimal with one important exception. Pierce, named colonel of the Ninth Regiment of the United States Army and serving with Winfield Scott, was present for all the battles of the war, including the storming of the castle of Chapultepec. Pierce eventually was promoted to brigadier general but because of a severe injury received at the

Battle of Contreras in September 1847 was discharged in 1848. The Mexican War proved to be unpopular with the people of New Hampshire, and in 1846, the legislature voted down a resolution approving the war. A similar resolution was passed by only a slim margin the following year.[14]

The annexation crisis and eventual split of the Democratic Party led to Amos Tuck of Exeter and John L. Hayes of Portsmouth founding the Independent Democratic Party. This weakening of the Democratic Party allowed the Whigs in 1846 to capture the governor's seat in New Hampshire. Though strange political bedfellows, the Whigs and Independent Democrats cooperated on a number of issues, the election of Hale to the U.S. Senate in 1847 being their primary goal. Hale's election was by far the single greatest political victory of the New Hampshire antislavery movement to date. The strange coalition led by Tuck resulted in a short time in the founding of the Republican Party.[15]

During the 1849 Congressional session, Representative James Wilson of Keene made this statement on the growing crisis over secession and slavery: "Gentlemen need not talk to me or frighten me, by thoughts about the dissolution of the Union. I do not permit myself to talk or even think about the dissolution of the Union; very few northern men do. We all look on such a thing as impossible. But, sir, if the alternative shall be presented to me of the extension of slavery, of the dissolution of the Union, I would say, rather than extend slavery, let the Union, aye, the Universe be dissolved. Never, never, will I raise my hand or my voice to give a vote by which slavery can or may be extended."[16]

Daniel Webster's support of the Compromise of 1850, which promised to uphold the Fugitive Slave Laws, caused an avalanche of criticism from the abolitionist radicals of the North. Whittier responded with his poem "Ichabod," which decried Webster's support of the Compromise.

> So fallen! So lost!
> The light withdrawn which once he wore!
> The glory from those gray hairs gone forevermore!
> Then pay the reverence of old days to his dead fame;
> walk backward with averted gaze, and hide the shame![17]

In 1850 New Hampshire's population was over 317,000, with Manchester, its largest city, numbering 13,932. Residents of Concord were happy that the telegraph, the invention by one-time New Hampshire resident Samuel Morse, had finally reached them and that Concord coaches could reach most parts of the state.[18] Prosperity was measured by vocational diversity and the proximity of the railroad making its way north. The coming of the railroad meant that New Hampshire could take to market its lumber, one of its greatest resources, and that merchants could order goods from Boston and have them on the shelves within a week.[19]

In 1851 America, still in the glow of compromise, for the first time in years felt optimistic about the future. But in 1852 New Hampshire was stunned by its loss of the Democratic favorite for president, native son Levi Woodbury, who died in September.[20] *Uncle Tom's Cabin,* published that year, was gaining nationwide attention. Also finally published that year was *Northwood,* a novel extolling the virtues of life in the north, written in 1827 by Sara Josepha Hale of Newport, who founded *Godey's Lady's Book.*[21]

The country's respite ended also in 1852, yet another election year when all the old problems again were brought to the national stage. The Democratic Convention opened in Baltimore on June 1, 1852, with a broad range of nominees. The 288 delegates from the thirty-one states adopted the rule that the nominee of the party must have the support of two-thirds of the delegates. None of the convention favorites—James Buchanan of Pennsylvania, Lewis Cass, formerly from Exeter but now from the Michigan Territory, or Stephen Douglas of Illinois—could garner the needed majority. Although New Hampshire's favorite son Franklin Pierce was not at the convention, his advocates were, and after the thirty-fifth indecisive ballot, they put his name forward as a dark-horse candidate. On the forty-ninth ballot, Pierce won his party's nomination with 282 votes. Pierce, already dubbed "Young Hickory from the Granite Hills," was in Massachusetts on June 5 when he was informed of his nomination. His wife, Jane, was less than enthusiastic.

The Free-Soil Party convention was held in Pittsburgh in August 1852. Two thousand delegates gathered in the oppressive heat at Pittsburgh's Masonic Hall to nominate their candidate. Former Farmington, New Hampshire, resident Henry Wilson was the convention president. The theme of the convention was one of opposition to compromise and slavery, with one placard stating, "NO COMPROMISE WITH SLAVEHOLDERS OR DOUGHFACES." Doughfaces were politicians who were seen to be either soft on slavery or too eager to cater to Southern political and economic interests. The convention nominated Hale on the first ballot with 192 of 208 votes; George W. Julian of Indiana was chosen as his running mate. Pierce and Hale, once the best of friends, were now playing out their political feud on the national stage.[22] In New Hampshire, one of the largest political rallies in the nineteenth century was held for Pierce in his hometown of Hillsborough, with over twenty-five thousand people in attendance.

On October 24, Daniel Webster died at his Green Harbor homestead on October 24, with his last words being "I still live." He is buried in the Marshfield, Massachusetts, cemetery, his grave marked by a simple granite block. Clay and Calhoun were already gone, and with the passing of Webster, the voices of compromise were lost.[23]

Election Day was close, but both major candidates had studiously avoided the issues. Whig candidate Winfield Scott further weakened his party by suggesting

FRANKLIN PIERCE. *Born in Hillsborough, New Hampshire, in 1804, Pierce was a leading Democrat in the state. Known as "The Young Hickory of the Granite Hills," he become the fourteenth president of the United States and served from 1853 to 1857. Photograph courtesy of Russell Bastedo and N.H. Division of Historical Resources*

that he might consider amendments to the Fugitive Slave laws. Pierce, who had a genial personality, pledged to support the Compromise of 1850 and promised to respect the rights of states.

Pierce won the electoral vote with 254 votes to Scott's 42. Scott and his Whig party carried only Vermont, Massachusetts, Kentucky, and Tennessee. Pierce received 1,601,474 votes, and Scott garnered 1,386,580. The next runner-up was Hale with 167,000 votes. Although receiving a majority of the electoral vote, Pierce was not given a popular mandate and was actually in the minority in many of the Northern states. Some Americans were dismayed that a virtually unknown Democrat from New Hampshire had defeated the popular Scott.[24] Pierce's Whig opponents maintained during the campaign that because of his inexperience he was unfit for office. A prominent Whig from Boston, Richard Dana, stated that Pierce was "a doughface militia colonel and a state politician."

Before Pierce could assume the presidency, a personal tragedy occurred that would have a profound impact. On January 6, 1853, the Pierce family was returning to Concord from a funeral in Boston when the train jumped the tracks near Andover and crashed. The only child of the president-elect, eleven-year-old Benjamin, was crushed to death before his eyes.[25]

Pierce traveled alone to his inauguration with a heavy heart to Washington. He had left his grief-stricken wife behind but would eventually send for her. On March 4, 1853, Young Hickory arrived at the East Portico of the Capitol to take the oath of office. The fourteenth president of the United States became the only president in American history for religious reasons "to affirm" rather than "swear" the oath administered by Chief Justice Roger Taney. Pierce opened his inaugural address: "It is a relief to feel that no heart but my own can know the personal regret and bitter sorrow over which I have been borne to a position so suitable for others rather than desirable for myself."[26]

The new president discussed the issues of expansion, the balance between federal and state's rights, slavery, and his fears over disunion: "With the Union my best and dearest earthly hopes are entwined. Without it what are we individually or collectively? . . . I fervently hope that the question is at rest, and that no sectional or ambitious or fanatical excitement may again threaten the durability of our institutions."[27]

Finally Pierce talked about the constitutional protection of slavery: "I believe that involuntary servitude, as it exists in different States of the Confederacy, is recognized by the Constitution. I believe that it stands like any other admitted right, and that the states where it exists are entitled to efficient remedies to enforce the constitutional provisions. I hold that the laws of 1850, commonly called the 'compromise measures' are strictly constitutional and to be unhesitatingly carried into effect."[28]

Pierce began his presidency with his confidence shattered by personal tragedy. Mrs. Pierce became obsessed with the notion that God had punished them through the death of their son. Jane Pierce went into seclusion and never appeared publicly again. Her place was taken at state functions by her relative and companion Abigail Means.[29] The assumption of the presidency by the Democrats marked the end of their long campaign to regain control from the Whigs and Zachary Taylor. In New Hampshire the Democratic Party was again on the rise, and old grudges were being settled. Charles Atherton replaced John Parker Hale in the U.S. Senate in 1852, and Amos Tuck was ousted in the congressional elections.

Tuck returned to Exeter, a discouraged but not a beaten man. To him the path was now clear. The Whig party had collapsed, and there was no party strong

Amos Tuck. *Born in Parsonfield, Maine, in 1810, Tuck became a leading Free-Soil and Whig politician in New Hampshire. He is widely regarded as one of the founding fathers of the Republican Party. Photograph courtesy of Exeter Historical Society*

enough to challenge the power of the Democrats. Tuck, determined to found a new party composed of all the remnants that had once opposed the Democrats, called an organizational meeting at Blake's Tavern in Exeter. Fourteen members representing Whigs, Independent Democrats, and Know-Nothings met on October 12, 1853. Included in their number were Hale, William Plumer Jr. of Epping, George C. Fogg of Gilmanton, and Asa McFarland of Concord. Because the meeting was held secretly, there were no official minutes recorded, and nothing was published in any of the newspapers, but Tuck did suggest that the new, united party call itself the Republican Party. Soon after the meeting, Dr. Daniel Batchelder, who had been in attendance, related the story to newspaper editor Horace Greeley, who was visiting his native town of Amherst, New Hampshire. Greeley, in June 1854 wrote an editorial in the *New York Tribune* endorsing the name "Republican" for the new party. Similar meetings held in Wisconsin and elsewhere did not convene until 1854, so it can be said with certainty that the Republican Party was indeed founded in Exeter, New Hampshire, in October 1853.[30]

The Know-Nothing, also called the American Party, used Pierce's appointment of James Campbell, a Catholic, as his postmaster general to attack the administration. Another boost for this party came with the visit in 1853 of the Papal Nuncio Monsignor Gaetano Bedini. From then on the Know-Nothings would be a continuous source of anxiety for Pierce in both Washington and at home in New Hampshire.[31]

Wishing to immediately gain laurels for his administration, Pierce sent James Gadsden to Mexico to settle a border dispute remaining from the end of the Mexican War. Mexico agreed to sell thirty thousand acres of land (now most of southern Arizona and part of New Mexico) for $15 million. This would have been a political coup for Pierce had not Sen. Stephen Douglas of Illinois introduced the Kansas-Nebraska Act. Pierce would inevitably see his plan passed but at a dreadful cost to both his presidency and the country. Douglas's plan, which began with a progressive dream of building a railroad to the Pacific Ocean, would instead exacerbate sectional tension. After a fierce debate, the Kansas-Nebraska Act passed by a margin of 113 to 100 in the House; and the Senate passed it 35 to 13 on May 24, 1854. Northerners were outraged that all the work of compromise of the past thirty-five years had been undone.[32]

Trouble began in March 1855 when the workers at the Amoskeag Manufacturing Company in Manchester marched in protest over long working hours. The average wage of a New Hampshire worker in the 1850s was $205 per year, $9 above the national average. Still, with twelve- to fourteen-hour workdays, workers felt that wages were not keeping pace with the demands placed upon them.[33]

The face of New Hampshire politics changed drastically in these years. Ralph Metcalf, the Know-Nothing Party candidate, was elected governor. The Whigs, Know-Nothings, and Free-Soilers were in control of the General Court but had not banded together fully under the Republican banner. Governor Metcalf and his Know-Nothings were staunchly antislavery men and champions of the temperance movement. The governor recommended and the legislature passed a tough law prohibiting the sale of liquor. Metcalf endorsed the law: "The welfare and prosperity of the state demand it, our social and domestic relations demand it, morals and religion demand it . . . and patriotism demands it."[34]

The opposition of the Know-Nothings was still the Democrats, and the organ that chiefly held the Know-Nothings to account was the Democratic, Concord-based *New Hampshire Patriot & State Gazette*. In the July 18, 1855, issue, the paper attacked the "Reform" legislature and promised, "It will be our duty to review the proceedings of this body and to expose to the people its misdoings and shortcomings."[35] There was a New Hampshire Democrat in the White House, but the gains of the Know-Nothings and the unraveling of the Democratic Party had significantly weakened the latter's power in New Hampshire. In June the New Hampshire General Court appointed Hale to the U.S. Senate.[36]

July was also an important month because of the appointment of Joseph C. Abbott of Concord as state adjutant general to oversee the level of military preparedness in the state, the lack of which can be directly traced to the state's failed militia system.[37] In the early nineteenth century, New Hampshire had a respected militia system that had grown since the American Revolution. The old militia system comprised forty-two regiments drawn up in eight brigades

in four divisions. One example was the Thirty-third Regiment, which was composed of men from the towns of New Durham, Alton, Milton, Middleton,
Brookfield, and South Conway.[38] The regimental muster that occurred in the fall
involved about one hundred men from six surrounding towns. There were
parades, food, liquor, auctions, and dancing but very little military discipline.
There was a sham battle, but the consumption of large amounts of food and
alcohol tended to turn these events into decidedly unmilitary affairs.[39] Enoch
Quimby Fellows, who later commanded two New Hampshire regiments in the
Civil War, described the militia as "barnyard cadets" because they were more
interested in show than in military discipline.

The average militia uniform was a blue or gray swallowtail coat, white pants
with a red stripe, bright brass buttons, and a large cap with a plume. The reten-
tion of some of these militia uniforms, which other states used as well, created a
great deal of confusion in the first battles of the Civil War, becoming such a
problem that regimental commanders instructed their men to wear cloth strips
of white or other colors around their arms to distinguish them from the
enemy.[40]

In 1847, 1848, and 1851 the New Hampshire legislature had tried to regulate
the militia, which was criticized not only by temperance advocates but also by
the participants themselves. During these years, regular training and regimental
musters began to fade. The militia days had provided enjoyment in a time when
people worked hard and had few diversions, but these gatherings had a serious
purpose, and "the abandonment of the muster days and the militia system left
New Hampshire totally unprepared for the Civil War."[41] In 1857 the militia system was changed by the legislature, which divided the state into six brigades and
three divisions.[42]

With the passing of the militia system, a number of citizens formed independent voluntary units for military instruction. At the beginning of the Civil War,
twelve such groups were throughout New Hampshire, including the Governor's
Horse Guard, which later became part of the First New Hampshire Cavalry in
the war and still exists. Other colorful names of volunteer groups were the
Mechanics Phalanx of Pittsfield, the Granite State Cadets of Nashua, and the
Gilmanton Artillery.[43]

Pierce hoped for renomination in 1856, but his connection with the crisis involving the Kansas-Nebraska Act precluded any chances of success. The Democrats would have to find someone else to carry their banner that year; the man
they chose was James Buchanan. Pierce left Washington with little sense of
accomplishment. He and his wife traveled and eventually returned to Concord.
Other than an embarrassing speech made on the State House lawn on July 4,
1863, in which Pierce predicted that the North could never win the war, the president sank into political obscurity. Franklin Pierce, New Hampshire's favorite son,

died in seclusion and was buried in Concord in October 1869, five years after the
death of his wife.[44]

Pierce's final message, which was read to Congress, was a virulent attack
against the Republican Party and all those whom he perceived as agitators. He
accused them of leading the country into "a furnace of strife." Under the guise
of freedom, Pierce said, the faction agitating for emancipation was not satisfied
with merely excluding slavery from the territories but wanted to destroy it in the
states as well. He told them that emancipation could only be purchased "at the
cost of burning cities, ravaged fields and slaughtered populations in a wild com-
plication of foreign, civil, and servile wars." It is astonishing that so much of
Pierce's prophecy came true in such a short time.[45]

In June, New Hampshire and other northern states passed personal liberty
laws, in direct defiance of the federal government. The laws gave fugitive slaves
the protection of the state courts and forbade state officers from participating in
the capture of runaway slaves. All blacks were given full citizenship status, and
black men were given the right to vote. New Hampshire had exercised its own
act of nullification in bypassing the federal fugitive-slave laws. The passing of the
personal liberty laws was expedited because of the evaporation of Democratic
and Know-Nothing power in New Hampshire.

The Republicans now controlled the state legislature and had been successful
in the reelection of all three of their congressmen.[46] The incumbent Republican
governor, William Haile, was reelected in 1858; Hale was returned for another
term in the U.S. Senate. The state also approved the construction of the Cog
Railway, which would run up the side of Mount Washington.[47] Representatives
George Fogg and Mason Tappan of New Hampshire were alarmed by the possibility of the annexation of Cuba by the United States and urged Hale to speak
out against it. Hale was personally convinced that Spain would never conclude
such a deal but mysteriously offered little resistance against the plan.[48]

The central event of 1860 was clearly the presidential election with its aftermath. However, things might have been different had Abraham Lincoln not come
to New Hampshire to visit his son at Phillips Exeter Academy. After the Lincoln-
Douglas debates, Lincoln began to receive invitations to speak outside of his
home state of Illinois. These invitations came from Ohio, New York, Pennsylvania, and his old friend Amos Tuck of New Hampshire. Lincoln still had no
aspirations for any office beyond that of senator and hoped to defeat Stephen
Douglas for his Senate seat from Illinois.

In 1859 Lincoln's oldest son, Robert Todd Lincoln, wanted to attend Harvard
but flunked the entrance examination. His father decided to send him to Phillips
Exeter Academy for a year of preparatory study before trying again for Harvard.
The father also felt that his son would be in good company with Tuck and his
Republican friends in New Hampshire.[49] In the fall of 1859, Lincoln agreed to

give a speech in New York City the following February and therefore decided to mix business with a visit to his son in Exeter. Because of his accommodating nature, Lincoln agreed to make eleven speeches in New England, four of which would be given in New Hampshire.[50]

On his way to New Hampshire, Lincoln gave his famous Cooper Union speech in New York on February 27, 1860. On that snowy evening, fifteen hundred influential New Yorkers crowded into the new hall to hear Lincoln give the speech that would be the pattern for the rest of his speeches that spring and eventually the platform of the Republican Party that year. The first half of his scholarly speech was a rebuttal of all the charges leveled against him by Douglas, and the second half was an address to the Southern people. In the latter section, he tried to allay the fears of the South that the Republican Party represented a threat to the Southern way of life.[51] Because of this masterful presentation, he became an instant favorite to deliver addresses in the upcoming-primary states of New Hampshire, Connecticut, and Rhode Island. Up to this time and well into the spring of 1860, the Republican favorite for president was still William H. Seward of New York.

Lincoln's first speech in New England was given in Providence, Rhode Island, on February 28. Lincoln then headed for New Hampshire and the long-awaited reunion with his son. Arriving in Exeter on Wednesday, February 29, Lincoln spent most of the afternoon and evening with Robert at Phillips Exeter. On the following morning, March 1, Lincoln set off for Concord via Lawrence, Massachusetts, for his first New Hampshire speech. Passing on the way through Manchester, New Hampshire's largest city at almost twenty-one thousand people, Lincoln and his son were joined by future governor Frederick Smyth, who implored Lincoln to speak in Manchester on his return trip.[52]

Lincoln spoke in Concord at the Phenix Hall on Main Street for over an hour. The hall was quiet, and Lincoln's effect on the audience was electrifying. On March 3, 1860, the *New Hampshire Statesman* said Lincoln's speech was "one of the most powerful, logical and compacted speeches to which it was ever our fortune to listen: an argument against the system of slavery and in defense of the position of the Republican Party. . . . We are not extravagant in the remark that a political speech of greater power has rarely, if ever, been uttered in the capital of New Hampshire." From Concord, Lincoln traveled back to Manchester where he spoke that evening. Smyth introduced him as "the next president of the United States." The Manchester *Daily Mirror* stated that Lincoln "displays more shrewdness, more knowledge of the masses of mankind than any public speaker we have heard."[53]

The reception of the audiences in Concord and Manchester made a definite impression on Lincoln. Prior to this time, he had been adamant in his belief that Seward would probably receive the Republican nomination and that he had not set his sights any higher than vice presidential. After these two speeches and his discussions with Smyth, an ex-mayor and strong party man from a large textile city, Lincoln began to consider his options for a run at the presidency.[54]

The next day, March 2, Lincoln toured various factories in Manchester and then set off for Dover, New Hampshire, again via Lawrence, Massachusetts. His speech in Dover was very similar to the Cooper Union one as well as his talks in Manchester and Concord. Lincoln's final speech was in Exeter on March 3. Lincoln stayed with his old friend and political colleague Amos Tuck.[55]

During his trip to New Hampshire, Lincoln had made four speeches to approximately six thousand people and spoken to and conferred with many of the people responsible for the founding of the Republican Party. Lincoln arrived in New Hampshire uncertain regarding his political future. When he left, he returned to Illinois with the newfound confidence based on the assurance of his New Hampshire political friends and backers that he could be a serious candidate for the presidency.

The delegates from New Hampshire who were to go to the Republican convention in Chicago were Edward H. Rollins as the chairman, Tuck, Benjamin Martin, Haile, and six others. The convention in May featured Seward, John C. Fremont, Salmon Chase, and Abraham Lincoln as serious candidates. No one garnered the necessary 233 votes to sustain a nomination on the first ballot. Seward led the pack but saw his lead slip in the second ballot. However, on the third and final ballot, Lincoln surged ahead, securing the nomination. All ten New Hampshire delegates eventually cast their votes for Lincoln. The Republican Party was now united behind a strong and charismatic leader. The Democratic Party was deeply divided over the issue of slavery, and its convention in Charleston, South Carolina, had ended with the complete rupture of the party.[56]

Interest in the election ran higher in the Southern states over the issue of what should be done if Lincoln actually won the election. Many of the Southern state legislatures called upon their governors to be ready to hold special conventions if Lincoln captured the presidency. As expected, none of the four candidates received a majority of the popular vote on Election Day 1860: Lincoln received 1,866,352 votes, Douglas 1,375,157, John C. Breckinridge 845,763, and Bell received 589,581. Fifteen states chose only Republican electors, so Lincoln received the majority of the Electoral College vote. Most of the Southern states opted for Breckinridge, who received the second highest number of Electoral College votes. Bell's votes were spread out among the sections, and he managed to carry three states: Virginia, Kentucky, and his native Tennessee. Excitement over the election waned in the North, but the result instantly threw the South into a panic.[57]

The results of the election in New Hampshire were proportionately higher for Lincoln. He received 37,519 votes, while Douglas, who was the only other presidential candidate to visit the state, garnered 25,881. Breckinridge, who was considered a Southern candidate, received 2,112 votes, while Bell ran a distant fourth with only 411. In Keene, New Hampshire, Lincoln garnered 635 votes, Douglas 244, Breckenridge 31, and Bell 5. Lincoln did not receive a mandate because his name did not appear on ballots in the South. The secession-minded legislatures of the South wasted no time in determining their course of action. South Carolina left the Union on December 20, 1860, with six more states following in the next two months.[58]

The country's worst fears were reality: the Union was threatened with division, and people in both sections pondered what was to come. Would the South be allowed to leave the Union and create a new country, or would the land be drenched in the blood of thousands to keep America under one flag? People in New Hampshire and the country at large turned to Washington and the inauguration of the man who would serve a deeply divided America.

By early 1861 the sections were alienated, North and South polarized on almost every issue. Two lifestyles had evolved with their own distinct cultures. The same language and the same faith bonded the country, but churches both North and South had differing interpretations of the will of God. Both sides became increasingly shrill in their denunciation of the other, with the South rapidly becoming the champion of states' rights and secession and the North standing for preservation of the Union and increasingly warming to the idea of restricting slavery. The two sections had grown so far apart in eighty years that they were now incapable of respecting or understanding each other. There were already two Americas even before South Carolina seceded.

All the compromising and competent statesmen who could have saved America were dead. The collision of the sections was now almost inevitable, and the horror of fratricidal war was about to engulf the country. The South welcomed the coming war as a chance to punish Yankee greed. On the other side the Mason-Dixon Line, it was believed that God was going to punish America for the abomination of slavery. New Hampshire, as well as the other northern states, waited and wondered if anything could save their country from the imminent disaster.

New Hampshire Responds to the National Crisis

Call back that morning with its lurid light,
When lips were mute and women's faces white,
as the pale cloud that out from Sumter rolled.

John Boyle O'Reilly, "At
Fredericksburg Dec. 13, 1862"

In December 1860, tension escalated in Charleston, South Carolina, when Major Robert Anderson moved his garrison from Fort Moultrie to Fort Sumter. This move caused more anger and frustration between South Carolina and President James Buchanan administration. The members of Buchanan's cabinet were split over Anderson's decision, prompting more resignations. Secretary of the Interior Jacob Thompson of Mississippi learned that Buchanan had dispatched the merchant vessel *Star of the West* to Charleston with troops and supplies. Thompson immediately telegraphed Charleston with news of the departure.[1] The *Star of the West* attempted to enter Charleston harbor on January 9, 1861, and a masked battery on the north end of Morris Island opened fire on the ship. Many of the shots missed, but two struck the vessel, causing it to turn back for New York.[2]

During January, Mississippi, Florida, Alabama, Georgia, and Louisiana also seceded. This action resulted in scores of federal forts and installations in the South falling into the hands of Confederate state militias. February began with feelings of confusion and frustration throughout the land. Amid the excitement of a peace conference in February 1861 in Washington, D.C., the state of Texas seceded.[3]

On the floor of the U.S. House of Representatives on February 5, 1861, Mason Weare Tappan of Bradford (he, Gilman Marston, and Thomas Edwards were all representatives)[4] delivered a memorable speech in which he expressed his fears for the Union: "If this government is a mere cobweb, with no power for its own preservation, it is utterly useless to try to tinker and patch it up by 'compromises.' If the Union is so utterly weak and helpless that the first breath of treason is sufficient to destroy its vitality, it will be good for nothing after it is saved, and the time spent in trying to save it will be worse than thrown away."[5] He offered advice for preserving the peace: "Firmness on the part of the Executive, and firmness and courage on the part of the people of the free States, is in my judgment, the best antidote for the insanity that prevails at the South."[6] Tappan summarized New Hampshire's position, "The people of New Hampshire are attached to this Union. . . . I believe the united voice of her people, irrespective of party, is for the 'Union as it is,' and our Constitution as our fathers made it. . . . New Hampshire was the ninth State—the last one required to complete the formation of the Union, and she will be the last to desert it in its hour of peril."[7] Tappan offered this prophecy for his country: "But I do not apprehend any serious collision. I do not believe that this land is to be drenched in the blood of fratricidal strife."[8]

In Concord, New Hampshire, Gov. Ichabod Goodwin[9] readied himself for the crisis he knew was coming. The Amoskeag Veterans and the Governor's Horse Guard were the only effective military organizations in the state.[10] Goodwin, a conservative businessperson and ex-Whig, sent Amos Tuck, Asa Fowler, and Levi Chamberlain to the peace conference in Washington, D.C., as representatives of New Hampshire. Goodwin was first elected in 1859 (governors then were elected for one-year terms). In his first message as governor, Goodwin emphasized New Hampshire's devotion to the preservation of the Union and the recognition of the rights of the states. He also stated that while those rights were recognized, New Hampshire would not accept the extension of slavery into free states.[11] Many in New Hampshire considered Goodwin a good choice for the position of secretary of the navy under Lincoln.[12]

On Saturday, February 9, Jefferson Davis was elected provisional president of the new Confederacy. Both presidents-to-be left their homes on February 11, 1861, to assume office in their respective national capitals.[13] Davis was inaugurated on February 18. Monday, March 4, 1861, was Abraham Lincoln's inauguration day. Many hoped Lincoln would break his silence, but his inaugural speech contained little in the way of new ideas for compromise or plans for dealing with the current secession crisis. The body of Lincoln's address was basically a statement on the inviolability of the Constitution and how he would uphold and enforce it. Referring to the act of secession directly, Lincoln stated, "Will you hazard so desperate a step while there is any possibility that any portion of the ills you fly from have no real existence? Will you, while the certain ills you fly to are greater than all the real ones you fly from, will you risk the commission of so fearful a mistake?"[14] Lincoln finished his inaugural address by asking for unity in the country, to be obtained through "the better angels of our nature." The entire address lasted thirty minutes, and then Chief Justice Roger B. Taney administered the oath of office.

On March 29, President Lincoln sent a naval squadron to Charleston, S.C., to aid Major Anderson at Fort Sumter. In order to confuse Confederate agents, false information was spread around Washington that Fort Sumter was being abandoned.[15] Captain John G. Foster from Nashua, New Hampshire, and a U.S. Army Corps of Engineers officer, had arrived at Fort Moultrie in November 1860 to make repairs and supervise other work on the harbor's defenses. When the U.S. garrison moved from Fort Moultrie to Fort Sumter on December 26, 1860, he was among those who made the transfer. As a corps of engineers officer, he did not serve under the direction of Major Anderson, the U.S. artillery officer who had commanded Fort Moultrie. Fort Sumter was a construction site and, therefore, under the jurisdiction of the U.S. Army Corps of Engineers and, therefore, Captain Foster. Because of the seriousness of the situation, Foster (and his command of two engineer officers and a group of civilian contractors) worked with Anderson. Part of Foster's job was to report to the Engineer's Headquarters in Washington, D.C. While it was not his responsibility to report on Southern militia movements, he, as a good officer, kept his superiors informed of the situation. In a message to his superiors on April 6, Captain Foster expressed skepticism over whether Fort Sumter could withstand a sustained attack.[16]

On April 6, President Lincoln sent state department clerk Robert S. Chew on a mission to South Carolina to inform Gov. Francis Pickens that an expedition was on the way to Charleston was to resupply Fort Sumter, not reenforce it. Chew was to explain to Pickens that if no force was used to stop the ships, no force would be used to reenforce the fort. Chew arrived in Charleston two days later and relayed Lincoln's message. Pickens's reaction was to order all forces in the Charleston area on immediate alert.[17] In his last dispatch from Fort Sumter, Captain Foster reported, "I am very busy and am doing all that can be done with the means dispensable."[18]

At precisely 4:30 A.M. on April 12, the Confederate batteries opened fire on Fort Sumter and for the next thirty-four hours battered the fort with their shells. Firing on April 13 was more accurate, and before long Anderson decided that the fort must be surrendered. Thousands of shells were fired, but no human lives were lost in this first engagement of the American Civil War. The only casualty of this engagement was a horse on the Confederate side. As soldiers were fond of saying at the beginning of a battle, "The ball had finally opened."[19]

Sixteen-year-old Elbridge J. Copp of Nashua, New Hampshire, was folding newspapers in the store owned by his brothers when the news came across the telegraph that Fort Sumter had been fired upon. Copp remembered that he was filled with intense excitement and an overwhelming desire to be a part of history. Older and wiser men in the Copp dry-goods store only shook their heads. Copp's uncle softly uttered, "We are going to have a terrible war."[20]

ADJUTANT ELBRIDGE J.
COPP, *Third New Hamp-
shire, Company F. Wounded
at both Drewry's Bluff and
Deep Bottom, Copp was
always close to the action. He
wrote his* Reminiscences of the
War of the Rebellion *in 1911.
Photograph from* Reminiscences
of the War of the Rebellion

On Saturday morning April 13, a rainy, overcast day, Concord received the news of the attack. Reactions varied between outrage and somber resignation. Only one subject was on the lips of New Hampshire citizens as they went to church the next day. Mass meetings were planned in cities and towns throughout the state to discuss how each locality would deal with the crisis.[21]

John Parker Hale, U.S. senator, had returned home to Dover after Lincoln's inauguration and was resting comfortably when the news was brought to him about Fort Sumter. Dover citizens implored Hale to speak to them. At a large meeting in Dover on Monday, April 15, he told them that if the secessionists were not defeated "then indeed have our Fathers lived and died to little purpose." When asked if he would give his services to the country, Hale replied in the affirmative and said, "I have no desire to outlive my country."[22]

The people of Dover then passed the following resolution: "Resolved, By the City Councils of Dover, that the sum of ten thousand dollars, or so much thereof as may be needed, be and is hereby appropriated for the benefit of the families of those who have responded, or shall respond to the call of their country."[23] That call was not long in coming as Abraham Lincoln proclaimed on the same day: "I, Abraham Lincoln . . . have thought fit to call forth the militia of the several states of the Union, to the aggregate number of seventy-five thousand, in order to suppress said combinations and to cause the laws to be duly executed."[24]

On Tuesday, April 16, Governor Goodwin sent the following letter to Joseph C. Abbott, adjutant and inspector general of the New Hampshire Militia: "Sir, The President of the United States having, in pursuance of the act of Congress approved February 28, 1795, called upon the State of New Hampshire for a regiment of militia, consisting of ten companies on infantry, to be held in readiness to be mustered into the service of the United States for the purpose of quelling insurrection and supporting the government."[25] Orders similar to Goodwin's were going out all across the North. In New Hampshire the negative effects of legislative tinkering with the militia system were now being felt. Goodwin later wrote, "When the Civil War broke out, there was no military organization in the State, except some few independent companies forming a regiment. Indeed there was little military interest. There was no course left to us but voluntary enlistment."[26]

Shortly after receiving Goodwin's letter of April 16, Abbott issued General Order No. 6, repeating Lincoln's proclamation and Goodwin's request for one regiment of infantry. In Hampton the militia unit known as the Winnacunnet Guards passed a resolution: "We the Winnacunnet Guards of Hampton, New Hampshire hereby volunteer our services to the Governor of this state and are ready to enter upon such duty as he may direct at notice." The militia company was added to the roster of men forming the First New Hampshire Volunteer Regiment.[27]

Men interested in volunteering for the New Hampshire regiment began eagerly searching for places to enlist. Two men visited a dry-goods store in Portsmouth and made inquiries about where they could enlist. One, an Irishman, had recently served in the English army; the other man had served in Texas. The Irishman stated that the American flag had at one time protected him, and now he was ready to return the favor.[28]

The adjutant general authorized the creation of twenty-eight recruitment centers in the state for enlisting those interested in serving in the three-month assignment in the regiment. The response of New Hampshire citizens was immediate and overwhelming. Between April 17 and 30, the recruitment centers enlisted 2,004 men. Over seven hundred came from the Concord, Dover, Manchester, and Keene areas. Militia companies, such as, the Abbott Guards, Cheshire Light Guards, and the Mechanics Phalanx, signed up as a whole unit. Men signed up from as far away as Lancaster, West Lebanon, and Claremont. A man from Littleton shouldered his musket and set off on his own to join the defenses around Washington. Three women without the benefit of disguise tried to enlist at one of the recruitment centers.[29] The ladies of Exeter called a meeting at the

Town Hall to make clothing for the troops. The Granite State Bank authorized a loan of $20,000 to the state for military purposes. Throughout New Hampshire, the popularity of Jefferson Davis was celebrated by burning or hanging him in effigy.[30]

The first blood shed in anger in the Civil War came on April 19, 1861, when, on their way to Washington, the Sixth Massachusetts Regiment collided with a crowd of secessionist protesters in Baltimore. Bricks were thrown, and shots exchanged, resulting in the death of four soldiers and nine civilians. Among the soldiers was eighteen-year-old Luther Ladd of Alexandria, New Hampshire, who, when the war began, had traveled to Massachusetts and enlisted for nine months in the Sixth Massachusetts Volunteer Regiment. During the riot in Baltimore, Ladd was struck in the head by a piece of masonry and while falling forward was hit in the thigh by a bullet that severed an artery. It is said that his last words were "All hail the Stars and Stripes." His body was brought home in May where it was briefly interred, later moved to Lowell, and buried under the Ladd-Whitney monument.[31]

Early Saturday morning, April 20, Professor Thaddeus Sobieski Lowe of Jefferson, New Hampshire, began a balloon flight from Cincinnati, Ohio. The intrepid New Hampshire aeronaut in his balloon *Enterprise* intended to fly to the Chesapeake Bay area. At twelve thousand feet over Ohio, the swift upper air current quickly propelled his balloon eastward,[32] but nine hours later Lowe landed his balloon not near the Chesapeake but, ironically, in Unionville, South Carolina. Backwoods people thought that he must be a devil descending from the skies. Lowe obtained a wagon ride to downtown Unionville where he was greeted with suspicion. Referring to the balloon, one of the townspeople shouted, "Only a Yankee could do something like that." Because Lowe was carrying northern newspapers, he was arrested and held as a spy, making him the first prisoner of the Civil War. Lowe's incarceration did not last long because word of his identity and scientific mission had reached understanding ears in South Carolina, and he was soon set free.[33] Patriotic passions in New Hampshire were running high in Nashua when a mob accosted a South Carolina man in the streets and threatened to hang him. Leading citizens managed to rescue the man and encouraged him to leave town.[34]

A fund-raising dance held in Nashua gathered $315 in donations, enough to provide 222 shirts, towels, and handkerchiefs for Companies E and F of the First New Hampshire Regiment.[35] Before the volunteers from the Town of Claremont left for the war, each was presented with a revolver, knife, Bible, two pairs of flannel pants, two flannel shirts, woolen socks, towels, and several handkerchiefs.[36] Many towns were either equipping their recruits with revolvers or considering an appropriation to do so. The *New Hampshire Telegraph* registered a different opinion on April 27, 1861: "The idea that every soldier for the war be armed with a revolver is giving place to one that an extra blanket is worth a good deal to a soldier. . . . An extra blanket, stockings and clothing will save more lives than revolvers."[37] The Town of Rollinsford elected to give its thirty volunteers revolvers at the cost of $525. The Town of Fremont voted to give all its departing soldiers a revolver as well but four months later at a special town meeting decided that it was too expensive and revoked the earlier vote.[38] The cost of outfitting depart- ing Dover soldiers totaled $27.51 per man: gun sling, 50 cents; haversack, 75 cents; cap, $1.10; shoes, $1.25; blanket, $1.87; two shirts, $1.92; knapsack, $2.25; blouse, $3.00; coat and pants, $7.00; and overcoat, $7.87.[39]

Orders were issued to establish Camp Union on the fairgrounds, about a mile east of the State House in Concord to marshal the new incoming recruits.[40] U.S. representative Tappan of Bradford, New Hampshire, who had been in the New Hampshire Thirtieth Militia Regiment, offered his help to Governor Goodwin, who immediately accepted him to lead the First New Hampshire Regiment. Tap- pan was regarded by many in New Hampshire as the best choice to assume the colonelcy of the First New Hampshire regiment.[41]

As the surge of patriotism in New Hampshire became a wave, Hale reported to Secretary of the Navy Gideon Welles that the enthusiasm of the people of New Hampshire was "unprecedented." Flags began appearing everywhere, and vendors made money on the sale of American flags.[42] Offers of help flooded in from all parts of the state. Governor Goodwin raised $680,000 from banks and influential businessmen. Downing and Sons of Concord received a contract for fifteen specially designed wagons. So quickly was the regiment equipped that on May 14, Quartermaster Richard N. Batchelder reported to Colonel Tappan that the regiment was ready. More men enlisted than were needed for the first regi- ment, so the thousand extras were sent to Brigadier General George Stark to Ports- mouth for a possible second regiment. Their new camp, Camp Constitution, was in the Rope Works building, near South Mill Pond, near the present-day Portsmouth Police Station.[43] The men of the Second New Hampshire Regiment discovered after they had enlisted that on orders from the War Department, the Second New Hampshire was to become a three-year regiment. In fairness the men were given the choice of serving out their nine months at Camp Constitu- tion or enlisting for three years. About five hundred men chose three years.[44] New Hampshire's first regiment in the Civil War was fortunate enough to have its own band, the Baldwin Cornet Band of Manchester. The First New Hamp- shire Regiment was officially mustered into the service of the United States on May 7, 1861, in Concord.[45]

In a letter to his brother in Holderness on May 6, 1861, Private Caleb Dodge of Company K of the First New Hampshire described his life at Camp Union: "I am writeing in a rather strange place for this is the first time that I ever wrote a letter in a horse stall for sutch is my home for the present. . . . I do not think that

I should do any diferent for it is a time when ever good and patriotic men will serve his Country to the best of his ability we have good quarters and a knuf to eat. I have got the best Capt on the field we went to Concord after our guns to day we are going to have our Uniforms tomorrow. . . . The tatoo has just been beat so I must put out my light and go to bed."[46] Dodge's background and physical characteristics were that of the typical Civil War soldier. He was a twenty-one-year-old farmer of modest means, a light complexion, brown hair, and blue eyes, who stood about five feet six inches.[47]

By early May, Thaddeus Lowe had returned safely from his flight to South Carolina. Upon seeing his old friend Murat Halstead, Lowe told him of an idea that he had formed on his trip back home. Lowe felt that his balloons could be used as observation platforms from which to watch the movement of Southern troops. Halstead, who was a friend of Secretary of the Treasury Salmon Chase, said he would petition the government on Lowe's behalf.[48] In Keene on May 6, two companies of volunteers headed for Portsmouth, their passage financed by several Keene banks, and the ladies of Keene quickly organized a Soldiers Aid Society to send boxes and supplies to the men training in Concord and Portsmouth.[49]

The commander chosen to lead the Second New Hampshire Volunteers was forty-one-year-old Colonel Thomas Prescott Pierce of Manchester. Pierce was content to lead the Second until he discovered that its service term was changed from three months to three years. Pierce resigned his command on June 4, 1861 and retired from military life.[50] Under Pierce, the 979 men of the Second New Hampshire camping in Portsmouth were trained in the military arts. Many of the farm boys and millworkers who composed the ranks of the Second were learning military discipline for the first time. When a Maine regiment passed through Portsmouth en route to Washington, some of the uniformed members of the Second were there to meet them. Their attitude after meeting the Maine men was that the war would be over before they would have a chance to take part in it.[51] This opinion was popular nationwide, but the *Exeter News-Letter* offered a different viewpoint: "From the items of news in our paper, our rulers at Washington are evidently preparing for a vigorous contest, which will be commenced at or near the Capitol. The news of the weeks that follow will be anticipated with great interest. *The war may be continued for a long time;* its fortunes and chances are proverbially uncertain and some reverses ought not to dishearten those who are sure that they have right on their side" (emphasis added).[52]

For the moment, the concern of most soldiers was the hardships of being a soldier. On May 9, 1861, twenty-one-year-old Private Thomas B. Leaver of the Second New Hampshire wrote his mother in Concord about army food: "Our food has varied very little from the following: Breakfast—one piece of white bread, ditto brown bread, generous piece of corned beef, butter and mug of coffee. Dinner the same."[53] Charles E. Jewett, a Gilford twenty-three-year-old private of the Second New Hampshire, did not seem too dissatisfied with camp life on May 11: "We have enough to eat and drink and enjoy ourselves first rate . . . beef and bread, hash soup and coffee twice a day. We drill four hours a day the rest of the time we have to stay about the camp. We have straw to sleep on and a blanket so we are pretty well provided for."[54]

A typical day for the recruits in the Second New Hampshire began with reveille at five o'clock in the morning. The men then had two hours to get themselves, their equipment, and their quarters in order. At seven, the men reported by company for breakfast. One hour later, the drums beat for assembly, and the men were assigned their duties and were inspected. Sick call was made to the officer of the day, and all who were ill were escorted to the hospital by an orderly. At nine o'clock, the recruits marched to the parade ground or, if on a Sunday, to church services. Lunch was at noon, and evening dress parade commenced at five. Dinner was served in camp at seven o'clock. The tatoo was beat at nine in the evening, and it was then lights out until morning.[55]

In addition to being the place where the Second New Hampshire gathered their forces, Portsmouth was also home of the Portsmouth Naval Shipyard. From the very beginning of the war, the shipyard was a hub of naval activity. The workers traveled across the Piscataqua River from their homes to the shipyard every day in a flotilla of sixty boats. One of the ships being constructed at the shipyard in May of 1861 was the USS *Kearsarge*. This steam-screw sloop would take its place in history alongside the USS *Monitor* as one of the most storied ships of the American Civil War.[56]

The uniforms of both the First and Second regiments were gray swallowtail coats and gray pants trimmed with red. Many of the Northern regiments adopted their uniforms after the style of their old militia units, most of which were patterned after the gray cadet uniform used by West Point. Some Southern regiments copied the blue coats used by the cadets at the Virginia Military Institute. The similarity of the blue and gray uniforms understandably led to great confusion during the first battles of the Civil War. Until the color problem was worked out, many regimental commanders had their men wear white or different colored armbands to distinguish them from the enemy.[57]

Camp life for the men in Concord and Portsmouth became both tedious and boring. When orders came in from the War Department that the First New Hampshire was to proceed to Washington immediately, there was cheering throughout the camp.[58] The men of the First New Hampshire said good-bye to friends and family and prepared to leave Camp Union on the morning of May 25, 1861. Tearful relatives and friends hovered around fathers, sons, and brothers departing for an uncertain future. Kisses and hugs were exchanged. Family members and soldiers clasped hands, made promises, and said their farewells.

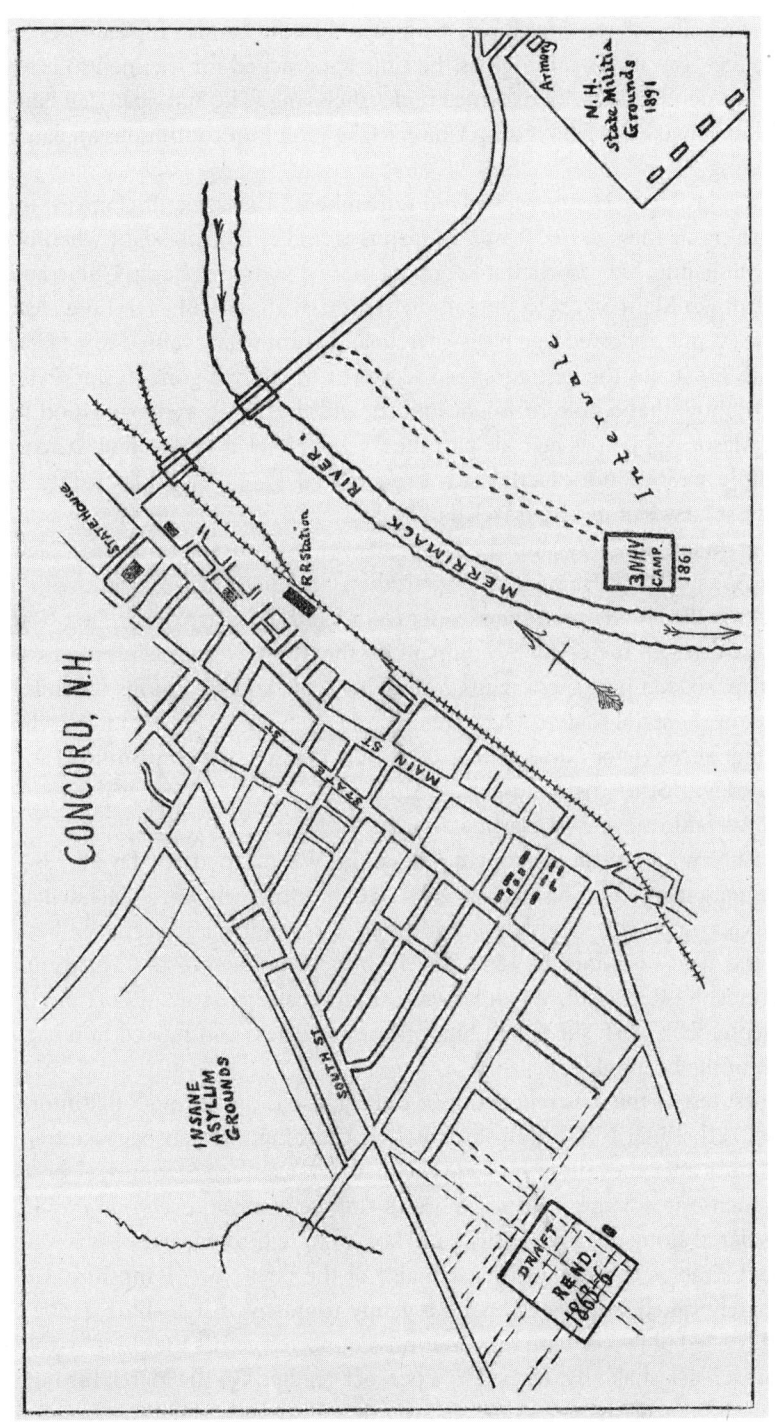

Concord Regimental Training Area. From Daniel Eldredge,
The Third New Hampshire and All about It, *1893*

Countless small packages and Bibles were placed in the hands of loved ones by their families. Emotions ran high as the time approached for the men to leave for the train depot. As the men formed ranks, they sang "The Star Spangled Banner" and marched away from Camp Union to the sounds of continuous applause and cheering.[59]

Newspaper editor Henry McFarland remembered the scene in Concord on that morning in May 1861: "It was an inspiring and reassuring sight when on Saturday morning, May 25, the 1st Regiment came down from Camp Union and marched down Main Street to the railway station, with its ranks reaching clear across the avenue, followed by a baggage train and outfit which caused some New Yorkers to say it was the best equipped regiment which had gone to war. I can see exactly how that whole regiment looked, and the figure and expression of Colonel Mason Tappan as he rode past the Phenix Hotel at the head of the column, a little anxious, not exactly ready to go, but ready to do a soldier's duty."[60]

The First New Hampshire traveled to Worcester, Massachusetts, then by boat to New York, and at every stop the regiment was fed and entertained. In New York the Sons of New Hampshire organization presented the regiment with a beautiful silk flag. A New York newspaper recorded the passage of the First New Hampshire through their city: "Accompanying the troops were one hundred sixteen horses, sixteen baggage wagons containing tents and provisions for thirty days, and one hospital wagon. There were also in attendance sixteen nurses, who took dinner at the Astor House. The troops were dressed in a gray uniform and were armed with Springfield muskets."[61] Among those sixteen nurses was twenty-year-old Adelaide Stevens of Nashua, the wife of Major Aaron Fletcher Stevens of the First New Hampshire Regiment. The couple was married on May 19, 1861, just seventeen days after Stevens was mustered into the regiment. Adelaide had elected to accompany her husband into the field as a nurse and served in both regular and field hospitals. In 1862 Stevens became colonel of the Thirteenth New Hampshire Regiment. When he was wounded at the Battle of Fort Harrison in September 1864, she found him on the battlefield and nursed him back to health in the hospital.[62]

The first test of the new regiment was during its passage through Baltimore. On May 27, the First New Hampshire was kept waiting for their baggage train for two hours after they disembarked. The march to Camden Station was tense, and the memories of the previous month's riot were still in everyone's mind. Tempers flared along the route, bricks and bottles were thrown, and insults were exchanged. Francis H. Pike, the drum major of the First New Hampshire who affectionately called him "Saxy," wore a gaudy uniform of light-blue pants, a double-breasted blue coat with brass buttons connected across the chest by gold cords, and a black shako hat topped by a peacock feather. On the march through Baltimore, Pike, sensing he had the security of a thousand armed men around him, cleared the way by waving a large silver-headed baton back and forth to clear the street. Along the route, he struck up the Baldwin Cornet Band several times with rousing renditions of *Yankee Doodle* and *Hail Columbia*. The First New Hampshire passed through the city without major incident.

The regiment arrived in Washington, D.C., on Tuesday, May 28, and went two miles outside of the city to a camp the soldiers renamed their Camp Cameron, probably after Secretary of War Simon Cameron. Tappan received a message from the White House complimenting the First New Hampshire on its smart appearance.[63] Tappan's first military orders in the field came from Colonel Joseph K. Mansfield on May 30: "Sir, I wish you to keep your pickets out to guard against surprise by approach from the direction of Harpers Ferry. If you have not a full supply of ammunition, you must have at least forty rounds the man in the future."[64]

When Colonel Pierce of the Second New Hampshire resigned his post on June 4, 1861, Gilman Marston of Exeter, the First District U.S. representative, took his place. He had served briefly in the defense of the nation's capital during Lincoln's inauguration, immediately returned to New Hampshire, and offered his services to Governor Goodwin. Marston, like Mason Tappan, had previous militia experience, serving as a general's aide in 1843. He had helped with the raising of the Second New Hampshire regiment.[65] Marston was commissioned colonel of the Second New Hampshire that, from then on, would be a three-year regiment. By June 5, Republican congressmen commanded both of the regiments of New Hampshire.[66] Six days after his commission, the people of Exeter presented a sword and other equipment to Colonel Marston.

Simon G. Griffin was another celebrated lawyer-turned-soldier destined to make his mark on New Hampshire's role in the war. Recognizing that war was imminent, Griffin began the study of military strategy and tactics. On the outbreak of war, Griffin volunteered as a private but was unable to find a place in the First New Hampshire Regiment. He was later appointed captain of Company B of the Second New Hampshire Regiment. By June 1861 this company was known as the "Goodwin Rifles." With the donations of friends and money from his own pocket, Griffin equipped his company with Sharps breech-loading rifles. Griffin later received the colonelship of the Sixth New Hampshire regiment and was promoted to even higher rank later in the war.[67]

Professor Lowe arrived in Washington, D.C., on June 5 for his appointment with Secretary Chase. On his way to the National Hotel, he noticed that Washington had become an armed camp. Thousands of soldiers were arriving in the city every day, the streets jammed with militia soldiers wearing uniforms of every color. Although he had competition, he felt he could persuade the government to use his balloons as observation platforms. The advantage of being able to observe one's enemy from the air could not be ignored.[68] Professor Lowe was busy during June, not only with a successful interview with Secretary Chase but also with an enthusiastic response from Lincoln. To demonstrate the potential of balloons for military purposes, Lowe made an ascent on June 18 with a telegraph in the basket with him. The excited professor sent the following wire to the Lincoln while aloft: "To the President of the United States: Sir: This point of observation commands an area of nearly 50 miles in diameter. The city with its girdle of encampments presents a superb scene. I have pleasure in sending you this first dispatch ever telegraphed from an aerial station and in acknowledging indebtedness for your encouragement for the opportunity of demonstrating the availability of the science of aeronautics in the service of the country."[69] The next day Lowe had a letter of approval in his hand from Lincoln, and although he met resistance from General Winfield Scott, Lowe was given permission to form a balloon corps for the use of the army. Lowe made many successful ascents for the Union army and provided it with much valuable intelligence.[70]

New Hampshire's second wartime governor was Nathaniel Springer Berry from Hebron, a Democrat-turned-Republican, who defeated General George Stark, 35,467 votes to 31,452. Berry assumed his office in June of 1861.[71] In his inaugural address, he stated that the acts of rebellion committed by the South were treason and ought to be suppressed. To this end he asked the state legislature to appropriate one million dollars and warned them against any "external mercenary efforts exerted in matters of legislation." Under Berry's administration, New Hampshire mustered in fourteen more regiments, the last one mustering after his term expired.[72]

Far from New Hampshire, the men of the state's first regiment in the field were anticipating their baptism of fire. Stephen G. Abbott, the chaplain of the First New Hampshire, delivered a memorable sermon just before the First was ready to break camp and march into Virginia. The chaplain prayed for peace but stated that if violence must come to the regiment, "He [God] would give to our soldiers a brave heart, a firm nerve, a steady eye, and send the missile straight to its mark."

On June 7, 1861, First New Hampshire Regiment's captain, Louis Bell of Chester, who would go on to command the Fourth New Hampshire Regiment, wrote to his wife, Mollie: "I am appointed General Captain of scouting parties. I see that the NH papers say we have been in a fight. We have not known it. No news here. You know far more about war matters in Chester. The enemy is at Leesburg or Leesville 25 miles from Washington but we are two to their one in numbers."[73]

The First New Hampshire marched to Rockville, Maryland. It was a hot day, and many fell out along the roads because of the heat. The baggage and supply wagons gave many footsore and hot soldiers a ride that day. The First was one of the regiments of the brigade commanded by Colonel Charles P. Stone.[74]

The First stayed only a short time at Rockville and then set off for Poolesville, Maryland, arriving on the June 15. The rumor was the Confederates were evacuating Harpers Ferry in order to move south to attack federal units along the Potomac River. Their aim was also to avoid being caught by Major General Robert Patterson's force coming south from Williamsport, Maryland, to capture Harpers Ferry. Major General Patterson was ordered to prevent the Confederates under Brigadier General Joseph E. Johnston from uniting with other Confederate forces around Manassas Junction, Virginia.[75]

On June 17, five companies of the First New Hampshire under Lieutenant Colonel Thomas J. Whipple of Laconia were sent to Conrad's Ferry, opposite Leesburg, Virginia, to stop a suspected river crossing by the Confederates. A musket duel ensued between the First New Hampshire and the Confederates across the river. After several hours the Confederates added a battery of artillery to the contest. By day's end the firing ceased but began again the next day until the Confederates withdrew. The Southerners admitted to several casualties. The men of the First New Hampshire survived their first battle unscathed.[76]

On June 20, 1861, Captain Bell wrote to Mollie from Conrad's Ferry: "I have not had a chance to write to you, blessing, for several days because, first I have had no paper—second we have ate, slept and lived in our entrenchments which as it is only three feet wide does not offer unusual facilities for correspondence. Particularly as every few seconds whiz goes a rifle ball over our heads or "thud" and a cannonball strikes our parapet. Now however since night before last we have killed and wounded 27 and not a man on our side has been injured. . . . I have not suffered a single moments ill feeling since I left Concord. We live well and have chicken, pork, beef, hardbread and beans."[77]

When Colonel Tappan discovered that firing was coming from Conrad's Ferry, he immediately began marching the remainder of the regiment to the aid of Lieutenant Colonel Whipple. When Colonel Stone was told of the movement, he ordered Tappan to return to camp.[78]

Major General Patterson, discovering that Harpers Ferry was abandoned, should have tried to overtake Johnston and stop him. On June 25, 1861, Patterson's superior and friend from the Mexican War, General Winfield Scott, urged him to cross the river and attack Johnston. Patterson, however, fearing that Johnston outnumbered him, chose to dig in instead. On June 30 Colonel Stone was ordered to take his brigade—First New Hampshire, Ninth New York, and five companies of a Pennsylvania regiment—and join Patterson at Harpers Ferry. Scott told Patterson that action against the Confederates at Manassas Junction was imminent.[79]

The First New Hampshire remained in the Poolesville area for twenty-one days, guarding fifteen miles of the Potomac River. The men understandably became restless, and a good deal of "foraging" took place. After Colonel Tappan received several complaints of missing geese, he had a talk with some of the suspected soldiers. Feigning ignorance for a while, one of the soldiers asked, "Did he say anything about his pigs?" Tappan, obviously amused by the incident, said nothing and went about his business. Even though the First New Hampshire had acquired the nickname the "New Hampshire Wildcats," the soldiers of the regiment were not above swimming over to the other side of the Potomac and fraternizing with their Confederate counterparts.[80]

At Camp Constitution in Portsmouth, the Second New Hampshire Regiment was still eleven days away from leaving for the war when Thomas Leaver wrote home on June 9 complaining of his boredom: "I am heartily sick of Portsmouth and want to be off for the seat of war. It is awful dull here pent up in this camp. . . . I used to think Concord a dull place but it is not a circumstance to Portsmouth."[81]

Eight days later, on June 17, Leaver was animated in his description of his imminent departure from Portsmouth: "I wrote to say that we will leave this one-horse town on Thursday of this week at 7'oclock in the morning by the eastern road direct to Boston. From there we shall proceed by the Old Colony road to Fall River where we shall take the boat to New York. . . . We shall pass through Baltimore with loaded rifles I hope. They are getting very ugly again and may mob us. Woe to them if they do. You must keep up a brave heart and look forward with hope until I shall return which will never be till the glorious stars and stripes wave over the *whole* land and not a part of it."[82]

The uniforms and equipment of the Second New Hampshire were virtually the same as the First. They were attired in the same swallowtail gray coat banded with red cord. Nine companies were armed with smoothbore .69 caliber muskets, which are only accurate at close range. Company B, thanks to Simon Griffin and the people of Concord, were equipped with Sharps repeating rifles. The old smooth-bore weapons were exchanged after First Bull Run for the more accurate Springfield rifled musket.[83]

In Portsmouth on June 10, 1861, the Second New Hampshire was officially mustered into the service of the United States. Charles E. Jewett of the Second was feeling optimistic in his last letter home while still in Portsmouth: "We expect to start next Thursday, we shall go by land for we want to march through Baltimore. . . . Tell Father that we are going down South and clear them all out in less than a year. I have got the promise of a shot at Jeff Davis and that is all I want."[84]

The day for the departure of the Second New Hampshire had finally arrived. Just as Thomas Leaver had told his sister in a letter earlier, the Second New Hampshire departed from the Eastern Depot on Deer Street in Portsmouth on the morning of June 20, 1861. The experiences of the Second New Hampshire and their journey to Washington were similar to those of the First New

Hampshire. The regiment arrived in Boston at noon and was marched to the Music Hall on Tremont Street, where a series of speakers that included Governor Berry, former governor Goodwin, and Governor John A. Andrew of Massachusetts addressed the regiment. The regiment then went to Faneuil Hall for a sumptuous banquet.

The Second continued south and arrived in New York on June 21. At every major stop, the regiment was greeted and provided with provisions from the local Sons of New Hampshire organization. The Second was accompanied on its entire journey by the Manchester Band, which stayed with them for nearly two weeks after its arrival in Washington. While in New York, the regiment was presented with its flag by Charles Soule of the Sons of New Hampshire. The regimental band played the national anthem, and the regiment marched up Broadway on its way to the railroad station. The Second New Hampshire experienced its first casualty on the way to Washington. While passing through New Jersey, Lieutenant Charles W. Walker of Concord fell from the train, receiving a fatal injury to the head. The passage of the Second New Hampshire through Baltimore occurred without incident. The regiment traveled through the city with the Seventeenth New York and a Pennsylvania regiment. The crowd that gathered to watch the passing of these regiments was grim but not hostile.[85]

Also writing on June 26, 1861 from Camp Sullivan was Second New Hampshire Private Charles Jewett of Gilford. He recorded the regiment's departure from Portsmouth and its passage through Baltimore: "We expected to be fired upon when we got to Baltimore but they kept perfectly quiet and it was well they did for if they had not Baltimore would ben no more for we had our guns loaded and 40 rounds besides we was all prepared for they had give out word that we could not pass but we marched down through the Citty. . . . We are right in sight of Arlington hight we have to be very careful how we go out for the enemy is plenty around here. . . . They are lurking around to see how strong we are. . . . They fire at our guards almost every night but they have not killed any yet here. . . . The first regiment are 35 miles from us. . . . We have got to go to the Citty today and be inspected by Old Abe."[86]

The Second arrived in Washington around noon and marched about a mile from the capitol to Camp Sullivan, named in honor of General John Sullivan, the Revolutionary War hero from New Hampshire.[87] On June 26, 1861, Second New Hampshire Private Enoch G. Adams of Durham described conditions in a letter to his mother and brother: "This camp. . . . is one of the loveliest places you ever saw. On a side hill in a grove of cedars is our camp. It is as romantic a place as ever I beheld. A beautiful oak overshadows with its cool boughs our tent. . . . There are more than 50,000 soldiers in the vicinity. More than 5,000 arrive everyday in Washington. They are discharging their guns and pistols of old loads—cooks are cleaning their culinary instruments—spades are rattling

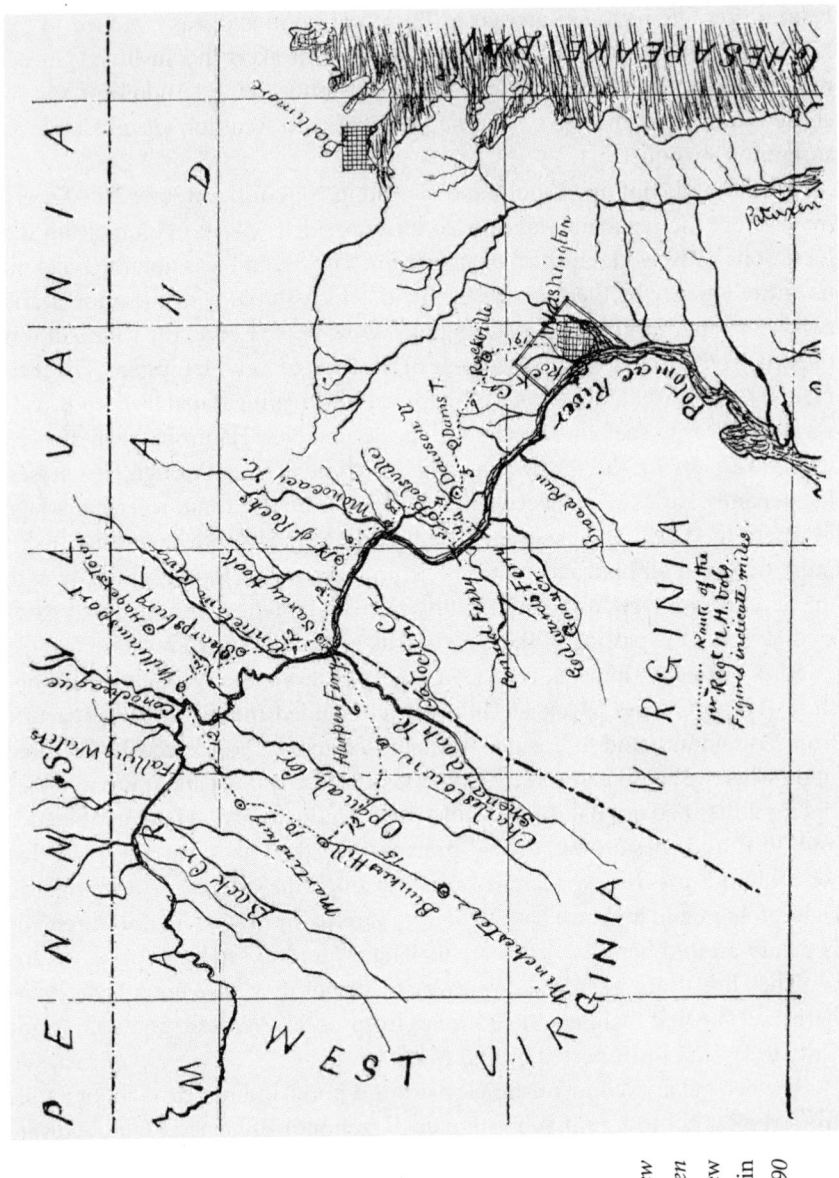

Route of the First New Hampshire. From Stephen Abbott, The First New Hampshire Volunteers in the Great Rebellion, 1890

digging trenches round the tents to carry off the rain when it comes. Horses are neighing—drums are beating, axes, hammers and saws are sounding, voices humming and the air fresh and balmy and redolent with the smell of cut cedars comes into the tent."[88]

Before the men of the Second discharged the old loads from their muskets, a stack of loaded muskets collapsed, with one going off. The ball went through the arm of Joseph Conner of Pembroke and resulted in his discharge from the regiment. A more serious event occurred late in June when Jonathan Calef of Keene wandered outside of the picket line and was accidentally shot in the neck while trying to come back through. Calef died in August 1861 and is buried in Washington, D.C.[89]

On arriving in Washington, the Second New Hampshire joined with the First and Second Rhode Island and Seventy-first New York to form the Second Brigade of General David Hunter's Second Division. With these units was the Second Rhode Island Battery. The Seventy-first New York was equipped with two Dahlgren howitzers. Colonel Ambrose E. Burnside of the Second Rhode Island was the brigade commander.[90]

On June 21, Haldimand Sumner Putnam, serving on the staff of Brigadier General Irvin McDowell, read the following letter from his father in Cornish, decrying the appointment of politicians to military command: "and say to Squire Lincoln that if he continues to make generals and colonels of his cronies, who have nothing more to recommend them than that they have been expert engineers on the 'underground railroad' . . . they will expect to be whipped of course."[91] It was true that many in the new volunteer army lacked regular military training, but experience became a good teacher. Besides Tappan, the First New Hampshire provided five future New Hampshire colonels. The Second New Hampshire provided two brigadier generals, five colonels, ten lieutenant colonels, eleven majors, and five surgeons.[92]

During the first week of July, the First New Hampshire left camp on the Maryland side of the Potomac and marched to join General Patterson's army. Colonel Stone's brigade caught up with Patterson midway between Martinsburg and Williamsport on the afternoon of July 8. Patterson skirmished with Johnston's forces on several occasions and fought a small battle at Falling Waters. Despite his orders to prevent Johnston's juncture with General Pierre Gustave Toutant Beauregard at Manassas, Patterson inexplicably decided to entrench and wait for a Confederate attack.[93]

On July 4, 1861, in Fremont, New Hampshire, the first Civil War riot to take place in New England occurred. Many Northern communities built custom-made flagpoles called liberty poles. The town of Fremont's was 150 high. The pole's dedication on July 4 turned out a large crowd, including several soldiers leaving for the seat of war. As the flag was raised, a Southern sympathizer in the crowd attempted to shoot at the flag. The riot broke out when the crowd attacked the sympathizer, and the soldiers helped break up the disturbance. One of the soldiers said, "We were going to fight the rebels but we had as soon commence here [Fremont] as anywhere."[94]

An order for Colonel Tappan on July 8, 1861, from Major General Patterson's headquarters in Martinsburg said the Confederates were expected to soon move and fast. The next day, Brigade Commander Colonel Stone raised expectations in the regiment with the following order to Colonel Tappan: "Commanders of regiments will at once make requisition on the Quartermaster for ammunition so as having their supply up to 70 rounds per man."[95]

On July 15, the First New Hampshire and the other twenty-five regiments of General Patterson's command marched for Winchester, arriving at Bunker Hill just outside the town. The expectation was that Patterson would either attack Johnston the next day or position himself in order to prevent Johnston from reenforcing General Beauregard at Manassas.

Between Martinsburg and Winchester, the division had skirmished with small pockets of Confederate resistance and encountered some runaway slaves. Many of the runways sought refuge in the Union camp, so General Patterson ordered, "Members of the Army have permitted Negroes to be dressed in the Uniform of the Army. This is prohibited and every officer is called upon to put an end to such degradation and guards are directed to take from Negroes Uniforms of the Army."[96]

On July 17, Patterson, stating that he believed Johnston had been reenforced with twenty thousand fresh troops, not only did not attack but also retreated in the direction of Charlestown. This move left a clear road between Johnston and Beauregard at Manassas. The First New Hampshire heard on July 20 that fighting had broken out around Manassas. That night the regiment was told to cook one day's ration and be prepared to march the next day. On the day of the Battle of First Bull Run, July 21, the First New Hampshire marched to Harpers Ferry and camped at Bolivar Heights. Except for a small movement to Sandy Hook, the First New Hampshire remained around Harpers Ferry until their term of enlistment ran out on August 2.[97]

Why did the First New Hampshire not have the opportunity to fight a pitched battle against Johnston's force? Thomas L. Livermore of the First New Hampshire explained, "Johnston, the rebel commander, had retreated to Winchester, and there he was on the 16th when we were lying still. He had 17,000 men and we had 20,000 or more. Patterson was frightened, or pretended to be, by an alleged report that Johnston had been re-enforced by 20,000 from Beauregard. He said the enemy had stolen a march on him. Johnston marched on the 18th for the Shenandoah with 8,000 men crossed it . . . and was at Bull Run before the fight opened on the 21st. The probability is that if Patterson had attacked, he would have at least prevented that junction. Bull Run would have been ours and mayhap the war would have been closed."[98]

The Second New Hampshire, destined to play a part in the Manassas battle, was on the march from Fairfax Court House toward Centreville on July 18. As the men of the Second marched toward their first battle, Charles Jewett of Company F wrote an excited letter home: "My Dear brother as we expect to go into battle to day I thought I would write a line to let you know whare I be we are between fair fax and menaset Junction we expect to have a hot battle at the Junction but we are good for it we have got about 150,000 troops with in six miles of thare this morning with any amount of artilery. . . . I don't know how strong the rebbels are we expect they are pretty strong we drove them out of fair fax. . . . I have got a good gun and a seven shooter besides and I mean to use them both . . . we begin to see something that lookes like war now and that sutes me."[99] Jewett and the rest of the Second New Hampshire became involved in the First Battle of Bull Run at approximately 9:30 A.M. on July 21 when the Rhode Island regiments, preceding them up the road, drew Confederate artillery fire. The Rhode Islanders were engaging in an exchange of musket volleys with the Confederates when the Second emerged into the same field to support them.[100]

Colonel Marston was wounded almost immediately and was carried to the rear. He was quickly bandaged and returned to the battle line to the delight of the men. "Now," Marston said, "the New Hampshire Second will have a chance to show what it is made out of." After the most recent exchange of musket fire, the Second, on the right of the brigade line, lay down to avoid the Confederate artillery. The Rhode Islanders were on the left. Lieutenant Colonel Fiske was swearing at the men of the Second for lying down but Captain Griffin of Company B ordered his men to lie down so they would not fire into the Seventy-first New York that had filed in front of them.[101] The Second was ordered forward across a small stream to join other troops on the right of the line. Captain Griffin was leading his men when a cannon ball struck a man from Company I two feet in front of him and "knocked him into a shapeless mass—it whirled him around and sent him about a rod to the right." The soldier was Harvey Holt of Lyndeborough, the first New Hampshire soldier to die in battle.[102]

Before Beauregard had been reenforced by Johnston, the Federals were exploiting their success, and it appeared as though they would win the day. Later in the day, the northern troops were in a highly disorganized state, as Captain Griffin describes: "Crossing the [Bull] Run we found Burnside with some of his staff trying to rally the troops and make a stand-we made every effort in our power to aid him but it was impossible. The men were completely demoralized. The retreat became an utter route."[103] Civil War historian William C. Davis praises the Second New Hampshire: "Indeed much of it [Burnside's brigade] had simply broken up, the men withdrawing without orders to sprint through the woods back to Sudley Ford. Only the 2nd New Hampshire remained organized, and Burnside would lead it personally through the remainder of the battle." Regarding the Federal defeat, Davis concludes, "There was no shame in being defeated.... Burnside's brigade, and particularly the 2nd New Hampshire had fought a good fight."[104] Captain Griffin desperately tried to keep the remnants of his company together, "but," he said, "the crowd of fugitives soon broke us up again and we drifted along, weary, hungry, footsore, ashamed, astonished and disgusted. Company B had gone out with eighty-two men and twelve had been wounded."[105]

New England Civil War historian Otis Waite gives the losses for the Second New Hampshire in the First Battle of Bull Run as seven killed, fifty-six wounded, and forty-six captured. Many of the men assumed captured actually died on the field. Martin A. Haynes, author of the Second New Hampshire regimental history, records the loss as nine killed, thirty-five wounded, and sixty-three missing, the last being all prisoners.[106] Private William F. Oxford of Portsmouth was wounded at the First Battle of Bull Run and captured by the advancing Confederates. Taken to Richmond, Oxford died one month later in a Confederate prison. The Second New Hampshire soldier was brought home to Portsmouth and is interred in Harmony Grove Cemetery.[107]

Colonel Marston, wounded early in the battle, was later taken to the surgeon's tent to have his arm treated. Marston gave his aide, young John Sullivan Jr. of Exeter, a revolver and instructed him to shoot any surgeon who attempted to amputate his arm. The surgeons were convinced that the colonel's arm needed to come off, but the presence of Marston's protector motivated them to save his arm. They operated, and the Colonel's arm was spared.[108]

Private Charles Jewett of the Second New Hampshire sought to find a reason why certain victory turned to humiliating defeat at First Bull Run: "I was in it Sunday about six hours the hottes battle that ever has been fought in the united states they say. . . . Thare is thousands of troops a coming in every day and I am glad to see them for that was wat we lacked the other day but we did not suppose they had over 30,000 but they had a bout 80,000 and that made quite a difference with us but we should have whiped them if it had not been for their 20,000 to reinforce when we had got pretty well tired out so we had to retreat."[109]

Back in Camp Sullivan, Enoch Adams of the Second New Hampshire recorded his opinions about their last battle: "We probably shall never have so dreadful a battle again. It is said the enemy suffered dreadfully 3,000 of them were killed. We shall in the future use batteries and cannons more."[110] In a short article written for the *Dover Gazette*, Adams gave this opinion of the battle: "The Battle of Bull Run was the wildest engagement ever fought on this continent. . . . There are 81 men missing from the Regiment. Six out of our company."

In his official report, Colonel Burnside praised Colonel Marston and the Second New Hampshire: "Col. Marston, of the Second New Hampshire, was badly wounded in the shoulder, but, notwithstanding, he remained in the saddle under fire after his wound was dressed, his horse being lead by his orderly. The regiment, under charge of Lieutenant-Colonel Fiske, conducted itself most gallantly. Both officers and men deserve great praise."[111]

Although the Union army had suffered a humiliating defeat at Bull Run, the men of the Second New Hampshire knew they had bravely acquitted themselves and brought honor to their state. After the First Battle of Bull Run, the regiment camped outside of Washington in Bladensburg, Maryland. During September, ninety-seven recruits under the able leadership of Sergeant Frederick Cobb of Keene joined the Second. During the fall and winter of 1861 to 1862, the Second New Hampshire and its brigade, now under the command of Brigadier General Joseph Hooker, practiced drilling and built fortifications around Washington. Under the direction of both Major General George B. McClellan and Hooker, the Union army received the training and discipline that it had lacked at the First Bull Run.[112]

By the beginning of August 1861, both sides viewed each other differently. The North realized that the South would not be easily defeated and that the war was going to continue longer than expected. The South now knew that the North was not about to let the South go its own way and was determined to fight to preserve the Union.[113]

Regardless of its duration, the war was over for the First New Hampshire Volunteer Regiment. Its ninety-day term of enlistment expiring, the regiment headed back to New Hampshire and was mustered out of service in Concord on August 9, 1861, although fully sixty percent of the men in the First New Hampshire enlisted in regiments raised later.[114] Some of the more prominent members of the First New Hampshire assumed command in other New Hampshire regiments. Lieutenant Colonel Thomas J. Whipple was commissioned colonel of the Fourth New Hampshire Volunteers. Major Stevens went on to command the Thirteenth New Hampshire. Adjutant Enoch Quimby Fellows became the colonel of the Third New Hampshire and later of the Ninth New Hampshire. Quartermaster Richard N. Batchelder was appointed captain and later attained the rank of brigadier general and chief quartermaster of the Army of the Potomac. Captain Louis Bell became lieutenant colonel of the Fourth New Hampshire and later its colonel. Captain Barton became lieutenant colonel of the First New Hampshire Heavy Artillery.[115]

Upon the arrival of the First New Hampshire back in Concord, an incident occurred that escalated into riot. The *Democrat Standard,* a newspaper published in Concord by John B. Palmer and Edmund Burke, was making what appeared to some citizens of Concord some rather harsh antigovernment statements.

Soldiers of the First New Hampshire, having recently seen copies of the newspapers, called on the Palmer family at their office, asked them to cease printing the paper, and were refused. A gun was discharged. The Palmers thought they had been fired upon so they returned fire into the growing crowd. Five shots were fired, wounding two of the recently returned soldiers. The small police force that had been barely keeping control of the crowd was overpowered, and the mob rushed into the office and ransacked the entire establishment. The Palmer family escaped through a side door, but their printing press and all of their equipment were burned in the middle of the street by the angry mob.[116]

About the time of the Concord riot, the First New Hampshire Light Battery, later known as Edgell's Battery, gathered in Manchester in August 1861 under the command of Captain George Gerrish. Edwin Hobbs and Frederick M. Edgell were first lieutenants of the battery. The battery enlisted 155 men and was equipped with six bronze rifled cannon, horses, carriages, and baggage wagons. The First New Hampshire Light Battery camped in the north part of Manchester on the fairgrounds. The city turned out to be an ideal place to recruit an artillery battery because it had a large labor force in the mills that knew machinery and how to repair it. The operation of an artillery battery required that its members be mechanically inclined, and Manchester provided a host of such skilled men.[117]

The second three-year infantry regiment raised in New Hampshire was recruited throughout the entire state. By order of Governor Berry, each man who enlisted in the Third New Hampshire Volunteer Regiment was paid a ten-dollar bounty by the state. The 1,047 men of the Third New Hampshire went into camp at Camp Berry in Concord and were mustered into the service of the United States on August 26, 1861. The regiment was given their canteens, haversacks, Enfield rifles, and other equipment. Up to that day, only a portion of the regiment had received their uniforms, which like the previous two regiments, were gray.[118] This regiment also had its own band, a twenty-four-piece group under the directorship of Gustavus Ingalls of Concord.[119] Twenty-year-old Daniel Eldredge of Lebanon, who enlisted with the Third New Hampshire on August 2, 1861, recorded in his journal before he left his hometown for Camp Berry, he met several returning veterans of the First New Hampshire, who told him about their experiences during their Southern Campaign. The soldiers also commented on some of the hardships of the life of a soldier in the field, recounting their distain for such things as wormy hardbread, maggoty meat, and ill-fitting clothes and shoes.[120] When the Third New Hampshire's formation was finalized, it was discovered that there were two hundred more men than needed for the regiment, so this group was sent to Manchester to form the core of the next three-year regiment, the Fourth New Hampshire Volunteers.[121]

Selected to lead the Third New Hampshire was Hawkes Fearing of Manchester, but he declined the commission. Appointed in his place was Enoch Quimby

Lieutenant Daniel Eldredge, *Third New Hampshire, Company K. Wounded at both Fort Wagner and then Deep Bottom, Eldredge left behind an excellent journal of his experiences and also became the regiment's official historian. Photograph from* Reminiscences of the War of the Rebellion

Fellows of Carroll County, who had attended West Point but left in his third year, his standing with his classmates fifth in conduct and eighth in general standing. This is a fine accomplishment—his classmates included Thomas Jonathan "Stonewall" Jackson, George McClellan, Jesse Reno, and Ambrose Burnside.[122] The *History of Carroll County* records the most probable reason for Fellows's departure from West Point: "While at West Point he [Fellows] became permanently deaf and could never hear commands but safely depended on his knowledge and his eyes to execute them at the proper moment. The affliction caused him great annoyance and embarrassment because of which he rarely attended public gatherings or reunions."[123]

On August 15, 1861, Governor Berry authorized the state to raise and equip the next two three-year regiments, the Fourth and Fifth New Hampshire Volunteer Regiments. The Fourth, under the command of Lieutenant Colonel Whipple, was directed to report to Camp Sullivan in Manchester.

Twenty-six-year-old George F. Towle of Portsmouth, who found himself at the beginning of the war deep in Texas, resolved to make his way back north to serve the Union cause. His journey took him from Bandera, Texas, on May 28,

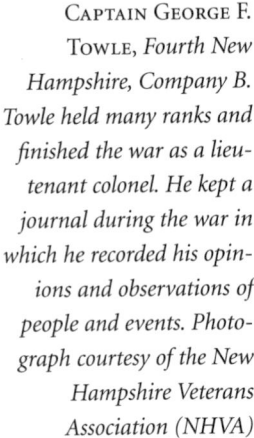

CAPTAIN GEORGE F. TOWLE, *Fourth New Hampshire, Company B. Towle held many ranks and finished the war as a lieutenant colonel. He kept a journal during the war in which he recorded his opinions and observations of people and events. Photograph courtesy of the New Hampshire Veterans Association (NHVA)*

1861, to Kansas in July. While in Texas, he was offered a commission in a Texas Confederate regiment. He recorded his reaction in his diary, which he faithfully kept through the entire war: "But I was a Union man. I could not fight against the promptings of my own heart. I could not fight against that flag."[124]

Arriving in New Hampshire, Towle explained, "The news of the Bull Run disaster, while it seemed to stun many made others but more eager to get into the fight. Sharing the feelings of the last, I hurried on to New Hampshire. The 3rd Regiment was in camp at Concord. I made efforts to secure a commission in this." Towle was later made first lieutenant of Company B of the newly formed Fourth New Hampshire Volunteer Infantry.[125]

On the Thursday afternoon of the August 29, 1861, the Third New Hampshire was reviewed and received their flag from Governor Berry. The ceremony was "hot and tedious." Two days later, Berry told Colonel Fellows to prepare the Third New Hampshire to leave for Washington.[126] Elbridge J. Copp of Company F remembered on their day of departure: "The scenes through the streets of Concord and at the depot while embarking on the cars shook the courage of many of the boys as the relatives and friends, fathers and mothers, brothers, sisters and sweethearts bade goodbye to the soldier boy, who was soon to face unknown danger."[127] The Third New Hampshire, three quarters of whom were farmers, laborers, or machinists, boarded the train in Concord for Washington, D.C., arriving there September 16.[128]

Back in New Hampshire, the Fourth New Hampshire was gathering and beginning to drill under the leadership of Colonel Whipple.[129] The Fourth was mustered into the service of the United States on September 18 and began preparations for leaving the state. September 26, proclaimed as a national day of fasting by President Lincoln, was also the day that the Fourth New Hampshire held its final review in Manchester. At the presentation ceremony, Governor Berry presented the Fourth with its flag. Fifteen-year-old Nellie Grace Willis, dressed in red, white, and blue, was named the "adopted daughter" of the regiment.[130]

In his diary Lieutenant Towle wrote, "Finally at 6 A.M. on the 27th, we struck our tents, formed line and marched down the main street of Manchester through the crowds on each side and at precisely 12 noon left for the seat of war. At last we were to really seek that enemy of whose powers we had heard so much since the lesson of Bull Run."[131]

September 26 also witnessed the official mustering of the First New Hampshire Light Battery in Manchester. The men were the first soldiers who were not in gray uniforms but were nattily dressed in short shell jackets with red chevrons, brass shoulder scales, and a shiny belt to hold their sabers. The battery practiced with old militia cannon on the shores of Lake Massabesic. The men were encouraged when their four new rifled guns and two twelve-pounder, smooth-bore howitzers arrived from Boston.[132]

September also saw the muster of the first of three companies of New Hampshire sharpshooters, initiated by Hiram Berdan, a native of New Hampshire living in New York. He had begun four months earlier trying to convince the War Department to allow him to raise a regiment of sharpshooters and after some initial resistance got the go-ahead, provided he could raise it in ninety days. Because of the short time frame, Berdan knew he could not raise all the men from just New Hampshire, so he sent out letters to all the Northern states requesting the help of their adjutant generals. Not one but two regiments of sharpshooters were formed, the First Regiment United States Volunteer Sharpshooters from New York, Michigan, Vermont, Wisconsin, and New Hampshire and the Second Regiment with companies from Minnesota, Michigan, Vermont, and Pennsylvania and two companies from New Hampshire. Requirements to be a sharpshooter included providing one's own rifle and getting ten shots inside a ten-inch target at both one hundred and two hundred yards. If the man was accepted, the government would give him a sixty-dollar allowance for use of his rifle.

The sharpshooter uniform was a departure from the standard gray of the previous New Hampshire regiments. In an attempt at camouflage, sharpshooter uniforms were green with a dark-green shirt and kepi. The uniform pants started as standard army blue but were later changed to green. The 350 men of the New Hampshire sharpshooter companies, as well as the other states', spent the winter of 1861–62 at Camp Instruction, Washington, D.C.[133]

In August, Edward Everett Cross, originally of Lancaster and just arriving from California, had met with Governor Berry to discuss how to raise the Fifth New Hampshire, the next three-year regiment. On August 27, 1861, Cross received his commission as colonel of the Fifth New Hampshire and immediately began organizing and making arrangements necessary for mustering his new regiment. The camp of the Fifth New Hampshire, located two miles southeast of Concord, was named Camp Jackson after the American hero of the War of 1812. On September 28, the first company entered the camp, and after a few days, seven hundred men were enlisted in the Fifth.[134]

As September turned to October, the people and the government of the United States were wondering how long the commander of the Army of the Potomac, Major General George B. McClellan, would need to bring the federal army to the level of proficiency where it could again engage the Confederates. In the South the Confederacy was desperately seeking ways to gain diplomatic recognition before the full strength of the United States armed forces descended on them.[135] The gathering of northern strength continued in Washington. Lieutenant Towle of the Fourth New Hampshire recollected, "The usual routine of drills prevailed in this encampment. Near us were the 2nd and 3rd New Hampshire and the 9th Maine with which the last two we were destined to be associated in many a battle. Not till Oct. 3rd did we receive our rifles, a Belgian arm of large bore .69 but one we found very effective."[136]

While the Third and Fourth New Hampshire drilled and waited for orders, New Hampshire men were in action in Virginia. In late September companies E and C of the First Regiment United States Sharpshooters were on a reconnaissance mission with General Smith near Lewinsville, Virginia, and saw their first action of the war and on return were in another on September 29.

Hiram P. Beede of Fremont, a member of Company E and present for these skirmishes, wrote in a letter home on October 4, "Least saterday night there was but one severely wounded and another slitly beside his eye. the papers did not tel the truth here aboat it. Thair was thirty-seven kiled at my knoledg and I don't know how many more and a grate many wounded. I was close to the dam when it was blode up."[137]

On October 9, the Fourth New Hampshire moved to Annapolis, Maryland, and became part of the Third Brigade along with the Sixth and Seventh Connecticut, Ninth Maine, and Forty-eighth Pennsylvania. Lieutenant Towle of the Fourth New Hampshire remarked on how the men began to wonder what they were preparing for, "Our days passed in constant and faithful drill, speculation prevailed as usual as to our destination, but beyond the fact of our going by sea, nothing further was known."[138]

A memorable incident during an inspection by Brigadier General Thomas W. Sherman. Sherman, known as a martinet, was not satisfied with the efficiency of the Fourth, and he began cursing at the officers. Colonel Whipple stood face-to-face with Sherman and screamed back, "G—d d——n you, General Sherman, I want you to understand this regiment was kicked out of New Hampshire without being given time to drill or even armed because it was suspected of being a Democratic regiment." Sherman, speechless, simply rode away with his staff to the next regiment. Whipple apologized to the men; General Horatio Wright had a word with him, probably a mild rebuke. Sherman never said another word and did not press charges against Whipple.[139]

In Camp Jackson, the men in the Fifth New Hampshire began to adjust to the discipline and regimentation of military life. On October 24, Colonel Cross received orders to report with his regiment to Washington. Concerned that he had not been given enough time to prepare and equip his men, he was able to gain a few days to organize the Fifth New Hampshire, which was mustered into the service of the United States on October 26, 1861. The Fifth struck their tents on Monday, October 28, and received their colors from Governor Berry and Adjutant General Anthony Colby. The 1,010-man regiment stayed overnight in Concord and was loaded into railcars for its long trip to the seat of war with a day's ration of dried beef and soft bread in their haversacks.[140]

The Sixth New Hampshire, the next three-year regiment to be formed, received the same $10 bounty as the others. The regiment, organized in Keene, was formed mostly by men from the western portion of the state.[141] Nelson Converse of Marlborough became colonel of the Sixth New Hampshire on October 26, 1861, when the man originally appointed colonel was not able to resign his post in the regular army. Converse, who had held several commissions in the New Hampshire Militia, was efficient in his efforts to raise and organize the regiment and held command of the Sixth New Hampshire until March 1862 when poor health compelled him to resign. Captain Simon Griffin, who had transferred from the Second New Hampshire to the Sixth and been appointed lieutenant colonel under Colonel Converse, became the colonel when Converse resigned. Griffin's record in the Second New Hampshire and the performance of his breechloader-equipped company had caught the attention of Brigadier General Hooker, who recommended him for promotion.[142]

The First New Hampshire Light Battery left the state on November 1, 1861, after an impressive march from Manchester to Nashua. In Washington their guns, which called for ammunition not then used by the U.S. government, were exchanged for six twelve-pound howitzers.[143]

COLONEL SIMON G. GRIFFIN, *Sixth New Hampshire, Field and Staff. Griffin was a captain at the start of the war in the Second New Hampshire. He bravely led the men of the Sixth New Hampshire in their charge against the Railroad Cut at Second Bull Run. Griffin finished the war as a brevet major general. Photograph courtesy of NHVA*

Winfield Scott's Anaconda Plan became the strategy for strangling the South's ability to maintain its war effort. Along the eastern coastline, the plan was to set up a blockade of southern ports, which would denying the Confederacy the imported supplies it so desperately needed. To maintain the blockade, the federal navy needed secure coaling stations along the southern coast. Captain Samuel Francis Du Pont was directed on October 12, 1861, to seize a southern port for a base of the South Atlantic Blockading Squadron; he decided on Port Royal, South Carolina, because "Port Royal alone admits the large ships."[144] Du Pont was given command of a mixed army and navy force whose equal had never been seen before. The naval force consisted of seventeen warships, twenty-five coaling ships, and thirty-three transports with a total of thirteen thousand men under the command of Brigadier General Sherman. A battalion of marines was also included because this was to be an amphibious operation.[145] Du Pont's flagship, the U.S.S. *Wabash,* was a thirty-two-hundred-ton steam frigate armed with twenty-eight nine-inch guns and fourteen eight-inch guns. The Third New Hampshire was quartered aboard the USS *Atlantic,* a side-wheel steamer that also served as the headquarters for Brigadier General Sherman. The Fourth New Hampshire was aboard the USS *Baltic,* also a side-wheel steamer, which carried all the horses of Wright's brigade and forty cannons. Another ship in the flotilla was the Portsmouth-built, fourteen-hundred-ton sloop USS *Mohican,* under the command of Captain Sylvanus W. Godon and boasting two eleven-inch pivot guns and four thirty-two pounders.[146]

The military force under Sherman's command consisted of three brigades: the First Brigade, under Brigadier General Egbert Viele, held the Third New Hampshire, Eighth Maine, and the Forty-sixth, Forty-seventh, and Forty-eighth New York Regiments; the Second Brigade, under Brigadier General Isaac I. Stevens, in which were the Fiftieth and 100th Pennsylvania regiments, the Eighth Michigan, and the Seventy-ninth New York; and the Third Brigade, under Brigadier General Horatio Wright and consisting of the Fourth New Hampshire, Sixth and Seventh Connecticut, and Ninth Maine regiments.[147]

On October 19, 1861, the Fourth New Hampshire struck tents in Annapolis and aboard the *Baltic* sailed down the Chesapeake Bay in company with the rest of the fleet. At Fortress Monroe in Maryland, the brigades were landed to exercise and practice drilling. The Fourth New Hampshire suffered its first casualty when twenty-three-year-old Private John S. C. Kelley of Derry succumbed to disease.[148] On October 29, the flotilla left Fortress Monroe at about seven in the morning. The *Baltic* had in tow the *Ocean Express* carrying twenty-five-hundred tons of ammunition and other ordinance. Lieutenant Towle of the Fourth recorded, "Going to his (General Wright's) stateroom one day with an officer who desired to ask some trifling information, I saw he was engaged over a map spread on his table. He covered it at once but not before I had seen that it was a map of the South Carolina coast. Our destination at last I said to myself. Somewhere along there we were going to make a landing."[149]

On the night of October 31, the *Baltic* ran aground off Cape Hatteras, North Carolina. The lines of the *Ocean Express,* still in tow, were cast off for fear of running into the *Baltic* and detonating the munitions.[150] Private Stephen J. Wentworth of Company F, Fourth New Hampshire, aboard the *Baltic* wrote to his parents back in Somersworth, "We sailed from Fortress Monroe one week ago. I have seen something of a sailors life during that time. The weather has been very rough and stormy. About four o'clock on Wednesday morning we ran on a sand bar off Cape Hatteras but got off without much damage."[151] Fortunately for the *Baltic* and its passengers, the sea was not very rough, and the ship was gently backed off the sand bar and floated freely in the deeper water. The *Ocean Express* was reattached, and the *Baltic* hurried to catch up with the fleet headed south.[152] Wentworth recorded his impression: "The next day the wind blew a perfect gale.

. . . I went up on deck about Midnight and for the first time in my life I know what it was like to see the waves run mountains high. It was a splendid but terrible sight. Our vessel is one of the largest ocean steamers and was tossed about like an egg shell."[153] Many onboard the *Baltic* voiced concerns for the smaller ships until a larger danger arose. The *Ocean Express* broke her tow cables in the heavy seas and was soon lost from sight. The *Baltic* itself because of its size and cargo weathered the storm rather well.

Towle relates that aboard ship, "Anxiety was felt for the *Coatzacoalcos* [carrying the Ninth Maine], *Governor* (carrying a complement of marines), *Isaac Smith* and *Mayflower* all of which were believed to have foundered but the fears turned out to be groundless. As it proved however, several ships were wrecked, the *Governor* sinking just as the last marine was being taken off and the *Union* (carrying a cargo of horses) going aground on the North Carolina coast."[154]

The seas were still heavy on November 3, and the fleet was still scattered by the storm. On November 4, the ships began assembling at the rendezvous off the harbor of Port Royal. The *Baltic*, ordered to look for its lost tow ship, returned the next day without finding the *Ocean Express*, carrying the bulk of the army's ammunition.[155] Du Pont was openly contemptuous of the multibranch nature of this expedition: "Soldiers and marines are the most helpless people I ever saw." That the storm had scattered the fleet, especially the ship carrying the army's ammunition, aided Du Pont's own plan. Feeling time was of the essence and because the rescued marines and several other ships needed for the landing had not yet arrived, Du Pont decided to attack the forts guarding the harbor with his warships alone.[156]

While the ships were waiting for their orders, and the gunboats were sounding the channel of the harbor, four Confederate gunboats appeared from the direction of Beaufort and came within range. Several shots were exchanged without effect on either side. Lieutenant Towle described the Confederate defenses, "Several guns were fired from a battery on shore. The strongest earthwork seemed to be on the point of Hilton Head, this was called Fort Walker-on the opposite point of Port Royal entrance, a small work known as Fort Beauregard stood over the bay. . . . But this last would fall of itself if Fort Walker were taken."[157] The forts were able to muster approximately fifty guns between them, but because of the distance, they could not support each other. November 6 passed without any activity, except for several more of the lost ships making their appearances.[158]

On November 7, 1861, Du Pont sent his ships in to shell the forts. Private Wentworth gave his impressions of the battle: "It was a glorious sight to see the bombardment. It lasted five hours and a half. The rebels fought bravely, but it was impossible to stand before the fire of the Frigates and gunboats. They rained a perfect shower of shells upon them."[159] Lieutenant Towle described the bombardment, "At 9:30 A.M. of the 7th, the fleet commenced shelling Fort Walker on Hilton Head. In the plan of attack, the gunboats formed a circle thus following each other in succession past the fort and delivering fire as they went by. Thus a continuous fire was kept up. Broadsides from the flagship *Wabash* hit the fort with a concentrated force. After nearly four hours shelling, Du Pont anchored the *Wabash* and poured in his broadsides upon the doomed fort which was then abandoned by its garrison being no longer tenable."[160]

The casualties among the fleet during the battle were light. Eight sailors were killed, and twenty-three wounded. The *Wabash* was struck thirty-four times, the *Pawnee* nine, and the *Bienville* five, with the *Mohican* sustaining minor damages.[161] The USS *Wabash* moved close to shore and landed sailors and the marine force to occupy Fort Walker. A staff officer of Du Pont's raised the American flag over the fort, closing the book on Du Pont's victory. Fort Walker was turned over to Sherman at sunset, at which time the army was finally permitted to land.[162] Lieutenant Towle remembered the singular honor accorded the Fourth New Hampshire and himself, "We were landed towards night in small boats, the first volunteer troops to set foot on South Carolina. I jumped into the light surf, the conviction flashed on me that I was the first volunteer Union soldier to stand on the soil of the Palmetto State."[163]

Private Wentworth remembered the same event with only a few differences, "We landed about eight o'clock in the evening. The night was a bright moonlight one. Our Reg't was the second to land. It was a laughable sight to see us land, two thousand men invading knee deep in the water, each one clinging to his gun with all his equipment—looked in the moonlight like a pack of peddlers."[164]

The Fourth New Hampshire spent the night in a sweet-potato field near the beach. Many in the landing force began to forage immediately. Parties of officers and enlisted men plundered Fort Walker. In one of the foraging parties was Private Wentworth, who described what he found, "Those who first got ashore got the best of it. They got gold and silver watches, revolvers, pistols, knives and everything you could think of. I did not get much. I got some knives and forks, plates, spoons and blankets. They were better than the ones I owned."[165] The Fourth New Hampshire had landed directly in front of the mansion and estate owned by Confederate Brigadier General Thomas F. Drayton, who was not only the commander of the military district that included his home in Port Royal but also was in command of Fort Walker. Drayton's brother, Commander Percival Drayton, was in command of the USS *Pocahontas*, which had bombarded Fort Walker. By daylight foragers were returning from Drayton's estate with geese, turkey, and sweet potatoes. Private Wentworth echoed the sentiments of his fellow soldiers when he said, "Ever since we got here we have lived like princes . . . you would have laughed to see the boys bring in pigs, pigs weighing between twenty-five pounds and two hundred pounds. We also get oranges and peanuts."[166]

The Third and Fourth New Hampshire regiments suffered no battle casualties from the action at Port Royal. On November 9, Admiral Du Pont came ashore, bringing the naval casualties in for burial.[167] The next three months witnessed the Third and Fourth New Hampshire regiments building fortifications and wharves, landing supplies, and drilling. At one of the daily inspections, Colonel Whipple asked a private why he had a dirty gun. The private sheepishly replied, "I know my gun is dirty but I've got the brightest shovel you ever saw, Colonel."[168]

In Keene the Sixth New Hampshire under Colonel Converse was mustered into the service of the United States in the last week of November 1861. The closing of November found the Fifth New Hampshire setting foot on the soil of Virginia for the first time. The regiment was in O. O. Howard's brigade and was placed in General Edwin V. Sumner's division. The Fifth, camping near Alexandria, Virginia, named their new camp Camp California and then went to work preparing their winter quarters.[169]

Writing from Hilton Head Island, Private Wentworth described some of the events in his camp: "There is not much new here. The work of fortifying the Island goes on rapidly. There has been one death in our company since we landed. Our Col. [Whipple] has seen service in the Mexican Wars and is well known as a brave man and a good soldier, but he has one failing. He is too fond of liquor. Thanksgiving Day he got a little too much aboard for his benefit. He followed it up the next day and got in a row with the officer of the guard, and I think he will resign. Sometimes we do not have anything to do, but eat and lay still for a week. It agrees with me, a soldiering first rate. I am as stout as a young jackass."[170]

The Seventh New Hampshire Regiment, also a three-year stint, was organized by Joseph C. Abbott, the former adjutant general of the state, who received permission to raise a regiment at federal expense; the same ten-dollar bounty would be paid by the state. The men began to gather at the camp of the Seventh, set up in Manchester and named Camp Hale. The colonelcy of the Seventh was offered to Abbott, but he turned it down, accepting the lieutenant colonel position instead. It was his desire to have a West Point graduate lead the Seventh.[171] Selected was First Lieutenant Haldimand Sumner Putnam of Cornish, who was in the U.S. Topographical Engineers and had served on the staff of General Irwin McDowell. Governor Berry offered the position to Putnam despite the latter's objection that he was too young, at age twenty-five, for the job. Organization of Seventh New Hampshire completed, the regiment was mustered into the service of the United States on December 14, 1861.[172] Thirty-five-year-old Calvin Shedd of Enfield enlisted in Company C of the Seventh New Hampshire in early

November 1861 as a private but was promoted almost immediately to sergeant. After giving his wife some advice on preparing their farm for winter, Shedd commented, "I am getting to be the most popular man in the Co if they could have their own way they would put me in Capt I think. All the Officers come to me for advice and the men call on me to decide all military questions that they have."[173]

In Hilton Head, South Carolina, Lieutenant Towle of the Fourth New Hampshire recorded an amusing story in his journal on December 7, 1861: "The Chaplain we brought out from Nashua was a Unitarian from Nashua—The Rev. M. W. Willis. Strong drink proved his rock ahead. He went in with full heading and stuck fast. Holding a glass half filled with whiskey to the light, he would exclaim 'If anything can make a man believe there is a God in Israel it is this,' He held out till December 15, when he was shipped back North—an expended Chaplain."[174] Towle also related the ongoing federal effort to blockade Charleston Harbor: "It seems prospects are afoot to close up Charleston Harbor. Odd-looking old vessels drop in occasionally. Relics of past ages. Old whalers from New Bedford that have pursued the Northern whale for years in more icy seas. Now laded with stones they are brought down to rest beneath these almost tropical waters on Charleston bar."[175]

The last New Hampshire regiment completed and mustered into service in 1861 was the Eighth New Hampshire. Raised at the same time as the Sixth and Seventh, the Eighth New Hampshire went into camp in Manchester at Camp Currier on the fairgrounds north of the city. Mustered in on December 23, 1861, the Eighth New Hampshire, under the command of Hawkes Fearing of Manchester was destined to serve in the far-off theater of Louisiana.[176]

In New Hampshire, the Portsmouth Navy Yard was proud that it had done more work from May to the end of 1861 than in any four-year period previously. When Abraham Lincoln took office in March 1861, only forty-two vessels were in commission. By the end of the year, that figure was 264. The Portsmouth Navy Yard was instrumental in making such an increase possible. One shining example of the Portsmouth Navy Yard's efforts was the sloop USS *Kearsarge*. This ship, destined to fight in one of the most famous naval battles of the Civil War, went from naval architectural plan to reality in only six months. The *Kearsarge*, named after a mountain in New Hampshire, was the sister ship of the *Mohican*, a recent participant in the Port Royal expedition.[177]

The middle of December was cold and snowy in New Hampshire. In this bleak and gray weather, the Sixth New Hampshire was ordered to break camp and proceed to Washington by the usual route of Worcester, Norwich, New York, Philadelphia, and Baltimore. The regiment and equipment all aboard, the engine picked up speed and left Keene behind on Christmas Day 1861.[178]

Eighteen-year-old, Sixth New Hampshire Private Samuel E. Douglas wrote to his father from Washington, D.C., on the last day of 1861, recounting the journey from his home in Keene: "I arrived here safe on Saturday the 28. . . . We took the Cars to Collins point in Connecticut and then took the Steamer to New York and then took the car to Washington we came through Philadelphia and Baltimore. . . . When we got to Baltimore the Stars and Stripes floated over Baltimore as we came through and hope it will float all over the Union."[179]

Camp life seemed to be a dismal experience for New Hampshire soldiers everywhere that winter, even in the relatively balmy climate of South Carolina. Private Steven Wentworth of the Fourth New Hampshire wrote a depressing report home to his brother on Christmas Eve: "Charley, do not enlist if you have got strong. Stay at home and remain so. If you come out here you would not stand one chance in ten in remaining well. There are a great many sick in the Reg't. Our principal living is hard tack and fried salt pork. The hard tack is so hard that we have to soak it to make is soft so we can eat it. The coffee is not fit to drink, At least I can't drink it. . . . This comprises a soldier's life. Have to go through this rain or shine, hot or cold. . . . I like it because I am doing my duty to my country. . . . So tomorrow is Christmas. I will close by wishing you a Merry Christmas and a Happy New Year."[180] Even despite these conditions, most men would have agreed with Thomas C. Cheney, a twenty-eight-year-old Manchester native who had enlisted in the First New Hampshire Light Battery in August 1861. He was now with the battery at Camp Du Pont in Munson's Hill, Virginia. In a letter home to his brother on December 19, Cheney repeats a refrain seen in many Civil War letters when asked if he would not rather be at home: "If I was at home now prephaps I could get Two Dollars a Day. I would like that first rate, but I want to see this wicked rebellion put down first. I don't care how soon we have a whack at them—, the Sooner the better."[181]

In New Hampshire, 1861 was the first year that the state officially recognized the Christmas holiday. In the winter camps of the New Hampshire soldiers, there were both idleness and anticipation. Charles E. Jewett of the Second New Hampshire wrote of both from Camp Beaufort, Maryland, on December 30, 1861: "There ain't any news to write everything seems to go on at a slow rate and I have got about tired of waiting for them to do something. . . . Some of them seem to think we have got into a scrape that we can't get out of easey but I don't see it in that light myself. The Army of the Potomac seems to be waiting for something but I don't know what."[182]

Jewett's Commander in Chief, Abraham Lincoln, was waiting, too. That fall, Major General McClellan had been supplying and giving his army the training that it so badly needed. Lincoln, who became more frustrated by the week at McClellan's inaction, could no longer contain himself in December when he heard that McClellan had taken sick. The president tried desperately to get someone to do something somewhere, but all the Federal forces had begun their winter hibernation.

The year 1861 ended for people in the North with sorrow, fear, and doubt over whether the country would be whole again. In the Confederacy there was also sorrow, fear, and doubt as to whether their new country would even survive.[183]

New Hampshire to the Front

CHAPTER 2

January 1862 to June 1862

Woe, woe to the traitorous children of Mars, who challenge this bird,
with his banner of stars; we will teach them this lesson, that truth
and the right, are ever triumphant, and must win the fight.

Anonymous, Union letterhead

January 1, 1862, in the camp of the Fourth New Hampshire at Hilton Head, South Carolina, began on an ominous note. Thirty-year-old Private John H. Whitehouse, who was posted to guard duty, was killed instantly when another soldier's gun accidentally discharged. His son, John H. Whitehouse Jr., was sent home disabled three weeks later. They had enlisted together at Somersworth in Company F, Fourth New Hampshire.[1]

Charles E. Jewett of the Second New Hampshire mentioned the ubiquitous mud along with a humorous comment about hard tack in his January 1 letter penned to his brother: "It has been so muddy here for two weeks past that we have not drilled but a little. We get plenty of mule meat as the boyes call it and hard crackers some of them are marked 18.10 other 75 B.C. meaning they say 75 years before crist but I am fatting up every day."[2]

On January 14, Colonel Haldimand Putnam and the Seventh New Hampshire left the state and were bound for New York, where they stayed four weeks before shipping off for the Florida Keys. Quartermaster Andrew H. Young, thirty-four years old and from Dover, described the departure to his son Hamilton, "We took down the big tents you saw at Manchester on one of the coldest mornings you ever saw, rolled them all up in a small bundle and put them on the cars, and all the rest of the things you saw, chests, beds, swords, guns, horses and saddles. We got started for Washington and all along the road wherever we went the boys swung their hats and the girls waved their handkerchiefs. But we did not go to Washington. We came to New York a place twenty times as big as Washington."[3] To his sister, Sergeant Caleb Dodge reported on the progress from New York City, "We had a tip-top time a comeing out here the boys were as stiddy as could be they are nothing like the 1st regiment the folks in New York that do not know us think that we are regulars we act so well."[4]

The Sixth New Hampshire under Colonel Nelson Converse did not stay in Washington very long before they were assigned to Brigadier General Ambrose Burnside's division in North Carolina and embarked for Hatteras Inlet, arriving January 13, 1862, after a fierce storm. Lieutenant-Colonel Simon Griffin recorded the passage: "We left in two boats, the *Louisiana* and the *Martha Greenwood*. *Louisiana* nearly capsized in the storm off Hatteras. Most of the regiment is seasick. The storm lasted eight days and two other vessels were lost."[5] The regiment could not be disembarked and had to stay on board for eight days and ride out the storm. During the journey south, 150 men from the regiment came down with measles. In the next two months, sixty men from the regiment died from a combination of fever and measles. Once ashore, the Sixth New Hampshire went into camp with the Eleventh Connecticut, Forty-eighth Pennsylvania, and Ninth and Eighty-ninth New York, all of whom would soon be fighting side by side.[6]

In the midst of a howling snowstorm on the morning of January 25, 1862, the Eighth New Hampshire Volunteer regiment under Colonel Hawkes Fearing struck its tents in Manchester and traveled by rail to Lawrence, Massachusetts, and then to Boston. Briefly quartered at Faneuil Hall, the regiment then went by boat to Fort Independence, Boston Harbor. The Eighth New Hampshire remained on garrison duty for three weeks, digging clams and drilling. The clams were a tasty supplement to the otherwise bland army diet.[7]

At Camp California in Fairfax County, Virginia, the Fifth New Hampshire continued to drill and train for the battles ahead. Private Lee C. Sears, originally of New York City, had enlisted in Company D of the Fifth in October 1861. Writing home on February 1, 1862, Sears shares his feelings of pride in the regiment and its colonel: "The regiment is one of the best in the army for drill, size and discipline. Our colonel [Cross] is an old Mexican veteran and a good soldier. He is a perfect gentleman, and one of my best friends. We use the Enfield rifle, and drill as light infantry. About seven-eighths of the regiment are shoemakers by trade, and a finer set of fellows one seldom sees."[8]

Sears was in error regarding the trade of his fellow soldiers. Farmers and tradesmen were evenly distributed throughout the regiment. What set the Fifth New Hampshire apart was that an unusual number of the men were taller than the average Union soldier height of five foot eight inches. Sears, wounded at the Battle of Malvern Hill on July 1, 1862, was appointed sergeant major on October 2. He was wounded again, this time seriously, on December 13, 1862, when the Fifth New Hampshire charged the Confederates at the base of Marye's Heights at Fredericksburg, Virginia. For his bravery Sears was appointed second lieutenant of Company F on December 14, 1862, but he suffered from his wounds and died on January 11, 1863.[9]

On February 13, the Seventh New Hampshire received orders to leave New York for Dry Tortugas, seventy miles west of Key West, Florida. Colonel Putnam and six companies of the Seventh left aboard the S.R. *Mallory;* the other four companies under Lieutenant Colonel Abbott left on the bark *Tycoon.* Both vessels left port on the same day but arrived seven days apart. While the *Tycoon's* voyage was shorter in duration, the ship experienced an outbreak of small pox.[10] The *Mallory's* longer time at sea was because of storms and days of buffeting by winds. The Seventh New Hampshire's duty at Dry Tortugas was to garrison and protect Fort Jefferson, a strategic fort in the Florida Keys and a distribution center for rations and ammunition headed for the federal forces in the Department of the South.[11]

From his new post at Fort Jefferson in Dry Tortugas, Corporal Caleb Dodge, Seventh New Hampshire, described his surroundings to his brother David: "Fort Jefferson is one of the largest forts uncle sam has got when it is don it will moant six hundred guns. it is one mile around and it incloses thirteen acars of land."[12]

On February 15, six companies of the Eighth New Hampshire Regiment left Boston aboard the *E. Wilder Farley.* This ship arrived March 15 at its rendezvous point at Ship Island, Mississippi, but the *Eliza and Ella,* with the balance of the regiment's companies, encountered hurricane-force winds that delayed its arrival until the end of March.[13]

The Eighth New Hampshire was assigned to Butler's Expedition against New Orleans. Capturing New Orleans, the largest city in the Confederacy, was the first step in gaining control of the Mississippi River from the south. The plan was that the combined efforts of federal forces coming south from Memphis and Northern armies pushing north from Louisiana would cut the Confederacy in two.[14]

At Hilton Head, South Carolina, the Third New Hampshire was still experiencing the monotony of its daily routine, the only event of consequence being that the regiment finally turned in its gray uniforms for federal blue. However, the Fourth New Hampshire was engaged in an expedition down the coast. Leaving at the end of January, the Fourth and other regiments sailed along the coast, landed at Warsaw Island, Georgia, and waited for their naval escort. On February 28 the ships went south to Fernandina, Florida, where a battle was anticipated, but upon landing, the troops learned that the Confederate forces had already evacuated the area. Fernandina was occupied and the Fourth New Hampshire became part of the garrison there.[15]

Writing to his family at the same time as Quartermaster Young of the Seventh New Hampshire was Sergeant Shedd, who chronicled the voyage south of the Seventh New Hampshire. He complained the meals were "poor at that and scanty since the men get over their sickness. The beef is so salt we cannot eat it.

I live on hard bread and a pint of the meanest coffee a day with some potatoes our pork is quite good tho fat but very bad to eat in this climate. We hope to fair better ashore. There are quite a no. of sharks swimming around the vessel they would like a Soldier to eat I suppose."[16]

Captain Towle, recently made captain of Company F, Fourth New Hampshire, recorded an unfortunate incident after the regiment occupied Fernandina. In mid-March the regiment's picket line on the outskirts of the city had been fired upon, forcing it to retreat to the city. Tension was already running high when members of Company G found a large supply of rum in one of the buildings. Most of the company became drunk and began looting the town. Towle was appointed as provost marshal with orders to quell the riot and restore the peace. Employing Companies H and K, he had the disorderly members of Company G surrounded by bayonets and the hotheads arrested. Private Martin J. Stanton of Manchester was accidentally shot by one of the provost guards during the riot. Soon after, all the companies of the Fourth New Hampshire, except E and F, under the command of Captain Towle, went south to Jacksonville, Florida.[17]

After arriving at Roanoke Island, North Carolina, on March 2, the Sixth New Hampshire reported to Colonel Rush C. Hawkins, the brigade and post commander. On March 8, Lieutenant Colonel Simon Griffin took six companies of the Sixth and joined General John G. Foster's expedition to Columbia. The report was that a sizable force of Confederates was gathering there, but no enemy troops were found. The force returned to camp.

On the same day as the expedition went out, Colonel Nelson Converse of the Sixth New Hampshire had to be discharged because of a disability caused by chronic diarrhea. Upon his return from the expedition, Lieutenant Colonel Griffin assumed command of the regiment. Griffin lamented in his journal that the same malady that had affected Converse had so weakened and demoralized everyone that only three hundred men were fit for duty. The Sixth New Hampshire had yet to suffer a single battlefield casualty.[18]

During their stay at Roanoke Island, the men of the Sixth New Hampshire, Company I, found a small, yellow Labrador puppy. "Old Jep" went everywhere with the regiment over the next two years, even following the men into battle. But on the morning after their engagement at Poplar Springs Church, Virginia, on September 30, 1864, Old Jep was never seen again. The men of the Sixth assumed that their valiant companion had fallen in battle.[19]

One of the three hundred men in the Sixth New Hampshire still fit for duty was Private Alvin A. Gove of Seabrook. In a letter home in March 1862, he expressed great confidence in Ambrose Burnside and passed along a camp rumor: "When we came here there was about 12,000 here but went with Gen. Burnsides to New Bern. Had a hard time taking that place but with Gen. B. for a leader we can do almost anything the report is that the Gen. has gone to Richmond and

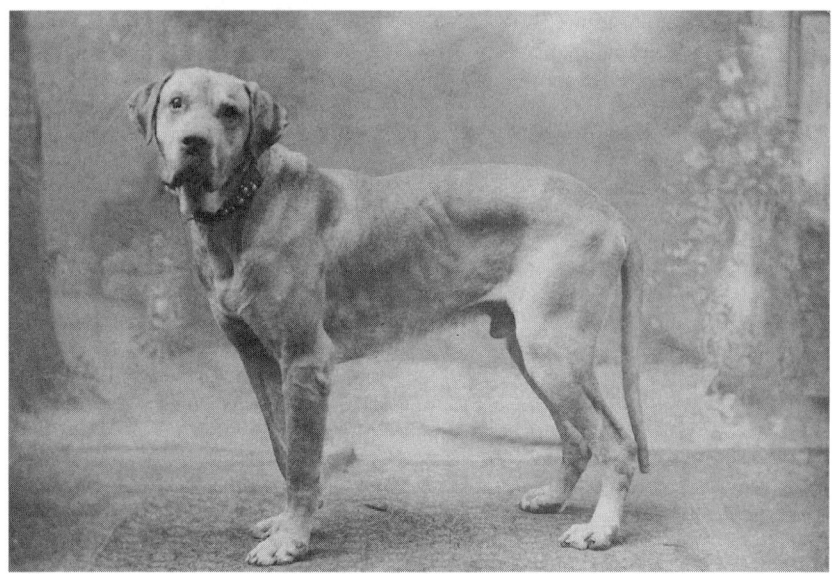

"OLD JEP." *This yellow, long-tailed dog was the mascot of the Sixth New Hampshire Regiment, Company I. The company found the three-month old puppy while at Roanoke, North Carolina, in 1862 and took the loyal dog everywhere over the next two years. "Old Jep" was not seen after the engagement at Poplar Springs Church, Virginia, and it was assumed that he was killed in the battle. Photograph courtesy of NHVA*

last knight the report was that he had taken Richmond but we can't hardly believe it as it seems almost to good to be true."[20]

Shortly after Colonel Converse was discharged from the Sixth New Hampshire, Colonel Whipple of the Fourth New Hampshire resigned command. Captain Towle of the Fourth New Hampshire recorded in his journal, "Colonel Whipple had left the 4th N.H. at Fernandina having resigned on account of certain affairs at Jacksonville into which he was drawn to act indiscreetly. We parted from him in regret." Towle registered his disapproval of Colonel Whipple's replacement: "Lt. Colonel Bell, a young man who owed his position to the political influence of the Bell family in New Hampshire succeeded Col. Whipple in command of the regiment."[21]

In their winter camp at Budd's Ferry, Maryland, the Second New Hampshire was busy building roads. With the coming of spring, the roads dried and became passable again, meaning the campaign season was about to begin.

From the Maryland side of the Potomac River, Colonel Gilman Marston and his officers could see that the rebels were hastily abandoning their camps on the opposite side of the river. The Second New Hampshire, along with the rest of the

First Brigade, crossed the river on March 9 and cautiously inspected the camps. The batteries were deserted. The Confederates had abandoned or destroyed a large amount of ordinance. The men of the Second cheered as the Stars and Stripes flew over the works so recently occupied by the Confederates.[22]

While searching the abandoned Confederate camp, a detachment of men from the Second New Hampshire found a ten-inch gun partially buried one mile from the river. One of the men in the party was twenty-nine-year-old Private Luther W. Fassett of Troy, New Hampshire, whose fate is described in his hometown's history: "The first soldier brought back for burial to Troy was Luther W. Fassett brother of D. C. Fassett, Co.E Second New Hampshire killed by rebels near Evansport, Va. April 2, 1862. Fassett with others had been engaged in digging for a gun that had been buried by the rebels after being abandoned. He and a companion, started back from where the men were engaged in digging to procure some shovels that were stored in a building about a mile away. They were met by three rebels in citizen clothes. Confronted with loaded carbines, Fassett surrendered but they sent a bullet through his body while his comrade made good his escape."[23]

In March 1862 the Third New Hampshire was involved in a mysterious expedition that was typical of Federal operations along the coastline of South Carolina and Georgia. Private Daniel Eldredge of Company K, Third New Hampshire, recorded this curious trek: "Embarked on lighters for some unknown point-towed by small steamers in the direction of Savannah. Landed on Mud Island where a battery had been erected to prevent the rebels from communicating with Fort Pulaski, bivouacked back at Dawfuskie."[24] The Third New Hampshire rowed in the distance in their unsteady boats and then marched twenty miles so they could raise the flag over a small part of the state of Georgia. During that time, five boats became beached, one returned, and the rest were fired on either by the Confederates or confused federal pickets. When the exhausted soldiers returned to their camp at Hilton Head, the expedition had already been dubbed "a Comedy of Errors."[25]

The beginning of March was cold and rainy in Northern Virginia when the Fifth New Hampshire began marching toward Manassas Junction for a much-anticipated engagement with the Confederates. At Manassas, the soldiers found that the Confederates had evacuated. The Fifth marched back to Fairfax and then were part of a reconnaissance in force on March 28 toward Rappahannock Station, where Brigadier Oliver Otis Howard's First Brigade (the Sixty-first New York, Sixty-ninth Pennsylvania, Eighty-first Pennsylvania, and the Fifth New Hampshire) met about five thousand men of Lieutenant General Richard Stoddert Ewell's division. Company A of the Fifth New Hampshire and about fifty federal sharpshooters were the first to encounter Ewell's Confederates who were hurriedly boarding trains. The skirmish line slammed into the Confederate rear guard just as they were setting charges and crossing the bridge. The bridge was promptly blown up, and the engagement settled into an artillery duel between the federals on the north side and the Confederates on the south side of the river. Amazingly, there were no casualties in either Company A or the other companies of the Fifth New Hampshire who served as flankers guarding the brigade.[26]

April began with the simultaneous movement of several federal armies. Major General McClellan commanded an army headed for the Virginia peninsula. Just before the Battle of Shiloh began on April 6 in western Tennessee, McClellan was laying out siege lines in front of Yorktown, Virginia, and planning to push up the peninsula and capture Richmond.[27] Sergeant Enoch Adams, a thirty-three year-old resident of Durham in the Second New Hampshire, wrote home before boarding the ship that would carry him to the Virginia peninsula: "I am well and in good spirits. I hope we shall have a fight. I want to distinguish or extinguish myself, one or the other. . . . The almighty will cover my head in the day of battle."[28]

About the same time as the Second New Hampshire was making its way to Yorktown, the Fifth New Hampshire was traveling from Alexandria, Virginia, to the Virginia peninsula. Colonel Cross left with six companies of the Fifth New Hampshire onboard the steamer *Donaldson,* and Lieutenant Colonel Samuel Langley departed aboard the *Croton* with the remaining companies.[29] History has recorded the drawn battle between the USS *Monitor* and CSS *Merrimac* in March 1862, but little is known about April's near confrontation between these ships in Hampton Roads. The Second New Hampshire had arrived at its camp eight miles from Yorktown, and Sergeant Adams of was on hand to witness the potential battle. In an April 14 letter to his mother, Adams described the action of April 11.

> At sunrise on the morning of the 11th I rose to look at the Monitor and Merrimac, the one our ironclad vessel the other that of the Rebels. The morning was magnificent. . . . Hampton Roads was full of vessels of every description and of different nations. When the Merrimac appeared around Craney Island. We ran our steamer under the guns of the Fort and we stood in expectation of seeing a greater naval battle than any ever yet recorded in history. The Monitor was floating round on the water like the oblong half of an eggshell, the spherical portion underneath. All above the water was a little narrow rim with a turret which it can pull in at pleasure as a clam can his head. A little pole in the stern with the American flag told whom it was ready to fight for. The Merrimac looked like a huge shed with nothing but its two roofs above the water. The iron plating was put on like slate shingles. It was followed by a flotilla of gunboats and resembled the Devil with his attendant angels. In comparison with this huge Goliath the Monitor appeared like a little David. Our gunboats were all cleared in expectation of a fight, and every man stood at his gun. The

Merrimac could get out to sea she could destroy New York City or any of
our seaports in a jiffy. But to do that she has got to get pass the Monitor and
between Fortress Monroe and the Rip Raps. But the fight didn't come off.[30]

The *Monitor,* on alert, had steam up in anticipation of another battle with the
Merrimac, but the latter proceeded no farther. The captain of the *Merrimac*
stated that he was waiting for the *Monitor* to come out and give battle. After this
brief standoff, the *Merrimac* returned to Norfolk.[31]

People at home in New Hampshire were hungry for descriptive stories like
the one Adams told about the *Monitor* and *Merrimac.* Susan B. Greene of Raymond asked her son William, serving with a sharpshooter regiment in Virginia,
not to hold anything back in his letters: "Don't deceive me Willie, but tell me as
it is. I am glad to hear, once more that you are alive and well. I hope I shall ever
hear such news from you-but I don't expect to. You must think that you would
be as likely to be killed as others when in battle. When those dreadful missiles
are flying in every direction. What a dreadful thing! Where will it end? How
many wretched Mothers, wives and orphans it is making."[32]

On April 18 from Camp Winfield Scott, Sergeant Adams reported to his
mother some details of the Yorktown siege: "An orderly sergeant of the artillery
was cut Square in two by a shell. Brig. Gen. Naglee just escaped death from a
forty-two pound solid shot which fell almost beneath his horse's hoofs. The balloon is up very often to keep track of them. No fifes are suffered to be played, no
drums beat, so every military maneuver is gone through like a pantomime. The
most sounds we hear are the rumblings of the caissons or artillery carriage and
the explosion of shells and the reports of cannon."[33] The balloon was the *Intrepid,* piloted by Thaddeus Lowe. During a flight over the Confederate lines at
Yorktown, Lowe said, "A hawk hovering above a chicken yard could hardly cause
more commotion." On one occasion during the Yorktown campaign, fellow New
Hampshire native Brigadier General Fitz-John Porter took an unescorted free
flight over enemy lines in the *Intrepid.* Although there were a few tense moments
when the balloon began to deflate too quickly, General Porter made it back safely.
The Confederates tried in vain to bring down the novel-looking aircraft, but their
muskets were ineffective, and they could not elevate their cannon high enough
to get a clear shot.[34] The first soldier from New Hampshire killed during the siege
of Yorktown was sharpshooter John S. M. Ide, thirty-two, from Claremont. While
exchanging shots from an exposed position on April 5, 1862, Ide received a fatal
head wound from a Confederate sharpshooter concealed some distance away in
a treetop.[35]

On April 18, the men of the Eighth New Hampshire on Ship Island, Mississippi, could hear the bombardment from the southwest by mortar boats under
the command of David Dixon Porter, the cousin of Brigadier General Fitz-John
Porter. The Union navy's first step to controlling the Mississippi River had begun

with David Porter's attack on the forts below New Orleans.[36] Aboard the USS *Cayuga* was Lieutenant George Hamilton Perkins of Hopkinton, New Hampshire, who had joined the navy when he was fifteen and gradually rose through the ranks, becoming a lieutenant in February 1861. Perkins described the action outside New Orleans in a letter home on April 20, 1862: "The bombardment of the forts commenced three days ago, and the first day we were in close action; but we all came out safe. Several of the vessels in the fleet have been struck and a few men killed and wounded. Today or tomorrow we start up river. The chain across it was cut last night, and I have no doubt but that the forts will be ours before tomorrow evening. The rebels are continually sending down firerafts, and the bombardment from the mortars goes on night and day, so that we have hardly any sleep. Unless we meet some unforeseen obstacle, New Orleans must fall."[37]

Southeast of New Orleans, Caleb Dodge of the Seventh New Hampshire, at Fort Jefferson at Dry Tortugas, described the troubles of his regiment: "This is a healthy place if we had not the small pox I don't think we should have lost a man but we have lost about twenty men with the small pox. We are in a barracks now it is a tip top place all the truble there is is the fleas and mosquetoes are so thick that we are most eat up with them. I have been up to the Capt and herd some news to day all about a big battle in Mississippi I hope it may prove true."[38] Dodge may have been referring to the bombardment of New Orleans, but because of the remote location of Fort Jefferson, he most likely just heard about the Battle of Shiloh that had occurred two weeks earlier in southwest Tennessee.

The following month, Sergeant Shedd of the Seventh New Hampshire was in good spirits when he wrote to his wife about Colonel Putnam's arrival: "Col. Put arrived yesterday I formed the Guard in good style & stood at Present Arms when he passed through the Sally Port he raised his cap to us & looked Bully & pleased the Regt think more of him than all the other Officers."[39] One of the most colorful characters of the Seventh New Hampshire was Heman Maynard of Lebanon, New Hampshire, to whom the men in Company C referred to as "Shaker," a reference to the Shaker country in northwestern New Hampshire. Sergeant Shedd said, "Shaker is busy Sundays and evenings teaching the slaves to read they are extremely pleased when they can spell words of three letters they astonish themselves in the progress they make."[40] Private Maynard, seriously wounded at the Battle of Olustee in February 1864, was discharged four months later.[41]

On April 23, Colonel Enoch Quimby Fellows, after applying for a sixty-day furlough, was relieved of the leadership of the Third New Hampshire by Brigadier General Horatio Wright. Fellows was suffering from neuralgia and resigned on June 26, 1862. During his command at Hilton Head and Edisto Island, Fellows had provided valuable information to his superiors regarding the deployment and strength of Confederate forces between Hilton Head and Charleston and had personally commanded several successful intelligence-gathering raids in the area.[42]

Outside of Yorktown, Virginia, Sergeant Adams of the Second wrote home on April 27 with great anticipation, assuming that a great battle was imminent: "I shall not disgrace you, you need not feel ashamed of my self devotion to the cause of my country. Please write oftener."[43]

As April gave way to May, New Hampshire troops were poised for action on many fronts throughout the South. In Virginia the Second New Hampshire was on the eve of its second major battle, while the Fifth New Hampshire was yet to be blooded. The Eighth New Hampshire waited to go upriver from New Orleans, while the Third New Hampshire stood only a month away from its first major engagement in South Carolina. After its baptism of fire at Camden North Carolina, during a small skirmish with the loss of one man, the Sixth New Hampshire rested on its arms during the month of May, and the Seventh New Hampshire remained on garrison duty at Fort Jefferson in Dry Tortugas, speculating how the war was developing elsewhere.

Writing from Camp Winfield Scott outside Yorktown, Sergeant Adams of the Second New Hampshire reported on May 2 that he thought the Confederates were almost finished.

It is reported that the Rebels intend to evacuate Yorktown. There won't be much chance for them when our mortars throw into them shells full of liquid fire. The shells, teakettles without any snouts as the boys call them have been bursting. Miss Dame, the Hospital matron told me one passed a few yards from her. There is no end to our mortars, and the siege of Sevastopol will be eclipsed by that of Yorktown: As the last battle of the revolution was fought here, I think the last battle of Secession will also be here, and a host of the leading traitors bagged. The eyes of all the world are on Yorktown today and millions of hearts are beating and swaying like pendulums between hope and fear at the name "Yorktown" I am glad I was not the last man to respond when my country called.[44]

Confronted with the possibility of being crushed between two federal armies, Brigadier General Joseph E. Johnston gradually withdrew from Yorktown, Virginia, on May 3 after a month-long standoff. Convinced that Johnston's troops outnumbered him, McClellan gingerly followed him up the peninsula toward Richmond.

On May 5, the advancing regiments of McClellan's army caught up with the Confederate rearguard divisions of Major General James Longstreet and Major General D. H. Hill just east of Williamsburg, Virginia. The battle fought centered on a line of defensive redoubts built previously by Confederate General John B. Magruder.

During the fighting at Williamsburg, the Second New Hampshire with other First Brigade regiments under the command of Brigadier General Cuvier Grover were advancing through a dense forest when they came under fire from Fort Magruder. The Second New Hampshire, emerging on the far side of the woods, encountered an obstacle of felled trees, which blocked the regiment's path but also provided some cover when the companies were in a shooting match with Confederates in their front and on their left flank. The first commissioned officer from New Hampshire to die in the war was Captain Leonard Drown, forty-one years old, of Penacook. Colonel Gilman Marston explains in his official report how Drown was killed: "Captain Drown had collected a company composed of his own men and those of other regiments, and bravely led them on to a body of the enemy, firing his revolver and cheering on his men, when the rebel barbarian in command exhibited a white flag, and cried out to him 'Don't fire, don't fire, we are friends,' at the same time directing his men to trail their arms. Captain Drown, believing they were about to surrender, directed his men not to fire, whereupon the whole body of the enemy suddenly fired upon him, killing him instantly, and also several of his men."[45] The bullet that killed Drown passed through his neck and struck the arm of Private Charles Holt of Antrim. The bullet was later successfully removed, and Holt returned to duty just in time to be wounded a second time at the battle of Second Bull Run.

The woods were filled with the screaming of men, the concussion of exploding shells, and the constant snapping and popping of musket fire. Small-unit actions and hand-to-hand combat were commonplace. Corporal John A. Hartshorn of Lyndeborough by himself skirmished with three Confederate soldiers. Hartshorn bayoneted one Confederate, swung around and shot another but could not react in time before the third Confederate shot him with a musket. Sergeant Adams was shot in the neck and on his way back through the lines met Captain Samuel Sayles of Dover. Adams was so covered in blood and caked with dirt that Sayles didn't recognize him. "Who is this?" asked Sayles. "It is I," said Adams. The sergeant's wound was treated, and from his Baltimore hospital bed, he wrote home on May 10, 1862: "I was in our battle at Williamsburg, the wildest fight on record. It occurred on Monday the 5th. I was wounded by a bullet or buckshot just behind the left ear running along the back of my head. It is still in. The Enemy shot me. It near cut the jugular vein. It cut some artery and I nearly bled to death and should if the wound had not been dressed. My deliverance was providential. My clothes, greatcoat, vest, shirt and pants are all clotted by blood. I am not disfigured anyway but the pain in my head is extreme. The Surgeon will not extract the buckshot for fear of pricking some artery and renewing the hemorrhage. I shall come on as soon as I can." Adams went home to Durham to rest and recuperate for three months and was back with his regiment in September 1862 as a new second lieutenant.[46]

Each time the brigade advanced or withdrew, the Second New Hampshire gained stragglers from other regiments broken during the fighting. Many incidents of heroism took place in the two hours that the Second was engaged in the forest. Lieutenant David Steele of Antrim and his squad through sheer gall and determination demanded and received the surrender of a force of Confederates roughly twice their number.

By 5 P.M. it appeared that the whole federal line would collapse from the pressure brought to bear when Confederate reinforcements were thrown into the fray. Arriving just in time, regiments from Brigadier General Kearny's division blunted the Confederate advance. From here Longstreet's exhausted troops were steadily pushed back until they disengaged and withdrew from the field. Johnston's rearguard action at Williamsburg was a victory for the Confederates in that it detained McClellan's army long enough for the main body of Johnston's army to withdraw farther west toward its new defensive line outside Richmond.

The Second New Hampshire and the rest of Hooker's Second Division, broke the Confederate line on May 5, inflicting punishing casualties on Longstreet's and Hill's divisions. The Second New Hampshire sustained frightening casualties in this one-day battle, with sixteen men killed, sixty-eight wounded (six mortally) and nineteen missing and assumed captured. Casualty figures for the entire Williamsburg battle vary, but it is generally agreed that the federals lost approximately twenty-two hundred killed and wounded, compared to the Confederates seventeen hundred.[47]

The Third Corps commander, Brigadier Samuel Heintzelman, lauded the Second New Hampshire in his official report: "In General Grover's brigade most of the regiments did very well—the Second New Hampshire particularly so, and it suffered greatly."[48] The Second New Hampshire was able to rest for the remainder of the month of May but would be in action again, participating in minor skirmishing with the Confederates during the Seven Days Campaign.

The Fifth New Hampshire on May 5 was east of Williamsburg on the Yorktown Road with the rest of Sumner's Corps when fighting broke out far in their front. The Fifth heard the sounds of battle about 9 A.M., and the division started marching toward Williamsburg. The men marched hard over roads that were rendered nearly impassable by the soaking rain. Arriving about 2 A.M. on May 6, the Fifth New Hampshire was too late to play a part in the Battle of Williamsburg because the Confederates had already retreated west.[49] The Fifth New Hampshire spent the month of May in pioneering and bridge-building duties. Thomas L. Livermore remembered the construction of a bridge that will always be associated with the Fifth.

On the [May] 28th Colonel Cross was ordered to construct a bridge over the Chickahominy capable of bearing up artillery and wagons. Large details were sent into the water, and there up the stream they cut logs and floated them down to the bridge. The work was mainly done in the water, sometimes waist-deep and amid mud and tangled underbrush. Details of the 64th and 69th New York were sent to aid us, and the colonel had a barrel of whiskey broached, at which the soaked soldiers could slake their thirst. By the evening of the 30th, whether three or five days, the bridge was completed seventy rods in length. General Sumner, I believe, christened it the "Grapevine Bridge." General McClellan says that it was the only bridge available as the rains had swelled the current so high that the rest were rendered useless.

The men of the Fifth New Hampshire had built the bridge that would carry them to their first major confrontation with the Confederates.[50]

While the Fifth New Hampshire was bridge building in Virginia, Quartermaster Andrew Young of the Seventh New Hampshire was explaining the meaning of the war to his young son Hamilton on May 28: "I expect by this time you know all about what this great war is about. A rebel is one who trys to injure or fight against his Government which has always used him well. Traitors are fighting to tear down the Government and good men are fighting to prevent it. But the war will do good. Those who have gone to the war will always remember how much labor it cost & how many lives it cost to save this good Government. And the boys will always remember how they staid at home & took care of their Mothers & Babies while their Fathers and Brothers went down to the war, and all will be better citizens."[51]

For the entire month of May, General McClellan and his army inched closer to Richmond. McClellan was constantly looking north for promised reinforcements. He placed three corps under Sumner, Porter, and Brigadier General William B. Franklin on the north side of the Chickahominy River to join forces with Brigadier General Irvin McDowell's First Corps when it arrived. However, McDowell did not come because Stonewall Jackson's campaign in the Shenandoah Valley had kept three federal armies at bay, and fears for the safety of Washington, D.C., kept McDowell's First Corps near Washington. McClellan later blamed his failure to take Richmond on the War Department's decision to withhold McDowell's Corps.

Taking advantage of McClellan's decision to split his army, Johnston promptly attacked the two federal corps that McClellan left south of the Chickahominy River. On May 31, Johnston ordered Brigadier General William H. Whiting, Major General James Longstreet, and Major General D. H. Hill to attack Brigadier General Erasmus Keyes's Corps near Seven Pines, Virginia. In the North this battle would be known as the First Battle of Fair Oaks, and in the south it was known as the Battle of Seven Pines.

While Majors General A. P. Hill and John Magruder screened the Confederate left flank, Longstreet's Corps was to attack Keyes's right flank and destroy his corps while D. H. Hill attacked from the left. The Confederate plan fell apart when instead of attacking at dawn as instructed, Longstreet delayed his attack until 1:00 P.M. Taking the wrong road, he delayed the progress of not only his corps but Whiting's division that was assigned to the attack as well. D. H. Hill alone slammed into the left flank of Casey's division.

Listening to the sounds of battle from across the river, McClellan instructed the Second Corps to help Keyes. In the First Division of the Second Corps was the Fifth New Hampshire Regiment. At approximately 2:30 in the afternoon, Colonel Edward Everett Cross and his men marched across the bridge over the Chickahominy River on their way to a sanguinary appointment at Fair Oaks Station.[52]

Confederate troops in Brigadier General W. H. C. Whiting's division finally attacked at Fair Oaks Station about 4 o'clock and by then ran into elements of Sumner's Corps that had just recently crossed the river. By dusk Confederate forces had made significant gains by smashing the federal right flank and forcing it into a defensive line near Fair Oaks. The fighting on May 31 subsided about 6:00 P.M. before the Fifth New Hampshire arrived on the field that night. The men in the Fifth were grumbling. A frustrated soldier in the Fifth loudly proclaimed, "This regiment never will get into a fight."[53] Livermore of the Fifth New Hampshire recounted the following day: "The light of day of June 1st, Sunday, had hardly crept around the shadows of the woods when over the railroad, a little to the left of our front in the woods, a thundering roll of musketry broke forth, and increased in noise until it was almost deafening. Bullets commenced to whiz over our heads in piping tones. General Sumner rode up to our colonel, and said in his deep voice, 'If they come out here, give 'em the bayonet.' The time was now come to shoot for country and liberty; we stood in our first field with the bullets whizzing around us. At length we moved in line of battle over the railroad."[54]

Again, as on the previous day, Longstreet was ordered to attack at dawn, the only difference being that Johnston had been severely wounded the previous day, and the army was in temporary command of Major General G. W. Smith. Fearing a large federal counterattack, Longstreet committed only two Confederate brigades to attack Fair Oaks Station. Brigadier General Israel Richardson's division stopped the Confederate attack. Known as Richardson's foot cavalry, the division included the famed regiments of the Irish Brigade and the Fifth New Hampshire.[55]

Early in the fighting, the First Brigade Commander Brigadier General Oliver Otis Howard received a wound to his right arm, but he stayed on the field directing the regiments of his brigade until he was hit a second time in the same arm. The ball so mangled Howard's arm that there was no recourse except amputation. Surgeon Luther M. Knight, a forty-nine-year-old doctor from Franklin who had joined the Fifth New Hampshire in September 1861, assisted the division surgeons during the operation. After Howard left the field, command of the First Brigade devolved on Colonel Cross, who ordered the Sixty-ninth and the Eighty-eighth New York of the Irish Brigade into positions on either side of the Fifth New Hampshire.[56] A member of the Irish Brigade writing a few days after the battle relates the desperate position of the Fifth New Hampshire.

> The scene of action was now on the railroad, distant from the open space in which we were in line. A few minutes after, an aide came for the Sixty-ninth (N.Y.) to support the Fifth New Hampshire, who were nobly holding their ground, thirty or forty yards in advance of the railroad, against a whole brigade. "You can not have the Sixty-ninth," said he (Richardson) "Take the Eighty-eighth." A short time only had elapsed, and on came the same aide, quicker than before for the Sixty-ninth, saying the 5th New Hampshire would be surrounded if not immediately re-enforced. True enough, when we reached the railroad left in front, we found that a rebel regiment had got around by the right of the 5th New Hampshire, and had them nearly surrounded, when we opened fire. We came at an opportune moment or they would have been cut to pieces.[57]

Livermore recalled the actions of the Fifth New Hampshire that day: "We had eight hundred rifles, and I never shall forget how we made those woods ring with our firing. The rebels opened at once and the bullets flew in myriads around us, humming deadly songs, hitting our men and splintering the trees around us."[58]

Born in New Durham and recruited for the town of Brookfield, Private James C. Chesley, forty-two, of the Fifth New Hampshire described the action at Fair Oaks: "The battle was tough at fair oakes station this station is on the York Town and Richmond Rail Road about seven miles southeast of Richmond we got the day and moved forward one mile and went to building breast works and they would shel us and we them and some of our men was killed."[59] Private Chesley wrote his letter home not even mentioning that he had been wounded in the Battle of Fair Oaks. He was too disabled to continue his duties and was discharged from the army in March 1863.[60]

After the battle, the Fifth retraced their steps back to and over the railroad. Livermore tallied up the cost of the Fifth New Hampshire's baptism of fire: "We moved into the open field whence we had moved at light and then counted our killed and wounded. The regiment had lost 186 all told and among them were Colonel Cross and Major [William W.] Cook." Cross and Cook had thigh and leg wounds.[61]

The Fifth New Hampshire fought directly against men of the Sixth Alabama, commanded by Colonel John Brown Gordon. Gordon took command of Rode's brigade when Brigadier General Robert Rodes was wounded. The Fifth New Hampshire and the Irish Brigade would face Gordon four months later in the Sunken Road at the Battle of Antietam.

The Battle of Fair Oaks, while a tactical defeat for the Confederates, resulted in General Robert E. Lee being placed in command of the Southern army. He ordered an immediate withdrawal toward Richmond. McClellan took advantage of the lethargy on the part of Johnston's subordinates to inflict sixty-one hundred casualties on them, but the federals lost five thousand men. This severe and clumsily fought engagement resulted in reinforcing McClellan's already over-cautious approach to the campaign.[62]

Several days after the Battle of Fair Oaks, Albert Taft of Nelson, New Hampshire, was opening a letter from his friend Gilman Griffin. The Taft family was still mourning the loss of Albert's brother Edward, recently killed at the Battle of Williamsburg while serving with the Second New Hampshire Regiment. Griffin had heard that Albert was determined to enlist in a regiment and take his brother's place. Griffin cautioned him, "While I am glad you are still patriotic, I wish to say to you, DO NOT GO BY ANY MEANS. Your health will not admit it. You could not lie on the ground or be exposed to storms or rain, or undergo the rapid forced marches, or any of the numerous hardships and privations of a soldier's life. Remember, Edward said that one out of a family was enough to go. So Goodell said to me, and so I say to you."[63] Griffin was referring to his brother Simon Goodell Griffin, the colonel of the Sixth New Hampshire Regiment. Twenty-four-year-old Albert Taft enlisted anyway along with other members of Kimball Union Academy. Taft joined the Ninth New Hampshire Regiment, formed in the summer of 1862. He contracted measles after the Battle of Fredericksburg in December 1862 and was transferred to a hospital in Washington. So disabled by disease that he never returned to duty, Taft was discharged from the regiment in November 1863. Taft's friend Gilman Griffin died later in 1862 at age forty-three.[64]

McClellan's campaign on the Virginia peninsula was the focus of attention throughout the North and in letters back to New Hampshire from soldiers in the field. Quartermaster Andrew Young of the Seventh New Hampshire writing June 6 from Fort Jefferson, Florida, was openly critical of McClellan's management of the army: "McClellan it was said was within three miles of Richmond which was three miles further off than when we heard from him before. With due respect for public opinion I must say that I think McClellan is too slow. He will probably take Richmond but he will do it so slow that it will lose very much of the moral fever. He has allowed them to retire all the way from Manassas so quietly with all their men & munitions that they will be as just as good condition to fight when they go out on the back side of Richmond as when they first started."[65]

While Young was writing down his opinions about McClellan's campaign, farther north, the Third New Hampshire crossed over to James Island, South Carolina, in the opening moves of the Battle of Secessionville. On the night of June 7, Major John Bedel, forty-two, of Indian Stream, New Hampshire was the general field officer of the day. Bedel had orders from Brigadier General Isaac Stevens to aggressively push forward the picket line to gain prisoners and information. The three-mile-long picket line had snaked back and forth for several days with each side advancing and then retreating without bringing on a general engagement.[66]

Guns within the Confederate fort and a nearby gunboat had the ability to shell the camps of Brigadier General Stevens. With permission from Major General David Hunter, Brigadier General Henry W. Benham advanced a battery forward to silence the Confederate batteries. Benham's battery succeeded in silencing the gunboat but not the guns in the fort. Hunter later gave Benham permission to conduct a reconnaissance of the area but not to bring on a general engagement.[67]

Bedel carried out his orders and advanced to where the Confederate works could be observed. He withdrew and reported his findings to Stevens, who promptly ordered Bedel to repeat the exercise, except that this time he was to draw the fire of the Confederate guns in the fort so they could be counted. Company C under Captain Michael T. Donohoe of Manchester was detailed for the return trip to the rebel lines. Bedel and Donohoe dashed through the open ground between the picket lines and with their company promptly drew fire from the Confederate fort. Bedel and Donohoe quickly retired with Company C back toward the Union line. When they looked over their shoulders, they saw that part of Company H and F had quit the picket line with the Confederates in hot pursuit. The rebels could see that they were rapidly approaching the federal lines and gave up the chase. Stevens's information-gathering expedition had been a success, and word that James Island was heavily occupied by Confederate troops was passed back to the headquarters of Brigadier General Benham.[68]

Benham was itching for a fight. Going completely against instructions from Hunter, Benham ordered a direct attack on the Confederate fort at Secessionville. Against the advice of Stevens and Wright, Benham ordered a frontal assault on the fort that anchored the Confederate right flank on James Island. In the fort waiting for the federal assault were elements of the First, Twenty-second, Twenty-Fourth, and Twenty-fifth South Carolina regiments along with the crack gunners of the Pee Dee, Charleston, and the Second South Carolina artillery regiments.[69]

At daylight on June 16, 1862, the federal assault column led by the Eighth Michigan Infantry attacked the fort. A ten-inch Columbiad gun in the fort erupted and tore massive holes in the Federal line. The Forty-sixth and Seventy-ninth New York, the Twenty-eighth Massachusetts, and the Seventh Connecticut gained the earthwork and engaged in vicious hand-to-hand combat with the Confederates. This attack was repulsed. The next wave advanced toward the fort. This wave included the Third New Hampshire, Forty-fifth and Ninety-seventh Pennsylvania, Third Rhode Island Heavy Artillery, and Sixth Connecticut. These units were also repulsed after multiple attacks.[70] Major Bedel described the early part of the attack: "The order to advance was repeated. Finally it was thrown forward and advanced as near to the battery as the marsh and creek would permit and opened fire upon, and at once silenced every gun in the battery and drove the enemy out of it, and so held it silenced for more than an hour against all odds. In passing into the field the regiment was enfiladed by a field battery with grape and canister, to which no attention was paid. Reenforcements from Charleston reached the enemy and the musketry became more gauling in front."[71]

About now the Third New Hampshire began to feel the effects of friendly fire. The regiment had pushed so far forward that shells from Stevens's artillery and federal gunboats in Stono River began falling on the regiment. At this point, with the regiment also running low on ammunition, Lieutenant Colonel John Jackson of Portsmouth asked for permission to withdraw, which Benham at first refused. As the situation in front of the fort deteriorated, Jackson was permitted to retreat.[72]

Daniel Eldredge of the Third New Hampshire was also present to describe the battle: "We marched in by the left flank so that in order to attack the command was 'by the right flank, double quick.' Just before this command was given we received a shot from a masked battery on our left which was aimed at our color bearer Corporal James Cassidy of Co. K striking him in the head with a fragment of shell cutting the scalp but not penetrating the brain. We arrived on a bank of a deep and muddy marsh that was impassable. When halted we opened a hot fire on the garrison of the fort. Gunboats began to shell and they struck as many Feds as Rebs. Stevens' brigade made the attack on the right and was repulsed with great slaughter."[73] Corporal Cassidy, born in Ireland in the war for the town of Dover, recovered from his wound and was wounded in two more battles before receiving a mortal wound at the Battle of Drewry's Bluff in May 1864.[74]

The Third New Hampshire abandoned the field piecemeal, as some of the companies did not hear the order to retire. Many soldiers stopped to fire one more round back at the Confederates. Those who were still close enough could hear the Confederates chanting, "Bull Run, Bull Run, Bull Run."[75]

Elbridge J. Copp of the Third New Hampshire summed up the human cost to New Hampshire: "Within the space of two acres more than a hundred of the men of our regiment lay upon the field dead or wounded."[76] A cannon shell literally tore thirty-two-year-old Captain Ralph Carlton of Farmington in half. Young Elbridge Copp of Carlton's regiment was horrified that he had been drenched by the captain's blood.

Sergeant Horatio C. Moore of Claremont wrote to his parents nearly a year after joining the Third New Hampshire: "We must clean out Charleston before, we go home. I shall never be contented to go home till we get one or more victories on our flag."[77] Moore, twenty-two, had a wound from a bullet that struck him in the head, passed through his cheek, and lodged in his throat. He lived for three days before succumbing to his painful injury on June 19.[78]

The Third New Hampshire went into the Battle of Secessionville with 26 officers and 597 men fit for duty. At Secessionville, 104 men were killed or wounded. Lieutenant Colonel Jackson in his report mentioned Captains Michael Donohoe, John E. Wilbur, and James F. Randlett as deserving special notice for courage under fire.[79] In a letter to Governor Berry, the overall brigade commander Colonel Robert Williams of the First Massachusetts Cavalry stated, "I do not believe it possible for men to have acted with more courage, and I desire to particularly call your attention to the marked gallantry of Lieutenant Colonel Jackson, Major Bedel and Captain [Josiah I.] Plimpton. Their conduct was even noticed by the enemy, as it was afterward stated at a flag of truce."[80] Private Eldredge criticized the leadership in the battle: "The whole fight in my opinion was a poorly managed one. Only 2 or 3 regiments ordered in at a time. And these were relieved by others who were so cut up they were inefficient."[81] Brigadier General Henry Benham was sent to Washington under arrest and was demoted to colonel, eventually leaving the service in 1882. Benham had been ordered to carry out only a reconnaissance in force but instead had brought on a battle that resulted in the loss of 683 dead, wounded, or captured Union soldiers.[82]

Because of the resignation of Colonel Fellows, Lieutenant Colonel John Henry Jackson was promoted to colonel. Major John Bedel became the new lieutenant colonel, and Captain Josiah I. Plimpton of Milford the major of the regiment. Before the end of the war, all of these men, including Colonel Fellows, would be in command of a regiment; one was to die on a blood-soaked field in Virginia.[83]

Near their camp in Fair Oaks, Virginia, Charles Jewett of the Second New Hampshire wrote home to his brother on June 19 about the eerie feeling of camping on a battlefield: "I shall be glad when we get out of this place for we are encamped rite on the Battle field whare they had Sutch a big slauter and you can hardly step without stepping on a grave and they were mostley buried on the top of the ground without being half covered up and many are not buried naw and it is very warm here naw and you can judge for your self that it ain't a very sweet smelling place about this time but I think there will be something done before long and I think if we have good Success in taking Richmon if thare is any left of the N.H. 2nd they will have a chance to go home."[84]

From the same battlefield and regiment, Captain Samuel Sayles of Company D Second New Hampshire wrote to his friend Sergeant Enoch Adams, who had been wounded at the Battle of Williamsburg and was convalescing at home in Newmarket: "We get whiskey rations everyday. The 2nd NH has grown frightfully small. But Whiskey is a great Institution. May it plentifully abound in wartime. I would tell you when Richmond will be taken if I knew, perhaps in the Year 1862 and perhaps not. Give old Joe Hooker enough and he would be in there tomorrow night. Bully for Old Joe, Gentleman Joe, He's a Brick."[85]

"Old Joe" Hooker, Grover's First Brigade, and the Second New Hampshire took part in the first of the Seven Days' Battles at Oak Grove, Virginia, near Richmond, on June 25, 1862. There had been light skirmishing for several days near the Fair Oaks battlefield when McClellan ordered Third Corps commander Brigadier General Samuel Heintzelman to clear out the Confederate pickets in the wooded area in their front. The soldiers became very excited at the prospect of this final push to Richmond because the tall spires of the city could be easily seen from the treetops.

At 8:00 A.M. on the 25th, Hooker's division attacked the Williamsburg road with Grover's brigade on the left and Major General Daniel Edgar Sickles's brigade on the right. This spirited attack quickly swept away the Confederate pickets but unfortunately slammed into the main Confederate line just a few miles east of Richmond that was held by a mixed force of Virginians and Alabamans under Brigadier General William Mahone.[86] By nightfall the lines had barely changed since the break of day, yet 626 federal and 441 Confederate casualties were on the field. The Second New Hampshire under Colonel Marston lost four killed and thirty-four wounded, of which four died later of their wounds. Seventeen of these casualties came from Company B alone when the company (armed with breechloaders) was called upon to clear out a troublesome nest of Confederate sharpshooters that had been delaying the advance of the First Massachusetts.

Among the New Hampshire casualties was Sergeant Thomas B. Leaver of Concord, the soldier who had been so uncomfortable and bored a year ago in the Second New Hampshire camp in Portsmouth and could not wait to leave. Leaver's body and that of Corporal George Damon of Penacook were brought to the regimental hospital and covered with blankets. Harriet Patience Dame, who had been nursing the wounded from the battle, lifted the blankets and recoiled in shock. She had been a neighbor of the Leaver family in Concord and had known Thomas from the time he was a boy. Dame carefully prepared the bodies of both soldiers and personally supervised their burial near the hospital. Burleigh Jones, twenty-two, of Hopkinton and Horace Lamprey, nineteen, of Concord, both of Company B, died of their wounds aboard the hospital ship *St. Mark*. Private Patrick H. Henaghan of Newmarket was killed instantly when a musket ball smashed into his forehead as he charged across a field.[87] The night passed with a casual exchange of picket firing until near midnight when both sides unleashed a huge volley against each other. The morning revealed that unknown Union officers had authorized a withdrawal from the lines that the Second and other regiments had fought so hard to secure the previous day.[88] In his official report on the Battle of Oak Grove, Colonel Marston stated, "Where almost every man performed his part well and according to the best of his ability it might be considered invidious to mention particular cases of gallantry and good conduct, which otherwise I should be glad to do so."[89]

June 25 to July 1 marked the critical battles of the Seven Days when the Confederacy appeared to be all but finished with its back to the gates of Richmond. The Fifth New Hampshire was in the battles at Savage's Station, the Peach Orchard, and Malvern Hill but had minimal casualties. In addition to the Battle of Oak Grove, the Second New Hampshire was present at the Battle of Malvern Hill and also experienced light casualties.[90]

One son from New Hampshire played a pivotal role in the Seven Days' Battle. Brigadier General Fitz-John Porter[91] rose to the pinnacle of his military career in summer 1862, only to be cashiered from the army six months later a broken and discredited man. He was responsible for the direction of the siege of Yorktown under McClellan while in command of the First Division of the Third Corps. Just before the Seven Days' Battle, he was placed in command of the Fifth Corps and led it at the battles of Gaines Mill, Mechanicsville, and Turkey Bridge. For his gallant conduct of the Fifth Corps during the retreat from Malvern Hill, Porter was promoted to major general. Fitz-John Porter had a brilliant future in the army, but his outspoken nature and his unswerving loyalty to George McClellan would eventually bring his downfall. After the Peninsula campaign, McClellan's popularity faded, and Porter made no secret of his disapproval of the Army of Virginia's commander John Pope.[92]

After a disastrous defeat at Second Bull Run, Pope went looking for a scapegoat, and he did not have far to search. He could not openly criticize the popular McClellan so he selected one of his minions. Pope charged Porter with disloyalty, disobedience, and misconduct in the face of the enemy. Pope was transferred to Minnesota to fight Native Americans, but the anti-McClellan faction remained in the War Department with Secretary of War Edwin Stanton as its unofficial leader. McClellan's perceived timidity at the Battle of Antietam and his lethargy afterward led to his removal from the army as its commander. After the exit of McClellan, there was little to prevent the War Department from ousting the remainder of McClellan's supporters. Fitz-John Porter, who had fought well at Second Bull Run, was ordered to hold his Fifth Corps in reserve at the Battle of Antietam. Had McClellan opted to use Porter's Corps instead, the next unfortunate chapter in Porter's life might never have begun. Porter was brought to trial and convicted by a panel that newspaper editor Alexander McClure said "had been studiously organized to convict." Porter was cashiered from the army in January 1863 and forbidden to hold any position "of profit or trust in the Government of the United States." Not until 1886 (under the Grover Cleveland administration) did Porter see his name cleared. He was restored to the rank of colonel without back pay. Historians generally agree that Porter would have gained little by attacking Jackson or Longstreet at Second Bull Run and that his men would have been needlessly sacrificed. Fitz-John Porter of Portsmouth died two years into the new century on May 21, 1901 at Morristown, New Jersey.[93]

Another New Hampshire notable whose reputation grew during the Seven Days was Harriet Patience Dame.[94] She joined the Second New Hampshire soon after it left the state, and unlike other nurses, she accompanied the regiment into the field. She was seen throughout the war nursing the wounded of not only the Second New Hampshire but also other New Hampshire regiments as well. She had no reservations about nursing the sick and wounded even though a battle was in progress all around her. The Confederates twice captured Dame during the Seven Days and Second Bull Run. After the Battle of Malvern Hill, Dame had lost her way and stumbled into a Confederate picket line. When she was taken to a Confederate officer, the following polite exchange occurred.

CONFEDERATE OFFICER: Got too far into Dixie, hey?
DAME: No, not as far as I'm going.
CONFEDERATE OFFICER: How far are you going?
DAME: As far as Richmond.
CONFEDERATE OFFICER: Ah, going as a prisoner?
DAME: No, I am going under the old flag.

At the end of this conversation, the officer was so exasperated with Dame's impertinence that he released her because it was apparent from her supplies that she was only a nurse who had been tending the wounded and not a great threat to the Confederacy.[95]

The second time Dame was captured, she was brought before no less a personality than Confederate General Stonewall Jackson. When brought to his tent, he silently regarded her for a moment, looked at her medical equipment, and then erupted in a towering rage. His anger was not directed at Dame but at her captors. "Take that lady back to the Northern lines." The soldiers quickly ushered Harriet out of the tent and politely escorted her back to the lines.[96]

Dame's tent burned on several occasions, and each time she managed to somehow replenish her medical supplies. She was observed by hundreds of soldiers caring for the sick and wounded on the battlefield at Gettysburg. Dame experienced the same hardship as the soldiers in the field, and she was remembered during and after the war as the Grand Dame of the Second New Hampshire.[97]

In St. Augustine, Florida, an event was about to take place in the camp of the Fourth New Hampshire that would carry extreme consequences for Colonel Louis Bell. Captain George F. Towle recorded in his journal his part in the controversy: "On the night of the 25th, I sent out patrols in an organized raid on the houses of ill fame. Orders were being given to arrest all found there. Six were raided and forty-three Negro women brought up to the guardhouse. On consultation with Col. Bell, I recommended that six of the most notorious of these with one infamous white woman be selected and put over the lines with four days rations of hard bread which was done. This action was the cause of much comment at Hilton Head where it was reported by lying rumor that we had delivered them up as fugitive slaves. But in fact there was really no enemy then in front of us."[98]

The Commander of the Department of the South, Major General David Hunter, much to the dismay of President Abraham Lincoln, had abolished slavery in his department. When Hunter discovered at his headquarters at Hilton Head in July the actions of Colonel Bell, he had him arrested. Captain Towle considered Hunter to be "an extreme favorite [of the administration] and a man destitute of any spark of chivalrous sentiment. He had very little sense anyhow."[99] That this was a totally innocent affair is apparent from the simple entry by Private Samuel Wilkinson of the Fourth New Hampshire in his diary for June 25: "Several Negroe girls put outside the Picket line this morning for being disorderly."[100]

By July 1, 1862, on the Virginia peninsula, Lee had pushed McClellan back from the gates of Richmond, and McClellan slowly crept back down the peninsula toward Harrison's Landing. The combination of Robert E. Lee taking command and the storied success of Stonewall Jackson's Shenandoah Valley Campaign contributed to McClellan's failure on the Virginia peninsula. Northern progress elsewhere was overshadowed by events in the eastern theater. Battles fought thus far were thought to be terrible, and people both North and South thought that they could not be surpassed in their intensity and loss of life. The next three months of the war would change their thinking forever.[101]

Into "a furnace of strife"

CHAPTER 3

July 1862 to September 1862

Faint the din of battle brays distant down the hollow wind
war and terror fled before, wounds and death remained behind.

"Carousal of Odin," *Poems of the*
Rev. Thomas Penrose (1782)

After the Eighth New Hampshire had been raised and mustered into service in 1861, all the recruiting offices in New Hampshire were closed under the assumption that no more men would be needed from the state. In May 1862 Governor Nathaniel Springer Berry received an order from the War Department in Washington asking for one more three-year regiment. Labor in the state was dwindling, and it was becoming more profitable to stay at home and enjoy the increase in wages than go off to war. In addition it was difficult to attract recruits with a bounty of only ten dollars. This was changed, and the bounty was doubled for individuals enlisting before July 1, 1862.

The ranks of the new regiment were thin when the recruits came into camp in Concord at the end of June. To further entice new recruits, the state bounty was increased to fifty dollars and sixty for anyone joining a regiment already in the field. The men already enlisted in the Ninth New Hampshire received an additional bounty of thirty dollars.[1]

With McClellan's failure to take Richmond came a new call from Abraham Lincoln for three hundred thousand more troops "to bring this unnecessary and injurious civil war to a speedy and satisfactory conclusion." For New Hampshire, a state of barely 310,000 people, the prospect of raising more regiments was a discouraging one. Governor Berry was faced with the nearly impossible task of providing Washington with five more regiments.[2] Recruiters had scoured the state offering higher bounties in order to raise the Ninth New Hampshire Regiment. Now, this effort would have to be redoubled to fill the new quota. There was tentative talk of a draft, but until then the recruiters would somehow have to find more men.

Initially Governor Berry had difficulty finding a suitable candidate to command the Ninth New Hampshire, but when he heard that Colonel Enoch Quimby Fellows of the Third New Hampshire had come home suffering from neuralgia, Berry offered him the colonelcy. Fellows accepted it on June 14 after resigning his commission in the Third New Hampshire. Josiah Stevens Jr. of Concord became the Ninth Regiment's lieutenant colonel and along with Fellows trained the new regiment throughout July.[3]

Lieutenant Thomas L. Livermore of the Fifth New Hampshire had received a minor wound during the Battle of White Oak Swamp, and as he lay on his cot recovering, he reflected on the recent campaign. Livermore's disappointment over the campaign was apparent: "And what had the army done? General McClellan found himself with nearly 100,000 good men in front of Richmond. Then after beating them off every time up to Malvern Hill and giving them a fearful whipping there, instead of advancing on them to take advantage of the victory he ordered us to retreat again."[4]

The hot July sun beat down on the Virginia countryside. Livermore and the Fifth New Hampshire were digging wells to get some cool, refreshing water when a surprise guest appeared. President Abraham Lincoln arrived on July 7 to inspect the camps. Livermore remembers that the president "rode by with an anxious but kind expression and we cheered him."[5] It was some time after the president's visit that the Second New Hampshire Regiment did not appear at one of the daily parades held in camp. Brigadier General Cuvier Grover sent for Colonel Marston to discover the reason for their absence.

GROVER: I noticed, Colonel, that your regiment was not out this morning. What was the reason?

MARSTON: The reason was, I did not order them out.

GROVER: You will order them out now, then, and remain under arms two hours.

MARSTON: I will do nothing of the kind.

GROVER: What?

MARSTON: I said the regiment will not be ordered out. If there is any fault, it is not that of my men, and they will not be punished. If you want the officers to parade, we will come out and stand as long as you please.

GROVER: I would have you understand, Colonel Marston, that I am the brigadier general commanding this brigade.

MARSTON: And I would have you understand, that I am a member of the body [Congress] that makes brigadier generals.

The matter was immediately dropped, and the regiment was not ordered out that day.[6]

In July, after the Battle of Secessionville, battle casualties and disease seriously depleted the ranks of the Third New Hampshire, who along with the entire force, were withdrawn from James Island and returned by steamer to Hilton Head. There the Third New Hampshire and the recently returned Fourth New Hampshire enjoyed a time of relative peace and quiet. The return to camp routine and military drill was supplemented with a sweeping religious revival in the camps.

The rivalry between the Third and Fourth New Hampshire was already common knowledge when an officer of the Fourth New Hampshire reported to Colonel Thomas J. Whipple that twelve men from the Third New Hampshire had been recently baptized. Whipple called in his adjutant and said, "Adjutant, they tell me that twelve men of the Third N.H. regiment have been baptized. I want you, sir, to detail fifteen men at once and see that they are baptized. I'll be d———d if the Third N.H. shall get ahead of the Fourth Regiment."[7]

When the Fourth New Hampshire was still in St. Augustine, Florida, in July, there was a drive to make many of the local inhabitants take an oath of allegiance to the government of the United States. It was hoped in Washington that if enough Floridians took the oath, then they could be brought back into the United States. This presaged Lincoln's Proclamation of Amnesty and Reconstruction that was offered to the Southern people in December 1863. The proclamation allowed that if ten percent of the voters in a state that had seceded took the oath of allegiance, then the federal government would recognize a new state government and welcome them back into the Union.[8] When an Episcopal minister named Standenmeyer refused to take the oath, Captain George F. Towle dispatched a squad under Corporal Stephen Wentworth to put Standenmeyer beyond the front lines. When Wentworth returned with Reverend Standenmeyer, the clergyman claimed status as a Prussian citizen. When he again refused to take the oath, Wentworth was ordered to put him over the lines. Standenmeyer told Towle before he left that he was going to Washington and report him to Secretary Seward. The reverend was never heard from again.[9]

Many of the people coming through the lines into the camps of the Fourth and Third New Hampshire were runaway slaves. What to do with these slaves was the topic of a letter written from the camp of the Third New Hampshire Regiment at Hilton Head by thirty-eight-year-old Private Edward F. Hall of Exeter: "Here are some of my 'Idees' on the great question. What to do with the Negro is the chief trouble in the war policy. Now I don't believe in 'Abolition' but in the progress of the war of course we shall find a great many Negros who have been left behind by their masters now something must be done with them. I say instead of taking soldiers from the ranks (to do disagreeable tasks) set the Negros at work to do it but as to arming them I don't believe in it."[10] Private Hall of Company B deserted in February 1864 and was returned to the ranks several months later. He received a severe wound at the Battle of Deep Bottom in August 1864 and was honorably discharged in October of that year.[11]

New Hampshire soldiers elsewhere were musing over why they were fighting at all. Sixth New Hampshire Sergeant George Upton of Derry wrote from Newport News, Virginia: "I came out here to help support the Constitution & Laws of our land and for nothing else, and if it is turned into some other purpose— then those that do it may do the fighting for all men, and if I had my say, in case of an abolition war—every abolitionist should be compelled to come out here and when here to be in the front rank."[12] Upton, thirty-two, died on July 31, 1864 from wounds received the previous day at the Battle of the Crater. Many New Hampshire soldiers fought to preserve the Union as it was, but there were also those who fought for moral, religious, and deeply personal reasons as well.[13]

Also writing from Newport News was Albion P. Thurston of Ossipee, a nineteen-year-old private in the Sixth New Hampshire originally from Freedom. On July 18, he apologized to his father that he could not be home in time for the harvest: "I should like to be at Home and help you do your work but I can't help it. I don't expect to be at home for 3 years unless I get discharged by sickness. You said that you would like to kill 2 Rebbels for you I will try to. Our living is very hard, you have no idea what we have to live on."[14] Private Albion Thurston was killed one month later in fighting at the railroad cut at Second Bull Run.[15]

In July the Fourth New Hampshire was busy skirmishing with the Confederates near Jacksonville, Florida. Private Samuel Wilkinson, Company F of Somersworth recorded one skirmish in his diary for July 17, 1862: "Our Company was in the Fort in a few minuates after the first gun. When we arrived at the Fort they were sheling the woods very briskly in the vicinity of the Jacksonville road about fifty heavy shells were fired. Some men were seen skulking through the Corn Fields and were fired upon by the Pickets. They invited the Pickets into the woods whare they said they would give them all the fight they wanted. Company I went out to day and burned a large house it belonged to one Fairbanks, who is in the Rebil army."[16]

Heat and disease kept the soldiers of the Eighth New Hampshire from doing much skirmishing in the area around Carrollton, Louisiana. Writing from Fort Macomb on June 20, 1862, New London Private Claude Goings complained that flies, mosquitoes, and bad water were the chief maladies of the average soldier: "Now I think the people of N.H. are quite intelligent but they don't know but a damned little about mosquitoes. We have bars here for the purpose of keeping them out of bunks but they are bound to come in and often times the whole Co. will be up all night. Our water here is very poor not so good as in a mud puddle there (N.H.) I don't drink any more of it than I can help."[17]

While death from disease was a constant companion for the New Hampshire soldier serving in Louisiana, it was not unknown in Virginia and elsewhere. While serving with the Second New Hampshire regiment in Virginia, Private Andrew J. Rugg died of disease after lingering for a while in the U.S. Army Hospital in

Philadelphia. Army Chaplain James H. McFarland was with Rugg when he died and wrote to Rugg's pastor, the Reverend James Barbour in Sullivan: "While we engaged in prayer he seemed to realize an unusual manifestation of the presence of God. He continued confiding and being happy in God til one o'clock this morning when he fell asleep in Jesus. His Mother informed me that she asked him whether he had anything to say to his young friends at home. His reply was tell them to strive to meet him in Heaven."[18] Captain Samuel P. Sayles of Company D, who had been kind enough to write to Enoch Adams while he was in the hospital, found himself writing a much sadder letter in the beginning of 1863 to Andrew Rugg's older sister Ellen in Nelson. Sayles would write many such letters before he himself received a serious wound at Gettysburg. Rugg started out with the Second New Hampshire as a musician, but when the regiment discovered it had too many musicians, it converted some, including Rugg, into armed infantry. In his letter Sayles reminded Ellen that Rugg "acted in a conspicuous manner, the part of a brave soldier and that while you mourn the untimely death of A devoted Brother, You have reason to be proud of his heroic life and the excellent character he has left his friends as a priceless legacy."[19]

By the end of July 1862, it was clear that McClellan would do no more against the Confederates on the Virginia peninsula. Lincoln then placed his trust and all the hopes of the North on a fellow Illinoisan, Major General John Pope.[20] The war was about to change, and for New Hampshire soldiers in the fields of Virginia and elsewhere, it was about to escalate in a violent and bloody fashion.[21]

Far removed from the events in Virginia, Private John McDaniel of Company D, Eighth New Hampshire was writing to his sister Sarah from Louisiana about a small but violent battle outside Baton Rouge between twenty-six hundred Confederate and twenty-five hundred Union soldiers on August 5: "There has been a great fight [at] baton rouge Our troops were Victorous Our general was killed Williams it is reported that the rebel General lovell was also killed as brecenridge had his arm shot of[f] it is reported that our loss is to or three hundred the enemy is supposed to [be] greater. I hope we shall go someplace where we get good water it aint much like the granit hills of NH it is all low flat level land. There is no hills here."[22]

The battle that McDaniel refers to was Major General John C. Breckenridge's August 5, 1862, attack on Baton Rouge, Louisiana. Brigadier General Thomas Williams was killed at the outset of the battle, but Major General Mansfield Lovell, who had been driven out of the defenses of New Orleans three months before, was not a casualty. A vice president under President James Buchanan, Breckenridge led the attack on Baton Rouge but did not lose an arm during the battle. McDaniel was nearly right about the casualties. The Federals suffered 84 killed, 266 wounded, and 33 missing, while the Confederates casualties amounted to 456. Private McDaniel leaves the mistaken impression that the Eighth New

Hampshire participated in this battle. Although they were only eight miles away, they did not take part but sixteen days later withdrew along with the rest of the federal troops back to New Orleans.[23]

Twenty-one-year-old McDaniel probably considered himself lucky that he did not number himself among the over two hundred soldiers of the Eighth New Hampshire who had taken sick that summer. The Northfield native's luck ran out, though, when he succumbed to disease in March 1863. Private McDaniel is buried just outside New Orleans in the cemetery in Chalmette, Louisiana. Because of the dangers from heat and contagious diseases, many New Hampshire soldiers could not be brought home for burial, but their home memorials are simple cenotaphs: "He sleeps in Southern soil."[24]

August was a busy month in New Hampshire for both recruiters and new soldiers. The Ninth New Hampshire's ranks were steadily growing when the next three-year regiment was created. The Tenth New Hampshire was formed with the intention of tapping the large Irish population in Manchester and other large cities in New Hampshire. Captain Michael T. Donohoe,[25] twenty-three, of Lowell, Massachusetts was serving with the Third New Hampshire in South Carolina and was considered an ideal choice to lead the Tenth New Hampshire. Respected legislator John Coughlin of Manchester was appointed lieutenant colonel. Six companies were drawn from the Manchester area alone, with additional men arriving from Portsmouth, Nashua, and Dover. The soldiers who enlisted in the Tenth New Hampshire began arriving at Camp Pillsbury in Manchester in the southeastern part of the city during the third week of August, and the entire regiment was completed and mustered into the service of the United States on September 5, 1862. By September 6,850 men had been raised and uniformed for the Tenth New Hampshire.[26] Raised under the same call for troops as the Tenth New Hampshire, the Eleventh New Hampshire, also formed in August, rendezvoused in Concord at Camp Colby, named after Adjutant General Anthony Colby.

The thirty-three men from Henniker who would form part of Company D of the Eleventh gathered in the town's common by the brick church and began marching to the railroad station at the end of town, accompanied by the Henniker Cornet Band. The throngs of people cheered, waved, and wished the departing soldiers well in their travels. The men from Henniker were only three months away from an experience that would change their lives forever. By the end of the war, only eight Henniker men from Company D would be alive to talk about that experience.[27]

The man Governor Berry chose to lead the Eleventh New Hampshire was Warner resident Walter Harriman, who was pleased to see his regiment filled in a near record eight days.[28] Moses Collins, a lawyer from Exeter, was chosen as Harriman's lieutenant colonel, and Littleton native Evarts W. Farr was selected

Colonel Michael T. Donohoe, *Tenth New Hampshire, Field and Staff. Donohoe was a captain in the Third New Hampshire before becoming colonel of the Tenth. He was wounded while leading his regiment at the Battle of Fort Harrison, Virginia, on September 29, 1864. Photograph from* Reminiscences of the War of the Rebellion

as major. In the course of its history, the Eleventh New Hampshire fought in nineteen different engagements, and its command, because of battle and politics, changed hands seven times. The Eleventh New Hampshire was mustered into the service of the United States on September 2, 1862, in Concord.[29]

Sharpshooter William B. Greene wrote to his mother Susan in Raymond about a skirmish the Second USSS ("United States Sharp Shooters") Regiment was involved in the day before the Battle of Cedar Mountain: "The Regt went out on a reconnaissance day before yesterday. They had a slight skirmish with a few of the Rebel cavalry. They took three prisoners from this Regt., one from Company C, one from Company E and one from Company F, a N.H. Co. His name is Murley and he is a sergeant. But they are all right. They will be at home soon for the enemy have got so many sick ones to take care of that they are letting all the prisoners go on a parole of honor."[30] The sergeant Greene refers to was Samuel F. Murray of Auburn, captured August 6 at Bowling Green, Virginia, and pardoned September 13. Captured yet again in 1864 outside of Petersburg, Virginia, Murray was brevetted a major for gallant and meritorious service.[31]

Greene wrote to his mother again on August 17 about a week after the Battle of Cedar Mountain between Major General Stonewall Jackson and Major

CAPTAIN SAMUEL F. MURRAY,
Second United States Sharpshooters,
Company F. Captured twice during
the war, Murray was brevetted a
major for gallant and meritorious
service. Photograph courtesy
of NHVA

General Nathaniel B. Banks. Again Greene did not see action, but he describes the aftermath: "I can now step outside my tent and look up on to the mountain and see right where the enemy had a battery stationed. The one that killed so many. The ground for two miles around here is covered with graves of soldiers killed and the carcasses of dead horses and, I tell you, if you want a good wholesome stink just go about a half mile above here and there you will get it. There is not much to be seen only horses and graves."[32] Exploiting Banks's lack of military experience, Jackson defeated him at Cedar Mountain. The Federal loss amounted to 2,353, with nearly 600 of the men becoming prisoners. The Confederates lost 1,300.[33]

Up to August 21, the Second New Hampshire was withdrawing along with the rest of McClellan's army from the Virginia peninsula. Embarking on the steamer *State of Maine,* the Second New Hampshire and the rest of General Joseph Hooker's division sailed north to reenforce Major General Pope's Army of Virginia. The small fleet arrived at Acquia Creek on August 23 and stayed there until it was decided whether to disembark the troops there or go on to Alexandria. During this stopover, the men of the Second jumped into the Potomac River to take a cooling swim. The drowning of Private James E. Seavey of Portsmouth darkened this happy scene. The men were soberly reminded once again that death could come at any time and not necessarily in the form of a bullet or cannonball. The fleet carrying the Second New Hampshire arrived at Alexandria on the evening of August 24, and during the next afternoon, the Second was herded aboard boxcars for transport to Manassas Junction.[34]

A week earlier, the Sixth New Hampshire had had a harrowing journey on the way from Newport News to Alexandria. In July the Ninth Army Corps was being organized under Major General Ambrose Burnside at Newport News. Colonel Simon Griffin of the Sixth New Hampshire used this opportunity to weed out ineffective company commanders and replace them with competent lieutenants. In mid-August, the Sixth was transported to Alexandria, like the others, to strengthen Pope's forces for the fight at Manassas. The sick and wounded of Burnside's Corps, including a number of Sixth New Hampshire men, were loaded on the *West Point* on August 13 and had an uneventful voyage past Fortress Monroe. That evening, the ship made its way up the Potomac and ran head on into the *George Peabody* coming down the Potomac with an empty cargo hold. The bow of *West Point* was split wide open, and the ship immediately began to take water. Instead of turning the boat toward shore and running her aground, the captain and first officer were seen swiftly rowing away from the boat as it sank. Corporal Curtis Parker, a twenty-two-year-old member of Company B from Woodstock, described what followed: "As we were now left wholly to our fate we got the ladies and children upon the upper deck and then tried to lower the remaining boat but in the haste and confusion the boat was lost and escape seemed hopeless. The water was full of struggling humanity. Those who could not swim or who did not get something on which to float soon disappeared beneath the water. George Smith and Hiram Pool of the 6th escaped by clinging to a door. One hundred and twenty were drowned, including all the ladies and a little boy." Some of the survivors were rescued by the *George Peabody,* which had not been as seriously damaged as the *West Point.*[35]

Earlier in August, the Third New Hampshire Regiment's Company H, now in South Carolina and under strength with about fifty men, was on outpost picket duty on Pinckney Island. The evening of August 6, Charles H. Drew of Concord, Joseph Witham of Nottingham, and James S. Wallace of Hooksett all decided to desert to the enemy. The night of August 21, a Confederate force of about a hundred men made an amphibious landing and ambushed Company H. The entire company was lost: killed were commanding officer, Lieutenant Joseph C. Wiggin of Sandwich, who had recently been promoted from sergeant, and Privates George W. Adams of Bedford, Charles O. Ring of Pittsfield, and Nathaniel Downs of Tamworth, with Wiggin and Ring both repeatedly shot and bayoneted. Privates Daniel Jefferson of Lisbon and Charles Morgan of Manchester later died from their wounds. Several other soldiers were wounded, and the remainder of the company, thirty-six men, was captured. Five Third New Hampshire soldiers managed to escape and get back to warn the outpost occupied by Company G.

Colonel Jackson immediately dispatched a force under Major Josiah I. Plimpton to the island to investigate. It was obvious from the reports of both Jackson and the Confederates that the Confederate force did not stay on the island long. It took the Confederates only thirty minutes from the time they landed to attack the Third New Hampshire Company, capture the prisoners, and leave the island. The aftermath was that only fourteen of the thirty-six men captured were paroled six months later. Some of their original numbers were not accounted for, while others were in the hospital or died of their wounds. A Confederate report discovered later confirmed that the three deserters gave the Confederates the exact strength and whereabouts of Company H.

Three extra paroled prisoners arrived with the men who had been captured on Pinckney Island. The three deserters, Drew, Witham, and Wallace, were immediately placed under arrest and sent to Fort McHenry in Baltimore. Drew and Wallace managed to escape, and Wallace fled to England. Drew joined a Maryland cavalry unit under the alias Henry White but his identity was discovered, and he was returned to Fort McHenry in November 1863 to await trial. Witham tried to atone for his sins and ended up serving for a brief time in both the Eleventh and Sixth New Hampshire Regiments. He retired after the war to his home in Epping, apparently with a clear conscience.[36]

The Ninth New Hampshire was preparing to leave the state on August 25. No new regiments had left the state since January, so there was a large turnout that morning to see the men off. The regiment had already received its rifles and had a full dress parade the previous day. A huge crowd jammed the area in front of the State House in Concord to witness the governor present the regiment with its flags. Corporal Albert Taft of Nelson recorded his impressions of that morning in his diary: "All hands busy this morning. Left Concord at 9 and a half o'clock. Arrived at the landing at 9 P.M. People in general & in Mass. In particular were very kind and I think patriotic judging from their conduct."[37]

Taft and the rest of the Ninth New Hampshire arrived in Washington on August 28. Taft wrote in his diary what happened the next day: "Hot and dusty. Were routed out in the morning at 3. Returned to camp, packed up and moved a few miles. Fight going on in the region of Bull Run. Firing distinctly heard."[38] Charles Moulton of the Second New Hampshire Regiment recorded the movements of the army as it made its way toward Manassas: "Wednesday Aug. 27. Pleasant. It is reported that the rebels are in our rear near Manassas Junction."[39]

After the Battle of Cedar Mountain, Confederate General Robert E. Lee saw an opportunity to deliver a knockout blow to Pope's army while it remained inactive on the line of the Rappahannock River. Lee gambled on Pope's inertia and sent Jackson's Corps on a flanking march around the right flank of the Union army. Hoping to get in Pope's rear and cut his line of communication, Lee assigned Jackson the task of taking and holding Manassas Junction until Lee could arrive with the rest of the Confederate army. Manassas Junction was a key railroad hub and Federal supply dump where the Orange and Alexandria and the Manassas Gap railroads met. Informed of Jackson's march, Pope mistakenly thought he was retreating to the Shenandoah Valley, and by the time he discovered the Confederate strategy, it was too late. Jackson was already at Manassas Junction plundering the supply dump and burning what his men could not eat or carry away. When Jackson heard the booming of Federal cannon, he knew that Pope had discovered his presence. He immediately ordered his men to dig in and create a defensive position in an unfinished railroad cut just west of the Warrenton Turnpike. Both sides were aware that they were about to fight a battle on nearly the same ground as First Bull Run.[40]

The Second and Sixth New Hampshire regiments, the First New Hampshire Light Battery, and three New Hampshire companies of United States Sharpshooters were about to take part in the effort to throw Jackson out of his defensive position.[41] The New Hampshire companies of the First and Second United States Sharpshooter regiments were almost continuously in combat from the Battle of Cedar Mountain on August 9 to the Battle of Chantilly on September 1. On August 19, the regiments served as the rear guard as the army withdrew behind the Rappahannock River. The three days from August 21 to 23 saw continuous skirmishing with the Confederates around Rappahannock Station. Corporal Julian P. Dodge of New Boston was wounded in this fighting but died in a firefight in June 1864 at Weldon Railroad, Virginia. William F. Gould was also wounded but survived the war. Skirmishing for the sharpshooters continued on August 25 at Sulphur Springs and on August 28 at Gainesville, Virginia.[42] Sharpshooter William B. Greene of Raymond described this protracted fighting to his mother, Susan:

> I have had a chance to do what I have always been anxious to do—sight my rifle on a rebel. After I left Cedar Mountain I went to Warrenton again and had four days battle on the way. We retreated from Cedar Mountain to Rappahannock Station where we were attacked and I tell you, it was warm work for a while. Our Regt. layed for 5 hours one day in a piece of woods and the rebels were shelling it all the time. A complete shower of pieces of shell, railroad spikes, small bullets etc . . . I did not get hit, but there are quite a number of our Regt. lay there now. One shell burst right in the middle of the Regt. and killed three men and wounded 7 more. It struck a man right in the bowels and burst in him and I tell you, it tore him up awfully. Another took a man in the nose and took his head right straight off.[43]

The first day, August 29, of the Battle of Second Bull Run was consumed by Pope's failed efforts to dislodge Jackson from his defensive position in the railroad cut. Pope sacrificed his army in a series of brutal uncoordinated attacks against Jackson's line. The Confederates repulsed six such attacks by the right wing of Pope's army. The Second and Sixth New Hampshire Regiments participated on the first day and sustained frightful casualties.[44] Pope's First Corps commander, Major General Franz Sigel, had been battling his nemesis from the Shenandoah Valley Campaign, Stonewall Jackson, since morning when Grover's brigade got the call that they would be the next brigade to try to penetrate the center of Jackson's line.

Grover's brigade marched down the Warrenton Road toward Groveton. The First Massachusetts hurried forward into the line. The remaining four regiments, including the Second New Hampshire under Colonel Marston, waited for the call to deploy. Grover received his orders to advance against the center of Jackson's line at about three o'clock. At the edge of the woods, he formed his brigade into two lines, the first comprising the Eleventh Massachusetts, the Second New Hampshire, and the First Massachusetts and behind them the second line with the Sixteenth Massachusetts and the Twenty-sixth Pennsylvania. Brigadier General Robert Milroy, whose brigade had been hammering at Jackson's line and the regimental commanders of Grover's brigade, met with the men and summarized the situation. The only way, he told them, they could carry the line was to charge the center. Colonel Marston told the Second New Hampshire to fix bayonets, Grover rode past each unit and instructed them to fire one volley and then charge the enemy. He gave the order to advance, and the men moved out of the tree line and into the open field beyond.

The Confederate musket fire that had dwindled to periodic popping and whizzing rose with a sudden crescendo when the first line of the brigade appeared in the open. One thunderous volley followed another as the brigade approached the Confederate line, composed of the Georgians of Brigadier General E. L. Thomas's brigade.

The Second New Hampshire fired one volley and charged at the Georgians with fixed bayonets. Not expecting the Federals to charge, the Confederates were completely surprised when the New Hampshire men came roaring up over the edge of the embankment and down into their trench. Men shot, clubbed, and bayoneted one another in fierce fighting. The Confederates were quickly thrown out of the railroad cut and withdrew to a second line of defense. The Second New Hampshire moved toward the second line, about one hundred yards beyond the railroad cut. Men on the left flank of the Second New Hampshire could see the men of the Eleventh Massachusetts pounding the Confederates in the trench, but soon these Confederates were also running for the protection of the second defensive line. The Second New Hampshire right flank saw the First Massachusetts struggling in the railroad cut. The Second New Hampshire had pursued the Confederates to the second line so quickly that the butternuts hardly had time to deploy before the Granite State men were on top of them again, shooting and clubbing away with the butts of their muskets. This second line also gave way. By now, however, the New Hampshire men were exhausted and disorganized. More importantly, the Massachusetts regiments on either side of them had been repulsed. The Eleventh Massachusetts on their left had been stopped at the second line by Confederate artillery, and the First Massachusetts on their right never made it out of the railroad cut. Brigadier General Maxcy Gregg's South Carolinians had advanced to seal the breech. The attack of Grover's brigade with the Second New Hampshire in the lead had been so successful that it threatened to sever the whole left wing of Jackson's line. The attack fell apart, and the Second New Hampshire found itself in mortal danger of not only being flanked but also surrounded. When they realized their plight, they turned and ran as fast as their feet could carry them back to the second Confederate line, then to the first, and finally down and over the railroad cut to safety.[45]

Sergeant Hugh R. Richardson of Company F of the Second New Hampshire wrote to the father of Private Charles E. Jewett of Gilford. Richardson and Jewett were in the same company.

> We got the order to March down to the woods and clear them if possible arriving near the edge of the woods we halted formed into line of Battle. was then ordered into the woods when we got the order to fix Bayonets then for charge Bayonets forward double quick we immediately received a sharp fire which we returned with spirit and our men advanced steadily and with the greatest coolness and bravery at the distance of some 3 or 4 hundred yards was a rail road wher the Enemy pourd in upon us a most destructive fire there was where Charles fell I saw him fall he fell flat upon his face turned partily over rolled back and died I was so busy in performing my duty I did not stop to examine closely but think he was wounded in the Head. Our men broke through two of their lines and rushed on to the third but was then compelled to retire out of the woods how ever not untille the Regt as well as Co had suffered severelly.[46]

Sergeant Richardson of Lancaster eventually rose to the rank of captain. He sustained a wound in the Peach Orchard at Gettysburg in July 1863 and survived the war.[47]

Grover's brigade rallied and reformed around their respective regimental flags in the field where they had formed to step off for the attack. The exhausted and wounded men glanced off to their side and saw the approach of Colonel James Nagle's brigade of the Ninth Corps. Men of the Second New Hampshire spotted the flags of the Sixth New Hampshire as they rushed forward to keep their appointment with Stonewall Jackson.

Now came the sad task of calling the rolls for the various regiments of the brigade. Out of 1,500 men put into the battle, 486 were killed, wounded, or

LIEUTENANT COLONEL
PHINEAS BIXBY, *Sixth New
Hampshire, Field and Staff.
Captured at Second Bull
Run, Bixby was exchanged
and was later twice wounded
in fighting around Petersburg. He finished the war
as a brevet colonel. Photograph courtesy of NHVA*

missing. Because of their place in the line and because they had penetrated the deepest into the Confederate defenses, Second New Hampshire lost sixteen killed, eighty-seven wounded, and twenty-nine missing; those of the Second mortally wounded raised the death toll to thirty-six. The Second New Hampshire was able to put barely 332 officers and men into the field that day. With their losses at Second Bull Run, the Second had been decimated And the Sixth New Hampshire was next into the fray.[48]

The Sixth New Hampshire, one of three regiments in Nagle's brigade, had been preparing for their role in the battle since 1:30 in the afternoon when they were instructed to fall in and move to the front. It was near four o'clock, and Nagle's brigade had not been put in yet. The men were becoming anxious at being idle for so long. Suddenly, their anxiety intensified when they saw the remnants of Grover's battered brigade and the Second New Hampshire limping back to their starting point in the clearing. Colonel Nagle gave the command to clear the woods in their front to get ready for the attack. The skirmishers moved out, and the brigade moved through the woods in two lines, the Sixth New Hampshire and Second Maryland in the first line and the Forty-eighth Pennsylvania in the second. The Forty-eighth became famous as the Pennsylvania coal miner regiment that dug and exploded the mine at Petersburg in July 1864.

The 1,500 man Union brigade quickly drove the Confederates out of the woods and back into the railroad cut. The order was to charge, and the Sixth New Hampshire surged forward to the lip of the embankment above the railroad cut. The men from western New Hampshire poured one volley after another into the struggling Georgians of Lawton's brigade. It was not long until they, too, broke and ran out the back of the railroad cut, and the men of the Sixth jumped in and out the other side of the cut after the fleeing Confederates.[49] Somewhere in the smoke and confusion of battle, the Sixth lost contact with the Forty-eighth Pennsylvania they thought were on their left. When Confederate units belonging to Bradley Johnson's brigade started shooting at the New Hampshire men from the left and rear, Colonel Simon Griffin, assuming the Forty-eighth on his left, went to see if he could stop this friendly fire. Lyman Jackman of the Sixth stated Griffin "took the flag, and, mounting an embankment waved it. But he received a murderous volley that convinced him that the stars and stripes had no friends in that quarter."[50]

The regiments of Nagle's brigade began to retreat as fast as they could. The Sixth realized that they were unsupported and fell back quickly, thus uncovering the flank of the Forty-eighth, which was actually on their right. It, too, fell back leaving the Second Maryland's left flank in the air.

"About 3 P.M. our brigade was formed in line of battle and ordered by Gen. Reno to clear the woods of rebels," wrote Private Jonathan Smith of Peterborough about the attack of the Sixth New Hampshire. "We had advanced about 10 rods into the woods when the rebels opened on us were soon discovered in a ditch or railroad track. We drove them out of that and we advanced some ten rods beyond it. Here we held our ground for half an hour under a most terrific fire which cut us down awfully. At last the rebels turned both our flanks and poured a fire into us from three ways. The men fell like grass before a scythe. And the order came to retreat. The moment the men saw their situation it was not a retreat but a flight. It was each one for himself."[51]

As was typical for the entire day, help arrived but too late to turn the tide of the battle. Regiments of Colonel Nelson Taylor's Excelsior Brigade arrived just as Nagle's brigade was leaving the field. Taylor's New Yorkers were soon forced to flee as the Confederate counterattack by Johnson quickly become general and swept everything in its path.[52]

The men of the Sixth New Hampshire made it back to the clearing where they had started after leaving a large number of their comrades dead, wounded, and missing around the railroad cut in the severe mauling by Johnson's Virginians.

The enfilading fire resulted in the loss of 66 dead, 130 wounded, and 30 missing. The Sixth New Hampshire had counted only 450 able men that morning; and now they suffered the loss of fifty percent of that. Thirteen of the twenty officers of the regiment were casualties in the Sixth New Hampshire's costliest battle. The ferocity of the contest lasted barely an hour for the Sixth New Hampshire, but the result was the loss of over sixty husbands, fathers, sons, and brothers from Cheshire County.[53]

That day the half-hearted demonstrations on the Federal side amounted to nothing. The piecemeal attacks of Pope on Jackson's left and center had produced nothing more than an enormous casualty list. And the day was not yet over.

Like the sharpshooters, the men of the First New Hampshire Light Battery had skirmished constantly for the past week and a half. At about 7 P.M., the First N.H. Light Battery, which had been attached to Brigadier General Rufus King's First Division, headed down the Warrenton Turnpike in search of Jackson's Corps. The Confederates were consolidating their lines, and Longstreet now had his corps astride the Warrenton Turnpike. Instead of finding a fleeing Jackson, the First New Hampshire ran headlong into the center of Brigadier General John Bell Hood's division. The skirmishing sharpshooters who had accompanied the First NH down the road, even with their repeating Sharps rifles, were no match for two brigades of Texans, Alabamans, and Mississippians who had been eagerly waiting to fight all day.

The Confederates quickly routed the sharpshooters and started to get dangerously close to Captain George Gerrish's battery. As the Confederates pushed inexorably forward, the battery started losing men to rifle fire. The battery's three Napoleon guns were not effective at long range, but as the distance closed between the advancing Confederates and the battery, Gerrish switched to canister, not wanting to lose the Napoleon guns. By then Privates William L. Babbet and Henry C. Parker were dead, and three others wounded. Gerrish ordered two of Napoleon guns to limber up and retreat while he stayed behind and shoved double canister down the barrel of the remaining gun. The Confederates of Colonel Evander Law's brigade swarmed over the position, and Captain Gerrish and ten others became prisoners. George Gerrish, a lifelong resident of Portsmouth, was paroled within three months and reported back to his battery.[54]

Private Thomas C. Cheney of Manchester was with the First New Hampshire Light Battery at Second Bull Run. In a letter to his brother David, Cheney recounted the battle along the Warrenton Turnpike: "Friday, all the AM forces were Marching by us for Bull Run, at Noon we were Ordered there also. There was heavy fireing all day at sundown we were ordered to open fire on Some Rebeles on an oposit hill who were supposed to be in a Peach Orchard and a Corn Field. We done so, but we had not fired but one or two Rounds before the Rebele Infantry opened on us, and Charged up the hill, on our Battery. The

Bullets flew around our heads like Bees when you have tiped their hive over. We fired till the Rebeles were so near to us that they touched some of our men with their Bayonets. We were Obliged to leave which we did suffering the loss of one Cannon and 10 men besides our Capt, 11 in all, and 4 men wounded."[55] Cheney offered his opinion of why the North lost the battle: "Saturday was fought the Big Battle, the Second Battle of Bull Run, and it has resulted adverse to our Armes. I and nearly all that Saw the fight Saturday lay the defeat to the bad Generalship of our Generals. Sigel handled his Troops well and held the Enemy at bey. The great failure was with McDowell, we have no faith in him, if McClellan had had the Command I think there would have been a different result."[56]

It did not take long for the recriminations and finger pointing to begin. The fate that befell Fitz-John Porter because of Second Bull Run, that is, that he was accused of cowardice for not attacking Longstreet, is well known. Colonel Simon Griffin in his memoirs of the war describes attending a meeting where Burnside, Porter, Reno, and Buford were discussing the current operations; Reno said, "We all know John Pope is the d——dest liar that is in the U.S. Army." Griffin also overheard Fitz-John Porter refer to Pope's threatened left flank: "I'll be damned if I'll go down in there, I'll get into a fight if I do."[57] Griffin made no pretense at hiding his opinions about his fellow officers: "It was common knowledge among us officers that Fitz-John Porter, [William B. Franklin and others of McClellan's pets refused to fight."[58]

August 29, 1862, had been the worst single day of the war thus far for New Hampshire. The army had to deal with a second humiliating defeat on the same ground. Generalship may have been suspect, but what was not in doubt was the personal bravery and valor of the soldiers. Many of their stories mention capturing flags, carrying flags, or planting flags in the works of the enemy. Private John Stevens of the Sixth New Hampshire Company E of Nelson distinguished himself by carrying the national flag forward after two other color-bearers had been shot down. Stevens was hit and fell holding the colors but quickly rose and started forward again. As Stevens weakened from his wound, another color-bearer relieved him of the flag and advanced. Arriving on the scene, Colonel Griffin saw Stevens leaning in great pain against a tree and trying to load his musket once more before he succumbed to his wound. When the battle was over for the Sixth New Hampshire, Griffin lovingly furled the bullet-torn flag and carried it back.[59]

The savage conflict among the blue and gray soldiers in the railroad cut was intensified by violent hand-to-hand encounters with bayonets, clubbed muskets, and even rocks. It would not be expected to find much mercy among men who were neither giving quarter nor asking for it. When Second New Hampshire Sergeant Frank C. Wasley of Manchester grappled with a Confederate in the railroad cut and relieved him of his knife, the outcome was almost certain. Wasley had bested the Confederate and was about to sink the blade into him when the Confederate cried out, "Oh, for God's sake—don't." Wasley stayed his hand and jumped out of the trench, leaving the startled but grateful Johnny Reb behind. Wasley, born in England, rose to the rank of lieutenant and received a severe wound in the Peach Orchard at Gettysburg the following July. He was honorably discharged from the army in 1864, having survived so many horrors of war.[60]

Far from his native Ireland, Private Thomas Burns of the Sixth New Hampshire, who had taken up a musket for the town of Swansey, was shot through the legs. He continued loading and firing on his knees until he received a musket ball to the head. Corporals M. W. Preston and William Talbot of the Sixth New Hampshire, both from Enfield, fought side by side until they were torn to pieces by a Confederate volley. Talbot lived in painful agony from his wounds until September 11, 1862.[61] Twenty-one-year-old Private Michael Dillon of the Second New Hampshire from Wilton was shot through the lungs in a struggle with the color-bearer of the Forty-ninth Georgia Regiment. He survived, worked in Washington for twenty-five years after the war, and received the Congressional Medal of Honor for bravery in action at the Battles of Williamsburg and Oak Grove.[62]

August 30, the second day of the Second Battle of Bull Run, witnessed the careless advance of Pope and the destructive attack by Longstreet on Pope's left flank, this crushing blow resulting in the collapse of the entire Federal line. The Union troops withdrew while a determined rearguard held off the Confederate pursuit.[63] Although the First and Second U.S. Sharpshooter Regiments suffered heavy losses at Second Bull Run, the New Hampshire companies lost fewer than five men between them. The sharpshooters withdrew along with the rest of the army after August 30, but unlike the rout one year earlier, this was an orderly retreat back to Washington.[64]

The 75,696 men under Pope's command sustained over 10,000 casualties, with an additional 6,000 posted as missing. Out of 48,527 Confederate soldiers who fought at Second Manassas, 9,108 fell dead or were wounded.[65] For its investment of blood and treasure, the North had precious little to show for its efforts that summer. Shocked Northern towns and cities reacted to the horrifying casualty lists. The Surgeon General begged the Northern populace to scrape lint for the production of bandages.[66] Private Smith described a soldier's perspective: "I don't believe half the men could stand it to march five miles If things go on this way a great while longer I shall begin to think that the North had better acknowledge herself handsomely whipped and give up the contest. Our only hope is McClellan!! The country stands just where it did a year ago minus 150,000 men."[67]

The importance of the army wanting McClellan back was not lost on Lincoln and the War Department. In a meeting in Washington on September 2, George McClellan was reluctantly returned to command of the army by Lincoln and Secretary of War Edwin Stanton, who were so opposed to the decision that their names do not appear on the order, only that of Henry Wager Halleck, general in chief of the United States armies. McClellan returned to the army on September 3 amid cheers and a thunderous ovation as he rode down the line of jubilant soldiers.[68]

Just days after McClellan took command of the combined armies, it became apparent that Robert E. Lee was marching toward Frederick, Maryland. The war was about to come to Northern soil. Lee did this hoping that his young country could gain foreign recognition and beleaguered Southern farmers could bring in a productive harvest from the fields of war-torn Virginia.[69] McClellan immediately sent Reno's Ninth Corps into Maryland in pursuit of Lee. The Ninth New Hampshire regiment under Colonel Fellows rushed to join their brigade. The regiment, which had left New Hampshire only a week and half before, now was on a forced march to catch up with their fellow First Brigade comrades in the Sixth New Hampshire, Second Maryland and Forty-eighth Pennsylvania.[70]

George Henry Chandler, twenty-three, of Concord, who just two weeks before had been appointed adjutant of the Ninth New Hampshire regiment, offered a sobering insight on September 3, 1862, from Arlington Heights, Virginia: " I can hardly give any opinion relative to the prospect of affairs: but have learned one thing. That this war is a big thing and that it is more of a task by ten times to subdue this rebellion than most people suppose. I don't know what the policy is to be, but it seems to me that it should be rigorous, decisive and immediately entered upon."[71]

During this time, recruiting continued for more New Hampshire regiments. By the beginning of September, ten companies for the newly formed Twelfth New Hampshire were raised and on their way to Camp Belknap in Concord. Raised primarily in Carroll and Belknap counties, the Twelfth New Hampshire would eventually earn the nickname "New Hampshire Mountaineers," not because they were from the mountains but because most of the men of the regiment averaged over five feet, eight inches tall.[72] Colonel Thomas J. Whipple of Laconia played a key role in raising the Twelfth New Hampshire and greatly desired to be commissioned as its colonel. Instead, Governor Berry decided to offer the colonelcy of the Twelfth to Captain Joseph Hayden Potter of Concord, then in the regular army. John F. Marsh of Hudson was chosen as the regiment's lieutenant colonel.[73]

During September, between the forming of the regiment and the appointment of Colonel Potter, the regiment was ably drilled and trained by the first colonel of the Second New Hampshire Regiment, Colonel Thomas P. Pierce of Manchester. Coming into camp in Concord at the same time were the men who enlisted in the Thirteenth New Hampshire Regiment, the fifth regiment raised in the late summer of 1862. The first company went into camp on September 11, its ten companies formed from recruits who were from seven counties of New Hampshire. Selected to lead the Thirteenth New Hampshire was Major Aaron Fletcher Stevens of Derry, New Hampshire, who had served in the First New Hampshire Regiment. Many of the companies of the Thirteenth New Hampshire began drilling in their respective towns before they started off for Camp Colby in Concord. George Bowers of Nashua was picked as the lieutenant colonel of the Thirteenth New Hampshire.[74]

The last of the three-year regiments to be raised in New Hampshire was the Fourteenth New Hampshire Regiment. The Fourteenth was established, and the men were brought to Concord and quartered in barracks on the same fairgrounds where the Twelfth and Thirteenth regiments were currently staying and training. The Fourteenth was composed mostly of men from southwest New Hampshire. Four companies were raised in Cheshire County and one each in Sullivan, Grafton, Coos, Carroll, Hillsborough, and Merrimack counties. Chosen for the colonelcy of the Fourteenth New Hampshire was Peterborough resident Robert Wilson. When the war began in 1861, he had been offered the command of one of the New Hampshire regiments then being raised but he refused the offer for personal reasons. In August 1862 he notified the governor that he was still available. Wilson's lieutenant colonel was Tileston A. Barker of Westmoreland, but when Wilson resigned in early September 1864, it was Major Alexander Gardiner of Claremont who assumed Wilson's duties as colonel.[75]

In the early morning light of Thursday, September 11, Colonel Harriman of the Eleventh New Hampshire had one more official duty to perform before his regiment left for the seat of war that day. Lieutenant Joseph B. Clark of Manchester was getting married that morning, and he wanted the colonel to perform the ceremony. Harriman brought the happy couple together, pronounced them husband and wife, and then set about the job of breaking camp with the Eleventh New Hampshire. (Lieutenant Clark received a frightful wound at the Battle of the Wilderness but was reunited with his bride in the summer of 1865.)[76] The regiment marched across the Merrimack River, through the crowds of people in downtown Concord, and on to the railroad station where the cars waited to transport them to Washington. Corporal Samuel Cooper of Manchester of the First New Hampshire Light Battery had time to appreciate the surrounding countryside as their cannon and wagons rumbled toward Frederick, Maryland: "Here in Maryland, the fences were up in their places, the woods were not ruthlessly chopped to pieces, but the farms looked smiling and fruitful, and the dwellings instead of being burnt down were neat and trim."[77] Newly arrived Eleventh New Hampshire Private Willard J. Templeton opined to his brother, "Since we entered Maryland everything looks shabby, dirty and old-fashioned. We don't see the thrift of New England here." A reason why Templeton may have held a negative opinion is that the reception of the Eleventh New Hampshire as it passed through Baltimore while not hostile was decidedly silent and cold.[78] Private J. Lewis Chase of South Newmarket (now Newfields) wrote to his father about the Eleventh's passage through Baltimore: "We started for Baltimore with 10 rounds ammunition ready for them. The boys were ready for it but they did not trouble us. There were a few of the roughs that balled [sic] out at us that was all."[79]

While the New Hampshire Regiments made their way through Maryland, the bloody and battered Second New Hampshire rested behind the lines outside Washington. The Second received praise from Hooker, who had just been promoted to major general and given command of the First Corps of the Army of the Potomac. In a statement to a New Hampshire reporter in Washington, Hooker said, "I know my men, and I think they know me. We have a perfect understanding of each other, and will work together, and I trust do our duty. Your New Hampshire boys (the Second Regiment) are my right hand men. They never fail me."[80]

In Maryland the distance between McClellan's leading corps, Jesse Reno's Ninth and elements of the Army of Northern Virginia holding the gaps at South Mountain was shrinking. On September 13 a copy of Lee's Special Order 191 was found in the Union camp. This was a copy of the disposition of all the parts of Lee's army in Maryland. McClellan at first reacted slowly but then pushed his troops forward.

The Battle of South Mountain began when divisions from Hooker's First Corps, Reno's Ninth Corps and Franklin's Sixth Corps clashed with Confederate brigades from Longstreet's Corps and Hill's Light Division at Turner's, Fox's and Crampton's Gaps at about 9 A.M., September 14. Lee's Army of Northern Virginia was strung out over a twenty-five mile area. Lee had sent Jackson's Corps to Harpers Ferry to neutralize that threat in his rear, and Longstreet had units as far north as Hagerstown. Lee became alarmed when he saw McClellan act with such uncharacteristic swiftness. Lee decided to turn and fight in the gaps of South Mountain, hoping to unite the separate wings of his army by delaying McClellan long enough. On September 15 as Lee approached Sharpsburg, he told his commanders that they would make their stand along the ridges outside the town.[81] At noon on September 14, Burnside ordered Colonel Fellows to go up a hill to silence a Confederate battery that had been particularly annoying. As the men of the Ninth New Hampshire filed forward, they could see Union soldiers trying to push their way through the mountain gaps in front of them. Ordered to load their weapons, many of the Union men had not received enough training to do so properly. Midway up the hill, Lieutenant Colonel Herbert B. Titus ordered the regiments to fix bayonets. Almost in one motion nine hundred bayonets flashed upwards and were attached to their muskets. Shells and bullets gnawed at the Ninth New Hampshire as it experienced its first battle. Men were falling dead and wounded when the order to charge was given.

The Ninth New Hampshire surged up and over the hill, sweeping everything in its path. They charged and ran so hard that they had passed nearly a quarter of a mile in front of the rest of the line. Orders were barked by officers to get back in line, and slowly by company, the Ninth reformed its badly disorganized formation. With twilight near Major General Jesse Reno rode by as the Ninth New Hampshire was regrouping and falling back. He asked Colonel Fellows what regiment it was. When Fellows replied, Reno said, "You made a gallant charge. I shall take great pleasure in giving you full credit for it in my report." Tragedy struck moments later when a thunderous volley erupted from the gathering darkness, throwing the men of the Ninth New Hampshire into confusion. Half of the men stood their ground and started firing back at the muzzle flashes. The other half broke and ran down the hill as fast as their legs would carry them. Some of them were rounded up and brought back, and the firing lapsed into a desultory fire that gradually died away at 9 P.M. The men of the Ninth New Hampshire suffered no casualties in this action but Major General Reno had been killed in the initial Confederate volley. Lieutenant Colonel Titus in particular had been upset with the behavior of the men that day. After making such a splendid bayonet charge in the late afternoon, he felt they had behaved shamefully when a number of the regiment had broken and run that night. He said to them, "I know you are green and haven't had much drill or discipline but. Don't you ever fire a gun again, nor change your position without orders."[82]

The Ninth had sustained twenty-six casualties. Private Joel S. Judkins of Kingston died of a thigh wound received in his first battle; Charles Judkins helped his wounded uncle down the hill and to a barn where the wounded were being kept. Enoch Haselton, a twenty-one-year-old private from Conway, died on October 1 of wounds he received on September 14. The first man of the Ninth New Hampshire wounded at South Mountain was Corporal Hiram Lathe of Manchester. Just as the men were stepping off to go up the hill, a bullet shattered Lathe's knee. His brother James came running over, taking out his knife, which he used to cut the bullet out of his brother's knee. James quickly bound the wound. The brothers were too busy to notice that the Confederates had just captured their older brother, Freeman L. Lathe, who was later released and survived the war.[83] It had been the first day that the men of the Ninth New Hampshire had seen action, and the veteran officers present that day felt that, despite the Ninth's unsteadiness, its men had acquitted themselves honorably.[84]

On September 15, brigades under Longstreet's Corps abandoned the passes and began falling back toward Sharpsburg, Maryland. Jackson, who had forced the surrender of Harpers Ferry the same day, headed north for Sharpsburg. Although Private Templeton of the Eleventh New Hampshire was not with the troops at South Mountain, he was confident enough to include in a letter to his brother, "The opinion here is that McClellan will bag the entire rebel army in

Maryland."[85] Corporal Samuel Cooper of the First New Hampshire Light battery said that on Monday September 15, "the cannonading was farther off, showing that Lee had retired from South Mountain Pass and was evidently planning to make a stand nearer the Potomac River."[86] Cooper continues with his description of how action around Sharpsburg began to escalate: "September 16th, rose at 4:00 A.M., marched at 6:30 A.M. The battle opened in our front at 9:00 A.M. with heavy cannonading, but the enemy retired again and we shortly crossed over Antietam Creek."[87] Another witness to this cannonading on September 16 was Second Assistant Surgeon William Child of the Fifth New Hampshire Regiment.[88] Dr. Child, writing to his wife about the terrible sights and sounds of the battlefield, was interrupted: "What more I was about to write above I have forgotten for just then bang-whiz came the shells and balls from a rebel battery about two miles away. . . . The sound of the guns and the screeching of the shells make a devilish music such as I never heard before."[89]

Healed from wounds he received during the Peninsula Campaign, Colonel Edward E. Cross was back with his regiment. Even before the Battle of Antietam began, Dr. Child noted that Cross was nearly wounded again: "The rebel sharpshooters sent some half dozen balls after me yesterday. The Col. was standing in the same place a little time after was hit on the shoulder taking out a bit of his coat but not wounding him at all."[90]

The bloodiest single day of the entire Civil War (and in all of U.S. history) was about to begin, and New Hampshire troops would be in all three phases of the battle, fighting from dawn to dusk. The First New Hampshire Light Battery was the first to see action that day and was still attached to Brigadier General Rufus King's First Division of the First Corps, now under the command of Major General Hooker. Hooker's Corps was deployed on the northern end of the battlefield facing south. As the men in Brigadier General James B. Rickett's Second Division advanced past the Poffenberger farm toward Miller's Cornfield, the blue troops drew artillery fire from the well-posted Confederate guns on Nicodemus Hill to the southwest.[91]

Private Thomas C. Cheney of the First New Hampshire Light Battery described the opening phase of the battle: "The next morning at just 6 Oclock our Battery was ordered forward about 100, yds in to Battery, that is to get in to posicion to fire. We had but just got into Battery when the Rebeles opned on us with one of their Batterys. We soon replied with earnest, and we were the first ones to commence the Battle on our side this day, Wednesday after one or one and half hours Smart firein we Silenced the Rebes Battery."[92] The First Corps artillery had been raking Miller's Cornfield and the approaching Confederates with such intensity that it led Hooker to state in his report, "Every stalk of corn in the northern and greater part of the field was cut as closely as could have been done with a knife, and the slain lay in rows precisely as they had stood in their

ranks a few moments before."[93] Private Thomas C. Cheney echoed his corps
commander's observation: "The Infantry had been having a fierce Struggle on
our left just through a piece of woods at 10 we were ordered on to this field at
one place where we crossed the field the Dead and Wounded mostly Rebeles laid
so thick that we had to move them to get along so as not run over them."[94]

In his diary Corporal Albert Taft of the Ninth New Hampshire recalled the
rainy night of September 16 and the following morning: "September 16—Were
a little disturbed by the shot and shell of the enemy. Changed our position once.
Got a few shells this way. Laid on our arms all night. September 17—The enemy
opened on us early this morning with their batteries. Ours have pretty much
silenced them now. We expect warm work before night." Perhaps referring to the
Battle of South Mountain three days before, Taft said, "We've had warm work &
enough of it too."[95]

After Jackson's men repulsed Hooker's First Corps attack, McClellan sent in
the Twelfth Corps under Major General Joseph K. Mansfield. The Confederates
also thwarted this attack, and Mansfield himself was killed. The next corps to be
sent against Robert E. Lee was the Second Corps, commanded by Major General
Edwin V. Sumner. The Fifth New Hampshire Regiment was in the First Brigade
of the First Division commanded by Brigadier General Israel Richardson.[96]
Colonel Cross and the Fifth New Hampshire were in good company because in
the Second Brigade of Richardson's division was the famed Irish Brigade, under
the command of Brigadier General Thomas F. Meagher. Richardson's division
had reached Antietam Creek on the evening of September 16. After ten o'clock
in the morning, the Irish Brigade attacked the North Carolinians of Brigadier
General G. B. Anderson's brigade in the Sunken Road, roughly in the center of
the battlefield. Meagher's Irishmen had been severely mauled and were falling
back. Next came Brigadier General John C. Caldwell's brigade, and the Fifth
New Hampshire opened their ranks to allow the bloody and torn Irish Brigade
through to the rear.[97] Thomas L. Livermore of the Fifth New Hampshire recalled
the scene as his regiment approached the battle line: "As we passed through the
ranks of the Irish regiment, they cheered us loudly, and in a twinkling we found
ourselves opposed to the enemy and under a severe fire. I never shall forget the
scene. We stood near on the edge of the sunken road which ran along the border of an extensive cornfield, behind us a hundred yards was dotted with the
dead and wounded."[98]

Soon after, Colonel Cross was grazed twice in the face by pieces of shell. He
reported in his journal, "My Reg't marched bravely up to the line of battle under
a heavy fire without faltering in the least. The enemy opened on us with shrapnel and cannister shot at short range. One discharge of cannister killed and
wounded eight men in one company (G.) & tore the state colors of my Reg't in
two pieces. I was also hit on the right arm."[99] The Fifth New Hampshire had only

been engaged for a short time when Colonel Cross was alerted by an officer that the Confederates were sending an entire brigade around the left flank, so, Cross wrote, "I instantly changed front forward on the 1st Company, by filing part of the Reg't & bringing the remainder forward into line. The movement was made just in time to save the entire Division from being outflanked."[100]

By this time the Fifth New Hampshire was in the Sunken Road and fighting desperately to repulse the Confederate counterattack aimed at reclaiming the road. Livermore recounted the scene that has become the most famous and most often told story about New Hampshire in the Civil War: "As the fight grew furious, the colonel cried out, 'Put on the war paint'; and looking around I saw the glorious man standing erect, with red handkerchief, a conspicuous mark, tied around his bare head and the blood from some wounds on his forehead streaming over his face, which was blackened with powder. Taking the cue somehow we rubbed the torn end of the cartridges over our faces, streaking them with powder like a pack of Indians, and the colonel, to complete the similarity, cried out, 'Give 'em the war whoop!' I have sometimes thought that it helped to repel the enemy by alarming him to see this devilish-looking line of faces, and to hear the horrid whoop; and at any rate, it reanimated us and let him know we were unterrified."[101]

Colonel Cross himself did not go into detail regarding this incident, but he did state that the Confederates "were advancing in line of battle yelling horribly, we met them with an awful volley, which smashed the Reg't in front of us, (4th NC) all to tatters. We now had sharp work for about ten minutes, both sides firing and cheering, but at length the enemy, broken by the close shooting of the federal troops wavered & fell back in disorder. In our first rush toward the enemy Corporal George Nettleton was injured by a piece of shell, but he gallantly remained on the field & brought off the State Colors of the 4th North Carolina Regt."[102]

When Cross had the roll called after this action, he found that eight officers and men had been killed, and 116 men were wounded. Corporal Nettleton, thirty, of Claremont, who later rose to the rank of second lieutenant, recovered but on December 23, 1862, died from a serious wound received during the Battle of Fredericksburg. Second Lieutenant George A. Gay of Newmarket, the soldier who had warned Cross of the impending Confederate flank attack, was killed when he was struck in the head by a shell fragment. The second phase of the battle was over, and the final act was about to take place farther south at the Rohrbach Bridge.[103]

To relieve pressure by the enemy on the Federal right, McClellan ordered Ambrose Burnside on the far left of the Union line to cross the Antietam Creek at the lower bridge and attack the enemy's right flank. This order was given to the Ninth Corps commander at 10:00 A.M. Burnside assigned the assault to

Brigadier General Jacob D. Cox, who used regiments from his own Kanawha Division, Brigadier General Orlando B. Willcox's First Division, Brigadier General Samuel D. Sturgis's Second Division, and Brigadier General Isaac P. Rodman's Third Division. The Sixth and Ninth New Hampshire Regiments were in the First Brigade of Sturgis's division commanded by Brigadier General Nagle.[104]

Opposing them were five hundred Confederates of the Second and Twentieth Georgia Regiments of Brigadier General Robert Toombs Brigade. Along with a small number of the crack Palmetto Sharpshooters, these Georgians, using the excellent position provided by the bluff above the west bank of the bridge, held off this combined Union force for almost three hours until the Georgians had to yield owing to casualties and lack of ammunition. By the time the bridge was taken by the Federals, there were as many Northern casualties as there were Confederates defending the bluff.[105]

Two attempts by the Eleventh Connecticut to take the bridge were thwarted by the Georgian's plunging fire, with the result of 139 casualties for this New England regiment and the loss of its commander, Colonel Henry Kingsbury. Regiments of the Third Division under Brigadier General Isaac P. Rodman were desperately searching for a place to ford the creek below the bridge.[106] Any Federal regiments that came out of the tree line on the east bank of the creek were immediately swept with musket fire from the Georgian position. Several Ohio regiments came down off the knoll towards the creek but were compelled to withdraw. Apparently, a frontal attack against the bridge was not going to work, so Burnside ordered Brigadier General Sturgis to take his division down to the creek and attack the bridge from the south end, going up the Rohrersville Road.[107]

Brigadier General Nagle's brigade—the Sixth and Ninth New Hampshire, the Second Maryland, and the Forty-eighth Pennsylvania—was next in line to try to take the bridge. As the brigade made its way up the road, the exhausted Georgians gathered ammunition from their dead and wounded comrades, rammed new charges into their barrels, and aimed their muskets down at the new group of blue-clad soldiers hurrying toward the bridge.[108] When the Sixth New Hampshire and Second Maryland reached the bridge, "the order of General Sturgis was to charge at once, so the regiments formed in line by the flank, side by side. They fixed bayonets, and, moving at the double quick, passed through a narrow opening in a strong chestnut fence-and charged in the most gallant manner directly up the road toward the bridge. As the attacking party, led by Colonel Griffin, debouched from the field into the road, the rebels, from their entrenched position, redoubled the fury of their fire, sweeping the head of the column with murderous effect. Of the first hundred men who passed through the opening in the fence, at least nine tenths were either killed or wounded."[109] The battered men of the Sixth New Hampshire, their assault shattered, took cover behind logs, stones, or anything else near the bridge that could give cover. The men in the Ninth New Hampshire and Forty-eighth Pennsylvania were providing covering fire for the Sixth New Hampshire the entire time. The rapidly dwindling Georgian force still held the high ground opposite the bridge despite being showered by Federal artillery from the knoll on the west bank of the creek.[110]

Burnside repeatedly asked McClellan for reinforcements, but he was refused even though Porter's Fifth Corps was available. McClellan did not want to weaken his right flank in case of a Confederate counterattack. Burnside vainly listened for the sounds of Rodman's advance south of the bridge.[111] Finally, the Fifty-first Pennsylvania and Fifty-first New York regiments under Brigadier General Edward Ferraro pushed their way to the bridge and made it across. The Ninth New Hampshire Regiment followed immediately over the bridge and rushed up the bluff to dislodge the severely weakened Confederate force.[112] This part of the Confederate line disintegrated, and the Federal force gradually pushed them back toward Sharpsburg. From there it was a short distance to the Potomac. A stunning Northern victory was tantalizingly within McClellan's grasp. He was just about to push Lee's entire right flank when disaster struck.

From behind Sharpsburg appeared the columns of Carolinians, Georgians, and Virginians of A. P. Hill's Light Division arriving from Harpers Ferry. Hill's men slammed into the exhausted Federal soldiers and pushed them all the way back to the west bank of Antietam Creek where action for Burnside's Ninth Corps ended for the day. Despite the involvement of other personalities in the drama, the Rohrbach Bridge would thereafter be known as Burnside's Bridge. A small force of Confederates had held off a superior Federal force until help could arrive. The Sixth and Ninth New Hampshire Regiments rested on their arms that night certain that the battle would be renewed in the morning.[113] Many of the men of both regiments before they fell asleep recounted the horrors of the day. Enfield native Private William French of the Sixth New Hampshire had been pinned down at the bridge and was firing from behind any kind of cover he could find. French had been busily exchanging shots with the Georgians on the opposite hill when Sergeant Howard Rand of Rindge appeared out of nowhere and sharing the same cover with French told him to load muskets for him because he was a better shot. Rand said, "Let me show you how it's done." French passed a musket up to Rand, who momentarily stepped from behind the tree to take aim at a Georgian across the creek. A Confederate sharpshooter had been watching Rand from across the creek, and when Rand stepped out, the Georgian fired. A bullet smashed into Rand's head and threw him over backwards on top of French. Both men rolled down a slight embankment, and French pushed the dead "marksman" off and took his place back at the tree.[114] War is replete with freakish accidents, but one of the more unusual ones happened to a pair of brothers in the Ninth New Hampshire from Plainfield. Privates Willard Humphrey and John Humphrey were providing supporting fire when both received odd wounds almost simultaneously. The right-handed brother had his right thumb shot off, and the left-handed brother lost his left thumb.[115]

The Ninth New Hampshire, a regiment mustered into service only six weeks before, lost ten men killed and eighty wounded. The Sixth New Hampshire, in reserve at South Mountain, suffered the loss of forty men killed and wounded at Antietam. The bloodiest day of the Civil War had been a tactical draw and had witnessed the death or wounding of over 23,000 men.[116] The First New Hampshire Light Battery, present at the battle opening, was also present at its closing. The battery was fortunate to lose only three men wounded and several horses throughout the day. Private Thomas C. Cheney of the battery described the unit's participation at the close: "We filled up with what Amunition we had in our Waggons and placed our Guns in Battery about 5'oclock PM. The Rebes opned on us or some Amunition Waggons in our rear with their Batterys. There happned to be 4 of our Batterys (ours included) placed along near together. We all opned on them it was the Smartest Cannonading I ever heard. This ended the fighting for the day."[117] The green-clad New Hampshire men in the sharpshooters were pressed into service as infantry during the morning's fighting in the bloody cornfield. The companies of the First Regiment were only lightly engaged but the New Hampshire companies of the Second Regiment saw serious action that day, losing twenty-five percent of its men, killed and wounded in fighting that swirled around the Dunker Church.

The Army of Northern Virginia remained throughout the day of September 18 but withdrew across the Potomac into Virginia the next day. McClellan claimed victory for the Union, but what remained were the horrible reminders of the battle. Dr. Child of the Fifth New Hampshire on September 22 tried to find words to describe the human wreckage after the battle: "Day before yesterday I dressed the wounds of 64 different men—some having two or three each. Yesterday I was at work from daylight till dark—today I am completely exhausted. The days after a battle are a thousand times worse than the day of the battle. The dead appear sickening but they feel no pain. But the poor wounded mutilated soldiers that yet have life and sensation make a most horrid picture."[118] Sarah Low, thirty-two, a Dover resident, would have agreed with Dr. Child. Low had left the comfort of her Dover home on the advice of a friend Hannah Stevenson, working in Washington, D.C., to come and help her with the sick and wounded. Low arrived in the capital on September 10, 1862, and began work the next day by changing the bandages of New Hampshire soldiers at the Union Hotel Hospital. In letters to her mother from the hospital in Georgetown, Virginia, Sarah described a nurse's duties but also aired her complaints about Dorothea Lynde Dix, superintendent of women nurses: "Attending to the wounds is only part of a nurse's duty, but it is the pleasantest part. Seeing that the ward is kept neat and that the incompetent attendants do their duty is the wearing part. Miss Dix assumes the authority of recruiting nurses but she has made the position of nurse uncomfortable by it, so much so that I could not have advised anyone to come."[119]

More New Hampshire soldiers and nurses would be coming to the war. The end of September in New Hampshire witnessed a flurry of activity in the training camps in Concord and Manchester. Private Alonzo Pierce of the Thirteenth New Hampshire wrote told his brother Hiram in Antrim about life from Camp Colby in Concord: "I will write a few lines to let you know how I like a soldier's life. Our food is wholesome and generally enough of it. It consists mostly of brown bread and baker's bread, beans and rice and cold meat. The 12th regt. are encamped right south of us and will probably leave the state this week. The Fourteenth are encamped right west of us. We are encamped about a mile from the city on a plain 6 miles square."[120]

While Private Pierce drilled with his comrades in the Thirteenth New Hampshire, farther south in Manchester, the Tenth New Hampshire Regiment was boarding trains for their journey south. The passage of the regiment was uneventful until one of the passenger cars jumped the track between Philadelphia and Baltimore. Unfortunately, Private John Cole of Manchester was thrown from the train and killed. At age forty-three, Cole was one of the older members of the regiment. The Irishmen of the Tenth were wondering if their luck had run out when they were involved in a second train accident the next day between Baltimore and Washington.[121] After their arduous journey, the Tenth New Hampshire arrived in Washington at three in the afternoon on September 25. The regiment spent the remainder of the month at Camp Chase in Arlington Heights, Virginia.[122]

The Twelfth New Hampshire on September 27 marched through downtown Concord to the railroad depot. The day was bright and clear, and the streets were crowded with hundreds of wives, sisters, fathers, and brothers of the men departing the state. On their way through Nashua, the ladies showered the soldiers with bouquets of flowers. A bouquet caught by Corporal Thomas E. Osgood of Bristol was thrown by an acquaintance, E. N. Ladd. Ladd's brother Luther of the Sixth Massachusetts had been the first soldier from New Hampshire to die in the Civil War when he was killed marching through Baltimore on April 19, 1861.[123] The Twelfth New Hampshire boarded the steamer *City of New York* for that city. On the day the regiment was boarding the train for Philadelphia, Governor Berry, on his way back home from Washington, visited the regiment. Instead of being cheered by the men of the Twelfth, he was greeted by cheers for Thomas J. Whipple and pleas to have Whipple appointed as their colonel. While the regiment waited in Baltimore, several shots rang out. The men of the Twelfth thought at first that this was a salute being fired by a New York regiment as it passed by. When the smoke and dust cleared, Darius Robinson of Meredith from Company I was dead on the platform. The somber men from New Hampshire arrived in the nation's capital tired, hot, and hungry and headed to their life at Camp Casey in Arlington Heights.[124]

Frozen Hell at Fredericksburg

CHAPTER 4

October 1862 to December 1862

And loving words shall tell the world their noble deeds,
who fought 'gainst the wrong
the flag of freedom first unfurled,
and suffering made the nation strong.

"Carousal of Odin," *Poems of the*
Rev. Thomas Penrose (1782)

While new regiments left New Hampshire for Washington, regiments already in the field received much-needed replacements. Private Ransom Merritt Neal of Claremont arrived at Hilton Head, South Carolina, to take his place in the ranks of the Third New Hampshire. Neal recorded in his diary on September 29, 1862, his first impressions of his new home: "Here I am spending my twenty-fourth birthday away down in Dixie. Little did I dream of this one year ago. I have been very busy putting my little tent in order. building a bunk for sleeping etc. assisted in my labors by a most obsequious little darkie. The tent occupied by three of us raw recruits is precisely six feet six inches square. So we find very little wasted room in our dwelling."[1] Despite his Spartan accommodations, Neal was able to see the natural beauty of his surroundings: "We are only five rods from the ocean at high tide. How I delight to sit in the tent door and gaze out upon its broad expanse. Then the mind goes out far beyond the strifes of Earth and all its cares are overlooked and forgotten. Ours is just now a quiet life."[2]

Adjutant of the Ninth New Hampshire, George Henry Chandler agreed with Neal: "Since our last battle (Antietam Sep 17) we have been leading rather a quiet life as far as outward demonstrations go, and have done more to perfect ourselves in discipline and drill than in six weeks previous."[3] Adjutant Chandler related President Abraham Lincoln's visit and review of the army after the Battle of Antietam: "Father Abraham passed close by us and looks careworn and thin as it appears to me. Gen McC. looks fat and hearty. We had a review by the President about ten thousand or more troops were in line besides artillery and cavalry."[4]

With General Robert E. Lee's Army of Northern Virginia back across the Potomac came a lull on the battlefields. However, there was great excitement in the North concerning the president's Emancipation Proclamation. There was action in Kentucky and Mississippi, but hostilities halted in the eastern theater. Once more, Lincoln begged General George B. McClellan to take decisive action against Lee. McClellan refused.[5]

In New Hampshire the government found that it had surpassed its quota for three-year men under the president's call the previous summer. The prospect of a draft loomed large, so when the call came for three hundred thousand nine-month troops, New Hampshire towns offered larger and larger bounties in order to attract new soldiers. In early October it was decided to raise three nine-month regiments, one from each of the three congressional districts. Much to the delight of the towns, the extra men who had enlisted for three years were counted toward the new quota of the nine-month regiments.[6] The men soon began to trickle into the camps at Concord and the first to arrive formed the core of the Fifteenth New Hampshire Regiment, with Colonel John W. Kingman chosen in October 1862 to lead them.[7] He stayed with the Fifteenth until he was mustered out on August 13, 1863. Of Kingman, Private Jonathan Huntington Johnson said, "We like our colonel very much. At first sight he appears to be a very good man, temperate and no swearing."[8] Kingman was such a man of temperance that he requested the officers of the regiment to sign a temperance pledge for their term of service. All of the officers agreed and kept their promise. It was said that the Fifteenth New Hampshire was probably the best-behaved New Hampshire regiment in the field.[9]

One of the three-year regiments still in New Hampshire was the Fourteenth. On October 3 while still at camp in Concord, Sergeant John Henry Jenks, a thirty-nine-year-old shoemaker from Keene, wrote to his wife, "You must try to keep up good spirits for I shall probably be back in Spring, if not sooner. Most of the folks think the war is most over. I hope it is for I had rather be with my family than on this business still I shall try and do my duty faithfully while I am a soldier."[10]

Soldiers in the Eleventh New Hampshire departed from Frederick, Maryland, too late to take part in the Battle of Antietam. McClellan and the Army of the Potomac stayed in the area of Harpers Ferry, while Lee remained with his army in the lower Shenandoah Valley. From his camp just outside Harpers Ferry, Private J. Lewis Chase of Company A of the Eleventh New Hampshire wrote to his brother Samuel on October 3 about the mood in the army at that time, "The old soldiers think that they are going to have a battle now that will tell the story. I hope they will."[11] On October 6, the Eleventh New Hampshire marched a short distance to Pleasant Valley, Maryland, and was brigaded with the Fifty-first Pennsylvania, Fifty-first New York, Thirty-fifth Massachusetts, and Twenty-first

Massachusetts.[12] Private John D. Purington of Company A expressed his displeasure with camp life in Pleasant Valley, "We haven't got enough to eat since we left Concord we fed one piece of beef two or three hard Crackers half pint of coffee one half the beef we cannot eat it, it stink. Your dog is used better than they use the poor soldiers." Private Purington did not have to cope with army life for long. Receiving a mortal wound at Fredericksburg on December 13, 1862, he died the next day. He is buried in the Locust Grove Cemetery in Newfields, New Hampshire.[13] Private Alonzo Pierce of the Thirteenth New Hampshire echoed the feelings of Lewis Chase, "The general impression among the soldiers of the Potomac is that there is to be a large battle come off soon. The soldiers are as determined to do their duty come what may. The rebels have the same love of country that we have and will fight for it."[14]

While some soldiers were looking ahead to the next battle, Dr. William Child of the Fifth New Hampshire was still thinking about the last one: "When I think of the battle at Antietam it seems so strange. Who permits it. To see or feel that a power is in existence that can and will hurl masses of men against each other in deadly conflict—slaying each other by thousands—mangling and deforming their fellow men is almost impossible. But it is so—and why we can not know."[15]

Letters from loved ones at home were an important part of a soldier's life and one of the few motivations that the men had for carrying on and suffering through the horrors and deprivations of war. Private Ransom Neal of Claremont confided in his diary how important letters were to him: "Oct.13. A mail and letters from home today. O, these home letters!—what an essential contribution are they to a soldier's happiness. We had just commenced our dinners today when the call came 'Fall in boys for letters.' Our knives dropped as though we had received an electric shock. The last half of our dinners was eaten cold."[16] Private Joseph F. Wentworth of Company G Twelfth New Hampshire described camp life and the weather: "We fare pretty well now sometimes we have rather poor grub and other times good. . . . it has been cold here for a day or two as it is generally in N.H. the middle or last of Oct." Wentworth related an incident that happened occasionally in the camps: "We herd the report of a gun and herd a ball whistle over head and herd a man screem I jumped and ran to the man and was the first one to get to him had his gun loaded with both hands over the muzzel and parts and puled it off and the hole charge went through the wright hand and bloded one finger from the left they had to cut off his write hand it looked hard."[17]

Writing on October 12 from St. Augustine, Florida, Second Lieutenant Calvin Shedd of the Seventh New Hampshire was very satisfied with his camp and their surroundings: "On the whole this is a very good place decidedly the best place the 7th has been in I wish I was rich enough, if I should live, to take you all here in the winter & live on Oysters, Clams, Fresh fish and Oranges the weather for two or three days has been splendid cool nights so that we can sleep." Shedd had quite a different opinion of the situation that Colonel Louis Bell and the Fourth New Hampshire had found themselves in earlier: "The Citizens like the 4th first rate for they used to abuse the Niggers & let the whites do just as they pleased, let them pass out in the lines pretty much as they liked when the 7th came here everything is changed Abbot [Lieutenant Colonel Joseph C. Abbott] and Put [Colonel Haldimand Putnam] just made the Men and Women take the Oath of Allegiance or go outside the Lines."[18]

While the men from New Hampshire serving in Virginia were given a respite from battle, it became the turn of the Third and Fourth New Hampshire in Port Royal, South Carolina, to face the battle's breath. These regiments were involved in a battle near the small village of Pocotaligo, also known as Coosawatchie, the objective being to destroy a bridge on the railroad line between Savannah and Charleston. On October 20 the Fourth New Hampshire was ordered to cook three days' rations and be ready to leave the following morning. The Third was ordered to take five days' rations and a hundred rounds of ammunition per man. The Fourth New Hampshire traveled via the steamer *Boston* to Hilton Head where they were loaded onto the gunboat *Conemaugh*. The Third New Hampshire traveled on a variety of ships, staying aboard overnight and in the early-morning hours of October 22 sailed thirty miles up the Broad River. Each man in the Third New Hampshire was given a bundle of pitch pine for burning the railroad bridge when they captured it. The entire expedition numbered over three thousand with two field pieces and two howitzers tended by men from the ship USS *Wabash*.

The Forty-seventh New York skirmishers were first to encounter the enemy, meeting the Confederates at about 1 P.M. After advancing about five miles, the Rebels made their first stand, and a fierce musket exchange occurred that left the Forty-seventh New York severely mauled,[19] and they fell back. The Fourth New Hampshire advanced in their place and threw out their skirmishers. Captain George F. Towle of Company G remembered, "Crossing the scene of the 47th fight, many evidences of its severity were seen in the blood still wet on the ground where groups of skirmishers had held position behind some giant pine."[20]

While the skirmishers were out, the Fourth New Hampshire formed their line between the Sixth and Seventh Connecticut and started forward all the while under a constant hail of shot and shell from the Confederate batteries. While they were dressing their line, several shells whizzed by and buried themselves in the ground behind the regiment. The regimental history of the Fourth New Hampshire recorded that a man could be killed just from the concussive force of the wind as a shell went by. The combined force of New Englanders fought a running battle with the Confederates until they came to a causeway that was heavily defended by some artillery pieces in a marsh. Union artillery was brought up, and the Confederate guns were silenced.

The chase began again but was significantly slowed when the Fourth New Hampshire line was broken up by the marsh. The men waded through waist-deep water and continued toward their objective, the heavily defended railroad bridge and causeway. Here the Confederates chose to stand and fight. The New Hampshire men heard the sound of trains approaching, which could mean only one thing: the Confederates were receiving reinforcements.[21]

The Fourth New Hampshire regimental history documents that when Colonel Louis Bell was wounded in the foot during the action, he was taken to the rear. Captain Towle of the Fourth believed that something different happened after the retreat was ordered, which he wrote in his journal: "Col Bell was nowhere to be seen. As it proved, he had lost heart and gone to the rear. He claimed to have been wounded but could show no bruise upon his person. Lamentable as the fact was, he had shown the white feather."[22] Colonel Bell apparently had no quarrel with Captain Towle because in his official report he stated, "I am proud to be able to say that I had no stragglers in my regiment and that no officer or soldier flinched." Bell also stated in his report that he had been "temporarily disabled." He did not mention a wound, but he did return to the causeway about five o'clock in time to lead the regiment back to its starting point.[23]

The Third New Hampshire was the last to land and supported the artillery and so was only lightly engaged. A brief bayonet charge was made over ground already contested, so the regiment's losses were light. The expedition failed to destroy the bridge.[24] A return raid was contemplated the next day but was cancelled. The Third and Fourth New Hampshire returned to Port Royal.

In its first action the Fourth New Hampshire lost three men killed and twenty-five wounded, and the Third New Hampshire suffered only a few wounded, but the total picture was somewhat bleaker. The Union paid for the destruction of a few railroad ties at Pocotaligo with the wounding or death of 340 men.[25] Sergeant David C. Hayes of Dover, one of the 294 men wounded during the Battle of Pocotaligo, was taken to the hospital at Hilton Head where he died on November 12, 1862. Hayes is buried in lot 1492 in the Beaufort National Cemetery in Beaufort, South Carolina.[26] Captain of Company A Third New Hampshire Rufus F. Clark sat at his desk to write a letter that was becoming more frequent: "On the 21st we were ordered on an expedition to Pocotaligo. Your husband was advised to remain in camp, and not accompany us, his appearance seeming to indicate that he could not stand the fatigue and exposure of the march. He went with us and the march hastened his end."[27] The man Captain Clark refers to is twenty-three-year-old Private Ransom Merritt Neal of Claremont, a printer and a skilled writer. He left vivid descriptions of his arrival and his life in camp at

COLONEL JAMES PIKE, *Sixteenth New Hampshire Regiment, Field and Staff. Pike was a Methodist minister and former congressman when he was called to lead the Sixteenth New Hampshire. This nine-month regiment had the distinction of having no battle casualties. It did, however, lose 210 men to disease. Photograph courtesy of NHVA*

Hilton Head. In his October 20 journal entry, Neal is positive and feels that he will be able to do his duty. Ten days later on Thursday October 30, his writing is shaky and almost illegible. The last entry in his journal simply says, "My wife Julia I'm going home. Sweet will be our meeting up yonder. God keep you my Julia. Your Merritt." Before the day was over, Private Ransom Neal suffocated and died from diphtheria.[28]

October 1862 had been unusually chilly in Louisiana, and the men of the Eighth New Hampshire were demanding overcoats if they were going off on an expedition. On October 27 in an open field at Napoleonville, the men awoke to a coating of ice nearly an inch thick. The battle that day at Labadieville, also known as Georgia Landing, was the first for the Eighth New Hampshire Regiment. The men of the regiment were advancing up the right bank of the Bayou Lafourche when they encountered two regiments belonging to General Braxton Bragg. On their side of the bayou, the Eighth New Hampshire under Lieutenant Colonel Lull had only a small cavalry force to lend assistance. The majority of the brigade was on the opposite bank with Colonel Hawkes Fearing.

The Eighth New Hampshire rushed forward over rail fences and through thickets, all the while exchanging volleys with the Confederates. Midway during the charge, Captain John Q. A. Warren of Nashua was killed. A concentrated volley from the graybacks shattered the flagstaff of the Eighth New Hampshire and left nine holes in the flag. The intensity of the charge by the New Hampshire men broke the rebel line but not without the cost of twelve killed, thirty-two wounded, and one missing in its baptism of fire. Also killed was Captain John Kelliher of Manchester. The Eighth New Hampshire would not see action again until April 1863 at Bisland, Louisiana.[29]

In Concord another nine-month regiment was being raised. The Sixteenth New Hampshire had the distinction of being the only New Hampshire regiment mustered after the First New Hampshire to suffer no battlefield deaths, but the Sixteenth lost almost a quarter of its men to disease. Five officers and 203 men succumbed to diseases prevalent in the swamps and river valleys of Louisiana. Men came from as far away as Germany, Austria, and India to serve in the ranks of the Sixteenth New Hampshire. Out of the original 914 men who enlisted to serve for just nine months, forty-four decided that they could not endure the depravations of a campaign in the Deep South and deserted.[30] The Reverend James Pike, forty-four, had offered his services as a regular foot soldier but was commissioned as the colonel of the Sixteenth New Hampshire on November 1, 1862.[31]

While the Fifteenth and Sixteenth New Hampshire drilled and trained in Concord during October and the first half of November, the Army of the Potomac was moving in Virginia. Private Horace H. Adams of Company G of the Tenth New Hampshire Regiment was wishing he could be back home in Portsmouth: "I suppose you have cold weather in New Hampshire now. I should like to be there and get some of Caleb's cider or a little Whiskey would be very acceptable at present."[32] From near Upperville, Virginia, Private J. Lewis Chase of the Eleventh New Hampshire on November 4 described the movements of the army in the latest campaign, "We have begun the marching a little. We march from 6 to 15 miles a day. We march almost everyday. It is hard work Mother. We live well now fresh meat Salt pork. We have got a spider that we carry with us and do our own cooking. Fry a hunk of pork then soak the hard bread then fry it. It goes good."[33] Private Harlan P. Knight of Nelson, making his way south to join the Sixth New Hampshire as one of its newest recruits, recorded his passage in his diary, "The difference between the buildings in Maryland and NH. Their barns are small and poor and their houses are poor compared to ours. Baltimore is quite civil, but it is very dirty."[34] Adams, Chase, and Knight, although they did not know each other and were all in different regiments, were about to be in the costliest battle to the state of New Hampshire during the Civil War. Two of them would survive the Battle of Fredericksburg, and one would survive the war only to die in a freak accident years later.

On November 9, Private Chase informed his mother of the progress of the Eleventh New Hampshire: "We are continueing our march toards Richmond. We march almost everyday."[35] The Eleventh New Hampshire was called out on November 10 to defend against an anticipated attack near Culpeper Courthouse, but the attack never materialized, and the regiment resumed its march to the northeast.[36]

While central Virginia experienced intermittent snow showers in the middle of November, the weather in Florida was still mild. On November 9, Quartermaster Andrew Young of the Seventh New Hampshire told his wife, Susan, in Dover that life was still very comfortable: "Oranges are now ripe & lemons and are so plenty that if you want one you have only to pick them. Maj. Henderson & myself are occupying the house of Maj. Corman, a Paymaster in the U.S. Army. Col. Putnam & Adj. Webber have one nearby & we all eat together. We have two colored girls 'Sally' & 'Lucinda' who are our cooks and are quite lady-like. They live in our kitchen. And a kitchen in the south means a house in the backyard. They are never attached to the main house."37 Colonel Putnam of the Seventh New Hampshire was happy that "the health of the men is improving decidedly. There has been a decrease in the morning 'sick report' one or two a day for a fortnight past, it is now below 60. I am now about 170 pounds in weight."38

While Colonel Putnam and Quartermaster Young enjoyed fruit and good health, the Fifteenth New Hampshire Regiment was formally mustered on November 12 into the service of the United States in the State House Yard in Concord. Colonel Kingman received the colors presented to the regiment by Governor Berry.39 The regiment left Concord on November 13 on orders to proceed to New York, remaining at Camp Nathaniel Banks in New York for the rest of the month. While in camp, Captain Jonathan H. Johnson described a curious weapon seen on the wagons: "It consists of one hundred rifles placed on four carriages, twenty-five to each, and they can fire them eight times in one minute. That makes eight hundred balls in one minute from them all a most dreadful engine of destruction."40 The weapon was known as a requa battery, which was used effectively by Union forces in siege operations such as those at Fort Wagner in the late summer of 1863.41

While the Fifteenth New Hampshire stayed in camp in New York, the Eleventh New Hampshire was still making its way, along with the rest of the Army of the Potomac, across central Virginia. At White Sulphur Springs, Private Willard J. Templeton of Hillsboro in a November 12 letter mentioned how the men supplemented their diet in Virginia: "While at Jefferson, our army was pretty short of provisions. We went right up to the house and meeting the Negro told him we must have something to eat. Two or three got hoe cake and milk. The rest of us shot the pigs that were running around the house where as in N.E. you see dogs, quickly dressed them and brought them into camp. And in 15 minutes 15 men were cooking liver or pork steak on our spiders or on picked sticks. Feel as well as ever in N.H."42

The Ninth New Hampshire was also on its way to Fredericksburg. Corporal Albert Taft of Nelson stated quite simply what the soldiers did for three straight days: "November 16, 17, 18—March, March, March." On November 19 he recorded, "Moved up to within a short distance of Fredericksburg. Here we are. Burnside orders Lee to surrender the city & Lee orders Burnside back. Our boys talk with the Rebs across the river."[43] Colonel Walter Harriman of the Eleventh New Hampshire detailed in his diary that on November 19, "We broke camp at six o'clock in the morning and marched, we hoped and believed for Fredericksburg. . . . On arriving on the bank of the Rappahannock . . . directly opposite Fredericksburg . . . the officers of the Eleventh came together . . . and grew eloquent over the prospect of the easy capture of the place. No rebels of any account are now there, the river can be forded without difficulty, and the men are ready for it." Harriman bitterly mused, "We must wait-wait for pontoons to cross on, which will be simply waiting for the rebel army to arrive and intrench itself."[44]

While on the march to Fredericksburg, the health of Colonel Enoch Quimby Fellows of the Ninth New Hampshire broke down completely. He had been steadily declining since the Battle of Antietam and on November 21 was relieved of command because of complications from neuralgia. Succeeding Fellows was Lieutenant Colonel Herbert B. Titus of Chesterfield. Josiah Stevens Jr. of Concord was promoted to lieutenant colonel.[45] In New Hampshire the Sixteenth New Hampshire Regiment readied to leave the city of Concord and headed out the same day for New York City, where they camped in Battery Park until their departure in early December for New Orleans.[46]

In a letter penned to his sister from his camp opposite Fredericksburg, Private J. Lewis Chase of the Eleventh New Hampshire described the late-November and made a prediction: "We have had a storm here. It has rained three days, awful muddy. Now it looks as though it would rain again before night. The mud is just like greese dab you all over. . . . We have 80 or so field pieces here of the citty. They say they can count 19 of their guns. If that is all they have got we shall not have much trouble in taking the citty."[47] Twenty-one-year-old Private Enoch F. Osgood of the Eleventh wrote home to a friend in Fremont on November 25 about the attack that all the soldiers knew was imminent: "I am now out on picit on the banks of the raphannock river, and the rebels are across on the other side, wee talk with one another, wee are expecting to atact the rebels every hour, wee have a very large force here and are puty sure to gain the victory." He was sarcastic in saying that he would enjoy a Thanksgiving dinner of "hard tac and salt pork." Private Osgood was killed in action during the Battle of Fredericksburg two weeks later.[48]

Private Harlan P. Knight of the Sixth New Hampshire confided in his journal on November 27: "I suppose it is Thanksgiving day today and would like to dine on chicken instead of hard bread. The Captain brought some beans for our supper. They were very acceptable." In a letter to some friends in Nelson on November 30, he said, "Our forces are rapidly concentrating in the vicinity and three

PRIVATE J. LEWIS CHASE,
*Eleventh New Hampshire,
Company A. Chase received a
severe wound to the face on
May 6, 1864, at the Battle of
the Wilderness. He survived the
war only to die with his wife in
1884, when the steamer* City of
Columbus *sank off the coast of
Massachusetts. Photograph
courtesy of NHVA*

pontoon bridges are being thrown across the River. Do not be alarmed if you should not hear from us for some time."[49]

A week after writing to his sister, Private Chase of the Eleventh wrote to his brother John about the growing anticipation around Fredericksburg: "We have been here over a week doing nothing. If they are going to do anything this fall I should think it time to be about it. There is a large army here now. The N.H. regts. are all around us. The 2nd 5th 6th 9th 10th 11th 12th are all here. I don't know when we are to move it don't look much like closeing up the war to me."[50] Chase was not completely correct in his estimate of the number of New Hampshire units present at Fredericksburg. Also on the field was the Thirteenth New Hampshire under Colonel Aaron Stevens and the First New Hampshire Light Artillery Battery posted on the extreme left of the Federal line under Major General William Franklin's Left Grand Division. Unknown to Chase was that the New Hampshire companies of the First and Second United States Sharpshooters were in the vicinity as well as members of the New Hampshire Battalion of the First New England Volunteer Cavalry. Chase's frustration with the Federal delay in attacking was shared by his colonel, Walter Harriman, who recorded in his journal, "The march had terminated not at Richmond, but at Fredericksburg; and there the army tarried three weeks." Harriman was of the opinion that the army should have attacked immediately or gone into winter quarters and that Burnside was also in favor of going into winter quarters. However, "the public mind was impatient, and Burnside was compelled to attempt an immediate advance. Though there were apprehensions of desperate, as well as, fruitless encounter, yet no adequate prevision was there of that magnified image of death which should loom so terrible on yonder plain and slope."[51]

While the Army of the Potomac prepared to cross the Rappahannock River at Fredericksburg, the Fifteenth and Sixteenth New Hampshire Regiments sailed south from New York for Louisiana, the Fifteenth in three separate vessels. Both regiments reached New Orleans two weeks after the Battle of Fredericksburg was decided.[52]

Writing to his brother Charles in early December, Private Alonzo F. Pierce of the Thirteenth New Hampshire described his march to Acquia Creek and the capture of some wild hogs: "We shall probably see an active campaign this Winter the way things look now. Artillery in the shape of long heavy siege guns have been passing within a short distance from Acquia Creek towards Fredericksburg—100,000 men are on the way to the heart of rebeldom." Private Pierce of Antrim, New Hampshire, fought in the Battle of Fredericksburg but died five days into the new year of 1863 from disease.[53]

Central to any discussion about why the Federal army did not win a victory at Fredericksburg is the issue of the pontoon bridges and Burnside's decision to wait for their arrival before attacking. Parties looking to exonerate Burnside point to Washington's deliberate delay with the pontoons or that the pontoons got stuck at various points along the road to Fredericksburg. Thomas L. Livermore, who was at the time of the battle a second lieutenant in the Fifth New Hampshire, proposed an intriguing idea that is rarely discussed: "There were the piers of the old bridge still standing and there was the expedient of covering them with timbers of the houses close at hand or cut from the woods close at hand, but that expedient was not comprehended in the strategy of General Burnside and we waited a month."[54] Opposite Fredericksburg, Private Chase of the Eleventh sent a letter home, this time to his brother Samuel about the turn of the weather on Monday, December 8: "Monday morning and cold enough to snow has layed on the ground ever since last Friday and the ground is all froze up solid. There is a large army here I can assure you. We have been here now some two weeks. What the delay is I do not know unless it was because the pontoon bridge did not get along."[55]

Despite the delay in attacking, confidence in Ambrose Burnside was high even as far away as St. Augustine, Florida. "We the Republicans in the Regt feel that the President is getting on the right track superceding McClelland," Seventh

New Hampshire Second Lieutenant Calvin Shedd wrote to his wife on December 11, "& hope Burnside push matters with a will and in accordance with his well known Energy."[56] Private Templeton of the Eleventh New Hampshire told his sister in Hillsboro about the opening stage of the battle for Fredericksburg on December 11: "We received orders this morning to march at sunrise for an hour before a tremendous canade had been going on at Fredericksburg mostly by our batteries on this side. It has continued with increasing vigor until now (11 AM) It reminds me of a heavy thunder storm except that it is one continued rumble."[57] Corporal Albert Taft of the Ninth New Hampshire made this brief record in his diary for December 11: "Cannonading commenced early this morning. Kept it pretty briskly all day."[58]

The pontoon bridges finally arrived but laying them across the river proved difficult because of Confederate snipers. Finally, at 4:00 P.M. on December 11, an amphibious force of Massachusetts and Michigan regiments secured a beachhead on the opposite shore so the bridges could be completed without hindrance.[59] Corporal Richard W. Musgrove of the Twelfth New Hampshire described the bridges as the regiment arrived at Fredericksburg: "On Friday morning, Dec. 12, we resumed the march towards Fredericksburg and halted on the bluffs opposite the city near the Lacey house. Six pontoons spanned the Rappahannock, three some distance below the city, and three between the city and the bluffs, where we were."[60]

Colonel Joseph Potter of the Twelfth was ordered just after noon to take his regiment across the bridge into the city. Just as the Twelfth approached the bridge, several Confederate cannonballs exploded in the midst of Companies B and K, and eight men were wounded, two of whom later died. Potter hurried his men off to the right and into a ravine. Another regiment took their place. The Twelfth New Hampshire withdrew about a mile from the riverbank and set up camp for the night. The day's events were apparently too overwhelming for some, because eleven men deserted during the night. The Twelfth New Hampshire did not cross the river until the following day.[61]

Corporal Taft of the Ninth New Hampshire marked the event in his usual succinct style: "Crossed over into Fredericksburg. Stay in the streets tonight. Quite mild."[62] The Eleventh New Hampshire also crossed on December 12, which Private Templeton of Company D related: "Went right across the river on the pontoon bridge and are now occupying the west part of Fredericksburg city. The rebels frequently throw shells on to the pontoon bridge and the opposite bank. We lay on the high bank of the river when they come to fast. The rest of the time we spent today pillaging the city. I have been in a good many houses. We find the most splendid furniture,—pianos, crockery and glassware. Tables all set and the victuals half eaten. Flour of the best quality and nice lard and our boys are frying fritters and donuts in any quantity. The relics of all kinds are collected by the boys. I didn't get much because I know we will be going into battle soon and they will only be an incumbrance."[63] Private Chase of the Eleventh scribbled off a simple note to his parents on December 12: "After the battle is over I will write particulars if I am alive and well. From your son Lewis."[64]

Before dawn on December 13, Union forces were ordered into positions. The First New Hampshire Light Battery moved forward to take its place along Bowling Green Road between Brigadier General Solomon Meredith's and Colonel William F. Rogers's brigades, which were in Major General Abner Doubleday's First Division of Major General John F. Reynolds's First Corps. These units faced the cavalry brigade of Brigadier General W. H. F. Lee.[65] A member of the battery recalled that around 7 A.M. as they passed a small rise, they saw white stakes driven into the ground: "As we passed them we received the compliments of the rebel batteries, who, knowing the actual distances were able to strike very close. In crossing one small knoll we lost several horses and had one gun carriage pole carried away."[66] Private Thomas C. Cheney of the First New Hampshire Light Battery said that on Saturday morning, "we moved further down to the extreme Left where our Division had gone, soon after we got there we opned fire."[67]

The Second New Hampshire was posted about one mile northeast of the headquarters of Left Grand Division Commander William B. Franklin. The Second New Hampshire along with three other regiments from Brigadier General Joseph Carr's brigade had been assigned to guard the lower set of pontoon bridges. In this position for the rest of the day, they witnessed the enormous struggle unfolding less than two miles to the northeast. At daybreak on the 13th, the Tenth New Hampshire was on picket duty with the Eleventh Connecticut and Twenty-first Massachusetts just east of Hazel Run along the Richmond, Fredericksburg, and Potomac Railroad line, which could be used to bring in a large Confederate force that might severe the Right Grand Division from the rest of the army. The rail line was being watched closely. The Thirteenth New Hampshire was posted on the western edge of town near the Gas Works with other regiments of Colonel Rush Hawkins's First Brigade. Two other Ninth Corps regiments, the Sixth and Ninth New Hampshire, were near Frederick Street and Princess Elizabeth Street, respectively. The Eleventh New Hampshire in Brigadier General Edward Ferrero's Second Brigade was at daybreak about one block north of the Sixth and Ninth New Hampshire, nestled snugly between the Fifty-first Pennsylvania and the Thirty-fifth Massachusetts. Colonel Edward Everett Cross and the Fifth New Hampshire were posted with the rest of the First Brigade of Brigadier General Winfield Scott Hancock's First Division on Sofia Street. The Twelfth New Hampshire under Colonel Joseph Hayden Potter finally crossed into the city early on that day, set up just east of Prince William Street, and only moved several blocks in the course of the day. The two deaths in the regiment were from the bombardment while trying to cross into the city the previous day.[68]

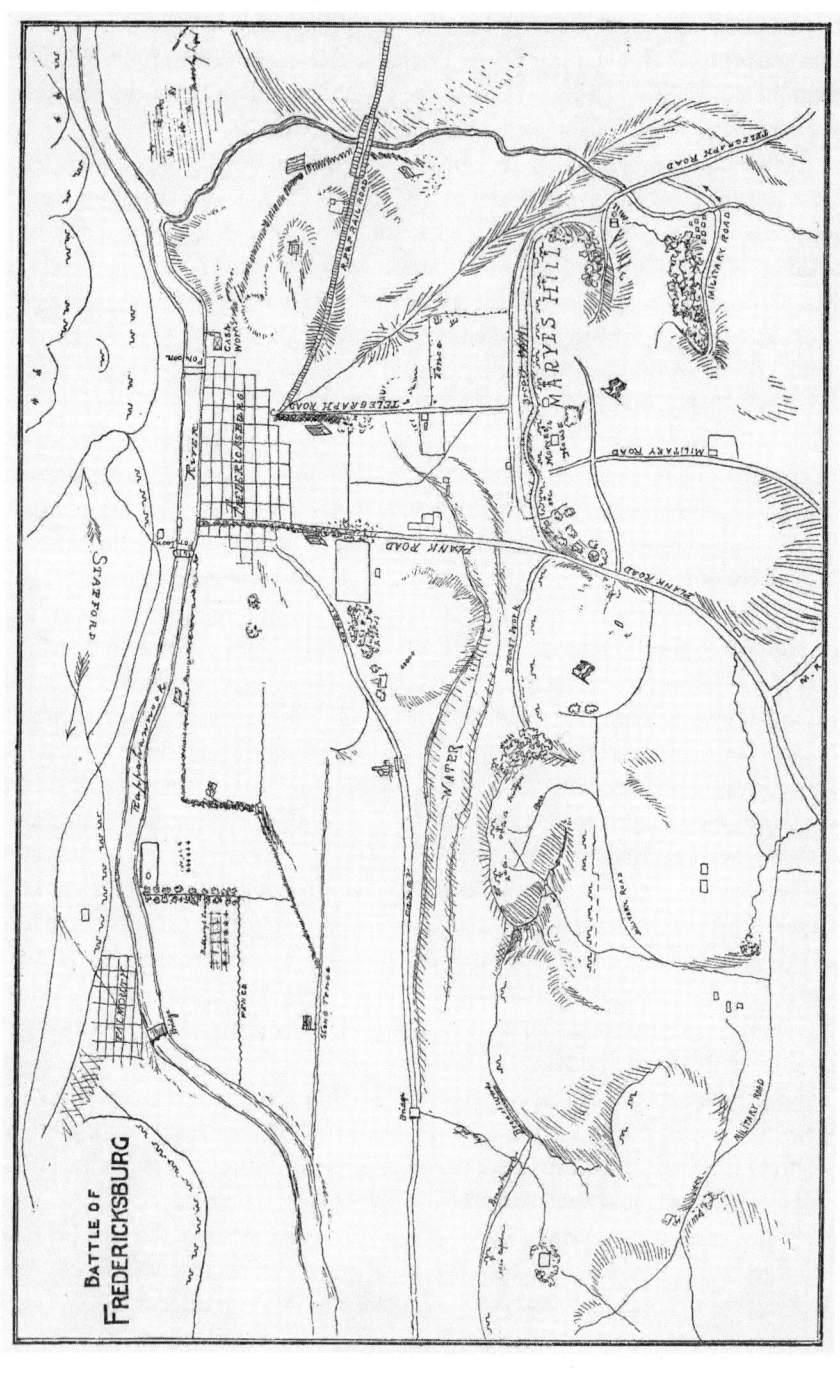

BATTLE OF
FREDERICKSBURG

Sensing that an attack was imminent, the Confederates unleashed an artillery barrage on the tightly packed Federal regiments in the town precisely at dawn. Several hours later as the clock approached noon, the first of Burnside's frontal attacks emerged from the city and made its way up the long sloping hill to Marye's Heights. Massed cannon fire from the Confederates met the regiments of Major General William H. French's division and tore huge holes in the lines. The blue-clad soldiers from Pennsylvania, New York, and New Jersey tried to hold their ground against the hail of lead pouring into them but their lines wavered and lost all semblance of formation.[69] Major General Winfield S. Hancock's division followed French's and was ordered to support him on the right. The Second Brigade under Brigadier General Thomas Meagher went in first, and the Irishmen fought valiantly. Directly behind the Irish brigade came Brigadier General John C. Caldwell's brigade with the Fifth New Hampshire on the far right of the line. Colonel Cross recounted the action as they met the enemy: "They opened on us with solid shot and shell, and before we reached the open fields several men were disabled. It soon became our turn to move forward. The Reg't rose up as one man and started forward. We were thus advancing when a shell exploded in the air directly in front of me a large fragment hit me on the breast, a smaller piece knocked out two of my teeth-& filled my mouth with sand; another bit struck me on the forehead, making a slight wound, another bit over the eye, and still another along the back of my hand. I was knocked clean off my feet & lay insensible."[70] Colonel Cross tried to get up, but another shell fragment slammed into his leg, causing him to collapse again. The ground was churned up all around him with bullet and shell fragments. Cross tried to go forward again but was knocked to the ground when his scabbard was hit. Spitting out blood, pieces of shell, and teeth, Cross resigned himself to lying still until the storm subsided. With Cross injured, Major Edward E. Sturtevant rallied the men and pushed them forward. The closer the Fifth drew to the stone wall, the clearer it became that unsupported they could not breach this formidable defense. After the loss of six color-bearers and Major Sturtevant, the tattered remnants of the Fifth New Hampshire withdrew.[71]

Second Lieutenant Livermore of the Fifth New Hampshire bitterly remembered, "Sumner, restrained by General Burnside from going across the river to head his lines, shed tears at the sight, and indeed it was a spectacle to provoke them from the sternest man, for five thousand men out of the old Second Corps were killed and wounded that day to no purpose and through the blunder of one man."[72] Out of 250 men that the Fifth New Hampshire had ready for duty that day, nineteen were killed, 154 wounded, and thirteen listed as missing. Cross

FACING: *Fredericksburg. From Leander Cogswell,* A History of the Eleventh New Hampshire Regiment Volunteer Infantry, *1891.*

reported, "Justice to the dead, the wounded, and the few unscathed of my regiment constrains me to express the opinion that no soldiers on any battlefield ever exhibited greater bravery or devotion. At the time of writing this report I have three officers and 63 enlisted men for duty."[73] The command structure of the Fifth New Hampshire had been all but wiped out: Colonel Cross was wounded, Lieutenant Colonel Samuel Langley had resigned earlier in the month, and Major Sturtevant and Captains John Murray, James B. Perry, and William A. Moore were all dead as well as several lieutenants. Cross himself lay on the battlefield for nearly three hours until he was found and brought to the rear. Lieutenant James Larkin of Concord led the remaining men of the Fifth New Hampshire from the field that day.[74]

Between noon and 1 P.M., the only other movement of New Hampshire units was the Eleventh New Hampshire in Ferraro's Second Brigade toward the center of town. All other New Hampshire units were in the same places they had occupied at daybreak. This day of carnage and misery for the sons of New Hampshire had barely begun.[75] Sergeant Charles C. Paige of the Eleventh New Hampshire explained what happened when the regiment received its orders to move forward: "At one o'clock we were ordered on to the field. We filed to the right going up a short street. Here our first to be wounded, Charles Lane was struck. Filing to the right, and obliquely, we went on to the field amid terrific musketry and shell missiles of death."[76] Private Lane of Candia was wounded and was transferred to the Veteran's Relief Corps. He survived the war and lived the rest of his life in Washington, D.C.[77] The sergeant described the battlefield of Marye's Heights: "From the river the ground gradually rises until the foot or base, of the Heights is reached; then an abrupt, steep slope fifty or more feet is reached on which crest are the cannon, while at the base of the Heights is a sunken road filled with infantry who had full view of us."[78]

"We rushed in on the keen run over fences, through mud holes in full view of the Rebel batteries and rifle pits which poured a perfect hurricane of shot and shell amongst us," Private Templeton recalled of the horror that awaited the Granite State men when they stepped out onto the battlefield. "We advanced under this terrific fire for nearly ¾ of a mile. We got dreadfully cut up going across the field. What made it worse for us, just as we were going on a Penn. Regiment broke their line and run past us for dear life."[79]

"Of course I had to be active and much in earnest to fire two hundred rounds from one-thirty o'clock to five-thirty o'clock," Sergeant Paige said about the duration of the fight for the Eleventh New Hampshire. "My knees were wet and covered with mud for I was on them most of the time. We were constantly expecting the Rebels to charge on us, and they did come over their works two or three times."[80] Colonel Harriman recalled, "How the minies whistled, and the shells screamed over our heads and through the ranks! How the case shot hummed and the splinters from the fences flew in our faces; while, as we neared the enemy's works, the canister was poured into our ranks and many of the boys fell killed and wounded. The ground behind every advancing regiment was dotted with blue coats, and gaps were made in the ranks that never could be filled."[81]

The Eleventh New Hampshire approached the sunken road. "We quickly advanced," Private Templeton wrote to his sister, "and filled the deserted line and the way we peppered the rebels for the first fifteen minutes wasn't slow! In half and hour the rest of our brigade came to our support. I fired my sixty rounds of cartridges and then lay in the mud and let the other regiments take the front."[82]

"Never can I forget the scene, or obliterate the horrors of that hour," Sergeant Paige of the Eleventh said about the battlefield. "The cannons were belching streams of lightning; solid shot fired point blank, striking the frozen ground ricocheting with streams of fire in their wake, and seemingly heating to a fiery molten color, the terrible missile of death, making more terrible the scene; shells bursting all around and a perpetual storm of leaden hail enveloping us, from which there seemed no escape, and I said to myself how hellish it seems; demons let loose with all the conceivable influences of that place where the fire is never quenched, could not have made more horrid a scene."[83] Fredericksburg was the first battle for the men of the Eleventh New Hampshire—40 men killed, 130 wounded, and 25 missing. Many of those wounded later died from exposure or expired from disease in January 1863.[84] After the war, a veteran of the Eleventh New Hampshire was speaking with two veterans of Longstreet's First Corps about the Battle of Fredericksburg. The two Southern soldiers remembered one particularly outstanding regiment they met that day. Dressed in a darker-blue uniform than the other regiments around them, the uniforms seemed almost black on the smoky battlefield. When the men of the Eleventh New Hampshire drew closer to the stone wall, the Southern soldiers remembered saying, "Boys they look too handsome to fire upon, but it must be done, let them have it." The soldiers said they expected them to break and run, because they could tell that the Eleventh was a new regiment. The Southerners complimented the Granite State boys for having a line that "was perfect and never wavered."[85] Immediately after the advance of the Eleventh New Hampshire, it was the turn of Nagle's brigade with the Sixth and Ninth New Hampshire to attack, with Colonel Samuel S. Carroll's brigade minus the Twelfth New Hampshire and Colonel James Barnes's brigade on their right.

Corporal Albert H. Taft of the Ninth New Hampshire wrote in his diary for December 13: "After breakfast hauled off alongside the river an waited till about two o'clock. Then filed up through the cross streets by company and formed in line of battle in the field back of the city. Marched in under a dreadful fire. Fought till dark and returned to the city."[86] In Simon Griffin's Sixth New

Hampshire, Nagle's brigade, was Private Harlan Knight, Company E, of Nelson, New Hampshire, who gave his perspective on the battle: "Between 12 and 1 we went into action and were under a heavy fire of artillery and muskets from that time till dark. Our boys fired their ammunition nearly all away and then drew back about two rods so as to give fresh troops a chance to take our places."[87] Most of the casualties of the Sixth New Hampshire came when the regiment stepped out onto the open plain. Cannon shells rained down on the regiment, killing and wounding men with each explosion. One shell that landed in the middle of Company K wounded Private Charles Gibson of Rindge. The regiment went forward without him and found cover in a hollow farther up the hill. A short time later, the men of the Sixth looked to their rear and saw the lone figure of Private Gibson running through the fields ducking and dodging explosions all around him. The regiment thought he was sure to be shot down, the intensity of fire shown by the number of clods of dirt thrown into the air by the bullets and shells impacting near him. Private Gibson received only a slight wound and was successful in reaching his comrades. He survived not only the battle but also the war. The number of men of the Sixth New Hampshire killed or wounded on December 13 totaled seventy-five.[88] Private Knight told his friends how he also sustained a wound: "I was near the brow of the hill and had just fired my rifle and dropped on my left elbow to load when a musket ball passed just under my head and struck me on the front of my shoulder and passed through my overcoat. Had it been a minie instead of a musket ball it probably would have wounded me badly. If you see my name in the list of wounded don't give yourself uneasiness on that account for it was nothing serious."[89]

The Ninth New Hampshire had moved out with the rest of Nagle's brigade and occupied the left of the line. Unfortunately, as the regiment drew closer to the Confederate line, it drew enfilading fire on its left. Lieutenant Colonel John W. Babbitt of Keene hurried the men along at the double-quick so they could gain the cover of a deep trench. As the men jumped into the trench, jagged pieces from an exploded shell tore into Lieutenant John Lewis of Lancaster, killing him instantly. Staying in the trench was suicide because Confederate cannon fire was now enfilading the trench that the men of the Ninth thought they had safely gained. They immediately scrambled up the fifteen-foot embankment, only to be met by a thunderous volley of Confederate musket fire from their front. The regiment started again at the double-quick across the open plain, still exposed to artillery and rifle fire. Sergeant Edgar Densmore of Company F, a veteran of the First New Hampshire Regiment, carried the national colors during the battle. When this twenty-one-year old Nashua soldier was shot dead, Lieutenant C. D. Copp of Company C, who was also from Nashua, grabbed the colors and carried them forward. Like the Sixth New Hampshire, the Ninth stayed in an advanced position until all its ammunition was gone. Only when night fell was it considered safe enough to withdraw the regiment. The Ninth New Hampshire lost eleven men killed, sixty-eight wounded, and twelve men missing and presumed captured.[90]

It seems that every battle of the Civil War has a fatuous argument associated with some aspect of it. At Fredericksburg, the debate has always centered on which Union regiment advanced closest to the stone wall. Regiments including the Fifth, Tenth, Eleventh, and Thirteenth New Hampshire regiments made claims that they left casualties closest to the wall. Such arguments are pointless, considering that thousands of men were killed and wounded all over the field that day. Valor and bravery of the Northern soldiers are not measured by where they fell but that they went forward without question into the jaws of death. Those soldiers from New Hampshire and elsewhere who participated in the last and least necessary charges at Fredericksburg were probably the most courageous on the field. The soldier who died from an infected wound one month after the battle in a hospital bed in Washington was just as brave as one who fell in front of the stone wall.

The First New Hampshire Light Battery remained on the far left of the Union line, making small adjustments to their position whenever Confederate counterfire became too deadly. But the movements were not enough, because the battery lost Private Thomas Morrill of Manchester to a cannon shell that tore through his body. The Confederate artillerists brought out two English Whitworth guns off to the battery's left and began raking the New Hampshire men with deadly accuracy. Private Charles A. Doe of Manchester was killed, and Private John Fish, also of Manchester, was wounded and died from it the following day. By the end of the day, the battery had lost three dead, twelve men wounded, including Captain Gerrish again, and sixteen horses.[91] About four o'clock in the afternoon, as the sky began to darken, Private Knight of the Sixth New Hampshire scribbled this observation: "They have been carrying the wounded across the river all day." Private Harlan Knight's wound was more serious than he led his family to believe, and he died on December 26 in camp at Falmouth, Virginia.[92]

About 5 P.M., after four previous, futile assaults on Marye's Heights, Brigadier General George W. Getty received orders to attack with his two brigades. One can only speculate about why this order was given at all when the battlefield was now dark and shrouded in a pall of smoke. The previously cool but mild day had turned bitterly cold since the sun had gone down. The brigades of Colonel Rush Hawkins and Colonel Edward Harland were ordered forward to attempt what thousands had failed to do throughout the course of the day.[93] The Tenth New Hampshire under Colonel Michael T. Donohoe and the Thirteenth New Hampshire commanded by Colonel Aaron Fletcher Stevens were in Hawkins's brigade along with Ninth, Eighty-ninth, and 103rd New York and the Twenty-fifth New

Jersey. The Tenth had for the majority of the day been on picket duty along the railroad, and the Thirteenth had been posted near the Gas Works.[94] Colonel Stevens stated in his report: "As the head of the column came in sight of the enemy at a distance of about three-fourths of a mile from their batteries when close to Slaughter's house it was saluted with a shower of shell from the enemy's guns on the crest of the hill."[95]

The pace was quickened, and the men began to discard anything that became a burden. Knapsacks, coats, and blankets were tossed on the way up the hill, the Twenty-fifth New Jersey preceding the Thirteenth New Hampshire and completely in their front. Having gained the shelter of the railroad embankments, the order soon came to charge. Colonel Stevens recalled, "The men sprang to their feet and moved forward at a run, crossed the railroad into a low muddy swamp on the left which reaches down to Hazel Run all the time the batteries of the enemy concentrating their terrible fire and pouring it upon the advancing line."[96] At some point during the charge, the line of the Twenty-fifth New Jersey on the right flank of the Thirteenth disintegrated, and a part of it started to retreat. Captain George Naylor Julian of the Thirteenth New Hampshire remembered, "We labored under great disadvantage having a cowardly regiment in front of us. The 25th New Jersey who broke and fled like a flock of sheep breaking through our ranks causing great confusion and breaking up our line so that our men were all broken up. Had it not been for this regiment in front of us the 13th NH would have seen the other side of the stone wall."[97]

Whether Captain Julian and the rest of Hawkins Brigade could have breached the wall is another matter. The Carolinians and Georgians who manned the stone wall were at times stacked four and five deep on their side waiting to discharge their muskets into the faces of the advancing New Yorkers and New Hampshire men. Colonel Stevens commented on the intensity of the Confederate defenses, "The powder from their musketry burned in our very faces and the breath of their artillery was hot upon our cheeks. The leaden rain and iron hail in an instant forced back the advancing lines upon those who were close to them in the rear. We remained about half an hour until we received orders to fall back."[98]

With the sudden withdrawal of the bulk of the Twenty-fifth New Jersey, the right flanks of both the Tenth and Thirteenth New Hampshire had been uncovered. By the time these two New Hampshire regiments had made it to the vicinity of the stone wall, it was almost totally dark, and the battlefield was a confusing mass of explosions, musket fire, and running men. Under these conditions, the chances of friendly fire were greatly multiplied.

In the dark the men of the Eighty-third Pennsylvania and Twentieth Maine of Stockton's brigade could not see that two regiments of Hawkins Brigade were dangerously close to their front left flank. Seeing flashes in the dark a bit more than a hundred yards to their left, the men of the Eighty-third Pennsylvania and

Twentieth Maine fired for the next seven minutes on what they thought were the Confederates but were the Tenth New Hampshire and the remnant of the Twenty-fifth New Jersey. The men of Hawkins Brigade yelled and screamed for the Maine men to stop but the volleys from their fellow soldiers and the Confederates in their front drowned their voices out.[99] "Upon arriving at a little creek or ditch, the enemy's fire was severe, and checked our progress and created confusion," Colonel Donohoe of the Tenth New Hampshire stated. "After some minutes, I succeeded in forming a portion of the line again, and crossed a fence, and found a number of the Thirteenth New Hampshire and Twenty-fifth New Jersey there. I proposed to the commanders that we should move on but a fire from troops in our rear caused me to change my mind."[100]

"The brigade received the fire of the Eighty-third Pennsylvania Volunteers and the Twentieth Maine Volunteers, who were on the left of General Couch's line which our right had overlapped," Brigade commander Colonel Rush Hawkins recalled.[101]

The friendly fire and the intensity of the Confederate defense caused the entire right flank of Hawkins Brigade to collapse, and it was compelled to withdraw. Nighttime and the smoke of battle prevented the casualty rate from being too high for these last two New Hampshire regiments participating in the battle. The Tenth suffered two men killed, thirty-one wounded, and six missing, while the Thirteenth suffered two killed, thirty-three wounded, and five missing.[102] Of the New Hampshire regiments involved in the Battle of Fredericksburg, the Second New Hampshire was lucky; only five men were wounded. Fredericksburg was a true baptism in blood for the Eleventh New Hampshire, for they suffered 195 men killed and wounded. Out of the total Federal loss of 12,653 men at Fredericksburg on December 13, New Hampshire lost 653 and lost scores afterward to wounds and disease. The men of this battle would remember and write about it for years.[103]

On December 13, it had both rained and snowed back home in New Hampshire. No one in Epping knew that Private James M. Sleeper of that town was dying on a frozen battlefield in Virginia with other men from the Eleventh New Hampshire. No one in Exeter knew that four students who had signed up for the war from Phillips Exeter Academy had all been seriously wounded.[104] "This cursed war is killing all of our best men," wrote Private J. Lewis Chase of the Eleventh New Hampshire to his father. Chase listed all the names of his friends who were killed and wounded. "Our company is all cut up 16 or 17 killed and wounded. They mowed us down awfully. I do not see how any of us escaped such a murderous fire as they poured into us. The groans of the wounded is enough to make your blood run cold. I don't know how I escaped."[105] Corporal Richard W. Musgrove of the Twelfth New Hampshire recorded in his diary for December 15, "Every dog in the city continued for hours a most dismal howling it seemed as if all the hosts of hell were let loose in the city."[106] "We had a fearful fight," Adjutant George Henry Chandler of the Ninth New Hampshire wrote home during the evening of December 18th. "The 11th in Ferraro's brigade suffered worse. Captain A. B. Shattuck of Manchester was badly wounded in the leg. It was amputated as a last chance. He died yesterday."[107]

Dr. William Child of the Fifth New Hampshire told his wife about his experiences in a makeshift hospital in Fredericksburg, the horror of his time in the city weighing heavily on him: "Three days at Antietam and one night in Fredericksburg have given me enough of battle. . . . I wish every person in Bath who has talked so savagely about this war could pass through one battle—see the suffering. Cad, It is beyond all description. If this war is from God—our sins as a nation must be great. When will it end."[108] From Armory Square Hospital on December 22, Sarah Low wrote to her mother, "Yesterday as we were giving out breakfast the bugle sounded again, a hundred more wounded had arrived and the floor was soon covered . . . the men speak of this battle as the greatest slaughter there has been."[109]

The Sixth New Hampshire under Colonel Simon G. Griffin was one of the last regiments to cross the bridges on the army's return to its camp at Falmouth. The men knew they had been defeated and were grumbling about where to lay the blame for the catastrophe. Colonel Griffin had already decided that it was Major General William B. Franklin's fault that he had not pressed the attack on the Federal left and come to the aid of Burnside. Of Ambrose Burnside, Griffin said, "He was too kind, large-hearted, optimistic and confiding to succeed as a great commander. Burnside was not clear, comprehensive and exact in his statements or instructions. Burnside gave Franklin a written order behind which he could shelter himself while he cut his commander's throat."[110] Major General Ambrose Burnside would receive more than his share of the blame for the defeat at Fredericksburg, the avalanche of criticism beginning almost immediately after the battle. A musician in the Eleventh New Hampshire, Ransom Sargent of New London said, "It really seems to me that Burnside must have seen what was apparent to almost everyone, the folly of making an attack under such circumstances, and I expect the next news we hear he will be superceded. Fredericksburg can never be taken by storm, as last Saturday's battle proves which cost New Hampshire the lives of more brave and true men than the whole accursed south is worth."[111]

Joseph Willey and Reull Willey of New Durham were both privates in the Tenth New Hampshire during the Battle of Fredericksburg. Joseph wrote to his parents about the recent battle: "We had a little fun with Rebs a Week ago yesterday and it was pretty hot fun to a recruit. We made a Charge on the Rebel batteries at dark and We heads to go back again. . . . Thare was not one killed nor wounded from New Durham the boys are well and ruged."[112] Private Chase also suspected that something had gone wrong with the Fredericksburg plan: "There is some mismanagement some way or the other. You seem to think the war is about through with. I think just the other way. It looks worse than it did when I enlisted." Chase also told his parents about the duty assigned to the Eleventh New Hampshire that became symbolic of the battle's end: "Last knight our regt. was ordered out to go down to the river and load the pontoon bridge the bridge was taken out last knight. It was loaded on to the wagons."[113]

Bitterness over the Federal loss at Fredericksburg turned to sarcasm in more than a few cases. Lieutenant Ben Calef of the Second United States Sharpshooters stated that the government "may find a good chance to have another lot killed off. . . . I would suggest their having it done in Central Park this winter. It would save much trouble and expense. Have no doubt Gen'l Lee would send a Division on to N.Y. They could select a position, post their batteries and men and then folks could see how it's done."[114] Dr. Child told his wife not to believe everything she read in the newspapers: "It is astonishing how different the idea conveyed in those papers [is] from the facts. It does seem as though the newspaper correspondents thought the people were fools—or simpletons. The facts are perverted. The truth is we made a great blunder. It was one of the greatest in the war."[115]

Almost every New Hampshire regiment lost dear friends and company commanders to death and wounds. Colonel Cross of the Fifth New Hampshire was seriously wounded again. Captain Horace Bacon of Company A Eleventh New Hampshire received serious wounds and had to go home. Captain Amos Shattuck of Company E was dead. Perhaps the loss felt most in the Fifth New Hampshire was that of Major Edward E. Sturtevant. Adjutant George Henry Chandler of the Ninth New Hampshire and Sturtevant, both from Concord, knew each other well. In letter home to his mother on Christmas 1862, Chandler lamented his friend's passing: "The late battle brought many civilians down from Washington to look after the dead and wounded. . . . Mr. Mitchell came down to get Major Sturtevent's body, which was unfortunately buried with hundreds of others in a field now in possession of the enemy, and can never be found. Concord people I am informed are much affected by his loss and would make any sacrifice to obtain his remains."[116]

New Hampshire regiments were also in Florida, Louisiana, Maryland, and South Carolina. The Fifteenth and Sixteenth New Hampshire were on their way to Louisiana aboard ships. "We arrived at Ship Island at about 12 o'clock last night," Captain Jonathan H. Johnson of the Fifteenth New Hampshire recorded in his diary for December 17. "This morning the weather is very fine. It seems like June in New Hampshire."[117] It was not long until Johnson was in camp near Carrollton, Louisiana, and met some friends from the Eighth New Hampshire. About the Eighth, he said, "A good many of their Regiment have died. I saw

George Rowe here today. He is very sick and feeble. I think it doubtful that he will ever get home again. Timothy Gleason is dead. He died about three weeks ago." Both Rowe and Gleason were from Raymond and were friends of Johnson. Johnson was correct about Rowe, who died of disease on February 13, 1863, in Baton Rouge, Louisiana.[118] Johnson, a forty-seven-year-old father of eight, who worked with his son George in a shoe shop in Deerfield before the war, confided to his diary, "I have seen a great many women out here but not any of them has any charm for me. They do not for one moment divert my mind from the wife I left at home in Deerfield."[119]

After the Federal withdrawal from Fredericksburg and the removal of the pontoon bridges, picket lines were established on both sides of the river. After the tremendous slaughter that had just taken place, Confederates and Yankees regarded each other warily from their side of the river. Soon sporadic conversations were struck up, and both sides agreed not to fire on each other. Christmas was coming.[120]

Christmas 1862 found Landsman Martin Hoyt of Newington aboard the USS *Kearsarge* in harbor at La Carraca, Spain. The sailors had been at sea for months. They had a forgettable Christmas dinner of salt beef, hardtack, and a plum pudding so overbaked that one sailor said they could have safely used it for a football.[121] Sarah Low probably had a chance to see President Lincoln that Christmas Day when he and the First Lady visited the hospitals around Washington. Armory Square Hospital and others were full to capacity with the wounded from the Battle of Fredericksburg. Private Chase, in camp opposite Fredericksburg, answered a question from his parents, "Homesick? No, I don't want to come home unless we all can." Chase went on to say how grateful he was for his Christmas presents, a new pair of socks and a handkerchief.[122] Christmas Day in the Federal camps opposite Fredericksburg was mild and sunny. Chaplain Gushee conducted divine services in front of General Nagle's headquarters. Christmas dinner for the men in the Ninth New Hampshire was beefsteak and potatoes, a welcome change from the monotonous diet of salt pork and hardtack.[123] Down at the riverside, with an uneasy truce in place, pockets of men, former and future enemies, gathered to exchange parcels of tobacco and coffee.[124]

The remainder of 1862 passed uneventfully for the men serving in New Hampshire's regiments. There were rumors of battle, but none materialized, and the men began to settle into their winter quarters. The last day of the year was cold and drizzly for the men in the sprawling camps opposite Fredericksburg. Even in this darkest and most depressing of times, the soldiers in the New Hampshire regiments clung to the hope that 1863 would be a brighter year and would bring a close to this dreadful war.[125]

"We poured a deadly fire into their ranks"

CHAPTER 5

January 1863 to May 1863

In the case of right engaged wrongs injurious to redress,
honor's war we strongly waged but the Heavens denied success.

Poems and Songs of Robert Burns

The first day of 1863 witnessed President Abraham Lincoln's Emancipation Proclamation go into effect. On the issue of emancipation, the abolitionists felt that the plan did not go far enough, because technically no slaves had been freed. For others, especially the soldiers in the field, it was viewed as a document that changed the focus of the war from one of preserving the Union to freeing the slaves, an idea that was not wholly acceptable to soldiers from New Hampshire or any other Northern state.[1] In camp opposite Fredericksburg, Private J. Lewis Chase of the Eleventh New Hampshire wrote to his parents on January 18, letting them know the condition of all the men from South Newmarket. Responding to a question in a previous letter from home about the men being homesick, Chase spoke for the average soldier when he said, "You spoke about their being homesick. I should think they were by the way they talk. They are down on Lincoln's proclamation freeing the nigers is what knocks them. There were 18 left one regt. night before last in our brigade. They were good fighting men but they are sick of it."[2] Private John H. Carr of the Thirteenth New Hampshire had a different take, which wrote to his friend George Beede in Fremont: "Whether the Emancipation Proclamation will cause an uprising among the slaves, remains to be seen, one thing I am sure of there will be no peace so long as slavery lasts. That cursed Institution is now totering on its last legs."[3] Corporal Claude Goings of the Eighth New Hampshire registered a strong opinion: "If I thought we were fighting to free them [the slaves,] I would throw my musket to the devil and leave."[4] From Port Royal, South Carolina, Third New Hampshire private Edward F. Hall described his feelings to his wife about Lincoln's proclamation: "The President's proclamation . . . was altogether unnecessary . . . those who think the abolition of slavery of more consequence than the Union are as much traitors as anybody else-they have no love for the constitution or the country, and have been disunionists for years." Hall explained why he wanted the country to be whole again: "Let me tell you that when this Union is divided, no one will tell where disunion will end, instead of two, there may be several different governments established on the ruins. New England may be left out in the cold."[5]

In New Hampshire the last of the nine-month regiments was bravely coping with the New Hampshire winter. Camped on the windswept Concord plain, the understrength Seventeenth New Hampshire Regiment shivered inside their rough winter quarters, ordered into camp in November to wait for the expected recruits. Unfortunately, for the Seventeenth, the last three nine-month regiments were filled in numerical order from the three congressional districts. The Fifteenth drew its men mostly from the first district, the Sixteenth the second, and any men from the third district automatically went to fill the ranks of these two regiments. Despite few volunteers remaining, the Seventeenth still raised over seven hundred men, who began their military training at Camp Colby in Concord during December.[6] Throughout January, the Seventeenth New Hampshire and its officers searched for the necessary recruits so the regiment could be officially mustered. An impending state draft created a great sense of hope that the last nine-month regiment from New Hampshire would soon see service, but the draft was abandoned, and orders were issued to reject all substitutes applying for enlistment on unfilled quotas. Substitutes were hired to take the place of soldiers or draftees. Because very few new volunteers appeared to join the Seventeenth, its officers and men were furloughed in February, allowed to go home, and then transferred to the other regiments already tested in battle.[7]

The men of the other New Hampshire regiments spent January in relative quiet. Private Jacob F. Chandler of the Eighth New Hampshire camped west of Baton Rouge described his New Year's celebration: "My New Year's breakfast was raw pork cooked on a splinter . . . for dinner salt junk and hard tack with Bayou Lafourche water, for supper hard tack and river water. . . . [Colonel Hawkes] Fearing rode out in front of our battalion in line and wished us very pleasantly 'A Happy New Year,' and we all greeted him with three hearty cheers." While on a march, Chandler said that the regiment encountered, "Our old battleground at Labadieville. . . . The fences were as we left them, broken down; even the dead horses were left unburied."[8] Captain Jonathan H. Johnson of the Fifteen, in camp at Carrollton, Louisiana, lamented the lack of letters from home, even though he had only been gone for two months. On January 4, 1863, he wrote home, "It cannot be that some of you do not have time. It must be neglect or accident."[9] Corporal Caleb Dodge of the Seventh chided his sister and the rest of his family, "I began to think that you were all dead for it is a long time all most three months since I herd from home. . . . We had chicken and plum pudding for thanksgiving dinner. We had a good time Christmas that is a grate day with the South."[10] On January 12, Jonathan H. Johnson recorded a sad first for the Fifteenth New

Hampshire, "The first death in the Reg. Occurred today. Charles Perkins from
Haverhill, NH belonging to Co. B." Perkins, thirty-one, died of disease in Carroll-
ton, Louisiana, and is buried in the cemetery in Chalmette, Lousiana.[11] John-
son's entry for January 14 discussed the prospect of the army moving upriver,
"The rumor is that we are to be ordered up the River to Baton Rouge or Port
Hudson. It is rumored that the rebels are concentrating a large force at Port
Hudson."[12]

Two events in January 1863 had profound consequences for the Army of the
Potomac. On January 19, the Federal army set out in good weather to cross the
Rappahannock River near the United States Ford. Major General Joseph Hooker
and Left Grand Division Commander William B. Franklin approached the ford,
but a sudden downpour followed by a savage winter snowstorm stopped the
movement cold. Men, horses, and wagons were stuck fast in the mud. The U.S.
Naval Observatory in Washington recorded a rainfall of two inches for the day
on January 21.[13] "We have had quite a snow storm," said Private Chase of the
Eleventh New Hampshire. "We have about six inches on the ground."[14] Private
Willard J. Templeton of the Eleventh New Hampshire also reported the weather:
"We had a severe rain storm lasting all Tuesday night Wednesday morning it
began to snow. It snowed all day and all night."[15] The weather's effect on the
army's move, Burnside's "mud march," was the subject of a letter by Lieutenant
Enoch Adams of the Second New Hampshire: "Last Tuesday we marched for
battle. We expected to cross the Rappahannock and attack the Enemy on the
flank. But the rains came on and the mud was so very deep so the artillery got
all stuck in the clay and the whole army was forced to return to their old
camps."[16] "I suppose you have heared of the intended move that was to have
been made and was made in part," Private Chase wrote to his father about the
failed move of the army. "Franklin and Hooker's divisions moved upon the right
and we were to try them in front again. Only for the storm there would have
been another big fight. . . . The ball was to commence as soon as it was light. But
they got stuck in the mud. Our artillery could not be moved. They had 16 horses
on a gun but could not move it a peg and consequently there has been no
fight."[17]

Burnside requested the removal of Hooker and Franklin, who, he felt, con-
spired against him. Lincoln relieved Burnside instead on January 25 and
appointed Hooker the new commander of the Army of the Potomac. The move
was met with mixed emotions in the ranks of the army.[18] "Now Joe Hooker has
command you may expect to see something snap. Some of us will get hurt,"
Captain Francis W. Butler of Bennington, Company K Fifth New Hampshire,
opined in January 1863 to friends back in Greenfield, New Hampshire. "I wish
he had been in command at Antietam and Fredericksburg." Captain Butler cam-
paigned with Hooker at the Battle of Chancellorsville and with Major General '

George Gordon Meade at the Battle of Gettysburg but died at Petersburg under the command of Lieutenant General Ulysses S. Grant.[19] Private Chase felt differently about Hooker: "I hear that Burnside has resigned and Hooker has command. I do not think that he can handle this army any better than Burnside. I do not think that any thing will be done of any consequence until another summer and get little Mack in command again. Then something will be done and not before."[20] Rumors among the soldiers were that the army was going to be divided. "It is reported that the Grand Army of the Potomac is to be broken up and some of it sent to Tennessee," Private James Howes of the Tenth New Hampshire told his wife. "I hope such will be the case, as I am tired of this spot having seen all that can be seen in this locality. Gen Burnsides has resigned and is superceded by Genl Hooker and I dare say that he will find us some work to do as he is called by all fighting Joe."[21] Division of the army was also on the mind of Dr. William Child of the Fifth New Hampshire: "The report is that this army is to be reorganized-a part sent south. But our Corps will be sent to the forts about Washington."[22] On Friday, February 6, the much-discussed division of the army began. To increase pressure on Richmond, Virginia, the Confederate capital, the Ninth Army Corps was transferred under the command of Major General William F. "Baldy" Smith to Newport News, Virginia. Private Chase informed his mother about the expected move, "I expect we shall move before night. We are under marching orders and have been for three days. I understand we are to report to Fortress Monroe as soon as we can have transportation there. The whole corps is ordered there and where then I know not. . . . I have got sick of the Virginia mud. It is just like greese."[23] Those who remained behind, especially the men in the Twelfth New Hampshire, were happy when 150 boxes arrived February 11 in camp. Private William P. Mason of Canterbury sadly described the condition of the contents of the box he received: "The Bred, Chickens, Pies, Pickels, Pudding, Apples, Sweet Cake, and also the Donuts wer spoiled. But what things were good, Could not be got here for $15.00."[24]

Far to the south at Camp Parapet in Carrollton, Louisiana, Sergeant Obadiah F. Rumrill of the Sixteenth New Hampshire was recovering from what he called "tyfo-malarian" fever. The Hillsborough native told his nephew about the lack of apples and cider but that oranges were plenty and "Gen. [Nathaniel B.] Banks as he was getting into his carriage last night near the Saint Charles hotel [New Orleans] was fired at by someone . . . but the ball passed by and done him no harm. I think there will be an attack made on Vicksburg soon for the troops are going up river."[25] During 1862 and 1863, the *People Journal* of Littleton, New Hampshire, received a series of letters from someone in the Sixteenth New Hampshire who signed the letters simply "Mascomy." This person regularly sent prosy reports on camp life in Louisiana and on February 28 sent the following report: "Occasionally looking across the high levee fronting our brigade encampment, the vision has been greeted by the sight of a gun boat passing up river—to join the great besieging army round Port Hudson and Vicksburg."[26]

From Newport News, Virginia, Private Chase described the passage of the Ninth Corps, "We left the next morning for Aquia Creek by rail. We then took transports by water for Fortress Monroe. We left the Creek Tuesday morning and arrived at the fort about midnight. We lay at anchor until daylight. We were then ordered to Newport News which was about two hours sail. We had a fine time comeing a smooth sea."[27] Private Reull Willey of the Tenth New Hampshire also made the trip to Newport News with the Ninth Corps and on February 21 expressed his dissatisfaction with his circumstances: "I wish they would settle it some how or the other for I have stayed as long here as I want to in this army among the damned lice I have to take my clothes off three or four times a week and hunt the Devils to get rid of them. . . . The boys are all smart at present and are like me they would all like to get home.[28] In a letter home from Falmouth, Virginia, Private William P. Mason of the Twelfth New Hampshire also displayed his anxieties: "I think I would be willing to stay this summer if we could give them one good sound pounding, & sink them forever into Oblivion. It seems to be wicked & cruel to have this government destroyed while the hands of those bloodthirsty villains & some our own officers & apastle of those men at Washington are dripping with the blood of thousands of our brave soldiers. The soldiers have a revenge against some of the officers as well as the rebs & would shoot their skin as full of holes that it would not hold corn. Col Potter as you say is thought considerable of by his men since the battle of Fred—he proved there & since to be a man with a long hert he uses us now very well. There is no doubt that he is a drunkard. He used us meen when we first came out here because they used to hollow Whipple so much."[29]

In the end of February from St. Augustine, Florida, Colonel Haldimand Putnam of the Seventh New Hampshire told his father about an event that nearly caused him to resign: "About two months ago a Presbyterian minister named Kennedy came here to look after the Negroes. . . . With him came a man named Billings formerly chaplain of the NH 4th now Lt. Col. of a Black regiment. . . . He took occasion on his return to Hilton Head to report certain things falsely. . . . Billings goes to Hilton Head and tells Gen. Hunter in effect that I am influenced by the women here."[30] Hunter's unilateral abolitionist policy making has already been discussed, and, in this particular case, he was unilateral in his abolitionist policy making and now used his staff to carry his draconian edicts to all the posts in his department, including St. Augustine. Hunter issued orders to Putnam to remove all citizens from St. Augustine who had husbands or brothers in the Confederate army. Putnam briefly considered resigning but instead, "I have concluded to . . . send a protest and remonstrance to Gen. Hunter which I think will cause the order to be rescinded," which it was.[31]

Two important events in the month of March 1863 were the Federal Draft Act passage and the New Hampshire gubernatorial election. New Hampshire soldiers in the field had plenty of opinions about both. The Federal Draft Act, which was made law on March 3, made all able-bodied men between twenty and forty-five liable for military service. The executive branch set quotas according to population and number of men currently serving for each Northern state. A focal point of controversy was that a draftee could hire a substitute for $300.00 to assume his military obligation. When the attempt was made to implement the draft in July 1863, riots broke out in Boston, New York, and Portsmouth, New Hampshire. In New York City, hundreds of people lost their lives, and a large part of the city went up in flames.[32] "The subject of the draft occasions some talk here," wrote Oran E. Randall of Chesterfield to his uncle Obadiah F. Rumrill of the Sixth New Hampshire. Back at home, "Some saying they had as lief die here as in the South, and some talk of Canada. At any rate the draft is attempted, is likely to cause some disturbance for a great many of the people are sick of the war. And who is not?"[33] Just as Randall's letter arrived at the camp of the Sixth, a letter arrived in Mason, New Hampshire, for the mother of Private Albert Austin, who asked her, "Remember me to all Mason boys and girls And tell them when I get home I will tell them all I know about Dixie and the Sunny South." Austin never had the opportunity to tell his stories because he died of disease just a few weeks before the Sixteenth New Hampshire was mustered out in August 1863.[34] A soldier in the Army of the Potomac was twice as likely to die from disease as from a battlefield wound. Austin's fate, as well as that of the soldier in the following letter, was common. Private Reull Willey of the Tenth wrote to his wife, "Pinkham is dead. He died this morning at 4 o'clock he had the typhoid fever. . . . We tried to have him sent home. . . . He wanted to be sent home to be buried. . . . They are going to send for his folks. . . . They won't discharge a man until he is dead." Private Justice Pinkham was from New Durham and died at age thirty-four.[35]

The race for governor in New Hampshire took on a special meaning for the men of the Eleventh New Hampshire Regiment. The Democratic candidate was Ira A. Eastman, and the Republican one was Joseph Albee Gilmore, and running as an independent was the colonel of the Eleventh, Walter Harriman. In early March, Private Chase of the Eleventh said he felt Harriman "will make a good governor but stil I would not vote for him. I have two reasons. One is we want him here to command the regt. The other is the third party. The third party is just no party at all."[36] On the subject of the election, Private Templeton also of the Eleventh flatly stated on March 3, "NH election comes off next week Tuesday. I hope the Copperheads will get so thoroughly whipped that they will not dare to express their traitorous sentiments in NH again." Correcting a mistaken impression, Templeton said, "I presume the Democrats say the soldiers if they were at home would vote against the Republicans. But there are but a few that would vote for the secesh candidate. . . . I heartily wish the Col would go to NH and enlighten the secesh who are indirectly giving aid and comfort to the rebellion."[37] The political outlook for the Republicans not only in New Hampshire but also the other northern states as well was particularly bleak, largely because of the Federal disaster at Fredericksburg. Nothing short of a miracle was needed to return another Republican to the governor's office. The Republican Party assigned William E. Chandler the responsibility of producing that miracle[38] and in 1863 nominated railroad executive and ex-Whig Gilmore as the party's standard-bearer and the favorite for governor. However, Chandler, not convinced that Gilmore could defeat Eastman single-handedly, devised a plan to organize some well-known "war Democrats" into a third party and run a popular candidate. Veteran politician and colonel of the Eleventh New Hampshire Walter Harriman became that third-party candidate. Chandler's mission to split the Democratic vote in New Hampshire was a success. Eastman received 32, 833 votes, Gilmore garnered 29,035, and Harriman managed to get 4,372. While on the surface it appeared that Eastman was the victor, because he did not gain a clear majority of the vote the election was thrown into the New Hampshire house. The legislature decided in Gilmore's favor with 192 votes to Eastman's 133. The eyes of the nation were on New Hampshire; the Republican Party members in both New Hampshire and Washington were delighted with the results, but they were also disturbed at the large number of Democratic votes, which led to the passing of a bill permitting soldiers in the field to vote.[39]

Eight of the sixteen New Hampshire regiments in the field were at Fredericksburg to give battle to the Confederates. In early 1863 those regiments, dispersed across a wide area, performed a variety of duties. Under Major General Hooker, who improved the soldiers' diets, the Grand Divisions of Burnside were broken up, and corps badges were assigned with red, white, and blue, signifying the respective division of the corps and bolstering the sagging morale of the troops after their dismal defeat at Fredericksburg. The corps insignia given to Major General Darius N. Couch's Second Corps was a trefoil. Because the men of the Fifth New Hampshire were in Brigadier General Winfield Scott Hancock's First Division, the color of their badge was blood red.

One of Hooker's favorite regiments, the Second New Hampshire, was ordered home for rest and recruiting and while there added 150 men transferred from the Seventeenth New Hampshire. Colonel Gilman Marston was promoted to brigadier general, Lieutenant Colonel Edward L. Bailey of Manchester became the new commander, and Major Carr became the new lieutenant colonel.[40] The Fifth and Twelfth remained in camp with the army at Falmouth, Virginia, while the Fourteenth was on provost duty in Washington. The Eighth, Fifteenth, and Sixteenth, on duty in Louisiana, were readying to march north. From Camp

Parapet in Louisiana, Private Albert McDaniel of the Fifteenth wrote to his sister Sarah about the death of their brother John, a private in the Eighth New Hampshire. McDaniel, nineteen, said that their brother "had his senses to the last. He talked about the folks at home. . . . He told me he should like to see Mother and the rest of the folks-but he sayed he Could not in this world but he wanted me to tell them to meet him in Heaven." Albert McDaniel of Northfield survived his tour of duty in Louisiana and was able to greet his sister the following August.[41] Getty's division of the Ninth Corps, of which the Tenth and Thirteenth New Hampshire were part, was detached and left at Suffolk, Virginia. General James Longstreet, who had General John Bell Hood's and Major General George Edward Pickett's divisions in the vicinity to block any Federal moves on Richmond, attacked Suffolk and laid siege to the city for the month of April and early May.[42] "Old Jeff and Co. would like to subdue the north or gain their independence and if the copperheads could rule they would let him have all he wants and more to for the sake of peace, peace at whatever cost, anyhow I want peace as much as anyone, I know what war is and the immense advantages and comforts of peace," Private John Harrison Foye of Rye wrote to his brother Samuel on April 5 from the camp of the Thirteenth New Hampshire in Suffolk. "But peace not by turning to a copperhead democrat and giving the south what they want but by sending shot and shell, grape and canister into the heart of the rebellion." Private Foye was killed less than a month later in fighting around Suffolk.[43] Also writing home from Suffolk on April 5 was Private Horace H. Adams of the Tenth New Hampshire, who told his friend William. "Last night it snowed all night and about 4 inches of snow fell, the weather out here is Just the same as it is north." He also reported on his tent mates Solomon Gray, Charles Muchmore, Andrew Whidden, and Sylvester White, all from Company G. Gray and Muchmore survived the war, but Whidden died in a southern prison camp, and White died from wounds received at the Second Battle of Fair Oaks in October 1864.[44] The remainder of the Ninth Corps, including the Sixth, Ninth, and Eleventh New Hampshire, proceeded to Kentucky to guard against rebel incursions and watch the Ohio border. "We left Newport News [Virginia] quite sudden," wrote Private Chase of the Eleventh New Hampshire from Paris, Kentucky, to his parents. "We left there in the cars to our present place. . . . We are to go to Mount Sterling to hold that. The rebs were there last week and burned a number of buildings. Som of Morgans gang of gurillas. We have got to fight them now. Stop them from making quick rades."[45] The Seventh New Hampshire remained at St. Augustine except for a small detachment that on April 7 accompanied the Third and Fourth New Hampshire on an aborted expedition to Charleston. The Fourth New Hampshire was ordered on April 4 to Hilton Head, where it was brigaded with the Sixth Connecticut and the third and fifth companies of the Seventh New Hampshire. Colonel Haldimand Putnam of the Seventh

New Hampshire commanded this brigade. While in Hilton Head, Putnam received a reassuring letter from Lieutenant Colonel Joseph C. ·Abbott, in command of the Seventh while Putnam was away. On April 1, Abbott told Putnam how he had given orders to "fit up the limbers for the howitzers so that they could be ready when needed. The hand grenades work well. I am satisfied that there is at present no rebel troops near here, but I should not think strange if Dickison [Confederate Cavalry Captain John J. Dickison] got back again in a week or so. In short, we are on the look out, and do not anticipate any trouble in thrashing anybody who has the temerity to attack us."[46] The grenades Abbott referred to were Ketcham percussion hand grenades, finned weapons made in one-, three-, and five-pound sizes and often as dangerous to the user as the intended victims because of the location of the fuse in the nose. Captain Dickison of the Second Florida Cavalry was considered the Nathan Bedford Forrest of the Southern theater because of his dashing guerilla raids against Federal camps.[47]

The principal event of April 1863 was the attack on Fort Sumter by Admiral Samuel Francis Du Pont. The attack by nine Federal ironclad ships on the fort in Charleston Harbor was a prelude to an amphibious assault by Federal troops. The ships were bombarded by cannon fire from Fort Sumter and Fort Moultrie and various other batteries. All the Federal ships were hit at least forty times, with the USS *Keokuk* receiving ninety and sinking the next day.[48] The Third and Fourth New Hampshire along with a small detachment from the Seventh New Hampshire were part of the Federal force. Colonel Louis Bell of the Fourth described the action, "In the attack we (the ironclads) made of Fort Sumter a day or two since the enemy sank the ironclad Keokuk but did not injure in the least degree the regular Monitors though they (the latter) had a much heavier fire on them than had the *Keokuk*." Bell said the Third New Hampshire "landed in the lower end of Folly Island and marched up to storm a battery on the lower end of Morris Island over the creek that divides the island in boats."[49] The Fourth New Hampshire stayed on their transports in Stono Inlet for six days awaiting the result of the Federal naval bombardment. Du Pont pronounced the expedition a failure on April 11 and stated that Charleston could not be taken at that time. The Third and Fourth New Hampshire, along with the other regiments in the expedition, were returned to Hilton Head.[50] Colonel Haldimand Putnam, who was in charge of one of the brigades, expressed his dissatisfaction to his father on April 11, "The Army, you see, has done nothing to speak of so far . . . for we don't believe that anything very serious was effected last Tuesday."[51] Apparently, Colonel Putnam was more dissatisfied than he let on because Lieutenant Calvin Shedd of the Seventh New Hampshire reported, "Put swore like a Trooper when he was ordered back here."[52]

A special visitor arrived in the Federal camp in Falmouth, Virginia, and on April 11, 1863, Private William P. Mason of the Twelfth New Hampshire described him to his friends in Canterbury: "The President has been here to review us, & he gave us his sincere thanks for neatness and good behavior. . . . He is a thin spare man with black eyes, black beard & black hair mixed with gray, he is a very sober man & caryes an expression of deap sadness upon his face, & looks pale. I am afraid it will be means of his deth he is to be pited."[53]

The boredom of provost duty in Washington was evident in this letter from Private Christopher Hoyt of the Fourteenth New Hampshire to his sister in Bradford: "We have not been paid of yet we haven't been paid for three months when they greed to pay us once in two months I wish that they was all in hell. The war and all folks in the capital it is nothing but a money making Expense of business the privates do the work and the big men get the pay. The city of Washington is nothing but a hogyard. . . . I would not give over forty cents for the whole city and I would not take the whole state of Mayerland as a gift."[54]

In early April the Second Brigade under Brigadier General Halbert Paine went to Algiers, Louisiana, and then on to Brashear City. The Federals found the Confederates strongly posted near Bisland. The engagement was primarily artillery, with the infantry of both sides playing only a minor supporting role. Deep trenches lined both sides of the Teche, and when the infantry was not busy supporting the artillery, they were in the ditches feasting on blackberries. Major General Banks did not press his attack, and the battle eventually fizzled out. The Union casualties numbered only 224, and the Eighth New Hampshire, which had the honor of having one of its flags reach the enemy's line, suffered one death.[55]

"Mascomy" described the first march of the Sixteenth New Hampshire: "Our farthest distance north of Baton Rouge was about 12 miles, yet we countermarched the roads more or less making one march of 17 miles in 14 hours, 6 miles of which was in mud from 3 to 18 inches deep. This would not be serious for troops experienced in retreats but for the maiden march of the 16th, it was more conducive to stiff joints, tired limbs and blisters than patriotism or perhaps profit."[56] From Winchester, Kentucky, Private Templeton of the Eleventh New Hampshire commented on his comrades in the Sixteenth: "I see by the papers that Banks had been pounding the Rebs beautifully. Probably the boys in the 16th Regt. have heard the whizzing little balls buzzing about their ears and the howling shells flying carelessly about. But they will have the satisfaction of writing home that they whipped the enemy in their first battle while we had to acknowledge we got terribly repulsed."[57]

In Falmouth, Virginia, the camp of the Army of the Potomac was stirring in the last two weeks of April. The men knew that once the roads were dry, a campaign was sure to follow. This one would be the Battle of Chancellorsville. "I should like to come home and would give anything in my power to have this war closed but I trust it is all coming out for the best I cant help thinking so but it seems hard to have to stay here and miss other things of orcurence at home but

Corporal Joseph F. Wentworth, *Twelfth New Hampshire, Company G. Wentworth was killed on July 2, 1863, in fighting in the Peach Orchard at Gettysburg. Photograph courtesy of Moultonborough Public Library*

Gods will be done," Corporal Joseph F. Wentworth of the Twelfth New Hampshire said on April 20, indicating his feelings about the war and the impending movement of the army. "It is summer like here we have been under matching ordors for a week with 8 days rasions."[58] Captain Thomas L. Livermore of the Fifth New Hampshire recorded, "In the last week in April we prepared for a march; rations for several days were distributed. . . . A large supply of ammunition was given out and the camp was broken up, and we started on what was evidently intended to be a regular campaign."[59] The Army of the Potomac was to travel up the Rappahannock, cross it, and crush Robert E. Lee and the Army of Northern Virginia from behind. Hooker's plan was a good one, but like all military plans, it depended on the enemy doing everything according to plan. As a portion of the army marched towards Chancellorsville, Virginia, Hooker's plan was already beginning to unravel. Left behind to demonstrate with the First and Sixth Corps opposite Fredericksburg was the Third Corps under Major General Daniel Edgar Sickles. To the men of the Twelfth New Hampshire, it seemed as though they were going to miss all the action. The men in the Fifth New Hampshire who were in a brigade of Major General Darius N. Couch's Second Corps had been posted in approximately thirty homes along Banks Ford to prevent the civilians from giving away Hooker's plan. The First New Hampshire Light Battery was still attached to Major General John F. Reynold's First Corps.[60] Intermittent rain showers fell from April 28 to 30. The U.S. Naval Observatory, Washington, D.C., recorded very heavy rains for both March and April. It was becoming increasingly difficult to move the army.[61] Sergeant Samuel Cooper of the First New Hampshire Light Battery described the opening of the Chancellorsville campaign: "We rose at midnight of the 28th and reached the bank of the [Rappahannock] river at 6 A.M. of the 29th, fired a few rounds into the enemy's rifle pits on the opposite bank, and then Gen. Meredith's brigade crossed the river. . . . We had a rainy night after crossing and were in a dangerous and uncomfortable position not knowing how large a force might attack us at any minute."[62] On May 2, Cooper said, at about 10 A.M., they "recrossed the river and with the whole First Corps made our way by the back roads to re-enforce Hooker's army at Chancellorsville by a forced march of sixteen miles, over fearful roads and through unfathomable mud."[63] The men of the Fifth New Hampshire had a higher priority—finding decent comestibles. Among the houses of the village they were garrisoning was a broken-down, abandoned mill. Bags of corn were piled everywhere, but there was no finished product to eat. Livermore and the men of Company K tackled the problem, and before long, the machinery of the mill was repaired, and the men were making hoecake.[64]

The Fifth New Hampshire had been under the command of Lieutenant Colonel Charles E. Hapgood since February 1863. Colonel Edward E. Cross, once again rebounding from serious wounds, returned to the army and was placed in command of a provisional brigade of three regiments, including the Fifth. On May 1 the happy time of milling for the Fifth ended when Cross gathered the brigade and marched it directly into battle at Chancellorsville just after 4 P.M. Colonel Cross stated that when he arrived at Hancock's position, he formed his brigade "with the 88th [New York] on my right[,] 81st [Pennsylvania] in the center & 5th NH on the left. The enemy soon opened a complete enfilading fire on us but fired too high." Cross withdrew about 2 A.M. on May 2 to a position just southeast of the Chancellor house and dug in.[65] Meanwhile, Hooker had ordered Sickles to leave his camp below Fredericksburg and march to Chancellorsville via the United States Ford. The footsore men of the Twelfth New Hampshire took up positions as did the rest of the Third Corps near Catherine Furnace, just southwest of the position occupied by the Fifth New Hampshire. Sergeant Richard W. Musgrove of the Twelfth New Hampshire remembered, "This was Saturday morning, May 2, and one of those beautiful mornings that come to Virginia at this season of the year, but beneath her skies were gathered two mighty armies of kinsmen, with all the modern appliances of war, determined on destroying each other."[66] The morning and afternoon passed with the Fifth New Hampshire occasionally shelled by the Confederates. The regiment suffered only two men wounded but experienced bombardment by everything from cannon shells to bundles of iron rasps.[67] The men of Sickles Corps heard the Confederates moving in their front and skirmished with them occasionally but were assured by their superiors that they had nothing to fear because the enemy was retreating, although the enemy in front of them was Stonewall Jackson's men. The superiors could not have been more wrong. It was true that the troops in their front belonged to Jackson, but Hooker ignored that Jackson was moving around Hooker's right flank. J. E. B. Stuart found that flank, consisting of the Eleventh Corps under Major General Oliver Otis Howard, in the air and not firmly anchored anywhere.[68] Jackson's men struck Howard's exposed flank like an avalanche. Colonel Hapgood of the Fifth New Hampshire made careful note, "At 6:45 P.M. the men of the 11th Corp began to come through our lines."[69] Colonel Cross's journal read, "A perfect panic took place and thousands of fugitives came back on my lines. I ordered my men to fix bayonets and drive them back, & we did stop & turn back more than 1000 officers & men."[70] Cross and his men found themselves in the midst of a maelstrom of running men, both friend and foe alike. As he did so often, Cross took the red bandanna out of his pocket and wrapped it around his head. He walked up and down the line of soldiers and tried to calm them so they would not be tempted to break and run with the other fleeing soldiers. By the time it reached Cross's position, the Confederate advance had lost its momentum in the dense woods and underbrush of the wilderness, and unit cohesion had fallen apart. With artillery fire the Union line repulsed the piecemeal and uncoordinated Confederate attacks.[71] "Our men behaved admirably," Thomas L. Livermore of the Fifth New Hampshire reported. "Neither the dangers or the panic affected them." While Cross attempted to both keep his men under control and to round up fleeing soldiers, a Union general of a German unit came rushing past. Cross drew his sword and chased after him. "Sare," the general said, "you do nod know who I am! I am a Prigadier Gineral!" Cross replied, "You aren't, you're a damned coward."[72] When the Eleventh Corps collapsed, the Twelfth New Hampshire was nearly overrun by the Confederate advance. "The 12th Regt. was hastily withdrawn," Sergeant Musgrove recalled in his memoir. "Cos. G and F came near being captured. . . . We marched, or double quicked, for nearly half a mile through the woods with the Johnnies on either flank, all unconscious of our presence."[73] At dusk, confusion still reigned, with the battle lines hopelessly tangled and overlapping. It was in this environment that Lieutenant General Thomas J. Jackson was shot by a North Carolina regiment while he was reconnoitering the front.

On May 3 Major General Stuart assumed command of Jackson's Second Corps and immediately moved to occupy the small village of Hazel Grove. From there Confederate artillery commanded the entire area around the Chancellor House. Soon after, an artillery shell struck a post that Hooker was leaning against and knocked him senseless. It was then that Stuart attacked and, listening to the advice the previous evening from Stonewall Jackson, began pushing the Federal forces back toward United States Ford.[74] During this withdrawal, disaster struck the Twelfth New Hampshire Regiment. The regiment, along with the others of Bowman's brigade, had fallen back at dawn to form new lines closer to the Chancellor house, the Eighty-fourth and 110th Pennsylvania on one side of a creek and the Twelfth New Hampshire on the other. When Major General Amiel Whipple ordered Colonel Joseph H. Potter to advance his men into the woods, fighting broke out in the front. Potter assumed that all the regiments of the brigade advance together,[75] and although the advance may have been coordinated, it was only for a short time. The advance was halted by Stuart's fierce attack toward Chancellorsville. The Eighty-fourth and 110th Pennsylvania broke under the weight of the attack and withdrew, leaving the Twelfth New Hampshire on the opposite bank of the creek to face the four Georgia regiments of Brigadier General George Dole's brigade alone.[76] Sergeant Musgrove of the Twelfth described the desperate position of his regiment: "We poured a deadly fire into their ranks and prevented for a time a further advance of this part of their line and here we held our ground till all the Union troops on our left and right had retreated, and the rebels had advanced to our rear on both flanks."[77] Another member of the regiment recalled, "As we expected, the enemy opened upon us from three sides, endeavoring to pierce our center, at the same time they were trying to flank us on our right and left."[78] "It was not long," Musgrove sadly recalled, "before one half of our men lay dead or wounded in a long windrow along our line."[79] Major George D. Savage of Alton received a severe wound to the jaw. Moments before, George's brother Moses, commander of Company A, had been hit in the head by a musket ball and died soon after. The elder Savage was wounded so badly he performed only light duties until his discharge in May 1864.[80] Company D Commander Captain O. W. Keyes of Ashland was shot through the heart, the impact of the bullet throwing him into the air. He was dead before he hit the ground. "Our men had sixty rounds of ammunition when we went into the fight," Sergeant Musgrove remembered, "and they stood in their tracks about an hour and half and expended all their ammunition."[81] During the fighting, Sergeant Joseph Stockbridge of Alton was apparently cool enough to stop momentarily and bite off a chew of tobacco. He calmly resumed firing and loading. Stockbridge was one of only four survivors of his twenty-one-man company.[82] At this point in the fighting, Colonel Potter was wounded in the leg and was captured. He was exchanged in October 1863, became provost marshal general of Ohio until September 1864, and was given a brigade command in the Eighteenth Corps in the Army of the James. It was then that the Twelfth New Hampshire was once again united with their commander.[83] Lieutenant Colonel John F. Marsh was severely wounded and never rejoined the regiment. Of the remaining officers, only two out of twenty-eight were left unharmed. Lieutenant Edwin E. Bedee of Meredith brought off the battlefield what was left of the Twelfth New

Hampshire and reported directly to Third Corps Commander Major General Sickles. Sickles asked Bedee, "What regiment, and where's the rest of it?" Bedee replied, "Twelfth New Hampshire, and here's what's left of it." Sickles turned and said, "Fall in, my brave men, and help us hold this line." Bedee's quick reply was, "But we're all out of ammunition, General." Sickles paused and then said, "Pass to the rear then, quick."[84] The Twelfth New Hampshire and the Third Corps at large sustained the brunt of the Confederate attack, and Hooker's army was gradually pushed back into a semicircle with one flank anchored on the Rappahannock and the other on its chief tributary, the Rapidan River. The Twelfth New Hampshire lost heavily at the Battle of Chancellorsville. Of the 550 men who went on the field of battle in the morning, three commissioned officers were killed and fifteen wounded; forty-two enlisted men were killed, and two hundred twelve were wounded; fifty-one men were listed as missing and assumed captured during the sweeping Confederate attack. Civil War historian Stephen Sears states that at Chancellorsville the losses suffered by the Twelfth New Hampshire were the highest that day of any regiment north or south.[85] Company E of the Second United States Sharpshooters, involved in fighting during the Federal withdrawal on May 4, suffered one casualty. Sergeant Samuel Cooper of the First New Hampshire Light Battery relates an incident about a particularly annoying Confederate sniper that was picking off gunners on units around him: "One of the U.S. Sharpshooters was sent out to fix the rebel who was constantly firing in our direction. He took off his cap and putting it on his ramrod showed it over the earthwork. Of course Johnny Reb let go at it. . . . Our sharpshooter . . . instantly perceived from the direction that his game was in the top of a thick bushy elm tree. . . . It was then the work of less than a second to aim his long telescope rifle at that tree and . . . down tumbled Johnnie like a great crow out of his nest and we had no more trouble from that source." Sergeant Cooper and the rest of the First New Hampshire Light Battery were fortunate in that they suffered no losses except a few horses in the battle.[86] Private Thomas C. Cheney of the First New Hampshire Light Battery said, "I will say however to commence with, that through the goodness of God I have passed through it all this far not rec as much as a scratch for which I feel to thank my Heavenly Father, neither has there any one in our Battery been hit or hurt."[87]

While the army was falling back toward the river on May 3, the Fifth New Hampshire was one of the regiments assigned the difficult and almost suicidal responsibility of fighting a rearguard action, as Colonel Cross recounts: "Our forces were now falling back along the whole line, & the rebels came on shouting furiously. . . . The rebels deployed from the woods in a line of double columns closed in mass. They halted, fronted & commenced to deploy but were driven back by a severe fire of grape & shell. . . . The Brigade was perfectly cool and steady."[88] The loss for the Fifth New Hampshire over the past three days was five men killed and twenty-seven wounded. Hooker, finally admitting defeat, withdrew across the Rappahannock on May 6 a beaten man, although he did not know why.[89] Colonel Cross in his regimental report gave his opinion of Hooker: "Hooker has not the amount of brains necessary to manage a vast army. . . . Hooker's popularity lay chiefly in the soft bread, potatoes & onions he issued. The army never believed him to be a great commander—never. His failure was predicted by thousands of officers & soldiers-from the first day he started."[90] Casualties for the Army of the Potomac had been staggering. Of 133,868 men in Hooker's army at Chancellorsville, roughly 17,000 men were killed, wounded, or missing.[91] The Twelfth New Hampshire had barely been engaged at the Battle of Fredericksburg—the Battle of Chancellorsville had been their actual baptism of fire. The loss of seventy-two men dead was the penultimate single day for battle deaths in a New Hampshire regiment. The tired, sore, and wounded soldiers from New Hampshire returned to their camps around Falmouth, only to find them broken up and sodden from rain. On the evening of May 6, the heavens opened up once again with lightning, hail, and drenching rain. It seemed to the men below that God himself was cleansing the tortured and bloody land.[92]

While the Battle of Chancellorsville was in progress, Longstreet ordered the divisions of Pickett and Hood to lay siege to Suffolk, Virginia, where the Tenth and Thirteenth New Hampshire were posted. Longstreet stated that while he thought that Suffolk could be taken, he did not think "we can afford to spend the powder and ball." Longstreet would break off the siege, but the unsuccessful attack began on May 4.[93] On April 17, Private Reull Willey of the Tenth had written to his wife, "We have had a rather hard time of it for a few days back the rebs have been trying to tare up the rail road between here and Norfolk and cut off our supplies but they have got defeated."[94] The reconnaissance ordered for May 3 saw the Thirteenth New Hampshire and three other regiments crossing the Nansemond River on the Providence Church Road in Suffolk, attacking the skirmish line of the Confederates and driving them back to their lines.[95] Private James Howes, an Englishman in the Tenth New Hampshire, described the confrontation, "There was a battle fought here yesterday but our regiment was not actually engaged in it although we had our share of the danger, we were doing picket duty and had some very narrow escapes. A man belonging to Company D was shot through the chest but is still living, he was not three yards from me . . . the 13th N.H.V. was at the fight and lost I hear, one Capt, 2 Lieuts & twenty men killed wounded and missing." The captain was Lewis H. Buzzell, thirty-one, of Barrington, and the official loss for the Thirteenth New Hampshire was thirty men killed and wounded.[96] One of the enlisted men killed along the Providence Church Road was twenty-one-year-old John H. Foye of Rye. Lieutenant Nathaniel Coffin of Company K expressed his grief in a letter to Foye's family on May 6: "Oh how I regret to say it—your beloved Son is a sacrifice to the cause of freedom. And yet he sleeps the sleep of the brave, beloved by all who knew him. . . . He shall be sent home if it is a possible thing. . . . Your brave son fell in the charge we made on a woods in front of the City of Suffolk. He died a patriot. . . . he is in another and better world why should we wish him here? . . . May Heaven heal the wounds caused in the hearts of Fathers, Mothers, Sisters and Brothers of our Country's defenders." Coffin was true to his word, and the body of John Harrison Foye was brought home for burial in Rye.[97] Dr. Child of the Fifth New Hampshire described his condition during the recent battle to his wife on May 7: "I am pretty well now, though not rested. We have not until last night taken off our clothes for the last ten days-and have not had more than two to four hours sleep each night. I lived most of the time on raw bacon and hard tack. During the time I had two drinks of whiskey. Such is war. I can not understand how we can endure so much as our soldiers do. But we do not know how much men can do until they are tried."[98]

Towns across New Hampshire did what they could to show their support for the health and well-being of the troops. In the town of New Ipswich, residents made comfort bags, which were constructed of strong fabric and typically contained a double fold of thick cloth, six sewing needles, black and white thread, a dozen buttons for shirts and pants, rolls of bandages, writing paper, a pencil, four envelopes, a piece of ginger root, and a Christian Commission leaflet. Professor C. T. Quimby, departing from town to work with the Christian Commission for the summer of 1863, was asked by the Soldiers' Aid Society to deliver the comfort bags and other items to the soldiers of New Hampshire in the field. By the time Quimby was ready to leave for the front, the townspeople had produced 280 comfort bags and 36 pairs of socks for the soldiers. Jars of pickles, jams, and jellies and bottles of wine and blackberry cordials were also taken along for the comfort of the New Hampshire men in the field.[99]

In the Federal Camp in Falmouth, Virginia, and elsewhere, soldiers were writing home about the recent Union defeat at Chancellorsville. "How do the people feel about the last effort of the Army of the Potomac?" asked Dr. Child of his wife on May 18. "Affairs appear to me in a rather bad condition. The last move was certainly not a success." Child said that the last rumors spread in the papers were false: "I hear that New England has celebrated the fall of Richmond. What gullibility! If someone should write that Prof. Lowe had carried the Confederate Capitol with Jeff. Davis off in his balloon and left them in the Gulf of Mexico it would be believed."[100] Private Chase wrote his mother about Hooker: "It seems that Hooker did not make out much in crossing the Rappahanock[.] When he can cross and whip them out there with his force he has got to fight. I have been there myself once. I do not care to go back again."[101]

One of the tragic consequences of the Battle of Chancellorsville was that Stonewall Jackson was wounded, and his left arm was amputated. Lost to the

Confederacy forever, Jackson died of pneumonia on May 10. A wave of sadness and remembrance swept the South. Private Samuel Wilkinson of the Fourth New Hampshire recorded in his diary on May 13, "The Flags or more properly speaking detestable rags were flying at half mast on Fort Sumpter. a report this afternoon that Stonewall Jackson is dead."[102]

In a May 16 letter to Governor Berry, Colonel Cross of the Fifth requested respite from the war for his men: "We have hard service, more so than any Rg't from the state. We are worn down—we feel entitled to a little rest. . . . We only ask 30 days." It is regrettable that this request was not granted until August 1863. By then Colonel Cross was dead, having fallen in the Wheatfield at Gettysburg on July 2.[103] By the middle of May, another New Hampshire colonel had been elevated to brigade command. Colonel Simon G. Griffin was promoted and given command of the First Brigade, Second Division, Ninth Army Corps. Taking his place in command of the Sixth New Hampshire was Phineas P. Bixby, thirty-four, of Concord. Bixby, as adjutant, had been captured at the Second Battle of Bull Run but was exchanged in October 1862 and appointed major of the Sixth. Bixby commanded the Sixth until he was wounded in July 1864 near Petersburg, Virginia.[104]

About twenty-five miles north of Baton Rouge, Louisiana, stood a Confederate earthwork fort protecting Port Hudson. The fort had been bombarded by a Union naval armada in March and early May; on May 27, General Banks's Nineteenth Corps was going to attack it, the opening act of what would become a month-long siege.[105] Participating in the attack were the Eighth and Fifteenth New Hampshire, with the Sixteenth New Hampshire posted nearby but seeing no action. By the opening day of the attack, Colonel Hawkes Fearing had been elevated to brigade command, and the Eighth New Hampshire was placed under the command of Lieutenant Colonel Oliver W. Lull of Milford. The Eighth New Hampshire was in the Second Brigade of the Third Division, and its strength had dwindled to a mere three hundred muskets ready for duty. The Fifteenth New Hampshire under Colonel John W. Kingman arrived at Port Hudson with only eight companies, two of them having been detached for provost duty in Carrollton, Louisiana. The men ready for duty in the Fifteenth numbered only 465, including the officers. The strength of the Sixteenth New Hampshire was so depleted by sickness in the end of May that Colonel Pike was only able to count on two hundred men and so the Sixteenth was assigned to guard duty at army headquarters.[106] Extensive earthworks had strengthened the fort at Port Hudson, and for three-fourths of a mile along its front were scores of chopped-down trees formed into abatis, trees placed with their tops toward the enemy to break up its advance. The fort that sat atop the bluff had dug in batteries that could sweep the riverfront below. It was estimated that as many as seven thousand

Confederates defended the fort on the hill against Banks's force of about twenty-two thousand.

On the morning of the attack, May 27, the Union brigades were formed in five lines fifty feet apart and one mile from the Confederate fort. Waiting in the woods between the Federal line and the fort was a strong force of Confederate skirmishers. The Federal lines began to move forward and soon came under Confederate artillery fire. Isolated pops and bangs from the woods merged into one steady roar of musketry as Yanks and Rebs exchanged volleys.[107] The first line of Federal troops was shot to pieces; many of the men broke for the rear. Fearing's brigade moved up and with the Fourth Wisconsin swept ahead, driving the Confederates through the woods and toward the abatis, which blocked their way to the fort. Lieutenant Colonel Lull waved the men forward and cheered them until a minie smashed into him, ending his life on the spot. Fearing's brigade pushed on through the felled trees and to the fort. The men of the Eighth New Hampshire climbed up the steep slope and went down into the fort itself. A fierce fight swirled around the Eighth's regimental colors now planted on the parapet. The next line of support did not arrive soon enough, and the Eighth New Hampshire was compelled to withdraw and trade shots with the fort's defenders for the remainder of the day. Six companies of the Fifteenth New Hampshire were also in the attacking lines; the four other companies were placed under Major John Aldrich of Gilford to serve as flankers and skirmishers. The portion of the Fifteenth New Hampshire in the attacking column passed the remnants of the other regiments who had attacked the fort and were repulsed. They, too, jumped out of the ditch and charged toward the fort. They were forced to withdraw before even reaching the parapet. It was here that Lieutenant Colonel Henry W. Blair of Plymouth received a severe wound to the arm. At dusk after a long day of heat, thirst, and death, the New Hampshire men and their comrades in the other regiments were withdrawn.

The losses of the Eighth New Hampshire for the day were staggering: Lieutenant Colonel Lull and the entire color guard except for one corporal were dead, and Captain George A. Flanders of Sanbornton and Lieutenants James M. Langley and William Jones were wounded. The regiment as a whole suffered twenty-five killed and over one hundred wounded. Numbers vary as to the losses of the Fifteenth New Hampshire on May 27. The Fifteenth's regimental history states that twenty-one men were killed and 148 wounded, while Augustus D. Ayling's *Revised Register* records seventeen killed.[108] Thus ended the first assault against Port Hudson. In the ensuing siege and subsequent attacks, the Federal army of Major General Banks lost three thousand men.[109]

"We are all going into Wagner like a flock of sheep"

CHAPTER 6

June 1863 and July 1863

Let us deprive death of its strangeness, let us frequent it, let us get used to it; let us have nothing more often in mind than death. We do not know where death awaits us: so let us wait for it everywhere. To practice death is to practice freedom.

The Complete Essays of Michel de Montaigne

In June 1863, after several battles around Vicksburg, Mississippi, the Union army under General Ulysses S. Grant was settling in for a siege of that Confederate stronghold. The Ninth Corps under General Ambrose Everett Burnside was moving into position to block any relief that might come from Brigadier General Joseph E. Johnston's army marching west from central Mississippi. Farther down the Mississippi River, troops under Major General Nathaniel B. Banks were preparing for another assault against Port Hudson.[1] In the North, people were talking about the next moves by Confederate General Robert E. Lee and Union Major General Joseph Hooker. Several days of the new month passed, and Lee started moving the Army of Northern Virginia west away from Fredericksburg. Because of Hooker's dismal performance at Chancellorsville, Virginia, rumors were flying in the camps and elsewhere that Hooker was about to be replaced. "I think it is awful strange we cant have enough men to whip th rebs," opined Private William P. Mason of the Twelfth New Hampshire on June 1. "We had ought to had enough to went into Richmond this spring & we might if we had men at our head good for any thing, I don't blame Lincoln, but I have not got but a dredful little confidence in [Secretary of War Edwin] Stanton or Halleck. If they had let Mc [George B. McClellan] alone we should been in Richmond long ago. It is enough to agrivate any boddy if they see a man is a going to do any thing they will remove him, now they talk about removing Hooker he lade the best plans of any Gen we have had in the feald yet."[2]

On June 1, Colonel Edward E. Cross of the Fifth New Hampshire penned a letter, mostly about himself, to his friend Murat Halstead of the *Cincinnati Commercial:* "My guardian angels (if there are such personages) or my destiny saved me. The end of my days was reserved for another, and I hope more fortunate occasion. For if I am to die on the battlefield, I pray it may be with the cheers of victory in my ears."[3]

The Twelfth New Hampshire, whose command structure was nearly wiped out at Chancellorsville, was under the command of Captain J. F. Langley of Pittsfield, one of the few officers not killed, wounded, or captured at Chancellorsville. The Twelfth broke camp on June 11 and started its march north. The Twelfth was in General Daniel Edgar Sickles's Corps but was now brigaded with the First, Eleventh, and Sixteenth Massachusetts, the Eleventh New Jersey, and Twenty-sixth Pennsylvania Regiments.[4] The Fifth New Hampshire was still brigaded with the same units as they had been at Chancellorsville, except the brigade was now commanded by Colonel Cross, and the Fifth New Hampshire was commanded by Charles E. Hapgood of Amherst.[5]

In New Hampshire, Concord native Joseph Albee Gilmore became governor in June 1863 and in his inaugural address said the people of New Hampshire "will never submit to an ignominious peace or a dishonorable surrender of our liberties. . . . They will stand up boldly and manfully to the contest, till victory crowns the efforts of our brave soldiers, and an unconditional restoration of the Union rewards their sacrifices."[6]

For the second assault on Port Hudson, Louisiana, Brigadier General Halbert E. Paine devised a plan that, while it was almost unheard of during the Civil War, would become quite common in the twentieth-century. For the attack scheduled on June 14, the Eighth New Hampshire and the Fourth Wisconsin, again the head of the column, would rush forward as shock troops. What was different this time was that behind them by only a few paces would be the men of the Fourth Massachusetts and 110th New York carrying hand grenades for tossing into the fort; these two regiments would join the first two in the charge. Following them would be four companies of men carrying four hundred sandbags to throw into the ditch around the fort so it could be easily traversed by the troops. Following up these lines, the last couple of brigades with fifty pioneers would dismantle the parapet so it could be better shelled by Federal artillery.[7]

Captain William M. Barrett of Company A was selected to lead the Eighth New Hampshire in the attack. At daylight on June 14, nearly three hundred Federal cannons opened a bombardment of the fort. The attacking columns were formed under cover about eight hundred yards from the fort. When the artillery barrage began, the first two lines moved out and rushed toward the fort. Just as in the first assault on the fort, the Eighth New Hampshire and Fourth Wisconsin reached the parapet again, due in part to the shock of having four Federal regiments, two tossing hand grenades, attacking on a narrow front. About a hundred yards from the parapet, Brigadier General Paine was shot in the leg and fell into a pile of dead and wounded men. After his loss, the assault fell apart.[8] The men of the Eighth New Hampshire and the other three regiments fought bravely for a short time, but because of the loss of Brigadier General Paine, the supporting regiments were not brought up in time, and the assault collapsed. These four attacking regiments were again repulsed with fearful losses. No flag of truce was raised for three days, and when it finally was, many of the wounded who lay on the battlefield had long since died. Some of the lucky ones including Paine were brought back to the lines the night of the attack. Paine's wound resulted in the loss of his leg.

The Eighth New Hampshire had entered the battle on June 14 with 217 men; 122 were killed or wounded. During the battle, Sergeant George S. Cobbs was captured and later regained on July 9. In May 1864, after the Eighth New Hampshire became a mounted regiment, a column was overrun when Confederate cavalry attacked it. Some of the Eighth New Hampshire men, including Cobbs, had dismounted briefly to rest by a tree. Cobbs and several others were captured, and when the Confederates realized that the Federal cavalry was going to return for the prisoners, one of them grabbed Cobb's revolver and shot him directly in the chest. The Confederates fled. Cobbs was found under a tree by the Federal cavalry, but he was already dying. His last words were, "John, they shot me with my own revolver." Cobbs died moments later.[9]

The Fifteenth New Hampshire also was in this second attack but again did not gain the parapet of the fort. Under Lieutenant Alfred B. Seavey of Gilford, fifty men from the Fifteenth and the same number from the Twenty-sixth Connecticut tried to gain the fort on June 13 but failed, with the loss of two killed and six wounded. Elements of the Fifteenth tried an end-run attack on the fort but could not breach a deep ravine beside the fort.

Farther up the river, George Henry Chandler, the adjutant of the Ninth New Hampshire wrote to his mother in Concord about the anticipated fall of Vicksburg: "We arrived here this morning and are encamped near the river in Louisiana about four miles from Vicksburg. . . . It would seem according to reports here as if the city must surrender within a few days still it may hold out longer but is doomed to fall eventually. The weather is hot and unhealthy and the water of the river bad for those not accustomed to drinking it."[10] Second Lieutenant Enoch G. Adams of the Second New Hampshire was concerned with the condition of his shoes: "My boots have burst out and my feet are sore. . . . I like to live where everything is moving . . . to be an actor in a great drama. . . . The papers are full of excitement over the raid of the rebels into Maryland and Pa. . . . It is reported we are to march for Leesburg. . . . We are assigned to the 3rd Brigade 2nd Division 3rd Army Corps. On our hats we wear a white diamond."[11]

On Saturday, June 20, the Eleventh New Hampshire moved their encampment one mile toward the Yazoo River. It was apparent with the massive and continuous bombardment of Vicksburg that the end was coming soon. The Eleventh was ordered to build deep entrenchments along their line to defend against an expected attack by General Joseph Johnston. Grant anticipated that Johnston might try to break the siege around Vicksburg and come to the aid of General John C. Pemberton, the Confederate commander of Vicksburg.[12]

Meanwhile, in the eastern theater in mid-June, after the Battle of Second Winchester, Lee's army slowly moved north across the Potomac River into Maryland and then Pennsylvania. Panic gripped the residents of south-central Pennsylvania and Washington, D.C., as well. Hooker wanted to send only a few corps to assist the militia in pushing Lee out of Pennsylvania. The strategy of "Fighting Joe" was to secure Harpers Ferry, cut off Lee's line of retreat, and deal with him on the way back to Virginia. President Lincoln and Henry Wager Halleck, general in chief of the United States armies, wanted Hooker to confront Lee immediately before he could turn toward Baltimore or Washington. It was decided to replace Hooker on June 27 with Major General George Gordon Meade.[13] Leaving his post also on June 27 was Colonel Walter Harriman of the Eleventh New Hampshire. Private Willard J. Templeton put forth the feelings of loyalty and devotion by the men of the Eleventh: "We yesterday lost our firmest friend and best officer, our beloved Colonel Walter Harriman having resigned his commission started for home yesterday afternoon. His leaving is caused such a feeling of sorrow & sadness as I never saw in our reg."[14]

News of the replacement of Hooker spread through the army quickly. "Today we learn that Gen. Hooker has been relieved of his command," said Dr. William Child of the Fifth New Hampshire on June 28. "Gen. Meade is said now to be in command. I am discouraged. We do not yet find the man able to conduct the war successfully."[15] Word of Hooker being replaced gradually spread throughout the country even as far as Mississippi. "I hear that Lee is comeing north," wrote Private J. Lewis Chase of the Eleventh New Hampshire in an undated letter included in his correspondence for June 1863. "The report here is that he is in PA and MD and that Hooker has been superseded if he has let Lee in there with his whole army He is not smart."[16]

Meade lost no time in putting the Army of the Potomac into motion. Sergeant Samuel Cooper of the First New Hampshire Light Battery recorded the activity of the army on June 30, 1863: "Reveille at 6, 'boots and saddles' at 9, but did not move into the road till 2 P.M. We then fell into the stream of moving troops, and passed through Taneytown, a lively little village one mile from the Pennsylvania state line. Here we turned off to the left, hearing that the rebels were in force in Emmitsburg, a village three miles west of us. Marched eight miles this day. At night we were mustered and paid for the months of May and June, a sure indication of a fight being close at hand."[17]

No soldiers from New Hampshire were involved in the fighting west of the site of the Battle of Gettysburg on July 1, 1863. Sergeant Samuel Cooper recorded the actions of the First New Hampshire Light Battery on that day: "Reveille came early on July 2 for the men of the First New Hampshire Light Battery. The soldiers barely had time for a cup of coffee before they were out on the road to Taneytown at 4:00 A.M. The battery arrived at their assigned station inside the Gettysburg Cemetery at about 11:00 A.M." Sergeant Cooper described the shape of the lines when the First New Hampshire Light arrived, "The rebel line of battle was very nearly in the form of a horseshoe and our lines were formed inside of that figure . . . the apex . . . in the Gettysburg Cemetery. On the left our lines terminated on a hill called Round Top."[18]

The First New Hampshire Light Battery was deployed with other batteries and held in reserve until they were needed to relieve disabled batteries. Finally, at 5:00 P.M., the battery was called up to replace one that had been withdrawn. The First New Hampshire Light was posted on an exposed knoll only three hundred yards from the Confederates. This immediately drew the attention of the Confederate gunners, and a fierce artillery duel commenced. "The ground was strewn with broken carriages, dead horses and dead and dying men," Sergeant Cooper related about the grisly scene that occurred in the cemetery when the battle was at its heights. "And to crown it all, and make the picture still more hideous, every few minutes a shell from the enemy would come tearing through the ground and knocking down the headstones would scatter the broken stone, the sand, earth and bones of the deceased among the living adding stench horror and sacrilege to the rest of the awful scene." Cooper was a part of the battles around Cemetery Hill until the Confederate attack was abandoned after dark. The Union batteries had been brought under intense pressure but did not break, and no part of their line had been flanked.[19]

At approximately 7:30 A.M., the Second New Hampshire arrived near Sherfey's peach orchard. Federal skirmishers beyond the Emmitsburg Road indicated that the Second should go no farther because the Confederates were nearby. Third Corps commander Major General Sickles had thrust his entire corps forward from the Round Tops in a forced reconnaissance. The divisions of John Bell Hood and Major General Lafayette McLaws were a short distance from the Union skirmishers behind the tree line.[20] Two hours later, the mists and rain of the morning were replaced by a clearing sky and brilliant sunshine. Sickles's second division, under Brigadier General Andrew Humphreys, was now posted along the Emmitsburg Road and facing west with its left anchored at the Sherfey House. The First Division, under Major General David B. Birney, was strung out beyond the Fairfield Road facing south.

The Second New Hampshire was detached from the brigade of Colonel George C. Burling and sent to assist the First Division First Brigade command of Brigadier General Charles K. Graham. The Seventh New Jersey was also detached, and the two regiments went on the double-quick to their new positions at the apex formed by the Emmitsburg and Fairfield roads, where the Second New Hampshire, detailed to protect Ames's First New York Battery, was with the Sixth-eighth Pennsylvania, Third Maine, and 141st Pennsylvania. Company B was detached from the rest of the regiment and was assigned the task of guarding the right flank of Ames Battery, working in the yard of the Wentz farm. These movements were accomplished by 3 P.M., and for the next two hours, the Second New Hampshire endured a continuous artillery bombardment while they stood guard over the First New York Light Battery. The colors of the regiment were shattered by a Confederate artillery shell.[21]

While the Second New Hampshire was engaged in this duty, showers of hot shrapnel from exploding shells cut into the ranks of the regiment. While Corporal Thomas W. Bignall of Gilsum was protecting the artillery battery, a spent piece of shell slammed into his cartridge box, igniting the contents. The cartridges that exploded for over thirty seconds tore Bignall's body to shreds, causing almost-instant death. Corporal Bignall, a solid veteran of the regiment who had served in the First New Hampshire before joining the Second in September 1861 and had been wounded at Second Bull Run on August 29, 1862, is buried in Gettysburg National Cemetery.[22] Sergeant James M. House of Company I also received a direct hit on his cartridge box. House, a twenty-two-year-old native of Manchester, was able to unsling the exploding cartridge box and discard it quickly enough that he suffered only one severe wound. He was fortunate enough to survive both the battle and the war.[23]

The First New York Light Battery put up a tremendous fight but eventually had to withdraw, as did the Third Maine. A section of Rodman guns replaced the departing New Yorkers. Colonel Edward L. Bailey of the Second New Hampshire felt that the guns were not being served well; discovering that two Confederate regiments were about to flank him, "I reported these facts to General Graham, and asked permission to charge, the enemy being close upon us—so near that the officer commanding the section of battery spiked his pieces, fearful that he should lose them." Graham's reply to Bailey was, "Yes, for God's sake, go forward!"[24] The Second New Hampshire rose and formed in line of battle. To the order "Forward, guide center," the regiment moved southwest through the peach orchard toward the advancing enemy. The Second's right flank was adjacent to the Emmitsburg Road. This aggressive assault convinced the Confederates to withdraw, but a new threat was beginning to materialize on the right flank of the Second in the form of Major General Joseph B. Kershaw's six South Carolina regiments.[25] To meet this new challenge, the Third Maine rejoined the Second New Hampshire on its left and the Sixty-eighth Pennsylvania on its right. Now it was the Confederate's turn to be trapped in a pincer movement. Kershaw's men fought desperately against this force and one under Colonel Philip Regis Denis DeTrobriand. However, with this advance came a tremendous cost.[26]

As the men from New Hampshire and elsewhere drew closer to the Confederates, they became perfect targets for the Confederate artillery. A massive barrage tore this brief northern offensive apart, causing the Third Maine and the Sixty-eighth Pennsylvania to withdraw, leaving the Second New Hampshire unsupported. Then the Confederate avalanche was released. Brigadier General William Barksdale's Mississippians slammed into the right flank of the Union position, which left Colonel Bailey no recourse but to slowly withdraw. The combined Confederate force eventually pushed up to and over the Emmitsburg Road and past the Sherfey house. The Second, along with the remaining Union regiments, fell back to a new defensive line.[27]

Just before the charge of the Second, Corporal John A. Barker of Manchester was hit in the top of the head by a piece of shell, fracturing his skull. Barker was carried to the rear by several other soldiers but was dropped along the way when a shell exploded nearby and killed one of his carriers, Private Charles Moore of Pembroke. Barker lay on the ground for some time and then began crawling in the direction of the Union lines. The surgeons needed to remove a circular piece of his skull in order to operate, but Barker survived both the operation and the war and became the city messenger for Manchester.[28] Private William F. Brown, considered by many to be the best marksman in the Second New Hampshire was captured during the battle and taken to Andersonville prison where he died in August 1864. Lieutenant Edmund Dascomb, an accomplished orator from Greenfield, received a severe wound on July 2 and died from complications eleven days later. Lieutenant Albert Perkins of Exeter was acting commander of Company D during the battle when a bullet shattered his left arm. The limb was successfully amputated, and Perkins was sent home but soon after died from complications of his wound. A loss that was greatly lamented in the regiment was that of Captain Henry N. Metcalf of Keene. The thirty-year-old printer was in the midst of realigning his company for the attack when he was killed. He had just redressed his line when he turned to Colonel Bailey and said, "How does that line suit you, Colonel?" Bailey replied, "Excellent," and then Metcalf was hit.[29]

In the fighting in the Peach Orchard on July 2, the Second New Hampshire suffered 48 dead, 145 wounded or missing out of the 354 men present for duty that morning, a staggering loss of over 54 percent of the regiment. The monument to the Second New Hampshire Regiment is located at the site where the men from the Granite State fought and died. New peach trees blossom and bear fruit every year as if in the fallen men's honor.[30]

On July 3, the second day of battle, about a half mile north of the position held by the Second New Hampshire, the Twelfth New Hampshire under the command of Captain J. F. Langley waited on the east side of the Emmitsburg Road. The Twelfth New Hampshire, also a regiment of Sickles's Corps, was part of what is known today as Sickles's Salient and was therefore in the midst of the same massive artillery exchange as the Second New Hampshire. The only difference was that the Twelfth was posted in a small apple orchard near the Trostle House, and most of the cannon shells passed harmlessly over them.[31] From the time that the fighting began in earnest in the south end of the peach orchard, the men of the Twelfth New Hampshire listened to the increasing sounds of battle. Because of the intensity of the Confederate attack, by 6 P.M. it became evident that the entire line of Sickles's Third Corps was rolling back on itself. Major General Sickles had been wounded and would lose a leg. Major General Birney was now in command, and the Twelfth New Hampshire soldiers were wondering whether they would be withdrawn or left alone to face the advancing Confederate tidal wave.[32] The answer materialized when two brigades of Major General Richard Heron Anderson's division stormed over a ridge in front of the Twelfth New Hampshire and slammed into the center of Humphrey's line. Just as the Twelfth New Hampshire and the rest of Brigadier General Joseph B. Carr's brigade faced the advancing Georgians and Floridians, Humphrey's left flank was in danger of collapse from the force of Kershaw's and Barksdale's attacks pushing north along the Emmitsburg Road. In order to avoid disaster, the order was given for Carr's brigade to change fronts to the rear. Before they could withdraw, the men of the Twelfth New Hampshire would have to literally turn their backs to the enemy. For one regiment to perform this dangerous maneuver in the midst of battle is difficult, but to demand an entire brigade to change front is almost impossible. The movement was carried out with only partial success, and not long after, the bugles called retreat, but it was already too late.[33]

Where the Twelfth New Hampshire was previously untouched by the effects of the artillery battle, now they were trapped in the jaws of a Confederate attack that threatened to exterminate the entire regiment. Just as the order was given to change front, a musket ball smashed into the head of Lieutenant Henry French of Pittsfield, then in command of Company F. He fell at the feet of Captain Nathaniel Shackford of Holderness, who had just given French his orders. Shackford, wounded at the Battle of Chancellorsville, received another at Gettysburg, and yet another at Cold Harbor. Miraculously, he survived the battles and the war.[34]

In the midst of the swirling maelstrom of battle, both the national and state flags fell to the ground. Sergeant William J. Howe, twenty-five, also of Holderness, was shot through the heart and fell to the ground dead, desperately clutching the flag of New Hampshire to his chest. Corporal Samuel Brown of Hebron came running up and attempted to raise the flag. Still weak from the effects of his wound at Chancellorsville, Brown was shot through the bowels and immediately fell dead. Carrying the United States flag was Sergeant Luther Parker of Hill, who fell with a shattered leg. He held the flag until someone could carry it forward. Parker died three weeks later from complications of amputation.

Corporal William T. Knight of Barnstead also died trying to save the colors.[35] The state and national colors were finally saved and carried to the rear by Sergeant Charles S. Emery of Canterbury and Corporal John R. Davis of Northwood. Emery was wounded at Cold Harbor and died of the effects of his wound two months later; Davis was later severely wounded at Drewry's Bluff but survived the war.

Private Charles N. Drake of Bristol received a severe leg wound on July 2 that required amputation. When asked by a friend years later if he knew what happened to his leg, Drake replied, "The hogs ate it up." All limbs, Drake said, amputated at the temporary hospital he was taken to were buried in a nearby shallow ditch. As it was common knowledge that wild hogs roamed the battlefield for weeks after the battle, Drake assumed that his leg had been dug up and eaten by hogs.[36] Corporal Joseph F. Wentworth of Moultonborough was killed on July 2 fighting in the ranks of the Twelfth New Hampshire. A fellow soldier stated that Wentworth "was a kind and affectionate brother, a steady young man, and a constant reader of his Bible."[37] One of the most heartrending incidents for the Twelfth New Hampshire at the Battle of Gettysburg was the story of when early in the evening Private Thomas A. Lawler of Allenstown found two of his friends, Private Albert D. Jones of Alton and Private Christopher C. Joy of New Durham. Lawler "found Dana Jones on the field. He was shot, as near as I can remember, with a rifle ball in the left breast. . . . He prayed and seemed reconciled to die. . . . He died about 12 o'clock as quietly as falling asleep." Lawler then turned his attention to Joy, who had also been shot in the chest. Joy, however, was in a great deal of pain. Lawler obtained some water and tried to make his friend as comfortable as possible, and Joy's suffering eased over the next two hours. Then he also slipped away. Lawler, the kind, Irish brickmaker from Allenstown, survived the war but only after sustaining wounds at the battles of Drewry's Bluff and Petersburg.[38]

Twenty-year-old Sergeant Jesse Dewey of the Second New Hampshire described the July 2 battle and aftermath: "The night found us all exhausted and hardly able to move; the reaction after such a fight is tremendous, and to be in all day without anything to eat, after being up at midnight and marching eight or ten miles, will take the life out of any man, and tonight we were tired, worn out and hungry. How good my cup of coffee tasted that night, and hard tack too—it was a luxury. We laid ourselves down to rest. . . . What a refreshing sleep, but there were less to wake this morning than there were yesterday, How thin our ranks looked; out of 360 we had hardly 100 men left."[39]

The Twelfth New Hampshire under Captain Langley started the day with 224 men fit for duty, but when the roll was called that night, twenty-six officers and men were dead, and seventy-three were wounded. In three hours 44 percent of the Twelfth New Hampshire Regiment were casualties.[40] Lieutenant Colonel

John F. Marsh, wounded at Chancellorsville, returned to the regiment soon after the Battle of Gettysburg and upon seeing the survivors of the battle cried like a child and said, "My God, is that all that's left of the Twelfth New Hampshire?"[41]

As the three-day battle in Pennsylvania raged, people throughout the country were beginning to realize that a conflict of extreme importance was being fought. Not everyone was optimistic about the outcome. A relative of Private Christopher Hoyt, then serving in the Fourteenth New Hampshire, wrote to her friend Lizzie, "They are having an awful battle in Pennsylvania, Lizzie—the rebels are there in all their strength & woe be to all who come in their way. I wish every abolishinst might be there now in Gen. Lee's way. I guess it would be the last of them, then we might have peace again but the Union is gone assuredly. There is no hope of saving that. It will soon be each state for itself. . . . The enemy march right along. . . . If they get to us I shall hail them as friends sooner than I should this cursed army of Republicans with Hooker or Meade at their head for they it is who have ruined the country."[42]

Earlier in the day on July 2, Thomas L. Livermore, previously of the Fifth New Hampshire Regiment, now chief of ambulances for the Second Corps, met Colonel Cross where the Fifth was posted on the left of the Second Corps. About this time, which Livermore remembers to be about 3 P.M., there was only light skirmishing in front of the brigade that Cross was commanding. Pointing to the ambulances, Cross said to Livermore, "We shan't want any of your dead carts here today."[43]

When Meade realized that his entire left flank was in danger of collapsing, he ordered Cross's brigade, as well as the rest of Brigadier General John C. Caldwell's division, detached to reinforce Major General George Sykes's Fifth Corps. The Second Corps commander, Major General Winfield Scott Hancock, riding by, said to Cross that Cross's actions on that day would probably earn him a brigadier general's star. Cross, full of dark foreboding, replied it was too late because Cross knew he would not survive the battle. The Third Corps's retreat turned into a rout, and Caldwell's division ended up going to the Wheatfield near Devil's Den instead to try to stop the Confederate onslaught.[44]

The Fifth New Hampshire, under the command of Charles E. Hapgood of Amherst, arrived in the Wheatfield at about 6 P.M. with only 177 men. Division commander Brigadier General Caldwell's report was: "I ordered Colonel Cross, commanding the First Brigade, to advance in line of battle through a wheatfield, his left resting on the woods which skirted the field. He had advanced but a short distance when he encountered the enemy, and opened upon him a terrific fire, driving him steadily to the farther end of the Wheatfield."[45]

The brigade commanded by Cross—Fifth New Hampshire, Sixty-first New York, and the Sixth-eighth and 148th Pennsylvania regiments—swept through the Wheatfield, the Fifth on the extreme left flank and Cross commanding from the right. As the brigade reached the trees, Confederate snipers were beginning to take a toll on the brigade and slowing it considerably. Cross could not see the left of the line that had entered the woods. Before going to inspect the far left, he told his staff, "Instruct the commanders to be ready to charge when the order is given; wait here for the command, or if you hear the bugles of the Fifth New Hampshire on the left, move forward on the run."[46]

Cross arrived on the left flank of the Fifth New Hampshire as the Confederates were moving around and through the rocks in the woods. Moments later, a sniper's bullet tore through Cross's abdomen just as he was exhorting his men to go forward. Cross was carried to the rear, and the Fifth New Hampshire held its position against the combined weight of an attack by the Fifteenth Georgia and First Texas of Hood's brigade.

Lieutenant Colonel Hapgood noticed the direction of the shot that wounded Cross and ordered fellow Amherst native Sergeant Charles Phelps of Company I to take the sniper out. Phelps waited for the sniper to show himself and gunned him down. Phelps also became a casualty in the woods of the Wheatfield on July 2. The Fifth held its ground until the other regiments of the brigade were withdrawn, and then it, too, left the field.[47]

Of the small number of men that the Fifth New Hampshire brought on the field, about 45 percent of the regiment's strength was gone: twenty-seven dead and fifty-three wounded. The most grievous loss was Colonel Cross, who, with a wound from a minie ball in the abdomen, lived until about 12:30 A.M. on July 3. His last words were said to have been, "I did hope I should live to see peace restored to our distressed country. I think the boys will miss me." He muttered several more references to his brave boys and died.[48] Colonel Cross was mourned as was Sergeant Oscar Allen of Croydon and Corporal Joseph Trickey, forty-two, of Rochester.[49] Cross had led his men to fame and glory on many battlefields, but the history of this famous regiment was not over.

Company E of the First United States Sharpshooters was involved in reconnaissance beyond the Emmitsburg Road on July 2 as well as some light skirmishing. New Hampshire companies F and G of the Second United States Sharpshooters participated in the delaying action in the ravine in front of Little Round Top. The fifty men of these two companies lost two men each. Colonel William C. Oates, the commander of the Fifteenth Alabama, wrote a post-war letter to Colonel Homer Stoughton of the Second U.S.S.S., "You and your command deserve a monument for turning the tide in favor of the Union cause." A monument to the Second U.S.S.S. stands on the site at Gettysburg National Military Park. It was the green-clad sharpshooters who delayed the Confederate attack long enough to allow the Third Brigade under Colonel Strong Vincent in general and Colonel Joshua Lawrence Chamberlain specifically to prepare the defenses on Little Round Top against the attack of Oates and his Alabamans.[50]

None of the three New Hampshire regiments that fought on July 2 was involved in the battle on July 3rd. However, Sergeant Samuel Cooper and the First New Hampshire Light Battery were thrown into the largest artillery duel yet seen in the war: "Friday July 3d, was a cool pretty morning," states Cooper, "or would have been had there not been a constant smoke of battle hanging like a pall over poor Gettysburg." Beginning at 4:00 A.M., the Confederates periodically shelled the extreme left and right of the Federal line until about 11 A.M. Many men in the First New Hampshire Light Battery thought this was a closing salute by the Confederates and that the battle was over. "Suddenly," Cooper wrote, "at 1 P.M. without a moments warning, the rebel batteries opened from all parts of their long line. The roar was ominous. The air was blue with sulphurous smoke."

The First New Hampshire Light Battery was moved back to its position at Cemetery Hill and went into battery. For the next hour the young artillerists from New Hampshire exchanged shots with the Confederate batteries on Seminary Ridge. At 3 P.M., the entire battlefield became silent. Major General Oliver O. Howard ordered the batteries under his command, including the First New Hampshire, to load their guns and leave several rounds by the guns. He then instructed them to run from their positions toward the woods give the Confederates the impression that the Union artillerymen were retreating.[51] Whether this ruse played any part in what happened next is pure speculation. Thirty minutes later, three Confederate divisions were ordered by Lieutenant General James Longstreet to attack the center of the Union line held by the Second Corps and Major General Hancock. Across the broad plain marched the divisions of Major General George E. Pickett, Brigadier General Johnson Pettigrew, and Major General Isaac Trimble. Sergeant Cooper described the reaction of the Union gunners: "Our expected signal was given, and rushing back to our guns, we gave them as warm a reception as we could; but when they still kept on, closing up the great gaps in their column, and the order was shouted from battery to battery, 'Load with canister!' then came a slaughter that was terrific. Hundreds fell and hundreds more . . . threw down their guns . . . saying it was much safer and easier to come our way than to attempt to pass back over that open field."[52] Thomas C. Cheney of the First New Hampshire Light Battery said, "We were able to give the Jonney Rebes the Whipping at Gettysburg that their army in Va. never got."[53] The casualties of the First New Hampshire Light Battery were comparatively light, with several men wounded and ten horses killed. After the failure of the Confederate assault, the Battle of Gettysburg closed, and the men from New Hampshire started to calculate the cost of the battle.

Counting all the regiments and units present for the Battle of Gettysburg, New Hampshire put about 950 men in the field on July 2 and 3. Of that number, 107 were killed, and 274 were listed as wounded or missing. Sources differ, but the average total loss at the Battle of Gettysburg was 23,049 for the Federals and 28,063 for the Confederates.[54]

Of New Hampshire's losses, Colonel Edward L. Bailey of the Second New Hampshire wrote, "For our fallen braves who have so gloriously perished fighting for their country we drop a comrade's tear. While we would extend our heartfelt sympathy to those dear ones far away who find the ties of kindred and friends thus rudely severed, and for those who must suffer untold agony and pain through long weeks of convalescence our earnest sympathy."[55]

Dr. Child of the Fifth described the battlefield at Gettysburg, "I have been over the field today. I will not attempt to describe the horrors of a battlefield. It has been one of the severest of the war. Dead men and horses cover the field three miles long and one mile wide. The stench is awful."[56]

In the west, Adjutant George Henry Chandler of the Ninth New Hampshire detailed the military situation around the embattled city of Vicksburg on the Mississippi River: "We . . . hold this position against Johns[t]on. We are cutting down all the trees for miles to give our artillery a good range and to obstruct the advance. . . . I am rather surprised that Vicksburg holds out so long. . . . It [Vicksburg] is filled with a brave and determined army and with desperate inhabitants who are determined to hold out to the last crumb . . . hoping for relief. . . . I don't think they will endure more than a fortnight, and as far as their being relieved by Johns[t]on I think that is out of the question." Chandler and Grant would not have long to wait. On July 4, twenty-nine thousand soldiers under Confederate Lieutenant General John C. Pemberton surrendered the city of Vicksburg to the Federals.[57]

On that same Saturday in Pennsylvania, the skies opened with a torrential downpour of rain on the blood-soaked fields of Gettysburg. General Lee took this opportunity to start leading the battered remnants of his army back to Virginia.[58]

In Concord, New Hampshire, the news of these two developments was slow in reaching the state. Henry McFarland in *Sixty Years in Concord and Elsewhere* chronicled the curious political rally on the Fourth of July.

> The great events were a painful shock to certain citizens of NH who were assembled in convention in the State House yard on the 4th of July. Former president Pierce was presiding. A portrait of Vallandigham, the chief Copperhead of Ohio, whom *The Statesmen* called "The Great Unpronounceable," was displayed on the platform. Voorhees of like repute in Indiana spoke. The government denounced, its Chief Magistrate contemned and the war declared a failure. Tidings of the victory at Gettysburg, which reached the platform, were pronounced an abolitionist lie to distress the convention. This meeting was

timed to give moral aid to Lee's attempt at invasion of the North and I never doubted that it was held on some hint obtained from Richmond.[59]

When news of the rally in Concord reached the soldiers in the field, it evoked responses similar to that of Private Templeton of the Eleventh New Hampshire: "It almost makes my blood boil with indignation to read such speeches as Franklin Pierce made at Concord."[60]

Second Lieutenant Enoch Adams of the Second New Hampshire expressed his relief at still being alive and engaged in a bit of bragging: "The good Lord has preserved my life through one of the most terrible battles on record. . . . I escaped without a scratch though passing through the greatest danger. . . . That battle has saved our country, and I am one of her saviors. . . . I have conferred eternal honor on my name and race by my heroic conduct. The boys say I behaved 'BULLY.' . . . We are now following Lee up closely."[61]

Charleston, South Carolina, was a city symbolic to both the North and the South. For the Confederates it was the birthplace of independence for the South. For the North it was the epicenter of treason and rebellion and had to be expunged. Changes in the Department of the South occurred when Major General Quincy Gillmore replaced Major General David Hunter as commander of the department in June 1863. Gillmore began planning the next offensive against Charleston immediately, because he knew that to take Charleston he first had to neutralize Fort Sumter in the middle of Charleston harbor.[62] Gillmore's plan, along with his naval counterpart Rear Admiral John A. Dahlgren, was for a two-prong, night assault from Folly Island to the southern end of Morris Island, with the navy in a strong supporting role. The attack was scheduled for the night of July 9. The crossing to be made under the command of Brigadier General George C. Strong from Folly to Morris Island would be a small-scale amphibious attack across Lighthouse Inlet.[63]

First Lieutenant Albert H. Jewett of Gilford, serving with the Fourth New Hampshire Regiment in the summer of 1863, described the feverish preparations for the attack: "On this island [Folly Island], we were encamped about two miles from the rebel fortifications, on the south end of Morris Island, and for several weeks, our regiment was busy constructing works on the northern extremity. . . . Folly Island was quite heavily wooded, and the works constructed were hidden from view of the Johnny Rebs. . . . We could see through the trees the city of Charleston . . . and curses loud and deep were pronounced on the hated place, the scene of the first assault on the beloved flag of our country."[64]

The pickets of both sides, separated by only fifty yards of water, exchanged goods, such as coffee, tobacco, and newspapers, with one another, the trading taking place in tiny boats between the two sides of the narrow inlet.[65]

On July 9, the Third, Fourth, and Seventh New Hampshire Regiments, along with other Federal regiments, were loaded aboard nine troop transports at James Island around 4 P.M. Preparations went on through the night, and the men sailed for the south end of Morris Island, accompanied by two gunboats, one monitor, one mortar schooner, and several dispatch boats. The attack of July 9 was delayed because more work had to be done. During the night of Thursday July 9 and early morning of Friday July 10, the masked batteries facing Morris Island were finished, and the brush and trees were cleared away. Sixty cannon lined up along the bank looking toward Morris Island. At dawn, a signal gun fired, and the cannons exploded in one thunderous volley.[66]

"At daylight this morning the long looked for report of Cannon came plainly to our East," reported Private Samuel Wilkinson of the Fourth New Hampshire in his diary about the start of the operation. "Our Batteries had opened on Morris Island the first report was received with Cheers from all the boys."[67]

The Confederates, caught completely by surprise, offered only weak resistance when the flatboats transporting the invasion force appeared from behind Folly Island. Like all amphibious operations, the Federal attack was weakest at the outset. Elbridge J. Copp of the Third New Hampshire related his terror as the landing proceeded: "A shell explodes in the boat next to my own, killing and wounding many. The boat sinks leaving a struggling mass of human forms in the water, reddened with the blood of the dead and wounded, but on, on we pull striking the beach, out jump the men, some in water waist deep."[68] Brigadier General Strong was so eager to get ashore that he jumped from his boat into water over his head. When he was next seen on the shore, he was leading the attack minus his hat and boots. Only some men from the transports were landed; the Fourth New Hampshire stayed behind. Those that did land were able to carry the Confederate entrenchments easily. The routed Confederate soldiers fled down the beach to the safety of Fort Wagner and Fort Gregg at the north end of Morris Island.[69]

Lieutenant Colonel John Bedel of Bath found some Charleston newspapers in the Confederate camp and ran down the beach while waving them and shouting, "Vicksburg captured! Great victory at Gettysburg!" This was the first news many of the men had of those developments, and they cheered wildly. Completely disorganized and with no military discipline, they followed Bedel down the beach toward Fort Wagner. Hoping to follow up their relatively bloodless victory at the south end of Morris Island, the invasion force charged pell-mell toward the Confederate fort. As the soldiers approached it, its formidable character was impressed upon them in the form of a perfect storm of shot and shell. Artillery fire rained down on them not only from Fort Wagner but also Sumter and the other Confederate forts. As the Third New Hampshire advanced up the beach, a Whitworth shot came screeching over from Fort Sumter. Passing between Colonel Jackson and Adjutant Copp, the shot decapitated a private directly behind them.

"Another man . . . had thrown himself to the earth to escape a shot or shell he saw coming, but he was directly in its path," Adjutant Copp related. "The ball striking the ground, bounding a hundred feet or more, struck the corporal in the back, killing him instantly." The impact of this shell buried Copp in sand. A piece of the shell grazed Bedel's leg and caused a painful wound.[70] In this opening engagement to conquer Morris Island, nine men of the Third were killed, and thirty-one were wounded.

An assault against Fort Wagner was planned for the next day, July 11.[71] Fort Wagner was a relatively small but heavily defended earthen fort at the northern end of Morris Island. It was supported by Fort Gregg, a half-mile away, and Forts Sumter, Johnson, and Moultrie in Charleston Harbor. Wagner, manned by fifteen hundred troops under the command of Brigadier General William B. Taliaferro, was also known as Battery Wagner and was festooned with eleven heavy fixed guns and several mobile field pieces. The fort also had the advantage of having a bombproof that could protect 750 men during enemy bombardments. Because the fort was constructed of earth and sand, which could absorb more force and could be more easily repaired than other materials. At the northern end of Morris Island, the fort's left side rested on the beach and the Atlantic Ocean, and its right was in a marsh along Vincent's Creek. What made any attack on Fort Wagner almost impossible was that the only approach to the fort in its front was across a eighty-foot-wide strip of land that had been seriously eroded. In addition a water-filled moat went across front of the fort, and its earthen walls sloped at an angle. During the night, Fort Wagner had been reenforced in expectation of an attack in the morning, and the defenders did not have long to wait. With his brigade Brigadier General Strong again led the assault against the fort. Elements of the Seventh Connecticut, along with the Ninth Maine and Seventy-sixth Pennsylvania were to attack the fort in the morning. The supporting column was the Third and Seventh New Hampshire, the Forty-eighth New York, and the Sixth Connecticut regiments.

The thirty-minute attack was a failure. The Third and Seventh New Hampshire regiments were never engaged because the assault was halted after the first wave amassed heavy casualties. On the Federal side, 339 men were killed or wounded; 12 Confederate defenders were hurt.[72] This attack, which accomplished little or nothing, could not be considered as anything more than a probing operation. Captain George F. Towle of the Fourth New Hampshire, although not engaged in this attack, had a definite opinion: "A hasty formation was lead to the assault on the morning of the 11th but was repulsed with loss, and our forces settled down to preserve their gains and hold their new position. For in front of them was renowned Fort Wagner, destined to hold us at bay through so many long and bloody days."[73]

In the last known letter to his father, Colonel Haldimand S. Putnam of the Seventh New Hampshire wrote on July 10 of recent events. "We crossed this island [Morris] on Friday last after an engagement of about three hours in which we were completely successful, capturing about two hundred prisoners and ten large cannon, driving the enemy to its stronghold Fort Wagner directly under the guns of Fort Sumpter. Our loss was slight. The next morning at dawn an attempt was made to carry Fort Wagner by storm and were repulsed with considerable loss."[74] Putnam was later elevated to brigade command with the Seventh New Hampshire, Sixty-second and Sixty-seventh Ohio, and 100th New York regiments composing Putnam's Second Brigade.

After the failure of the July 11 assault on Fort Wagner, it was generally assumed that Dahlgen's monitors would reduce the fort. Surprisingly, Quincy Gillmore ordered a second attempt to carry the fort by storm, this time set for July 17. Gillmore, a highly qualified and experienced engineer, had plenty of time to examine the ground leading to the fort.[75] His men would have to squeeze through the same bottleneck of land they negotiated one week ago. Gillmore delegated responsibility for the attack to recently arrived Brigadier General Truman Seymour. Seymour in turn chose the ever-reliable Brigadier General George C. Strong. Gillmore was still relying on a heavy bombardment from the forty-one land-based guns and the floating firepower of Dahlgen's five monitors, five gunboats, and the USS *New Ironsides*.[76] After seven days of steady bombardment from the water, Gillmore planned to hit the fort with three brigades totaling five thousand men, the first brigade with seven regiments under Brigadier General Strong, including the Third New Hampshire and the Fifty-fourth Massachusetts, the second with four regiments under Colonel Putnam, including the Seventh New Hampshire under Lieutenant Colonel Joseph C. Abbott, and the third with four regiments under the command of Brigadier General T. G. Stevenson.[77] The Fourth New Hampshire Regiment was held in reserve. Captain George F. Towle of the Fourth described how the troops got ready: "In the meantime our forces on Morris Island were hard at work entrenching and placing guns in position against Fort Wagner, preparatory to another assault."[78] But, as Sergeant Daniel Eldredge recorded on July 17, "The severe duty for the past week preyed upon us to the extent that many . . . were conveyed to the hospital never more to join us."[79]

"The 'Ironsides' a broadside ironclad with six guns on a side crossed the bar on the 16th," Towle continued. "The assault on Wagner had been set for the 17th, but rain delayed. A very heavy shower occurred again on the 18th."[80] The men of the Third New Hampshire had been forbidden to sit down or sleep, but they snatched small naps leaning against their muskets or each other. By 3 A.M.

the drenching rains, Eldredge recalled, ruined all of the ammunition, and if the Confederates had come out of the fort and attacked them, they would have had little to defend themselves except their bayonets. The troops were withdrawn from their jumping-off positions. On July 17, the men of the Third New Hampshire spent most of their time drying their clothes and ammunition. Regrettably, only a small percentage of the precious powder cartridges could be salvaged.[81]

Early on July 18, the Third and Seventh New Hampshire were moved forward again to their attack positions. The artillery duel had already begun. The men of the Third looked out to their right and saw the *New Ironsides* and her small fleet of monitors moving into position to bombard Fort Wagner. "At noon time the iron clad fleet moved up off Wagner and simultaneously with our land batteries open fire on the fort," Towle wrote. "The roar of the artillery is indescribable," Adjutant Copp of the Third New Hampshire said. "The heavens seemed to have been rent in twain and the very earth trembled under our feet. . . . This cannonading went on all day long. . . . We waited on the sands of the beach . . . watching this terrible bombardment."[82] At first, the Confederates in the fort returned the artillery fire of the Federals and cheered whenever one of their shells hit its mark, but the intensity of the fire of the land and sea attacks forced the fort's defenders to take cover in their bombproof. Many of the artillerists and soldiers chose to stay outside rather than endure the intense heat and maddening concussions inside the bombproof.

As the shelling against the fort continued, the Federal gunners became practiced at skipping their cannon shells against the water and ricocheting the shells into the walls of the fort with great effect. Twice Federal shells knocked down the fort's flag, each time the Federal soldiers thinking that the fort's defenders had had enough and were surrendering. The Federals were crestfallen when both times one of the intrepid Confederate gunners emerged from the bombproof and waving the flag wildly back and forth firmly planted it back in the parapet. Knowing that the Confederates were far from surrendering, Gillmore directed the bombardment to continue until nightfall when the darkness would help, at least partially, to hide his troops from sight of the Confederate gunners in Fort Wagner and the other Charleston forts.[83]

Like Quincy Gillmore, Colonel Putnam was trained in engineering at West Point. When he arrived at the front before Fort Wagner, he took in the entire scene at once—the ocean on the right and the marsh on the left that had severely eroded the beach and in the middle that small deadly gap of eighty feet that he would have to squeeze his entire brigade through. Major General Gillmore had seen the same scene as Putnam but was apparently driven by a different set of motivations. It was Gillmore's assignment to conquer Charleston, and the door to that city was through Fort Sumter. In order to pass through that door, he needed the key, and that key was Fort Wagner. The obvious answer to Putnam

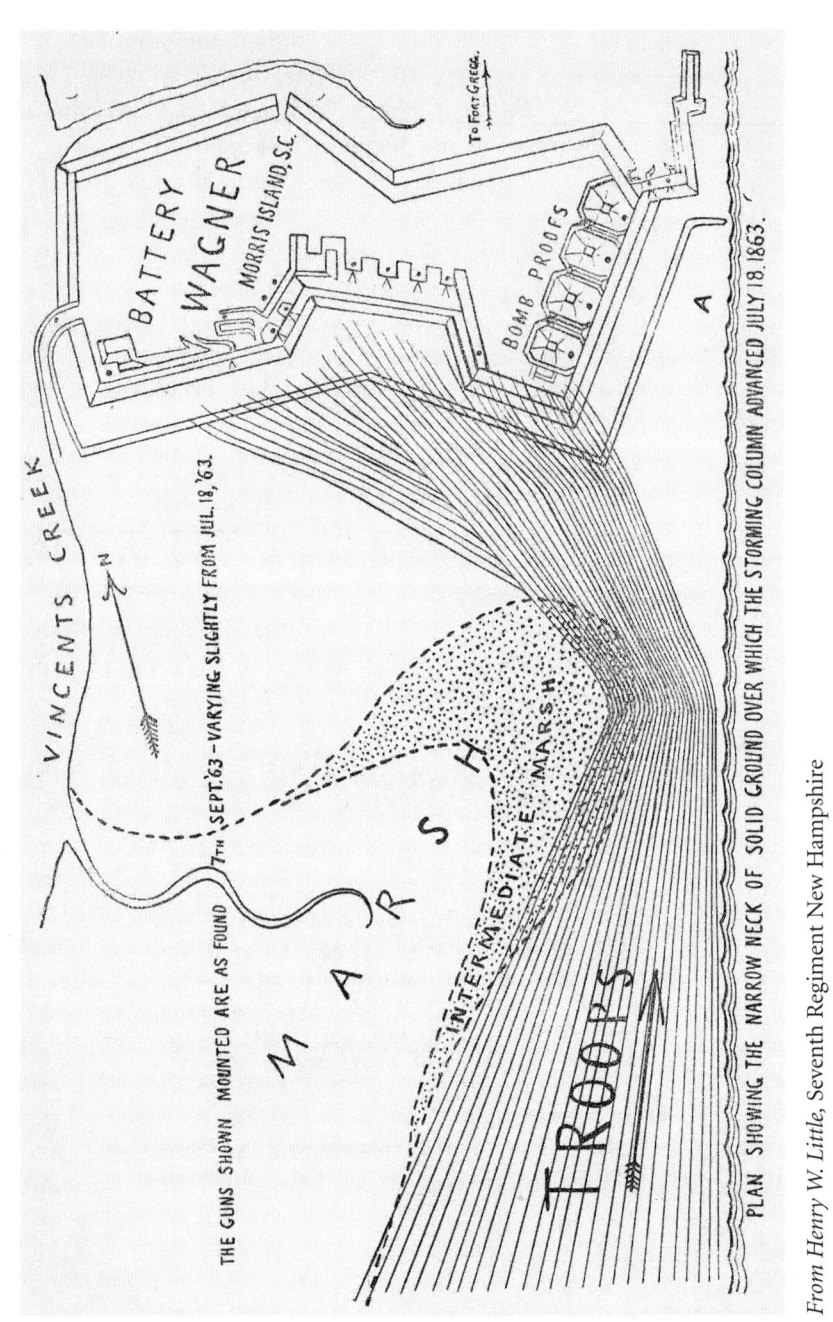

From Henry W. Little, Seventh Regiment New Hampshire
Volunteers in the War of the Rebellion, *1896*

was to lay siege to the fort, surround it so no supplies could reach it from Charleston, and wait them out. Sieges, however, take time and are not nearly as glorious
as a frontal assault, so Gillmore insisted on the attack.

Toward dusk, Gillmore called Brigadier General Seymour and his brigade
commanders together to give them their final briefing for the evening's assault.
Putnam spoke up that he was highly doubtful that the attack would succeed. Seymour, convinced that they could carry the fort, interrupted Putnam. Gillmore
did not change his plans. The attack would go ahead.

When Putnam returned to prepare his brigade for the attack, he saw his friend
Major Thomas A. Henderson of the Seventh New Hampshire, who with Lieutenant Colonel Abbott was busy getting the depleted regiment in line. Dysentery
had reduced the Seventh New Hampshire on July 18 to only 480 officers and
men. Henderson asked about the attack, and Putnam replied, "I told the General
I did not think we could take the fort, but Seymour overruled me; Seymour is a
devil of a fellow for dash." He paused for a moment and looked sadly at Henderson, "We are all going into Wagner like a flock of sheep."[84]

In Strong's First Brigade, along with the Third New Hampshire was the Fifty-
fourth Massachusetts, one of the new "colored" regiments and under the command of Colonel Robert Gould Shaw of Boston. Shaw had requested and was
granted the honor of leading the attack on Fort Wagner. Brigadier General Strong
reviewed the front line of the Fifty-fourth and stopped at the color guard. He
pointed to the color-bearer and said, "If this man should fall, who will carry the
flag?" Without a moment's hesitation, Colonel Shaw stepped forward and said,
"I will."[85]

It was well after dark before the order was given to advance. "The 54th rushed
forward with a yell of desperation echoed by our own regiment," remembered
Sergeant Eldredge, "and successively through the whole force."[86] The Fifty-fourth
led the way and directly behind them came the Sixth Connecticut in column on
the right, the Ninth Maine in the center, and the Third New Hampshire on the
left.[87] Inside Fort Wagner, the shell-shocked men of the Seventh and Twenty-
first South Carolina Infantry and the First South Carolina Artillery poured out
of their bombproof after eleven hours of continuous shelling amounting to nine
thousand Federal shells. The artillerists manned their guns and immediately
poured a hail of shot and shell into the advancing columns as they squeezed
through the gap.[88] After passing through the bottleneck of land, Lieutenant
Colonel John Henry Jackson of the Third New Hampshire ordered Lieutenant
Colonel Bedel to take a portion of the regiment around the left flank to see if
they could gain entrance to the fort from there. Bedel set off, but halfway to the
fort, the regiment came under a severe bombardment from the fort and had
mistakenly run into a minefield. Bedel continued but his ad hoc force took cover
in the sand dunes. Bedel reached the fort, and when he turned to give his men

COLONEL JOHN H. JACKSON, *Third New Hampshire, Field and Staff. Jackson became colonel of the Third when Enoch Fellows resigned his command after Antietam. Jackson was badly wounded in the attack on Fort Wagner on July 18, 1863. Photograph from* Reminiscences of the War of the Rebellion

orders, he found that he had become separated from them. Seeing a small group of men advancing on the fort, he assumed they were part of the Third New Hampshire. He could not have been more mistaken. The men running for the fort were Confederate riflemen who had abandoned their rifle pits outside the fort. Thinking they were his men, Bedel fell in with them but realized his error too late. Bedel went into Fort Wagner not as a combatant but as a prisoner. The Confederates held Bedel prisoner for seventeen months. He was paroled in December 1864 but did not return to the regiment until April 1865.[89]

The Fifty-fourth Massachusetts entered the fort and even fought on top of the bombproof inside the fort. But Colonel Shaw had been killed on the parapet, and the regiment's organization was shattered. The valiant regiment of freedmen from Massachusetts lost 272 men, or 40 percent of its strength.[90] "The scene was truly exciting, the carnage terrible, the fire deadly, hot and like hail," described Sergeant Eldredge of the Third about the battlefield before him. "The colored regiment broke and ran through our ranks after gaining the parapet but rallied again soon after. . . . My regiment was completely broken up and almost disheartened. The iron storm was too much for the troops to withstand."[91]

Brigadier General Strong personally led the Seventy-sixth Pennsylvania forward and received a severe wound to the thigh. He suffered with his wound and died two weeks later. Colonel Jackson, seeing that the attack was falling apart, halted the advance of the Third New Hampshire, and they did not enter the fort.[92] At this point in the fight, Sergeant Eldredge said, "I was struck in the foot with grape shot. My foot was taken instantly from under me my boot ripped from toe to heel." Eldredge was told to go to the rear to seek treatment. Along the path on the beach, he encountered a grisly scene. Scores of men were lying on the beach dead or wounded: "The rising tide slowly but surely drowning those who lived."[93]

In this first attack the Third New Hampshire suffered the loss of eight killed and forty-seven wounded, among them Colonel Jackson. It was now time for Colonel Putnam to lead his brigade forward against the fort.[94] The colonel was busy giving his regimental commanders their final instructions. The First Brigade had already gone forward and was engaged at the fort. He periodically looked out at Fort Wagner. The Confederate fort presented the image of a medieval fire-belching monster thrown up from the infernal regions. The bursting shells from the fort, as well as the covering fire from the forts in Charleston harbor, lit the sky like lightning and blanketed the battleground in an eerie shroud of smoke. Putnam was now ready to move his brigade forward against the fort. He regarded the ocean with its lapping waves on the right and then the men of his Seventh New Hampshire, about to participate in their first battle, in the front of the brigade. He had given orders that all muskets were to be uncapped, that is, the percussion cap that ignited the powder was not in place—the charge was to be made with bayonets only—which meant that the men could expect to be fighting in close quarters. The soldiers of the Seventh New Hampshire obeyed this order from their commander and took the caps off their muskets. The 100th New York, directly behind them, did not. Colonel Putnam mounted his horse and started his men forward through the narrow gap that he knew would result in the death of many of his soldiers.[95]

The bottleneck on the beach was actually narrower than expected, recalled Sergeant Henry F. W. Little of Manchester, who won the Medal of Honor for his actions outside Petersburg in 1864. Only six undersized companies of the Seventh New Hampshire could pass through the space; the others needed to go through en echelon behind them. After passing through the gap, the men lay down in the sand until Colonel Putnam rode up behind them on his horse and ordered them to charge.[96]

The regiment took casualties even before they reached the fort, whose cannons blasted forty-two-pound shot into the regiment's advancing lines. Upon reaching the fort, Lieutenant Colonel Abbott desperately tried to maintain order and discipline, but the obstacles of the wooden spikes in the water-filled moat totally disrupted any attempt at keeping the regiment together. Just before the men of the Seventh barreled down into the moat and tried to gain the parapet, a thunderous volley tore into them. New Hampshire men fell dead and wounded from a fusillade of bullets poured into them by the 100th New York directly behind them. The colonel of the regiment later said he had not heard Putnam's order to uncap their weapons, and in the darkness he thought the Seventh New Hampshire was the enemy coming out of the fort.[97] Regimental level action stopped as the Seventh became engaged in a series of small battles fought inside the fort and atop the bombproof. When Colonel Putnam, delayed because his horse had been shot from under him, finally entered the fort, he tried to rally a confused mob of soldiers of a host of regiments, including some from the First Brigade. A small amount of cover was near one corner of the bombproof, where he made a stand and drove back several determined Confederate attacks. He hoped to hold out long enough for the Third Brigade under Stevenson to come to their relief. Officers and men of the Seventh New Hampshire and the mixed brigade had been holding out for a short time when a musket ball hit Colonel Putnam in the head and instantly killed him.[98] Major Butler of the Sixty-seventh Ohio, being the highest-ranking officer still standing, surveyed the situation and determined that help was not coming. He turned to the Seventh's Captain Augustus Rollins of Rollinsford and ordered the retreat. The remains of the Seventh New Hampshire jumped over heaps of dead and dying bodies as they made their way over the parapet and out of the fort. Behind them, Lieutenants Henry W. Baker, Alfred N. Bennett, Perley B. Bryant, Virgil H. Cate, and Andrew J. Lane were all dead. As the Seventh and the remnants of the other regiments made their way back, they encountered Stevenson's brigade, which had not been committed when it was determined by Major General Quincy Gillmore that the fort could not be taken.[99]

The wounded included Lieutenant John H. Worcester of Hollis, whose left leg was shot up on the parapet; he could not move when the Seventh retreated. Found the next morning by the Confederates, Worcester was taken to Charleston, where his leg was amputated. He was returned under a flag of truce on July 25 and put on a ship headed north with other wounded from the recent battle. The next evening, gangrene set in, and Worcester died the following morning. Before he died, he turned to another wounded soldier, "Give my love to my men and say to them that I shall be with them no more, and tell my friends at home all you know of me." Lieutenant Ezra Davis of Nashua died aboard the same transport only a week later. Captains Leavitt and House both died soon after the battle.[100]

The Seventh New Hampshire in its first battle was engaged about an hour and a half in fighting at Fort Wagner and lost 218 men killed, wounded, or

All maps, pp. 171–74, from Daniel Eldridge, The Third New Hampshire and All about It, *1893*

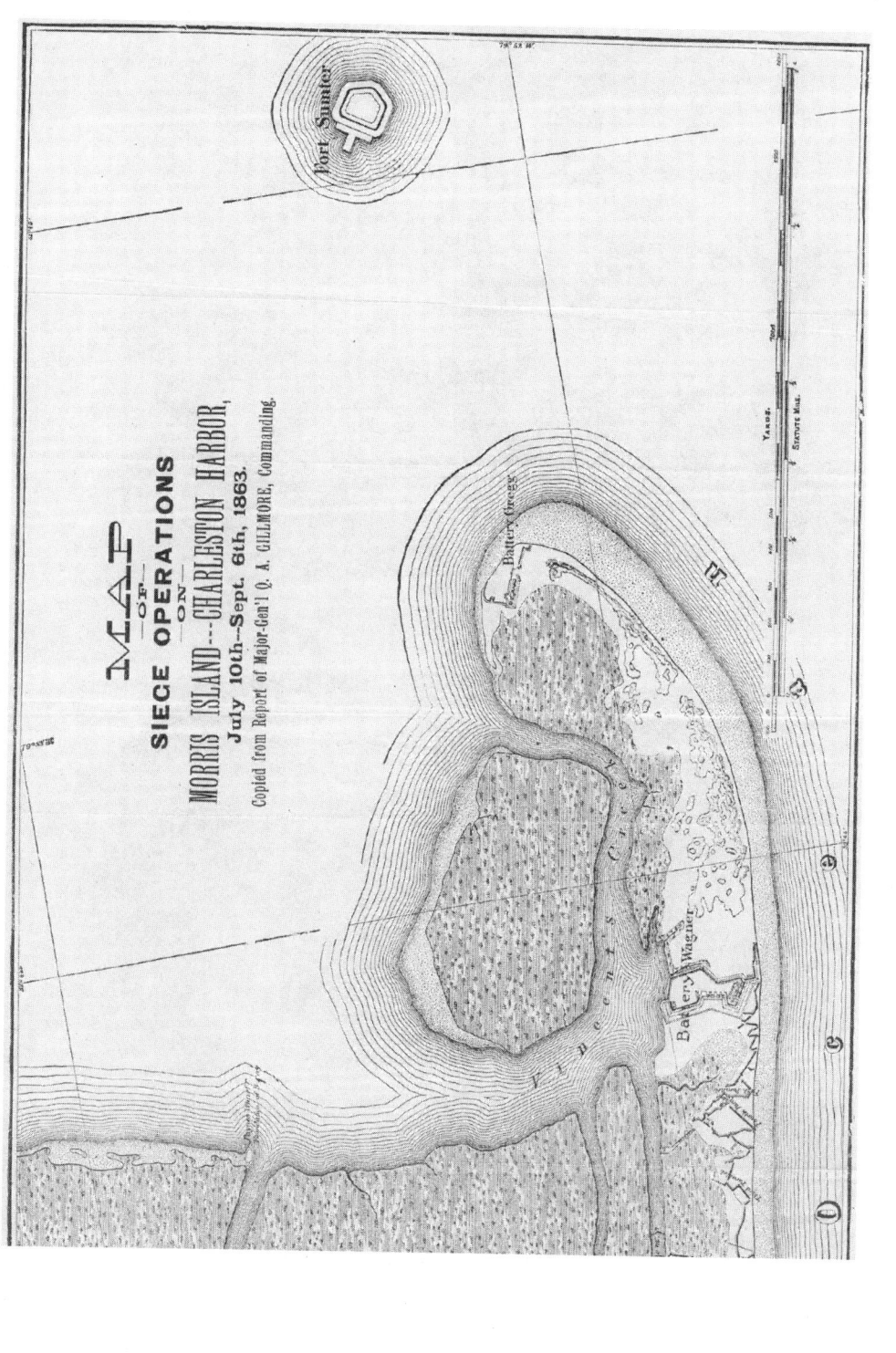

MAP
—OF—
SIECE OPERATIONS
—ON—
MORRIS ISLAND--CHARLESTON HARBOR,
July 10th--Sept. 6th, 1863.
Copied from Report of Major-Gen'l Q. A. GILLMORE, Commanding.

Fort Sumter

Battery Gregg

Battery Wagner

Vincents C'k

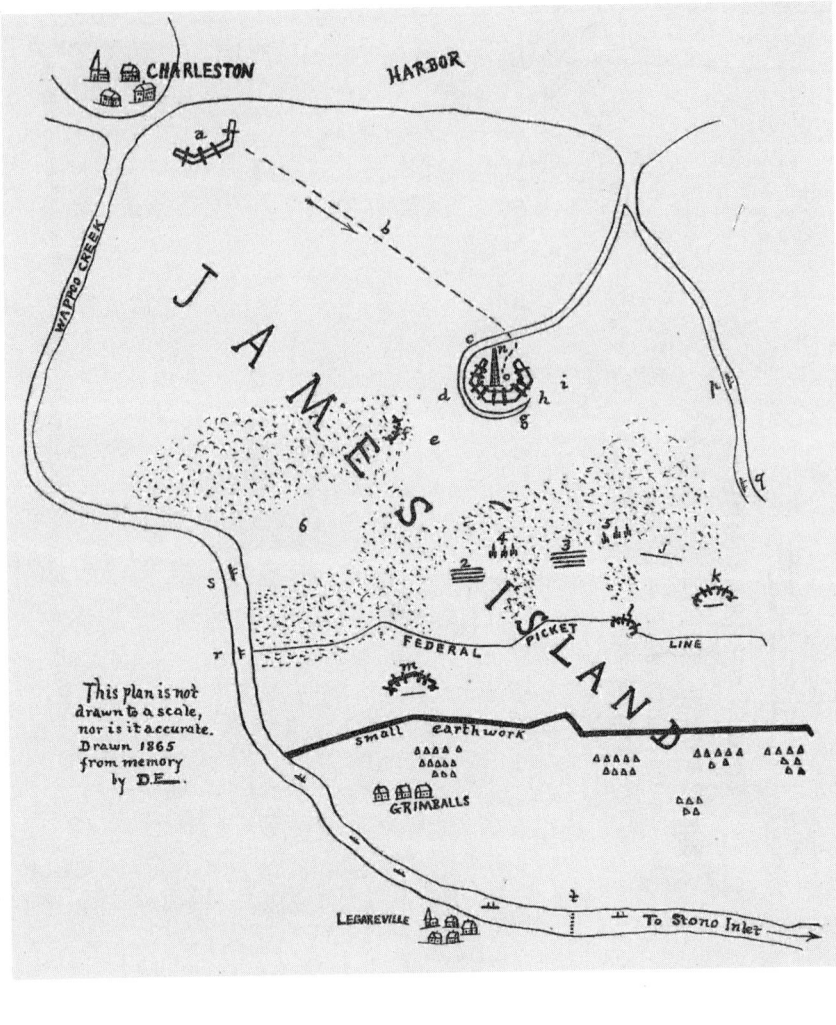

CHARLESTON   HARBOR

WAPPOO CREEK

J A M E S   I S L A N D

a

b

c
d   e
f
g   h   i

p

q

6

2   4   3   5

j

k

l

s

r

FEDERAL   PICKET   LINE

m

This plan is not
drawn to a scale,
nor is it accurate.
Drawn 1865
from memory
by D.E.

small   earthwork

GRIMBALLS

LEGAREVILLE   ⊥   To Stono Inlet

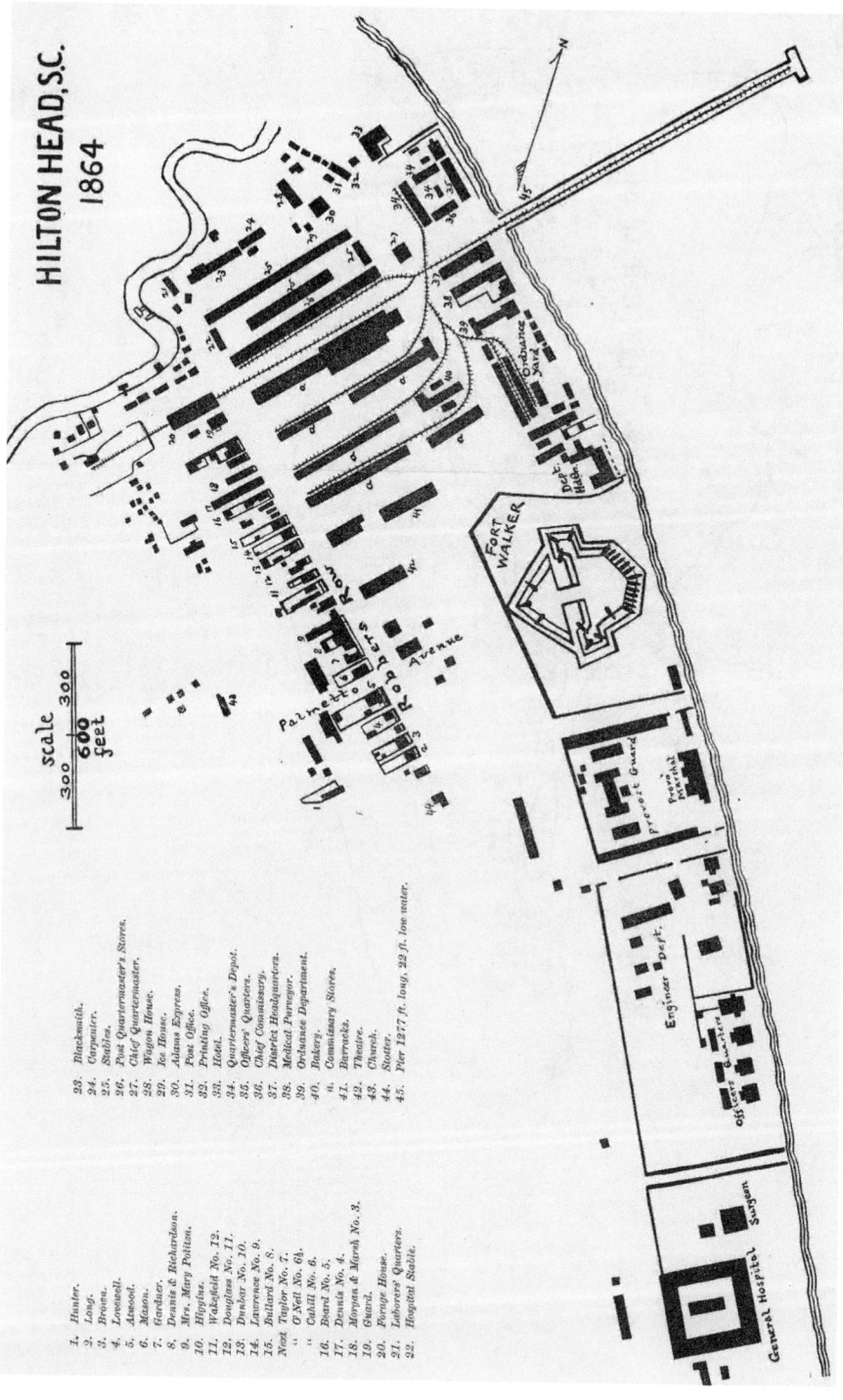

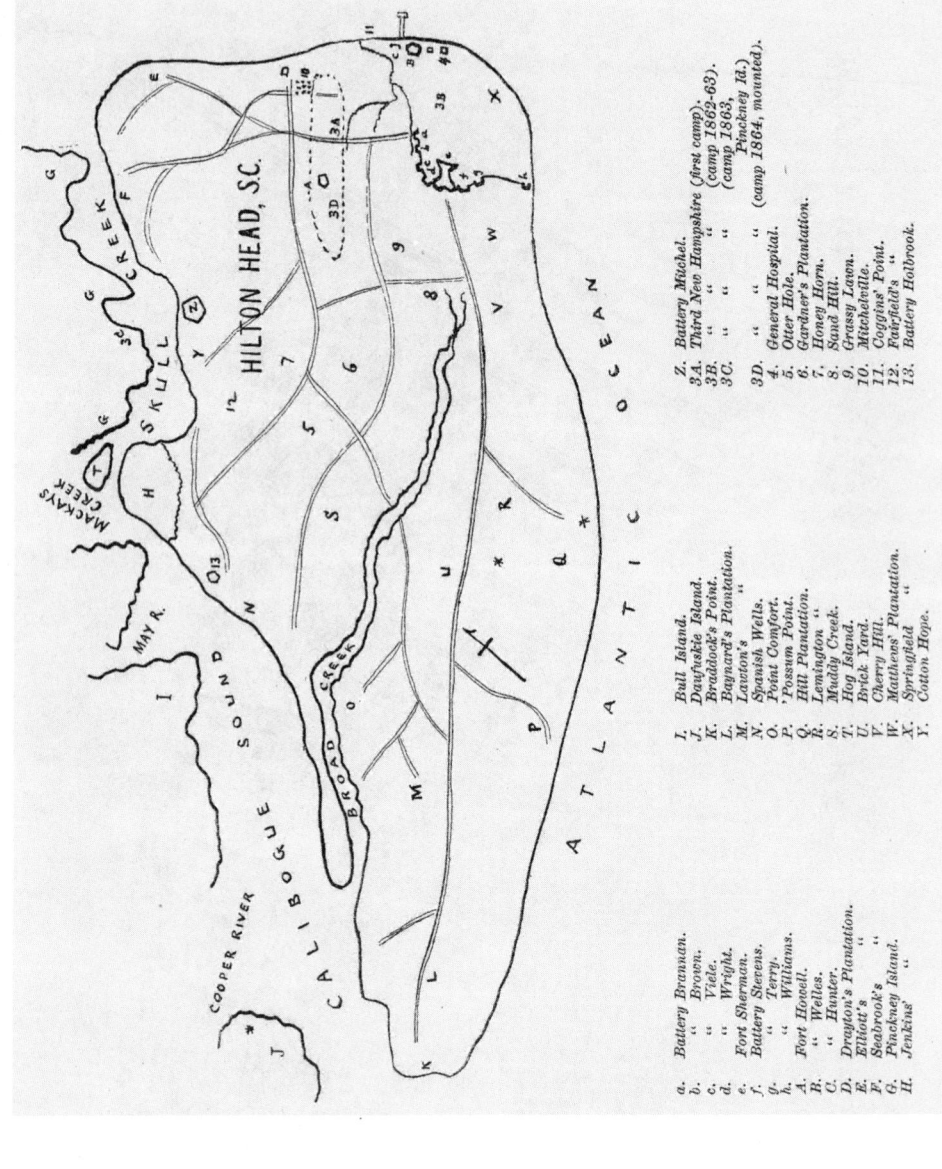

HILTON HEAD, S.C.

a. Battery Brannan.
b.   "   Brown.
c.   "   Viele.
d.   "   Wright.
e. Fort Sherman.
f. Battery Stevens.
g.   "   Terry.
h.   "   Williams.
A. Fort Howell.
B.   "   Welles.
C.   "   Hunter.
D. Drayton's Plantation.
E. Elliott's   "
F. Seabrook's   "
G. Pinckney Island.
H. Jenkins'   "

I. Bull Island.
J. Dawfuskie Island.
K. Braddock's Point.
L. Baynard's Plantation.
M. Lawton's   "
N. Spanish Wells.
O. Point Comfort.
P. Possum Point.
Q. Hill Plantation.
R. Lemington   "
S. Muddy Creek.
T. Hog Island.
U. Brick Yard.
V. Cherry Hill.
W. Matthews' Plantation.
X. Springfield   "
Y. Cotton Hope.

Z. Battery Mitchel.
3A. Third New Hampshire (first camp).
3B.   "   "   "   (camp 1862-63).
3C.   "   "   "   (camp 1863, Pinckney Id.)
3D.   "   "   "   (camp 1864, mounted).
4. General Hospital.
5. Otter Hole.
6. Gardner's Plantation.
7. Honey Horn.
8. Sand Hill.
9. Grassy Lawn.
10. Mitchelville.
11. Coggins' Point.
12. Fairfield's   "
13. Battery Holbrook.

Lieutenant John H. Worcester, *Seventh New Hampshire, Company H. Worcester was severely wounded in fighting inside Fort Wagner on July 18, 1863. He was captured and taken aboard the steamer* Cosmopolitan, *where he died of his wounds on July 26. Photograph courtesy of NHVA*

captured. Eighteen officers of the Seventh were hit, with twelve being killed, mortally wounded, or captured. The regiment had the unfortunate distinction of suffering seventy-seven men killed at Fort Wagner, the highest death toll for a New Hampshire regiment in a single battle for the entire war. The total loss for all Federal forces engaged at Fort Wagner on July 18 was 1,515 killed, wounded, or captured. Confederate casualties were relatively light at 147.[101]

Several contradicting stories exist about Colonel Putnam's burial site. The body of Colonel Cross of the Fifth New Hampshire was returned to Lancaster after the Battle of Gettysburg for burial but no such claim can be made about Colonel Putnam's body being returned to Cornish after his death at Fort Wagner.

In the Seventh New Hampshire regimental history published in 1896, author Henry Little included a story about Confederate Colonel Robert Houston Anderson, a classmate of Putnam's at West Point. Both graduated in 1857. Anderson, who did not take part in the battle, visited the fort the following day and was told by a fellow officer that Putnam's body (identified by a Seventh New Hampshire prisoner) was waiting in a trench to be buried. Anderson viewed the body and said, "I cannot say that I recognized my friend in the corpse pointed out. . . . In 1857 . . . he wore no beard. . . . The size, hair and complexion of the body pointed out to me agreed with my recollection of my friend." Anderson personally buried Putnam's body in a single grave on the seaward side of the fort. This would have been fine if the story ended here, but Little confuses the issue by stating that the man Anderson identified *might* have been Colonel Shaw of the Fifty-fourth Massachusetts. Little relates a story by another witness claiming that under a flag truce, the Federals were given a body thought to be that of Colonel Putnam but really wasn't and that this body was taken to Beaufort, South Carolina, and buried in the cemetery there.[102] Six years separated 1857 from 1863, and it is true that Putnam had no facial hair in 1857. His last picture shows a finely groomed mustache and long sideburns, but the high cheeks and facial features are noticeably unchanged. This makes the following story a bit more credible than the one in the regimental history.

In 1911 Brigadier General George P. Harrison, who had participated July 18 in the battle at Fort Wagner, was attending a convention of the American Bar Association in Boston. Harrison, a colonel at the time of the battle, was assigned the duty of burying the body of Colonel Shaw of the Fifty-fourth Massachusetts. He somewhat shamefully told the reporter that he was ordered to bury Shaw with about twenty of the Fifty-fourth's black soldiers on top of him. It was understood that because of the nature of Shaw's regiment, the Confederates would return the body of any officer to the Federals under a flag of truce *except* Shaw's. Harrison recalled with extreme clarity the visit of Colonel Anderson to the fort the next day. Harrison states that while they were viewing the piles of bodies in the trenches, Anderson "came upon the body of General [*sic*] Putnam, lying dead. Anderson recognized an old comrade in arms of the days before the war, and falling right there upon his knees, hugged the body to his bosom."[103] The facts indicate that the bodies of Putnam and Shaw were probably not confused, but they do not establish a burial place for Putnam. What is definitely known is that because of the absence of his body, Colonel Putnam's gravestone in Cornish, New Hampshire, is a simple cenotaph. It can be speculated that Colonel Putnam's body may have washed out to sea when large portions of Morris Island were eroded away or, more comforting, is that it was indeed his body that was brought back under a flag of truce and is safely buried in Beaufort, South Carolina.

After July 18, Gillmore reluctantly agreed that siege warfare was the only way that Fort Wagner could be taken. He immediately started the troops digging zigzag trenches toward the fort. The Union forces slowly made their way toward the fort with the help of a rolling sap (a large wicker cylinder that protected the sappers or soldiers) and requa batteries, a volley gun of twenty-five stationary rifle barrels mounted on a carriage like a horizontal xylophone that fires 175 shots per minute. This type of trench warfare went on until September 1863, when the fort was finally taken after the Confederate forces abandoned it.[104]

Newly seated Governor Gilmore then turned his attention to the problem of how to properly administer the new draft that was about to go into effect in July

14. On July 10, the New Hampshire Legislature passed a resolution calling on the governor to contact the War Department in Washington concerning the inequities of the coming draft. The legislature's chief concern was that the draft would be disproportional and would unfairly drain the manpower of those cities and towns that had already supplied their quotas of soldiers for the war.[105] Gilmore immediately sent the resolution to Secretary of War Edwin Stanton in Washington, who replied that the draft could not be changed because it was a law enacted by Congress that the draft would be made by each state's congressional district and not town by town. Stanton did say that he would submit the question to the judge advocate general for review. Gilmore acted on this by suspending the draft in New Hampshire until he received a clear directive from Washington.[106] Provost Marshal Fry informed Gilmore that the War Department would be willing to credit those towns that furnished a surplus of men.[107]

Dissatisfaction with and resistance to the draft reached such intensity that a massive riot broke out in New York City in mid-July. Boston experienced some minor unrest, and Portsmouth, New Hampshire, had a minor disturbance. In anticipation of more trouble, the aldermen of Portsmouth banned all public meetings. In defiance of this order, Democrats held gatherings to compose anti-draft resolutions. Tension in the city was rising. The next day at the Old Customs House, the order was read: the First Congressional District was to provide 1,968 men. No disturbance transpired because a company of marines was on hand to keep order. An announcement was read from the governor postponing the draft until the next day. The next day, another announcement from the governor arrived—he was in negotiations with the War Department to amend the draft and that it had been postponed again, this time for a week. This proved too much for some citizens to bear, and violence broke out soon after. Rocks were thrown and windows smashed. Gunfire erupted, but no one was killed. The mob in the downtown area ebbed and flowed throughout the day until a dramatic confrontation in the evening between the police and a mob of about one hundred people. Again, shots were fired, but no one was killed, thanks to the timely intervention of Mayor Jonathan Dearborn and the marine contingent from the Portsmouth Navy Yard.[108]

For days afterward, the partisan newspapers in the area tried to affix the blame for the riot. The *Portsmouth Chronicle* blasted the Copperheads for inciting the riot, while the *States and Union* blamed the city government for not maintaining order. There had been some injuries, but no deaths, and Portsmouth reluctantly accepted the draft when it became evident that the terms were not going to change.[109]

By the end of July, news of the dissatisfaction and unrest regarding the draft reached the soldiers in the field. One of the members of the Fourteenth New Hampshire, which was stationed in Washington, D.C., and had not yet seen action, was upset about the news. "Are they ever going to draft in NH?" asked Company I's Private Christopher Hoyt. "I wish they would and if they resist dam them shoot them they got us out hear and don't care how long we haft to stay."[110] Private Horace H. Adams of the Tenth New Hampshire, while concerned about the disturbance over the draft, seemed resigned that it would go through anyway: "You wrote me about the riot in Portsmouth NH I heard little something about that by the Papers some of the boys got there was also a big one in new York I was very sorry to hear of it as it puts a bad look on things just at Present but never mind they will be put down. Its no use to Kick against the bricks."[111]

After the Battle of Gettysburg, the Second and Twelfth New Hampshire regiments had been detached and sent to Point Lookout, Maryland, to perform guard duty at the prisoner-of-war camp there. Gilman Marston arranged for these battered regiments to be taken out of the line for a long rest. The Fifth New Hampshire went home to New Hampshire to rest and recruit for four months, and then joined the Second and Twelfth at Point Lookout.[112]

Before the fall of Vicksburg, the Ninth Corps under Ambrose Burnside had been assigned the task of preventing Major General Joseph Johnston from breaking Grant's siege of the city. Now that Vicksburg had fallen, the Ninth Corps that contained the Sixth, Ninth, and Eleventh New Hampshire regiments marched east from Vicksburg in pursuit of Johnston. The men made a grueling fifty-mile march before catching Johnston at Jackson, Mississippi, as Ransom Sargent of the Eleventh New Hampshire described, "The first day we marched about 20 miles and many men struck dead on the road" from sunstroke.[113] At Jackson a short engagement resulted in few casualties to the New Hampshire troops involved. Sergeant Charles Paige of Candia left an account of the Eleventh New Hampshire at Jackson on July 19, 1863: "After several days of fighting, Johnston evacuated his troops from Jackson. Burnside was then ordered to report back to Milldale, Mississippi. The return march proved to be harder than the combat in which they had been engaged." Ransom Sargent observed, "Nearly everyone was glad to get out of this mean country where it is almost impossible to get water and hot enough to melt anyone."[114] "We . . . arrived back here last Thursday," said Private J. Lewis Chase of the Eleventh New Hampshire about the march back to Milldale. "We had a hard time it was some 45 miles march and it is verry hot here and we suffered a great deal of our water that we had to use part of the time was such that the horses would not drink only to prevent them from chokeing to death it was rough I can tell you."[115] Colonel Simon G. Griffin of the Sixth New Hampshire described the march and journey upriver just concluded: "It was the most disastrous campaign to the health, strength, numbers and morale of our men that we ever experienced. They were attacked with fevers, congestive chills, chronic diarrhoea and kindred diseases. Many died, others were ruined in health and constitution. The sickness on the boats was terrible and universal. Every night as we lay up on account of low water, there was a burial party ashore."[116] The campaign of hard marches without adequate potable water took its toll on the New Hampshire troops of the Mississippi campaign. While casualties were light in the actual fighting, they were heavy during the march and return trip to Kentucky. Then the enemy was malaria, dysentery, and typhoid fever.[117]

Hard marching that summer was not reserved just for the Sixth, Ninth, and Eleventh New Hampshire regiments. After the Siege of Suffolk, the Tenth and Thirteenth New Hampshire regiments, which had been detached from the Ninth Corps, found themselves in the Seventh Corps. The Tenth and the Thirteenth were involved in a raid on July 4, 1863, the objective of which was to cut the rail lines north of Richmond while Lee's army was far to the north and occupied in Pennsylvania. When the troops approached the railroad bridges, they found them too heavily defended and retired for the long march back to Portsmouth, Virginia. This was called the "Blackberry Raid" because of the abundant presence of that fruit.[118] The terrible reality was that it was anything but a picnic. After leaving the railroad bridges behind, the Tenth and Thirteenth destroyed a few smaller bridges and marched for Hanover Courthouse. "We started and marched about ten miles the first day the Sun was very Hot we Had to Throw Blankets Knapsacks and everything away," Private Adams of the Tenth said. "A Great many died along the road from Sunstroke."[119] "On this . . . march the men suffered terribly from thirst," said S. Millett Thompson of the Thirteenth New Hampshire, "and actually dipped water out of puddles in the middle of the road, and drink it, after hundreds of horses, mules and men had splashed through it—'horse coffee,' as the boys called it." The men had left on their mission on June 30 and were back in camp on July 13, having marched 175 miles. This series of forced marches resulted in roughly half the Thirteenth New Hampshire becoming sick.[120]

One of the least chronicled parts of the Civil War is the ongoing riverboat war that took place up and down the Mississippi River. Lieutenant Commander George Hamilton Perkins of Hopkinton took part in many of these running battles on both land and water. Perkins was aboard the USS *New London* as she was returning to New Orleans. Passing Whitehall Point, Louisiana, he expected no trouble because he had passed the area five times without incident. However, on the night of July 20, 1863, batteries at Whitehall Point fired on the ship while Confederate sharpshooters raked her decks. The effect was immediate; shots penetrated the *New London,* and the boiler exploded, scalding six men. The ship was out of control and soon grounded. Still in range of the batteries, Lieutenant Commander Perkins fired off rockets asking for assistance, but none came. Sailors on the *New London* were being picked off one by one. Many abandoned the ship altogether. Perkins lowered several boats and tried towing the *New London* out of range of the Confederate guns. While this operation was underway,

Perkins landed some men on the shore with muskets to keep the Confederates pinned down. He also sent messengers downriver to ask for help. The situation became more desperate when a messenger returned with not only the bad news that no help would be coming but also that a sizable Confederate cavalry force was bearing down on them. Lieutenant Commander Perkins, determined to save his ship and crew, set off on horseback in search of help.

Finding the USS *Princess Royal* several miles downstream, he signaled to the boat for help. After discussing his plight with the captain, Perkins took a small body of troops back up the river to help him save his ship. He found that his ship was gone. He deduced that one of the other messengers had been successful and that the *New London* had been rescued and towed to safety. Perkins later found that the USS *Essex,* a nearby ironclad, had taken the *New London* in tow and brought her all the way to New Orleans.

Perkins, relieved his ship and crew were safe, soon realized he was far behind enemy lines. He turned the horse loose and got a ride from an old man driving a rickety wagon. Perkins tried to disguise himself by turning his coat inside out; he kept his pistols cocked under a small blanket. It appeared that he would make good his escape when he saw a cavalry detachment galloping after them. He assumed that they had been alerted and were searching for him. The driver lashed the mule, and the chase was on. As they approached the Federal lines, the blue-clad troops realized what was happening and came out with a cavalry unit of their own to meet the young lieutenant commander. The Confederates, not realizing that they were the ones riding into the trap, were surrounded and captured. Perkins was safely escorted back into the Union lines. Upon his arrival in New Orleans, Perkins reported to Rear Admiral David Farragut, who, although not entirely pleased with his methods, complimented Perkins for his daring and reassigned him to the USS *Pensacola.*[121]

The month of July 1863 had seen New Hampshire men fight and die in Virginia, South Carolina, Pennsylvania, and Mississippi, including Colonels Putnam and Cross. Many soldiers fell wounded in several campaigns and were sickened in forced marches. The sons of New Hampshire at Gettysburg, Fort Wagner, and Jackson covered themselves courageously in glory and gained everlasting gratitude and respect from the people of the Granite State.

"Our force was at work throwing grape and canister"

CHAPTER 7

August 1863 to December 1863

And glistening eyes shall throb with tears at names that, stamped on history's
page, shall aye go ringing down the years, the heroes of this patriot age.

Georgia Drew Merrill, *History of Carroll County, New Hampshire,* 1889

During July 1863, the Union had been victorious nearly everywhere. In some
sections the war seemed already won, but in others the war was far from being
concluded. "What do you think of the rebellion now don't you think it is about
played out," wrote Private J. Lewis Chase, somewhat optimistically now about
the North's chances for victory. "If it is not when for God Sake is it going to it
has been the talk a long while they can not hold out much longer but they seam
as good as ever."[1]

Corporal Myron W. Harris of the Twentieth Maine Regiment had left his
home Hudson, New Hampshire, to enlist in a Maine regiment. On August 13
from Beverly Ford, Virginia, he wrote to his father in Hudson about life in that
storied regiment: "I have been in several scrapes since the first of June. I was in
the Battle of Middleburg and the Battle of Gettysburg. The hardship of our
summer campaign has reduced our regt. to a very small number. Now after losing nearly one hundred and fifty our number out of but little more than 300. I
have stood all our hardships as well as the best of them and got through our different scrapes without getting a scratch."[2]

Writing on August 13 aboard the USS *David Tatum* was Adjutant of the
Ninth New Hampshire George Henry Chandler, who said about life on the Mississippi River, "We have had a great deal of sickness within the past month. Four
of the 7th Rhode Island have died on this boat since we started. We stop at night,
bury them on shore and keep along as if nothing has happened. Half the officers
and men are sick on board today. I don't know what is to be done with us now.
We are not fit for active service."[3]

On August 17, the Union forces on land and sea began a massive bombardment of Fort Sumter, Fort Wagner, and Battery Gregg. Private Samuel Wilkinson
of the Fourth New Hampshire in his trench on Morris Island, South Carolina,

needed no reminder that the war was still a very serious concern: "Our Batteries opened on Sumpter from all of our heavy Guns the small guns and Mortars on Wagner and Greg. Some of the shells made beautiful music as they passed over us. Sevral men were wounded and some killed Sumpter did not fire a Gun 46 large holes in Sumter."[4] Watching the same bombardment was Captain George F. Towle of the Fourth New Hampshire. After a day of severe shelling, Towle remarked, "Sumter's clear outline begins to look jagged and rough."[5] Two days after the bombardment started, Private Wilkinson offered a unique opinion on the condition of Fort Sumter: "Sumter looks very much like a raw potato after being picked by the chickens."[6] Corporal Caleb F. Dodge of the 7th New Hampshire was so excited by the bombardment of the forts that he wrote to his sister back in Holderness that she could "expect to hear that we have by the first of September got possession of Charleston."[7]

For the first time since the summer of 1861, a New Hampshire regiment was due to be mustered out. Such was the case for two, the Fifteenth and Sixteenth New Hampshire, whose enlistment ran out in the end of July 1863. The surviving members of the Fifteenth New Hampshire left Louisiana on the USS *City of Madison* with a large number of sick onboard. Thirty sick soldiers were left at a hospital in Memphis, where nineteen of them later died. Nine soldiers died before they reached Cairo, Illinois. Several sick members of the Fifteenth died on the train from Cairo to Concord, New Hampshire. The Fifteenth New Hampshire was mustered out of the service of the United States at Concord, having suffered 30 deaths in battle and 115 from various diseases.

The Sixteenth New Hampshire started for New Hampshire later than the Fifteenth and was too late to participate in the gala celebration put on by people of Concord. Having seen no combat whatsoever, the Sixteenth New Hampshire suffered no battle casualties but appallingly lost 210 men to disease, ironically roughly the same casualties as the other New Hampshire regiments. The Sixteenth New Hampshire's surviving 602 members were mustered out in Concord on August 20, 1863. This left only the Eighth New Hampshire Regiment in Louisiana to serve the remainder of its three-year term.[8]

Back home, the celebration set for the men of the Fifth and Fifteenth New Hampshire on August 8, 1863 was a lavish one. Main Street and the area around the State House grounds were decorated. Militia units from around the state as well as the Dover Cornet Band were present. Governor Joseph Albee Gilmore gave a brief welcoming statement, and Lieutenant Colonel Charles E. Hapgood of the Fifth New Hampshire and Major John Aldrich of the Fifteenth returned the greeting. The brief procession followed with the Governor's Horse Guard, the wounded of the two regiments, and distinguished guests and ended at the State House lawn where a banquet was held. Congressman Edward Rollins addressed the gathering and spoke eloquently about Colonel Edward Everett Cross, Major

Edward E. Sturtevant, and William Foster. Also on hand to address the crowd was Colonel Walter Harriman of the Eleventh New Hampshire and U.S. senator John Parker Hale.[9]

The return of the Sixteenth New Hampshire to Concord on August 14 led to a special celebration in its honor. Members of the Fifth New Hampshire escorted their returning comrades into town and to the ceremony at Phenix Hall. Fifty-one men of the Sixteenth unable to attend were taken to a wing of the City Hall especially constructed as a hospital. Seventeen of them died before they could see their homes again. The hospital, with room for one hundred patients, was full of sick soldiers until September 1863.[10] A large crowd of people waited at the train station to greet Colonel James Pike and the men of the Sixteenth New Hampshire. The soldiers then paraded into Phenix Hall for a fine dinner. Governor Gilmore, looking out over the audience, said, "We realize that there is no regiment which has gone from our State that has suffered more from sickness and fatigue, or done more irksome duty than the 16th. As I look at your ranks I think of the large number that are left behind who sleep in death. The State of New Hampshire will spare no pains nor expense to give a substantial welcome to its returning volunteers." Colonel Pike of the Sixteenth New Hampshire took the podium, thanked the governor for the hearty welcome, and said, "Though we have not been in positions where we could win for you and for ourselves imperishable renown, as has been the case with the 2nd, 5th and other New Hampshire regiments, yet we have the proud consciousness of knowing that we have always gone where we were ordered. Our decimated ranks show that the cup of sorrow has often been placed to our lips. We trust the people of New Hampshire will not forget our sleeping heroes, nor fail to protect and care for their mourning kindred and orphaned children." The members of the Sixteenth New Hampshire then departed to the sound of a brass band, were given a furlough for one week, returned again to Concord, and were officially mustered out of the service of the United States.[11]

One man who did more than his share to preserve the memory of New Hampshire soldiers in the war as well as those from other states was John Badger Bachelder. New Hampshire born, Bachelder has the distinction of being the first official historian of the Battle of Gettysburg. When the war began in 1861, he joined the army as a civilian and followed the army, making sketches of the various battlefields. Bachelder returned home for a brief time, but after the Battle of Gettysburg, he hurried south to see the battlefield. Bachelder remembered, "The debris of that great battle lay scattered for miles around. Fresh mounds of earth marked the resting-place of the fallen thousands, and many of the dead lay yet unburied." He spent the next week on horseback touring the battlefield and making drawings from one end of the battlefield to the other. He spent time with the soldiers in the hospitals, and when they were well enough to move, he took them to the fields where they had so recently fought so they could show him where their units had engaged in battle. Bachelder completed his map, and it was published the fall of 1863.

The map did not mark the end of Bachelder's research on Gettysburg. He continued interviewing soldiers who had been at the battle. In 1873, after nearly one thousand personal interviews, he published *Gettysburg, What to See, and How to See It.* Bachelder, a lifelong member of the Gettysburg Battlefield Memorial Association, added significantly to the body of knowledge of the battle until his death in 1894.[12]

Soon after the Battle of Gettysburg, plans were made for a National Cemetery in Gettysburg. Ira Perley of Concord was appointed the commissioner from New Hampshire to attend to the burials of the men of the Granite State. An appropriation in 1864 for $1,815 paid for monuments and gravestones in the cemetery. The following year, another $705 was allocated for markers for the forty-nine men from New Hampshire buried in the National Cemetery.

Governor Gilmore had promised to spare no expense in taking care of the soldiers of New Hampshire but the ballooning war debt of the state was making it increasingly difficult to do so. New Hampshire's debt in 1861 was $30,000 but had risen to an alarming $1,825,000 by mid-1863. Added to the state's financial burden was the final call for the draft; the state needed to produce five thousand men. Tensions were already high over the draft, and the violence in Portsmouth and other Northern cities added to the anxiety. In a letter to the *Belknap Gazette* on August 22, 1863, a soldier from the Twelfth New Hampshire, who signed his letter as "JOE," echoed the opinion of many New Hampshire soldiers in the field, "We are now watching with interest the progress of the draft in the several Northern States. The heart of the soldier is stirred with indignation, against the base hearted villains, who are preaching up opposition to the draft. The voice of the army is unanimous upon this point."[13] Lieutenant Andrew Jackson Edgerly of the Fourth New Hampshire had unwittingly become involved in the intense political environment in New Hampshire the previous spring. While on leave from his regiment, Edgerly had voted the Democratic ticket and had persuaded others to vote likewise. Someone reported him to the War Department in Washington, and through the office of the adjutant general in New Hampshire, he was discharged from the army. He was discharged "for circulating Copperhead tickets and doing all in his power to promote the success of the Rebel cause in his State." This action caused an avalanche of criticism from the Democrats, who charged that the government "falsely assumed the cause of the Democratic Party to be the rebel cause, thereby indirectly charging nearly one-half of the people of New Hampshire with the guilt of treason." An investigation by a Congressional committee fully exonerated Lieutenant Edgerly of any wrongdoing. The young lieutenant moved to Massachusetts and, ironically, became that state's adjutant general in 1874.[14]

By the first week of September 1863, the siege lines constructed by Major General Quincy Gillmore's men were getting closer to the walls of Fort Wagner, South Carolina. The Union troops on Morris Island anticipated another attempt to take the fort. "Our parallels are so close that we can jump at one step into the ditch," Captain Towle of the Fourth New Hampshire remarked. "A crisis is certainly near."[15] The plan called for the Third New Hampshire and the Ninety-seventh Pennsylvania regiments to storm the fort from the sea face and cover one hundred picked men as they forcibly spiked (plugged) the Confederate guns. Stevenson's brigade, which contained the Fourth New Hampshire and Ninth Maine, would enter the fort immediately after them. The task of the Third Brigade would be to swing around to the left and enter the fort from the rear.[16]

The attack began the early morning of September 7 when the men of the Third New Hampshire filed into the advanced trenches. There was no noise; Fort Wagner had become quiet as a tomb. Before long, rumors were passing down the lines that the fort was evacuated. Orders were given to move against the fort, and the men of the Third New Hampshire scaled the walls. They reached the parapet and looked down into the fort. The men carefully entered the bomb-proof and found only a few wounded men that the Confederates had left behind.[17] This was all too good to be true, but then the men in the Fourth New Hampshire made a gruesome discovery. Private Wilkinson felt that the fort had been abandoned because "a large burying ground in the rear of the Fort had been so disturbed that it was imposable for any human being to live near it. This was partley what made them leave sometimes one shell would strike in the burying ground and turn up a dozen half decomposed boddies at one time. It was more horrable than can be explained."[18]

Because it was still dark, no time was wasted in moving on to Fort Gregg. Men of the Fourth New Hampshire scaled the walls of the fort, again without firing a shot. This fort had been abandoned as well. The arrival of dawn halted the celebration of the men and made them realize that as the sun came up, they would be in full view of the other Confederate forts and be perfect targets. The majority of the troops withdrew, leaving a small force inside Fort Gregg and several regiments in Fort Wagner.[19] As most men of the Fourth New Hampshire made their way back to the safety of their siege lines, they strayed into a minefield on the far side of Fort Wagner. The area around the fort had become so transformed by the continuous shelling that even the Confederates did not remember where they had planted mines. This was evident when on September 6, a company from the Third New Hampshire captured over sixty Confederate soldiers in their rifle pits near the fort who were fearful of leaving the safety of their trench, lest they step on a mine. These early landmines, or "torpedoes" as they were called, were detonated when a soldier stepped on a small glass vial planted at ground level. The liquid in the vial ran into the explosive device, which then detonated. Corporal William Rich of Somersworth stepped on such a mine and lost a leg. (Later, he was awarded a Gillmore Medal for gallant and meritorious service in operations during the Charleston campaign. This singular medal of honor was created by Major General Quincy Gillmore for action in this theater of the war. Twenty men in both the Third and Fourth New Hampshire regiments received Gillmore Medals as did eighteen from the Seventh New Hampshire).[20]

The Federals wasted no time in pressing their advantage. Rear Admiral John A. Dahlgren formed an all-navy plan that included a landing made by his marines on Fort Sumter. Gillmore had a similar plan, only it involved the army being towed in barges and landed at Fort Sumter. The two military chieftains refused to cooperate, and the only coincidence is that both operations were planned for the same night. Gillmore ordered his commander to withdraw if it looked as though the navy would land first. The two independent attacks took place, and the navy indeed arrived first. Luckily for the men waiting to be landed in the army barges, they were ordered to return. The Confederates at Fort Sumter, with its garrison at the walls, were totally prepared for the marine landing. Grenades and successive volleys tore into the ranks of the hapless marines, killing and wounding almost 150 officers and men. The attack was a total failure. No New Hampshire troops were lost in this uncoordinated and foolish attack.[21]

Aboard the USS *Kearsarge,* the men from New Hampshire, such as, Martin Hoyt of Newington, were both elated and troubled about entering the French port of Brest. Their captain, John A. Winslow, had heard in Feroll, Spain, that the Confederate cruiser CSS *Florida* was headed for that French port, and he set off after her.

Upon arrival on September 17, one year after the Battle of Antietam, Winslow found the *Florida* already docked and undergoing repairs. The *Kearsarge* docked only a few hundred yards away from her prey in this neutral port. One day after Christmas, Winslow left the port and held station at the harbor entrance, waiting for the Confederate cruiser to emerge. He sailed back and forth for two months until the exasperated captain discovered that the *Florida* had evaded him by leaving the harbor through one of the back channels. At the same time, the captain of the CSS *Alabama* turned westward and started for France. She, too, was badly in need of repairs and needed to find a safe port. The *Kearsarge* remained off the coast of France waiting and hoping to catch any Confederate ships in the area.[22]

In the middle of September, Adjutant George Henry Chandler was coping with a painful case of scurvy. He had asked to be relieved of his duties so he could return to the Ninth New Hampshire Regiment, then posted at Paris, Kentucky. He had been on the staff of Colonel Joshua K. Siegfried of the Forty-eighth Pennsylvania. "The disposition of troops are as follows," he wrote his mother. "The Sixth New Hampshire to Frankfort to relieve the 2nd Maryland and the 9th to Paris. This brought me on his [Siegfried's] staff with the prospect of a march to Knoxville which I didn't much fancy."[23] Chandler would get a long time to rest because the Ninth New Hampshire was kept on guard duty in Paris for the remainder of the fall and winter. The Sixth New Hampshire also remained behind at Camp Nelson in Frankfort, Kentucky. While at this post, nearly every man of the Sixth New Hampshire reenlisted for a second term of three years. This regiment also remained here for the fall and early winter.[24]

Private Chase, writing from London, Kentucky, revealed the position of the Eleventh New Hampshire Regiment to his parents on October 1 and the progress of the army as it moved toward Knoxville: "The papers stated yesterday that the advance of the 9th Corps had reached Knoxville troops pass here most everyday about five hundred cavalry encamped here last night on their way there and Monday night there was about 4,000 of infantry stayed here. If we can just whip them out down there this thing is about played out. Georgia and Tennessee seems to be the battleground. . . . You may look for hard fighting in Georgia and Tenn. Gen. Burnside is a tough cuss."[25] The boys in the Eleventh New Hampshire would find out how tough they were when on October 15 they were finally ordered to catch up with the rest of the Ninth Corps. For the next twelve days, the regiment marched over difficult mountain roads into Tennessee with only half rations and were pelted by harsh rainstorms the whole way. It was a good omen that only two men had to be left behind, and only a few men reported sickness at the end of the march to Knoxville.[26] Private Willard J. Templeton of the Eleventh complained of the difficulty of the march but rejoiced that the regiment "found quite a quantity of apples of the most delicious sort." The Eleventh had finished a grueling march of two hundred miles with only three hundred men left for duty.[27]

As 1863 neared its close, the hospitals in and around the Washington, D.C., area were full with the product of the past year's business of war. Thousands of men lay in overcrowded wards, each fighting his own private war with his wounds. Many won their fight, but too often after an extended period of suffering, they died. Sarah Low of Dover was on duty at Armory Square Hospital in November. One patient, she said, "took his first walk on crutches with a man on each side to keep him steady," and another had "a ball taken from his back which was split in two parts of the bone, two deep incisions were made in his back and the hunting for the two pieces was long and painful but he did not groan or even make a face."[28] Low was amazed with the courage of her patients: "One reason that our soldiers bear suffering with such wonderful fortitude is because they are so well educated and read so much, it helps to take their thoughts from their pains."[29]

In his camp near Knoxville, Tennessee, on November 1, 1863, Private Chase reported the arrival of an important person: "Day before yesterday I went to the citty and who should I see but Gen. Burnside he and his whole staff came in on the cars. I do not think Burnside was obliged to fall back I think he is trying to get a better hold of them and I think he is going to use a little strategy." Chase echoed the excitement and anticipation in camp: "It has been some time since we have seen a brush and I for one should like to have a pop at them. I hope Burnside will get them where he wants them soon it is evident that there will be some hard fighting down here."[30]

Corporal Plumer Small also of the Eleventh New Hampshire explained to his friend at home in Fremont why the Union army was having supply problems outside of Knoxville: "We got half rations it is a very long and hard road to draw suplyes over and they can not get them along but as soon as they get the railroad open through to Chattanooga they can get plenty here. The rebels hold the railroad between us and there."[31]

November 4, 1863, was the beginning of the Knoxville campaign when Major General Braxton Bragg detached seventeen thousand men and gave them to Lieutenant General James Longstreet to drive Burnside out of East Tennessee. It was a campaign destined for failure because Bragg and Longstreet personally disliked each other, and Bragg did not give Longstreet a sufficient number of troops to deal with Burnside, who was waiting with nearly thirty thousand men all around the Knoxville area. Even with such an advantage, Burnside, who assumed the Confederates would send more men, contemplated a retreat back to Kentucky. This threw Washington into a panic, and frantic telegrams both from the War Department and Grant told Burnside to stay and hold his ground. Grant promised assistance as soon as he dealt with Bragg at Chattanooga, Tennessee. Bragg committed a serious error by detaching so many men from his command. Grant saw this and intended to make him pay for such a foolish mistake. Longstreet arrived near Loudon, Tennessee, on the Little Tennessee River on November 14, and the race for Knoxville was on.[32]

"The fighting and retreat commenced Saturday the 14th of November," Sergeant Charles C. Paige of the Eleventh New Hampshire said. "It seems that part of the enemy's forces had crossed the river by daylight and an order had been given by our Generals in command to retreat and a stampede was the result. The trains, artillery and infantry were started for Knoxville a distance of twenty-five miles."[33] Private Chase told his sister Sarah on that day, "We have heard the booming of cannon all the foor noon at times it is reported here that the first division has crossed the river again down near Loudon and I think it is so for the firing today comes from that way if that be the case we shall probably go down there soon."[34]

Burnside arrived from Knoxville to personally supervise the retreat of the army back to Knoxville. All day November 15, the two small armies paralleled one another in their mad dash for the possession of Knoxville.[35] "It was a very interesting, vivid and exciting scene to me to witness the maneuvering of troops, the break-neck rush of batteries," Sergeant Paige commented about the fighting withdrawal. "The firing was more than I ever expected to behold. The rebels followed and skirmished with our forces until they were two miles below Concord and fourteen from Knoxville. A field fight took place, and the enemy tried to flank our forces. It is reported by many officers that an army was never maneuvered in a more splendid manner than Burnside directed his."[36]

Campbell's Station became an important road hub for both armies on November 16. Burnside, who now had to realize that he had to fight this campaign on his own without any help from Grant, was cognizant that he was opposed by probably the South's most skilled general next to Robert E. Lee. Burnside got the army up early and on the road on November 16. It wasn't going to be easy and would prove to be a race in slow motion. The roads were a mass of sticky, red Tennessee mud. The Federal general's luck held, and his blue-clad soldiers gained the important crossroads barely fifteen minutes ahead of Longstreet's advance column. The two armies clashed in a brief engagement between the roughly fifteen thousand men of Longstreet and the seven thousand of Burnside's army. The Federals lost 31 killed, 211 wounded, and 76 captured, with no loss of New Hampshire troops. The Confederates suffered 22 killed and 157 wounded, with 174 men becoming Federal prisoners. Burnside's men fought this delaying action until nightfall and with the dawn of November 17 began to withdraw again into the defenses at Knoxville. Longstreet followed hard after him, and in a brief cavalry engagement, Brigadier General William P. Sanders of Kentucky was killed (a lunette, or three-sided fort, in the northwest section of the Knoxville defensive perimeter is named after Sanders). As Burnside's men filed into their prepared defenses and made ready for the siege to come, Longstreet warily approached this outer ring of federal outposts that led to Knoxville. Fort Sanders, he decided, would probably be the easiest to overwhelm and made preparations to attack it.[37]

From November 18 on, as Longstreet's siege took shape, the Eleventh New Hampshire was involved in a variety of duties, including acting as a garrison around all the locomotives and rolling stock that had been pulled inside the perimeter. The less-desirable duties of the Eleventh were the wielding of the ax to build defenses and the frequent use of the shovel to dig trenches. The men of the Eleventh got very little sleep at this time as they were shuttled from picket to fatigue to garrison duty almost constantly. The supply pinch was felt almost immediately. The Eleventh New Hampshire was reduced to quarter rations of a small amount of corn meal, a miniscule chunk of pork, a bit of sugar, and a small ration of coffee. Tobacco, when available, was a much sought after commodity.[38]

The rains came again during the afternoon and evening of November 20, making all but the paved roads around Knoxville an impassable sea of mud. The people who were caught in the crossfire of two armies desperately tried to save all they could. Private Templeton of the Eleventh New Hampshire had genuine sympathy for the local residents: "The citizens are engaged during the night in moving off their goods, the rifle balls whizzing over their heads and shells dropping about added to the excitement of teamsters, citizens and mules. It seems too bad for such splendid dwellings to be destroyed, dwellings as richly furnished as the finest dwelling houses in N.E." Templeton was in obvious disapproval of the behavior of the soldiers that to him seemed reminiscent of the sacking of Fredericksburg in December 1862: "The citizens are not able to get much of their property into the city and the contents of parlors, chambers, closets, cupboards and cellars are pillaged by our soldiers. Whatever they want is carried off, the remainder trampled under foot, broken or destroyed." Seventy-five homes and other buildings along the siege lines were destroyed as the contesting armies fired tons of ordinance at each other. Templeton concluded his observation for November 20, "It seems too bad to see the most elegant furniture, the choicest libraries and the nicest wearing apparel all left to be destroyed by the flames."[39]

While the Eleventh New Hampshire was engaged at the Siege of Knoxville, the Eighth New Hampshire was in continuous movement during the fall of 1863. "We have been scouring the country west of the Miss. River from Brashear City to Opelousas a distance of nearly 150 miles," Private Martin Jones, twenty, described to his uncle back in Alton on November 25 what life in the field was like for the Eighth New Hampshire. "We gather the Corn and Potatoes for miles around whenever we make a halt. This is the business of our large army." The many Confederate prisoners "look pretty rough being badly clothed and oft times hungry. We send them immediately to N. Orleans for safekeeping."[40]

The seriousness of war was often punctuated by light-hearted banter between the two sides. On November 22, the Confederates opposite the Eleventh New Hampshire at Knoxville were going to great lengths to demonstrate their new blue overcoats that they had recently captured. "Where are your overcoats?" the rebels taunted. The Yankees replied with a few pops from their muskets. The Confederates called back that they would capture the Yanks and take them all to Richmond. "Can't see it," was the New Hampshire men's reply. "Hey, Yank, got any hard tact?" The Yanks replied that they had none but did have plenty of whiskey and tobacco. The ambitious Confederates then announced that they were going to capture General Burnside and use him to exchange for General

John Hunt Morgan. The Eleventh replied, "Can't see it." These Confederates would not need to capture Burnside because six days later Morgan and six of his officers escaped from their prison cells in Columbus, Ohio.[41]

An attack was made on the skirmish line held by the Eleventh New Hampshire and Second Maryland at dusk on November 23. The Maryland regiment and a part of the Eleventh were ousted from their picket line and withdrew to a new line of trenches closer to town. The Confederates immediately began digging their own trenches on the line abandoned by the Federals.[42] Reading the reports coming from Knoxville, Grant was satisfied that Burnside was grappling with a sizeable Confederate force under Longstreet. Now was the time to break the siege of Chattanooga while Bragg was in a weakened condition. Grant gave Brigadier General George Thomas permission to advance his men. The Battle of Chattanooga was fought over the next three days, ending with the Battle of Missionary Ridge on the November 25. Bragg withdrew his army, and the state of Georgia was then wide open to invasion. Five days later, General Bragg asked to be relieved of command of the Army of Tennessee. The authorities in Richmond accepted and replaced Bragg with General Joe Johnston.[43]

At dawn on Thanksgiving Day, November 26, a counterattack was launched against the Confederates. The Eleventh New Hampshire, Twenty-first and Thirty-fifth Massachusetts, and Forty-eighth Pennsylvania threw the Confederates back and regained the old rifle pits that they had had to suddenly leave three days before. Private Templeton of the Eleventh New Hampshire lamented the lack of a Thanksgiving feast, "Woke up with the prospect of a poor Thanksgiving dinner. The boys shot a hog last night and I got enough for my breakfast. But black bread is a poor substitute for potatoes."[44] Life was apparently a little easier at Point Lookout in Maryland than around the siege lines at Knoxville. The New Hampshire troops guarding the Confederate prisoners there had some hope for a decent meal that Thanksgiving. For Dr. William Child of the Fifth New Hampshire, holiday dinner was "a turkey, plum pudding, custard, apple pie, bread, butter, potatoes and tea."[45]

After twice rejecting the idea of attacking Fort Sanders, Longstreet finally decided to make the attempt. The attack began in the pouring rain on November 28, "a very rainy day," Private Templeton remembered, "but the pickets are shooting considerable, I suppose to keep up their courage for it rains in torrents, about dark the rebels commenced to shell Fort Sanders and continued the bombardment all night. . . . At a little before daylight [on November 29] Longstreet ordered three of his choicest brigades to charge on Fort Sanders."[46] "The rebs made a desperate attempt to take one of our forts," Private Chase of the Eleventh wrote to his parents in South Newmarket, "but were repulsed in the attempt with great slaughter. They made the charge before light with eleven regiments on the strongest part of our lines and were nearly cut to pieces. Their loss was over one thousand. . . . Around the fort where they charged was a ditch dug about five feet deep. Before they got to the ditch our folks had a lot of telegraph wire all wound around amongst the stumps when they got to that they fell against it in a heap."[47] Among the eleven regiments Chase mentioned were the Sixteenth Georgia and the Thirteenth and Seventeenth Mississippi Regiments. The morning was frosty and wet but the attack went forward and did become temporarily hung up in the wire strung around the tree stumps. What seriously impeded the attack was the slope of the ditch around the fort. The ground was slippery from sleet, and the ground was churned up and muddy.[48] Private Chase explained that when the Confederates reached the trench, "our force was at work throwing grape and canister. The ditch was piled full of their dead and wounded the most of them shot through the head. The rebs planted three stand of colors on the fort but they could not stand."[49]

Some of the Confederates gained the fort when they "would actually take hold of the muzzles of the guns to pull themselves up into the fort," said Private Templeton. "A Lieu. climbed up in this way and cried out 'I am the man to whom this fort is to surrender.' 'The h—— you are,' answered the gunner as he touched off his piece blowing the lieutenant into a thousand pieces."[50] The Georgians and Mississippians made it to the parapet, planted their flags, and were even fighting for a short time inside the fort, but they could not hold out and had to retreat. Many who withdrew became mired in the trench and could not escape. Almost two hundred Confederate soldiers were captured unharmed in the ditch.[51] "The [Federal] captain of a battery burned himself by lighting the fuse of his shell and holding them in his hands until they were about to explode," Chase wrote. "Then he would toss them down amongst the cusses and slayed them in great style."[52] The ghastly scene that must have rivaled that of the Sunken Road at Antietam, as Private Templeton recalled, "I am informed nearly 700 dead and wounded in front of the fort. The ditch was full of dead and wounded in every possible form and laying in every shape three, four and five deep."[53]

After the attack, Burnside offered a truce so the Confederates could remove their dead and wounded. Private Templeton went out to the fort to watch the grim process: "The rebels were busy in removing their dead and wounded," said Private Templeton, who went out to the fort to watch the grim process. "Some of our boys were voluntarily helping them. It was a sad sight to see so many brave men cut down, the flower of the Southern army, the heroes of probably a dozen battles."[54] "You ought to have seen the ditch after they got the dead and wounded out," said a shocked Private Chase, also viewing the same scene of so many dead and wounded. "The ground was covered with blood. We captured six or seven hundred stand of arms. The piles of guns and cartridge boxes covered the ground well enough."[55]

Longstreet had decided he had seen enough. At the end of the assault, he had been handed a telegram that announced the defeat of Bragg at Chattanooga. It was clear to him that he could not stay. The Siege of Knoxville was finally lifted on December 4 with the withdrawal of Longstreet's army.[56]

Writing to his wife in Westmoreland, New Hampshire, Private Elisha Douglass of the Ninth New Hampshire, related some events after the battle: "Thare are a good many troops going back from Noxville women and children very poorly dressed of the children barefooted and bareheaded you don't know anything about the misery this war has caused." On May 12, 1864, Private Douglass died of wounds sustained at the Battle of Spotsylvania.[57]

The Federals were fortunate in that their loss for the attack on Fort Sanders was about a hundred, only twenty of those dying in defense of the fort. Actual Confederate losses came to about eight hundred with two hundred of those being captured. The Eleventh New Hampshire Regiment suffered one combat death during the siege. Private John M. Smith of Raymond was killed on November 22 in a skirmish between picket lines. Because the regiments had not been supplied in nearly five months, uniforms were in rags, and shoes were in pieces. Like Valley Forge, the men were leaving bloody tracks in the snow until one creative soldier found a supply of green hides, and the regiment was able to construct crude moccasins. This marked the last campaign for New Hampshire soldiers in 1863.[58] The men now began working on their winter quarters and would time to reflect on the past year and what would lie ahead for them. "I shall live I guess to come home & we will have a good time when I do," Private William P. Mason of Canterbury predicted to his mother from his camp at Point Lookout. The Twelfth New Hampshire. "Who merits the glory but God. Is prosperus & will prosper us & a greater & mightier nation will arise from our ashes than America has ever yet been."[59]

The year 1863 ended on a sad note for the men of the Third New Hampshire. Born in St. John, New Brunswick, Private John Kendall of Company G had signed on with the Third New Hampshire as a substitute for Plainfield. In early December, Kendall was caught in the act of desertion. Captain Towle of the Fourth New Hampshire served on his board of court-martial and recounted how Kendall came down from New Hampshire with other bounty men and promptly attempted to desert. Kendall stripped off his clothes and swam to James Island from Morris Island is the testimony. Members of the Ninth Maine later spotted him. When he was summoned, he told them a fantastic tale that he was really an English captain of a blockade runner. The soldiers escorted him to Brigadier General Alfred H. Terry, and Kendall told him the same story, complete with military information about Charleston's defenses. While Terry decided what he wanted to do with Kendall, he had him put in the provost marshal's guardhouse. Kendall's luck ran out when he was recognized by several soldiers of the Third

New Hampshire, who were not only on guard duty at the Provost Marshal's post but had also made the trip from New Hampshire with him. The court-martial found Kendall guilty and sentenced him to be shot. On the day of the execution, the entire army on Morris Island turned out to witness the death of the deserter. Great importance was placed on the ritual of execution to teach the soldiers the serious consequences of desertion. Kendall appeared in an open wagon sitting on the coffin he would be buried in. The procession made its way down to the beach, where all ten thousand soldiers and the firing squad were formed in an open square. The firing squad was composed of twelve men, nine of whom had live rounds in their muskets, three had blanks. None knew who had the loaded muskets so they would not know if theirs was a bullet that struck the deserter. As the wagon passed in front of the Third New Hampshire, Kendall cried out for mercy but was met by stony silence.[60]

Adjutant of the Third New Hampshire Elbridge Copp was on hand to witness the execution. In the last moments of the deserter's life, Copp said, "The prisoner's coat and cap removed, then blindfolded and made to kneel on his coffin, facing inward, he keeping up the same indifference to his fate to the last. The sword of the Lieutenant then descends, quickly followed by the sharp report of the rifles, the man pitches forward over his coffin in instant death. The whole army was then marched past the body where it lay upon the beach as it fell, and back to their several camps."[61]

In Louisiana the Eighth New Hampshire regiment was being converted to cavalry in expectation of the coming Red River Campaign. Hereafter known unofficially as the Second New Hampshire Cavalry, not every one of its members was happy about the change. To Sergeant Claude Goings, it represented more work and was not the easy ride that many of the men thought it would be. "It is true that we shall not have to walk so much," said Goings, "but will have to take so much care of our horses that it cannot be much easier for us. . . . This will be hard on an old Regt. whose time is more than half out."[62]

At the end of December the boys from New Hampshire, who were spread out in camps from Virginia to Louisiana, sat down to their Christmas dinners. The men aboard the USS *Kearsarge* then sailing off the coast of France enjoyed a dinner of roast goose and condiments. The Confederates were lucky if they had bread and a little bacon.[63]

As the old year ended, the New Hampshire soldiers reminisced about the loss of many friends and comrades. The Southern armies had been defeated on many battlefields. The grinding pessimism at the end of 1862 was replaced at the end of 1863 by guarded optimism, guarded because the veteran New Hampshire men knew that many months of hard fighting were ahead.

"He did all in his power
to rally his command"

CHAPTER 8

January 1864 to April 1864

I hear even now the infinite fierce chorus,
the cries of agony, the endless groan,
which, through the ages that have gone before us,
in long reverberations reach our own.

Henry Wadsworth Longfellow,
"The Arsenal at Springfield," 1912

By January 1, the boredom of camp life had permeated all the theaters of war. In South Carolina, Captain George W. Towle complained in his journal, "On the 3rd, my rival for Major of 4th NH was very drunk, Capt. Sawyer of Dover. . . . Last night the 4th NH band serenaded Gen. Stevenson who is sick and expects to go North. The command of the brigade now devolves on Col. Bell 4th NH and one more incompetent can scarcely be found."[1]

While Captain Towle was trying to cope with his personal problems, a significant event was transpiring on Morris Island. Fourth New Hampshire Private Samuel Wilkinson's brief entry in his diary for January 12, 1864 was, "The Good old Flag the Stars and Stripes was raised on Fort Strong [formerly Wagner] at 1 oclock to day a Salute of 41 Guns was fired and our Band was present."[2]

Corporal Horace H. Adams of the Tenth New Hampshire wrote home to his brother in Portsmouth about camp life in Virginia, the weather, and his predications for 1864: "Everything is Quiet, nothing to Disturb the monotony of camp Life The weather continues very good for this time of year. Some days we go in our Shirt sleeves. William it is now 1864 and we can begin to think about coming home but we have got Some time before us Yet. I think next Summer that we Shall have to catch it pretty Hard but we have got to take it as it comes hot or cold."[3]

Daniel Eldredge of the Third New Hampshire, upon recuperating from his wounds in New Hampshire, was commissioned a second lieutenant on the recommendation of Colonel John Henry Jackson to Governor Joseph Albee Gilmore. Eldredge's first duty upon reporting was to escort Colonel Jackson and a large group of recruits for the Fourth and Seventh New Hampshire, as well as for the Fifty-fourth and Fifty-fifth Massachusetts colored regiments, back to South Carolina. Second Lieutenant Eldredge remembered in his journal that the ship contained a mix of black, white, army and navy passengers. Although the passage went well for those on the upper decks, Eldredge recorded that because of the presence of liquor, there were several disputes and disagreements among the whites and blacks on the lower decks.[4]

The substitutes intended for the Seventh New Hampshire were accompanied south by Lieutenant Eldredge and arrived in camp on January 21. The official historian of the Seventh New Hampshire commented on the reliability of these new men by saying they were "no improvement upon those who had heretofore joined us. They were evenly distributed among the different companies, and quite a number were invariably in the guard-house."[5] These substitutes coupled with several unfortunate events and faulty command decisions would contribute to disaster for the Seventh New Hampshire within a month.

In the end of 1863, Abraham Lincoln announced a second proclamation. Known as the Proclamation of Amnesty and Reconstruction, Lincoln hoped to work in concert with Unionist groups in the various Southern states and start bringing them back into the United States. By the end of 1863, the only seceded state that remotely appeared to be ready for this step was Florida. It was perceived by the authorities in Washington, along with some overly optimistic Unionists in Florida, that this operation could be carried out with a minimum of risk. The dividends of such an operation could be enormous. Florida had become the commissary of the Confederacy. It provided large amounts of beef, lumber, turpentine, and cotton. Florida also had the weakest defenses and had been successfully blockaded. The year 1864 was an election year, and restoring a seceded state, especially one with so many raw materials, would go a long way toward bolstering up Lincoln's sagging chances at reelection.[6]

On February 4, 1864, orders were received by Brigadier General Truman Seymour, then in command at Hilton Head, South Carolina, to take certain regiments from his command and proceed to St. Helena Island, South Carolina. Included in the fourteen units selected were the Seventh New Hampshire, Seventh Connecticut, and the Fifty-fourth Massachusetts. The expedition needed to be highly mobile, so the men were told to pack light and take only sixty rounds of ammunition.[7] The Seventh New Hampshire and her sister regiment, the Seventh Connecticut, boarded the steamer *Ben Deford* on February 5 for their journey south. These two regiments spent so much time together in action that they referred to themselves as the Seventy-seventh New England Regiment.[8] The expedition proceeded up the St John's River without incident on February 9. The men, who had little to do except admire the countryside, were deeply impressed by their surroundings on their trip upriver to Jacksonville. The city was entered, and Seymour's force of fifty-five hundred men and sixteen cannon headed west toward Lake City on February 11.[9] In December 1863, the Seventh New Hampshire had received Spencer repeating rifles in the hope that they would become a mounted regiment like the Eighth New Hampshire. By the time that the regiment left for the expedition to Florida, they had not been supplied with horses, but they took their fine carbines with them.

In a decision that would have a serious impact on the coming battle, Seymour ordered that half of the Seventh New Hampshire had to exchange their rifles with the Fortieth Massachusetts. This regiment was already mounted but had old and out-of-date Springfield rifles. A witness to this exchange wrote to the *Boston Journal* in February 1864 as to why this was a bad decision: "Our men were obliged to exchange their favorite pieces for the old guns of that regiment [the Fortieth Massachusetts], many of which were so damaged as to be perfectly useless. I counted more than twenty in our company that were entirely useless. Many of them had no ramrods and others no locks. It should be stated that they had no bayonets, that most important part of the weapon, having been thrown away by the mounted men as useless and cumbersome."[10]

The Seventh New Hampshire was already laboring under the disadvantage of having three hundred raw recruits in its ranks. Having never seen battle, these men were not the volunteers of 1862 bursting with patriotic enthusiasm but a polyglot of substitutes and bounty men from Canada and Germany, the majority of whom would rather have been anywhere else on Earth than going somewhere they might get shot.

Colonel Joseph Hawley of the Seventh Connecticut was made commander of the brigade in which the Seventh New Hampshire was serving. When the order came down to exchange rifles with the Fortieth Massachusetts, Hawley could have effected that exchange with his regiment, the Seventh Connecticut, but he made the Seventh New Hampshire give up its rifles instead. The seeds of ill will between Hawley and Colonel Joseph C. Abbott of the Seventh New Hampshire had already been sown before the battle began.[11] The exchange of rifles with the Fortieth Massachusetts took place on February 13 near the town of Sanderson in Florida. Seymour's force was now fifty miles from Jacksonville and penetrating deeper into the interior of northern Florida. The expedition that was supposed to land and move into Florida with great secrecy had not been a secret since before it landed. Confederate coast watchers in South Carolina spotted the flotilla of ships heading south and alerted General Pierre Gustave Toutant Beauregard's headquarters. He knew an invasion was coming but did not know where. Beauregard immediately began to detach and divert Confederate regiments to the southern part of Georgia. Before long every move of Seymour's force had been observed, and on February 19, a force of almost equal size gathered just east of Olustee under the command of Brigadier General Joseph Finegan. Finegan carefully positioned his two brigades of Georgia and Florida regiments astride the rail line with impassable swamps on both flanks. The Federals would have to attack in the center on a narrow front.[12]

The Battle of Olustee, or Ocean Pond as the Confederates knew it, began on February 20 when two companies of the Seventh Connecticut, which had been thrown forward as skirmishers, made contact with a unit of Confederate cavalry. The Rebel horsemen immediately fell back three miles toward Olustee and their prepared positions. Seymour moved his men forward, and when it was reported that a large number of the enemy was ahead, he brought up a battery to probe the position. The return fire of the Confederates promptly answered the union artillery. Fighting intensified around three o'clock when Seymour brought up the rest of the Seventh Connecticut. The regiment still retained its carbines and was able to do good work against Brigadier General Alfred H. Colquitt's Georgians until the center of the Seventh Connecticut became too extended to the front and had to be withdrawn.[13]

Just as the Connecticut men fell back, the reinforcements that Colquitt had asked for arrived. He had the Sixth, Sixty-fourth, and Twenty-eighth Georgia form on the north side of the railroad and the Nineteenth Georgia on the south side. Seeing this deployment, Seymour had Hawley bring up the rest of his brigade that included the Seventh New Hampshire. The New Hampshire men moved up to support a battery, and then disaster struck. To this day historians are still trying to understand what made the Seventh New Hampshire Regiment totally disintegrate under fire and flee for the rear. The answer most likely lies in a combination of variables involving Colonel Abbott, Colonel Hawley, the newly arrived substitutes in the Seventh New Hampshire, and the bad rifles that the regiment had been given.

In his report Colonel Hawley stated that his brigade "met the skirmishers of the 7th Connecticut falling back, firing before the enemy, who showed, I judge, two battalions in line. I distinctly ordered the 7th New Hampshire to deploy on the eighth company, which would have brought the left of the line near the pond. Somebody must have misunderstood the order, for a portion of the regiment was going wrong, when myself, staff and Colonel Abbott repeated it vigorously, but vainly. All semblance of organization was lost in a few moments, save with about one company which faced the enemy and opened fire. The remainder constantly drifted back, suffering from the fire which a few moments' decision and energy would have checked if not suppressed." Hawley accused Abbott indirectly of not doing enough to rally the broken ranks, although elsewhere in his lengthy report he praised Abbott: "He did all in his power to rally his command."[14]

Abbott may have done everything he could, but the origins of the panicked retreat of the Seventh New Hampshire were in the initial deployment and not what was done afterward. In Abbott's report to Hawley, he stated, "The order was given by myself to deploy upon the first company and the deployment commenced. At this moment I was informed by yourself that the deployment was not as you intended, and I at once commanded, 'Halt; front.' But the fire of the enemy had now become very severe."[15] Herein lies the first mistake. Abbott should have known that his deployment would mean that the left flank of his regiment would have been in the air rather than firmly anchored on the pond as Hawley directed.[16]

Chaos now reigned on that part of the field, and only about one hundred men of the Seventh remained to exchange fire with the Confederates; the rest had fled for the rear. The unidentified correspondent who wrote to the *Boston Journal* contributes to understanding the problem. Referring to the faulty weapons, he stated, "It is very easy to imagine how any men must feel when ordered up in front of the enemy with no weapon in his hand. It would be very natural for him to feel useless in the struggle, and self-preservation would occur to him very soon. His reasoning would be, I am of no use, and why should I stand here for the sole purpose of being shot?"[17]

For one half hour after the Seventh New Hampshire fell apart, its officer tried desperately to rally it. While the Seventh was being reformed, Brigadier General William B. Barton's brigade of New York regiments was brought forward to plug the gap. The brigade formed on the right of the Seventh Connecticut. The Georgians tried desperately to flank this new brigade and slowly pushed them back. Finally, after three hours of continuous combat, the Confederates were running low on their ammunition. With the appearance of Colonel James Montgomery's brigade and the Fifty-fourth Massachusetts, it appeared as though the tide of the battle would turn.[18] Just as the Federals began to move forward, Colquitt received fresh reenforcements and pushed the Federals back again. Sporadic fighting went on until dark, and then Seymour withdrew his force. The Federals had lost 203 killed, over 1,000 wounded, and 500 missing. Of those who were posted missing, 184 were from the Seventh New Hampshire who had been deployed too close to the Confederate line. It has been documented that of that number, 112 were taken to Andersonville Prison, and 43 of them died from causes such as chronic diarrhea and scurvy. The Confederates lost 934 killed and wounded in the battle.[19] William Nulty in his book *Confederate Florida* had this to say about the Seventh New Hampshire at the Battle of Olustee: "To have then attempted to deploy them too close to the enemy's lines while under fire after their leaders had given them conflicting orders borders on the criminal. A crucial stage of the battle was the breaking of the 7th New Hampshire, a setback which could have been prevented."[20]

Years after the battle, Colonel (then Brevet Major General) Hawley wrote, "Col. Abbott of the 7th N.H. misunderstood my orders for deployment. I attempted to correct it. The regiment broke but they reformed and did excellent service on our right flank."[21]

In April 1864 Lieutenant Daniel Eldredge of the Third New Hampshire was part of a detachment that was assigned temporarily to the Seventh New Hampshire. Eldredge described this experience as unfortunate: "I say unfortunate because of the necessity to drill under the Col. of the 7th [Abbott] and I felt equally fortunate that I did not belong to the regiment." Eldredge went on to say that Abbott would often use abusive language and swear at his men. This was one more indication that this was not the Seventh New Hampshire commanded by Colonel Halimand Sumner Putnam during the better days it spent at Fort Jefferson on the Dry Tortugas.[22] Lieutenant Charles H. Farley had fought side by side with Colonel Putnam until he fell at Fort Wagner. A Confederate bullet tore through Farley's coat, and one was deflected by his pocket Bible. He escaped injury and retreated with the remnants of the Seventh New Hampshire. In the Battle of Olustee, Farley was mortally wounded early in the battle and was on the ground until the advancing Confederates captured him. They later carried him back to Lake City, Florida, for treatment. Two women, formerly from New Hampshire, took him from the hospital to their home. With the help of a Confederate army surgeon, they tried to heal him, but Farley died from his wounds on February 24. He was buried in a cemetery in Lake City but was later disinterred and his body brought home to Hollis. The Reverend Day of Hollis said at Farley's memorial service that he "was calm, self possessed and trustful in that Providence in which he had been taught to believe. . . . His courage was never doubted."[23]

One of the most curious stories to come out of the Olustee campaign was the story of a substitute from Company D of the Seventh New Hampshire named James Flynn. a forty-year-old tailor who lived in New York City. When the war began, his fifteen-year-old son ran off and joined the army. Flynn, in pursuit of his son, joined up also, briefly served with a New York cavalry unit, and was discharged. Flynn then made his way to Concord, New Hampshire, but by then for unknown reasons had changed his name to Arthur Bailey. In another curious twist, Flynn, (then Bailey) joined the Seventh New Hampshire in October 1863 under the name of a distant Irish relative named John Hill.[24] Flynn (as Hill) made his way to the Seventh New Hampshire and fought at the Battle of Olustee. The regimental history of the Seventh New Hampshire lists Hill as being killed in action at Olustee. This is not accurate, because there is a surviving letter from James Flynn to his wife dated March 30, 1864, posted from Tallahassee. Flynn (Hill) was wounded and become a prisoner at Olustee. He was taken with the other Seventh New Hampshire prisoners to Andersonville or Savannah. Descendants of the family said they believe that he might have escaped, but he was never heard from again.[25] In the official list of Union soldiers buried at

Andersonville, the New Hampshire section records no death or grave number for a James Flynn or John Hill. However, grave number 3346 is assigned to A. Bailey, Company C Seventh New Hampshire. Bailey is cataloged as dying on July 15, 1864 from diarrhea.[26] There is no mention of an A. Bailey in either the regimental history of the Seventh New Hampshire or the official register for New Hampshire soldiers. There was a Charles Bailey in the Seventh New Hampshire, but he had been captured in July 1863 at Fort Wagner and was already dead when the Battle of Olustee was fought. Chances are very good that Private James Flynn was buried under the name of Bailey and is buried in the cemetery at Andersonville.[27]

While many critics have scrutinized the Battle of Olustee and laid the blame for a Federal defeat at the feet of either Colonel Abbott of the Seventh New Hampshire or Colonel Hawley, the brigade commander, there are those who placed the blame higher. Captain Towle of the Fourth New Hampshire felt the blame belonged with Truman Seymour. Towle wrote on February 24, 1864, "We are getting vague and uncertain reports as to Seymour's defeat in Florida. He was 'unlucky' again of course. [Towle refers to when Seymour was in command of the assaults on Fort Wagner.] It is said he was advancing with no skirmishers out. In this way Seymour ran into the enemies position who at the proper time opened fire on the column obliquely in flank. The 7th NH suffered most and it is said did not stand up well."[28] The reasons why the Seventh New Hampshire did not stand up well were because of conflicting command decisions, three hundred recruits who had not been tested in battle, and half of the regiment having substandard or completely useless weapons.

In the camp of the Second Corps, feverish preparations were underway in the end of February for a gala celebration and military ball. Captain Andrew Young recounted to his wife Susan in a letter that all the Dover, New Hampshire, luminaries, Washington elite, and military brass that were in attendance: "I have been to Washington & brought up Mrs. Hale [U.S. senator John Parker Hale's wife] & the girls & they are here now. Also Captain Hall & Sarah Low & Miss Lowell of Boston. The Hales came up Saturday. The great Ball came off Monday night. . . . All the Generals of this army, the vice president, a large number of senators & Representatives in Congress several governors of States & their families was present. Genl. Warren commanding the Corps lead the first dance with Mrs. Hale & Genl. Meade took her to the supper table. Sarah came down to examine the Hospital Dept. I have shown her everything. Especially the Ball. Today Genl. Meade reviewed our corps for the benefit of the Ladies."[29]

Writing several days later, Sarah Low left a much more detailed account of her trip to the battlefront and the big dance. After leaving Armory Square Hospital in Washington, she remembered that it took six hours for them to make the trip by train from Washington to Brandy Station and then by horse to the Second

Corps headquarters. Her description of the surrounding countryside is particularly vivid: "On we went through fenceless country that would have seemed an uninteresting plain if it had not been for the associations connected with it. . . . We saw an unburied horse lying on the ground and sometimes a half eaten one."

Upon arrival at the camp they were met by Captain Andrew Young and Colonel Batchelder who made their quarters available for the visiting ladies. Sarah described where the gala ball took place: "The hall was decorated with regimental flags. Some of which were in shreds and some brilliant new ones belonging to regiments just returned from furlough. There are very few line officers here, they are most all generals with their staffs. General Meade, General Berry and Generals Sedgewick, Wright, Humphreys and Webb. General Kilpatrick is as ill looking a man as I ever saw. We watched a long conversation between Meade and Kilpatrick as they stood apart from all others. They were evidently describing movements." The day after the ball, Sarah, her party, and her escorts went to the corps hospital and were reasonably impressed: "The next day Miss Lowell, Lucy, Captain Young, Mr. Hall and I accompanied by the medical director of the corps went to visit the Corps hospital. They could take such good care of the men that they had not sent up those wounded at Mine Run 2 or 3 weeks ago."[30]

The Lucy that Sarah refers to is the daughter of Senator Hale of Dover. There is strong speculation that Lucy Hale was the girlfriend, if not the unannounced fiancée, of John Wilkes Booth. As Booth lay dying from his gunshot wound in the yard of the Garrett Farm, history records him as looking at his hands and saying, "Useless, useless." There are those who speculate that he might have been saying, "Lucy, Lucy."

Sarah left the hospital, then attended the grand review conducted by General George Gordon Meade, and made the amusing observation, "Vice President [Hannibal] Hamlin seemed to be taking a nap on his horse. We were very much entertained with his dancing the night before." Sarah and her party returned to Washington the next day.[31]

As the weather turned warmer in Washington and the soldiers prepared themselves for a new campaign, the men of the Fourth New Hampshire stationed at Beaufort, South Carolina, were already off on another raid. The year 1864 was a leap year, and Principal Musician Elias A. Bryant of Francestown wrote home to his sister on February 29 about their latest expedition: "We have just returned from a scout and expedition. . . . We were ordered down to Hilton Head . . . then kept on down to Fort Pulaski and ran up one of the rivers to within eight miles of Savannah and landed on White Marsh Island."[32]

The Eighty-fifth Pennsylvania Regiment accompanied the Fourth New Hampshire on this adventure and were detailed to land on the back of the island to cut off any Confederate reinforcements from arriving from Savannah. They were unsuccessful, and, consequently, the Fourth New Hampshire came under severe fire from several batteries. The accompanying Federal batteries returned the fire, and the Confederates withdrew, not knowing the landing party was so small.[33] Private Samuel Wilkinson in his unique prose described the action as it unfolded: "Just as the first Boat got near the shore about fifty Rebel Pickets arose and fired a volley at the Boat and skedadelled. The men landed as fast as posable and started after them. The Rebs opened with 2 pieces of Artilery our Forces followed them acrost the Island and took 17 Prisoners and lost one Lieutenant. About half our Regt. had got landed when we got orders to leave the Island."[34] Bryant gives the reason why the Fourth New Hampshire needed to leave so quickly: "They had lots of men and we could hear the cars as they came in with more; kept rushing them in." The Fourth New Hampshire was ordered to Jacksonville to reinforce Seymour's force falling back from its defeat at Olustee. The regiment was then safely returned to Beaufort by the end of the month.[35]

Captain George F. Towle of the Fourth New Hampshire, who did not seem to have a good opinion about many people, made this sarcastic remark in his journal for the next to the last day of February: "Admiral Dahlgren has gone North. We can spare him now and ever more. I suppose he wants to go back to Washington to experiment blowing putty through a tube. It is all he is fit for."[36]

The beginning of 1864 also marked the end of the three-year term of service for the Third and Fourth New Hampshire regiments. From January 1 to March 1 in the Third New Hampshire, 270 men reenlisted and so were entitled to a thirty-day furlough. Colonel Jackson, compelled to resign because of ill health, had turned over command of the Third New Hampshire to Major Josiah I. Plimpton of Milford. Almost four hundred men in the Fourth New Hampshire reenlisted and started packing their bags in early March. The two New Hampshire regiments would ship out together for the trip home.[37] Captain Towle of the Fourth New Hampshire noted the departure of the two regiments: "The reenlisted veterans of the 3rd and 4th NH have gone north on furlough by the same boat. The 3rd unarmed, 270 men and the 4th with 400 taking their arms aboard. This made some chaffing between the two regiments."[38]

One reason for the Third New Hampshire veterans leaving unarmed was that on March 1, it was changed to a mounted regiment. The unit was then known as the Third New Hampshire Mounted Infantry. Horses arrived for the regiment on March 7, and the two flanking companies were issued Spencer repeating rifles. The unit served briefly in the Jacksonville area until ordered to Gloucester, Virginia, in mid-April. There they were reunited with the veterans returning from furlough and were converted back to foot soldiers. At the same time, the remainder of the Fourth New Hampshire under Lieutenant Colonel Jeremiah D. Drew was ordered to Gloucester, Virginia, as well. They, too were met by the returning veterans of the regiment and became part of the First Brigade, Third Division, under Brigadier General Adelbert Ames. Both of these New Hampshire regiments were now part of Major General Ben Butler's Tenth Army Corps.[39]

In March 1864 a variety of strange stories appeared in the newspapers in New Hampshire about substitutes and deserters. A soldier in the Sixth New Hampshire complained to the *Rochester Courier,* "We have lost about 175 or 200 of our new recruits. Reckoning at about what they cost we call it only about $200,000. We have a few of them in prison but my opinion is that a large majority of them ought to have been there and kept there instead of being sent out here. Most of the officers and men look on it as an insult to have such men sent here."[40] A singular and fascinating story is the account of Private Horace B. Mandeville of the Fourteenth New Hampshire. Born in Liverpool, England, Mandeville was a substitute who enlisted for the town of Pittsfield. On a transport from Boston to Fort Monroe, Mandeville was overheard saying that all of "his friends were in the Southern Army and that he gloried in them, and never intended to fire a gun for the d——n Abolitionist Government and that he would be in the Southern Army only it paid much better being a substitute in the Northern Army." Mandeville's superiors were satisfied that this kind of talk was seditious so he was tried and convicted on that charge and put in prison in Albany, New York, doing hard labor for five years.[41]

A writer on the staff of the *Rochester Courier* made this ironic prediction that appeared in the March 25 edition: "When this cruel war is over and the student of history carefully sits down in future years to read its stirring tales, he will, perhaps, be surprised at the frequent changes of military commanders, especially in the Department of the East."[42]

Military activity in Virginia was beginning to increase in the first part of March 1864. The multitude of skirmishes that New Hampshire troops found themselves in are too numerous to document. Private Adams of the Tenth New Hampshire described a skirmish near Julian's Creek that his regiment was involved in along with the Ninth New Jersey and Fifth Pennsylvania Cavalry: "There was two or three wounded and one Killed belonging to the 9th N Jersey. None from our Regiment. . . . Some of the 9th New Jersey that was brought in wounded, was asked if our regiment was there. he said yes and that they were doing well he said there was a Grey-Headed man out thar. He meant Towle [George W. Towle, father of Captain George F. Towle of the Fourth New Hampshire] and that he was Singing out two to them to deploy as Scermishers. And that he was putting them through the mill. He can risk old members anywhere, but you Know there is a Great many Subs. among them. So it makes it bad for the old members but I would risk old Georgy with the Regiment anywhere."[43]

The First New Hampshire Cavalry was mustered into the service of the United States but could trace its origins back to the beginning of the war. In the fall of 1861, the War Department ordered the six New England states to raise a cavalry regiment that would be known as the First New England Cavalry. Each state was to provide two companies for a total of twelve. The cavalry arm of service soon became very popular, and all the states except Rhode Island and Vermont were able to raise cavalry regiments of their own. Rhode Island was able to raise eight companies and New Hampshire four, which combined to become the First New England. Major David B. Nelson of Manchester commanded the four companies of New Hampshire troopers.[44]

The First New England was quartered in Pawtucket, Rhode Island, and was ordered to Washington in March 1862. Soon after their arrival, the name of the regiment was changed to the First Rhode Island Cavalry. This caused a great deal of concern among the New Hampshire companies, who felt that they had no identity and no ties to their home state. The four New Hampshire units were known as the New Hampshire Battalion and while in service as the First Rhode Island, saw action from Front Royal in 1862 to Gettysburg in 1863. The New Hampshire Battalion lost fifteen men while in the First Rhode Island.[45]

In January 1864 these four New Hampshire companies were permanently detached and used as the core of the First New Hampshire Cavalry. The First New Hampshire fought at White Oak Swamp in Virginia in June 1864, losing eight men killed. The regiment was mustered out in July 1865, having lost a total of twenty-three men killed in battle. The unit also lost fifty-three men who died in Confederate prisoner-of-war camps.[46]

One of the unique units to be raised during the war was the Dartmouth Cavalry, which formed Company B, Seventh Squadron of the Rhode Island Volunteer Cavalry. The company was composed almost entirely of college men from Dartmouth College in New Hampshire and Norwich University in Vermont, with also several from Bowdoin, Williams, and Amherst colleges. The unit was mustered into service in July 1862 and mustered out in October of the same year. The Dartmouth Cavalry operated mostly in the lower Shenandoah Valley near Winchester and Harpers Ferry, suffering only one death in its term of service.[47]

Preparations were being made in the Army of the Potomac for the coming spring campaign. In the Second Corps headquarters, Andrew Young of Dover wrote to his wife about his quartermaster's duties: "There are some indications of an early campaign. U. S. Grant is coming next Tuesday. . . . I took an account of stock yesterday and found I had 138 mules—37 horses 32 teamsters, 7 hostelers 2 forage masters—2 clerks, 4 negroes, 5 cats 2 dogs 7 hens & a crower—all in good condition and ready to march."[48]

The winter had been mild in and around Point Lookout, Maryland, and the prospects for escaping winter were very good. Then, just as now, nature intervened, and everything was changed. A severe winter storm hit the Chesapeake Bay on the afternoon and evening of March 22. Gusting winds blew the heavy, wet snow into and against the tents of the Second and Twelfth New Hampshire regiments. The men were thoroughly surprised by this sneak attack by Old Man Winter that deposited five- and six-foot drifts of snow in their midst.[49] The chaplain of the Second New Hampshire set the stage for "the skirmish": "The great snowstorm of March 23, 1864 and the hotly contested snowball battle the next day between the 2nd and 12th regiments, which lasted for hours and resulted in bruised limbs and blackened eyes, was another episode to which reference will not soon cease."[50] The official historian of the Second New Hampshire who was present for the great "battle" describes how it began: "Three or four men from each regiment got to pitching snow at each other in play; others joined in, and in a little while a battle royal was on. Tents were wrecked, bones broken . . . and teeth knocked out—all in fun." The historian was impartial enough to recognize that the Twelfth New Hampshire won the snowball battle, but he included that the Second performed some brilliant flanking maneuvers.[51]

In the beginning of April 1864, New Hampshire troops were scattered all the way from Concord, New Hampshire, to Louisiana. The coming spring campaign meant that the armies would once again begin to gather. The Second, Fifth, and Twelfth New Hampshire regiments that were on duty at Point Lookout, prepared to rejoin the Army of the Potomac in northern Virginia, north of the Rapidan River. The reenlisted veterans of the Third and Fourth New Hampshire at home on furlough left to join the remainder of their regiments, also headed for Virginia from Florida and South Carolina. The Eighth New Hampshire was serving in Nathaniel Banks's Red River Campaign around New Orleans. The Ninth New Hampshire packed up from its camp in Kentucky and headed east. The Tenth and Thirteenth New Hampshire regiments were already in Portsmouth, Virginia, while the Eleventh New Hampshire, still outside Knoxville, Tennessee, started to make its way toward Virginia, also. The Fourteenth New Hampshire was the only New Hampshire regiment sent away from Washington. It was scheduled for a brief tour of duty in Louisiana.[52] The logistics of Union regiments was little changed from previous years of the war. This year there was one significant difference: Grant.

Ulysses S. Grant was made General in Chief of the Armies of the United States in March 1864 and was in charge of supervising the overall strategy of the war. Although the Army of the Potomac was under the command of Meade, Grant traveled with it and directed the movement of the armies from there. After a long succession of army commanders had tried and failed with their strategy of capturing Richmond, Virginia, Grant believed that General Robert E. Lee's army—not Richmond—was the key to Union victory. His strategy for 1864 would reflect this radical change of thought.

Grant intended to hit the Confederates in several places at once. He hoped by launching a four-pronged attack that he could pin down and thereby outmaneuver his opponents in the field. The Army of the Potomac was to cross the

Rapidan River and move through the Wilderness against Lee, while Butler and his Army of the James would threaten Richmond from the south. General William Tecumseh Sherman was slated to invade Georgia, and Major General Phil Sheridan was to occupy the Shenandoah Valley and prevent any men or supplies from there reaching the Army of Northern Virginia.[53]

On April 7 the Second New Hampshire left Point Lookout for its new camp at Yorktown, Virginia. This was the second campaign to begin in this location for the veteran regiment. Unlike the first time they arrived here, when the regiment was new and full of fresh volunteers, the regiments suffered one hundred desertions by the new substitutes. Most of these were rounded up and held for trial. In 1864 desertion had reached epidemic proportions. Something had to done, so several cases were chosen, and these men were made examples of.[54]

Substitutes Henry Holt and John Egin, both of the Second New Hampshire and both from England, were tried and sentenced to death. The scene of execution was a large, open square with the condemned men's regiment directly in front of the spot where they would be shot, and the remainder of the troops surrounded them. A source of extreme shame for the veterans of the Second New Hampshire was that armed soldiers surrounded the men in the Second, and a cannon was trained on the regiment in case anyone decided to desert during the execution. The condemned men rode into the square on top of their coffins. The sentence was read, the men blindfolded, and then they were shot. The men of the Second New Hampshire were made to walk past the bullet-riddled, lifeless bodies, and proceed back to their camp.[55]

Several days later, on April 29, this entire scene was repeated in Williamsburg, Virginia, when two more Second New Hampshire substitutes were tried and shot. James Scott of Scotland and Owen McDonough of England were caught outside the Union lines trying to paddle up the Chesapeake Bay. Regimental chaplain John Wesley Adams remembered that before the sentence was carried out, he told Scott to "forget what is about you now, and look only to Jesus and all will be well." The two men thanked Adams for ministering to them, and they shook hands. Again, the heads were covered, the commander's sword went down, and the rifles went off. McDonough and Scott fell backward into their coffins, and as Adams said, "The stern penalty of military law was paid."[56]

On April 16, while a portion of the Third New Hampshire was still in Jacksonville, Florida, Private Alphonso Osborn recorded in his diary that Company F Lieutenant Henry Miller was shot while trying to desert to the enemy. Actually, Private Henry Miller, a substitute from Canada, had deserted and was brought back and shot later.[57]

It was determined by the Lincoln administration early in 1864 that France might intervene in Mexico and possibly threaten Texas. To prevent this eventuality, the War Department authorized a second Red River campaign for the dual purpose of taking Shreveport and occupying a portion of southeast Texas. Major General Nathaniel P. Banks was the senior commander in that theater of operations and was therefore selected to lead the invasion.[58] The overall plan was for Banks to take his army up the Red River from Alexandria, Louisiana, with Admiral David D. Porter's gunboats supplying cover from the river. The Eighth New Hampshire, which was still mounted, supplied six hundred men armed with Sharpe's rifles. Reaching Alexandria on March 19, the Eighth New Hampshire joined with regiments sent down from Vicksburg by Sherman. The whole force of twenty-six thousand was coordinated and ready to start up the Red River by the end of March.[59]

The Eighth New Hampshire (Second New Hampshire Cavalry) had been lightly skirmishing with the Confederates for the past week and for the first week of April as the expedition moved forward. The Confederates gave ground continuously until Banks reached Mansfield, or Sabine's Crossroads, on April 8. Here the Confederates under Major General Richard Taylor had dug in and had a very strong defense.

The Eighth was sent around the right flank to protect the main body of the Union advance. Instead, it ran into a heavily defended position and held for two hours until reinforcements and a fresh supply of ammunition could be brought up. A Confederate counterattack routed the Union cavalry and pushed it back in a disorganized withdrawal that disrupted the sparse formations of infantry that were coming to its aid. The retreat soon became general and the defeat total. Banks lost a total of twenty-two hundred men killed, wounded, or captured. As in the Shenandoah in 1862, he lost scores of wagons full of supplies, ordnance, and, most precious of all, hundreds of prisoners. Forty-seven of those prisoners came from the Eighth New Hampshire, including Captain Dana W. King of Nashua. King was also wounded and, with the rest of his fellow captives, was taken to the Confederate prisoner-of-war camp at Tyler, Texas. He stayed there until he was exchanged in October 1864.[60]

Private Abraham Lefebre of Nashua was one of five New Hampshire cavalrymen killed that day at Sabine's Crossroads. Taylor had crushed and routed two full divisions of Banks's men with only half of the force that Banks had in the field. The Confederate drive and pursuit were halted the next day at Pleasant Hill, but the retreat of Banks's defeated army continued.[61]   .

Sergeant Claude Goings of New London remembered the terrible slaughter over those two days in April: "Soldiers say who help Bury the Dead that a Person might for half a mile on one Part of theis line walk on Dead Bodies and not touch the ground. Our army was so much cut up by the first Days fight that it was obliged to retreat here under cover of the gunboats."[62] Conditions worsened during the retreat, and Corporal Jacob F. Chandler wrote home to Concord that they had been reduced to eating "raw corn on the cob when we could get it. I saw a twenty-dollar bill offered for one half hard-tack which had been run over in the road and picked out of a wheel rut. It warn't for sale."[63]

The Red River Campaign had been a disaster for Banks, and the War Department removed him from command. He left the army soon after and served six terms as a U.S. representative from Massachusetts.[64]

Writing home from Grand Ecore on April 18, Corporal Chandler described the compliment paid to the Eighth New Hampshire/Second New Hampshire Cavalry by outgoing Fourth Brigade commander Brigadier General Nathan Dudley: "Our General Dudley made a big farewell speech to us last night, and gave the regiment a good deal of praise. He said that if it had not been for the 2nd N.H. his brigade would have been taken prisoners, and if it had not been for his brigade, the whole of Banks' army would have been destroyed."[65]

About two weeks later, Dover nurse Sarah Low had the opportunity to meet President Lincoln. She recorded in her diary on April 20, "We attended the President's reception last evening. I was never in such a crowd before. We went first to the reception room. Mr. Hale introduced me to the President who said, 'How do you do marm.' The ladies say that the reason he said so was because he thought I was Mr. Hale's venerable mother. Then Mr. Hale introduced me to Mrs. Lincoln. She shook hands with me and asked Mr. Hale after his family."[66]

In the middle of April, more New Hampshire troops were in motion headed for Virginia. The remainder of the Fourth New Hampshire left South Carolina on April 18. Captain Towle described the passengers aboard their ship: "About 9:30 A.M. we sailed from Hilton Head on the side wheel steamship 'Northern Light' for Gloucester Point, Va. We have on board Gen. Terry and Staff. Col Plaisted—the 7th New Hampshire—the 115th & 117th New York Volunteers in all about 1600 men crowding the steamer densely."[67]

Towle's ship arrived at Fort Monroe on April 21. There General Terry reported to Major General Benjamin F. Butler, who ordered him to report to General Major W. F. Smith at Yorktown. Upon arrival in Yorktown, Towle had a pleasant surprise waiting for him: "We reached there in the afternoon and soon heard of my father who is a captain in the 10th New Hampshire now at Yorktown in the 18th Corps." The ever-opinionated Captain Towle made mention of Butler's arrival in Yorktown: "In the morning went over to Yorktown to see my father—on my return saw Gen. Butler at the landing a theatrical looking figure in gold lace and satin. He looked like anything but a soldier."[68]

As the New Hampshire regiments gathered at Yorktown, they were given their new assignments. Butler commanded the Army of the James, and his two corps commanders were Quincy Gillmore and W. F. Smith. Smith, commanding the Eighteenth Corps, received the Fourth, Tenth, and Thirteenth New Hampshire into its ranks. Colonel Joseph Hawley commanded the Second Brigade of the First Division of Gillmore's Tenth Corps. The Third and Seventh New Hampshire were both assigned to Hawley's brigade.

These New Hampshire regiments and the Army of the James were headed for the peninsula between the James and Appomattox rivers, known as Bermuda Hundred. Butler's orders were to put pressure on Richmond and capture either it or the valuable railroad hub at Petersburg.[69] Second Lieutenant Daniel Eldredge of the Third New Hampshire, who had fully recovered from his painful foot wound, described the march of the Third to Bermuda Hundred. It was a scene that would be repeated many times by many regiments on the march. He stated that even before they had marched one half mile, a number of men had already fallen out to start lightening their loads. The first things to go were any extra pairs of boots or shoes. Eldredge remembered that at one mile, he dumped his extra socks and razor strap. At one and one half miles, he discarded his knapsack but kept his greatcoat, blanket, and letters. As the march wore on, items that were thought to be dear at the beginning of the march quickly became a burden. Soon, pictures, letters, razors, and the great coat were all disposed of. The marching columns were discarding everything that was not totally necessary. Eldredge arrived at Bermuda Hundred with only his gun, a rubber blanket, tobacco, and his canteen. Second Lieutenant Eldredge wrote in his journal, "At the end of the march the road was strewn with every conceivable article, which a soldier could carry. A line of blankets that could stretch for miles."[70]

The men of the Fourth New Hampshire received a grim reminder in mid-April that death could take them at any time. In a freak accident, Private Henry W. Winkley, a twenty-one-year-old, Irish-born substitute, was killed when he fell from the yardarm of the ship that was transporting the regiment to Virginia.[71]

Part of the contentious relationship that was to grow between Butler and his corps commanders was because Butler, having no formal military training, was a political general appointed by Lincoln. Early in the campaign, Gillmore and Smith suggested that if Petersburg was the target, they could build a bridge east of that city to cross over. According to Smith, Butler replied that he "would not build a bridge for West Point men to retreat over." The Army of the James, which included the Third, Fourth, Seventh, Tenth, and Thirteenth New Hampshire regiments, had an appointment within the month at a spot roughly seven miles south of Richmond known as Drewry's Bluff.[72]

Sophia Dodge had been concerned for several months about her brother Caleb of the Seventh New Hampshire; he was listed as missing after the February Battle of Olustee. Caleb Dodge had chided his sister in early 1863 for not writing more—she now was writing to everyone she knew to discover her brother's whereabouts. On April 23, 1864, Sergeant Paul Whipple of Company K Seventh New Hampshire, sent her a letter from his home in New Boston: "Friend Sophia, I received your letter last evening. I was glad to hear from you. . . . He [Caleb] was taken prisoner at the battle of Olustee, Fla. . . . I think he must be a prisoner in Georgia. . . . Caleb was a good Boy and was thought a great deal of by the Boys in the Co."[73] Sophia continued to send out inquiries as to the location and condition of her brother, but it would be some time before she discovered that her brother had died at Andersonville prison in Georgia, on July 20, 1864.[74]

At the end of April, the Ninth Corps was moved from Annapolis to Arlington Heights. The men in Sixth, Ninth, and Eleventh New Hampshire knew that battle was not far off. Private J. Lewis Chase of the Eleventh New Hampshire wrote to his brother John about the impending movement: "There is to be a forward movement on Richmond and we are to take part in it. As we passed Willard's Hotel yesterday we had a sight of Abraham Lincoln the first time I ever saw him he and Burnsides were talking together. We have got to see some hard times this summer. They told us in Washington that we were either going to take Richmond or els get a whipping. I hope and think it will not be the whipping there is a pile of men that are going to take part in this movement. I hope we may be successful. . . . Every man is to have forty rounds of cartages and I suppose you know what that means it means a fight well fight it is then."[75]

Private Thomas C. Cheney of the First New Hampshire Light Battery noted to his sister in a letter on April 28 that many New Hampshire troops were gathering near his camp in Stevensburg, Virginia. He gave her an imaginative description of Grant's strategy: "Gen. Grant is takeing the right course. . . . The Head of the Rebelion is in Va., but [bit] the Head off and it will be an easy matter to lop off the Monsters limbes, and Grant is concentrateing a large force here to strike of the Monsters Head this Summer if possible."[76] The twenty-eight year old artillerist from Manchester got to see the end of the rebellion but not before receiving a serious wound in fighting along the Po River in May 1864. The fighting in May would be worse than anyone ever expected.[77]

"Our regiment had
the toughest time"

CHAPTER 9

May 1864

> *The fire of God is fallen from heaven . . . and*
> *I only am escaped alone to tell thee.*
> Job 1:16

The last day of April, 1864, Major George Henry Chandler of the Ninth New Hampshire wrote to his brother William about the feverish preparations in the camps around Bristoe Station, Virginia: "You may be surprised to see where we have turned up and so are we. Heavy trains of soldiers and supplies are passing all the time. The Army of the Potomac is being largely enforced."[1] A few days later, another letter to William speculated on the future of the Ninth Corps: "It is not at all evident what is to be done with our corps and the plan of the expedition by water may yet be carried out or we may form a column to attack Lee's army at Fredericksburg or elsewhere on the right flank. . . . Lee may be prepared to hear from us anywhere within the next ten days."[2]

Gillmore Medal recipient Second Lieutenant Stephen J. Wentworth of the Fourth New Hampshire was at camp at Gloucester Point, Virginia.[3] To his mother, he described his feelings about the impending march and about the many deserters that still plagued the ranks: "You must not be worried about me if you do not hear from me for a long time, for when we commence marching it will be hard telling when we can get a chance to write. Several of us was out last night waiting for deserters. As soon as we commence marching I expect they will desert by dozens. There is not scarcely one of the subs that can be trusted. Some of them are perfect cut throats, and I would shoot one of them if I caught him deserting as quick as I would a dog."[4]

The First New Hampshire Light Battery was ordered on May 3 to be ready to move at 8:00 P.M. The battery headed out on schedule and about midnight pulled off the road to allow the infantry to pass. "During this halt a mule team attached to a wagon in one of the ammunition trains got frightened and ran in among the batteries," Sergeant Samuel Cooper recorded, "causing a stampede of battery horses, by which many gun-carriages and caissons were run away with and several overturned, injuring five or six of our men."⁵ This was the beginning of Ulysses S. Grant's Overland Campaign. As the First New Hampshire Battery rounded up its horses and carriages, the Army of the Potomac—over 120,000 strong—began marching toward the fords of the Rapidan River in Virginia. In the cool, moonlit night, the long columns trekked through the countryside and crossed the fords with all the sounds of an army—the clopping of hooves, the jangling of horse tack and tin cups, the swearing of teamsters, and the low thumping of thousands of feet marching on the road or the splashing of thousands making their way across the river.

The fords were Germanna Ford and Ely's Ford, about twelve miles below General Robert E. Lee's right flank. The Fifth Corps under General G. K. Warren and the Sixth Corps under General John Sedgewick crossed at Germanna, and Commander Major General Winfield Scott Hancock's Second Corps crossed at Ely. As the sun rose, the long, compact, blue ribbons of soldiers made their way down the roads of the Wilderness to their assigned destinations. Warren was ordered to Wilderness Tavern via the Germanna Road where it crossed the Orange Turnpike. Hancock with his Second Corps was to proceed directly to Chancellorsville. General Grant had moved around Lee's flank, and the Army of Northern Virginia responded quickly by dispatching Lieutenant General Richard Stoddert Ewell from Orange Courthouse to intercept the invading Yankees. The battle-hardened men under Lieutenant General A. P. Hill closely followed Ewell.⁶

After their midnight halt, First New Hampshire Light Battery proceeded again at 3 A.M. and crossed the river at 11 A.M. on May 4 at Ely's Ford. The exhausted men of the battery arrived at the front yard of the Chancellor House at 3 P.M. and spent the night. Up at dawn, the artillerists limbered up again and headed out at 5 A.M., traveling for five hours until they reached Todd's Tavern. There the unit went into position in front of a heavily fortified Confederate position. "Our position was in the very heart of what was known as the Wilderness," said Sergeant Cooper of the battery, "and we were close to the plank road, facing south, in a little clearing, where the trees had been felled and rolled together to form breastworks at the time of the Battle of Chancellorsville the year before. These logs were now dry as powder and took fire upon the first discharge of our guns."⁷

From the time the Eleventh New Hampshire left Bristoe Station at 10 A.M. on May 4 to when they filed into line of battle in the Wilderness on May 6, the footsore Granite Staters had marched fifty miles. By the time the Ninth Corps reached the battlefield, the Battle of the Wilderness had been underway for an entire day. The Ninth Corps men took up positions to reinforce Hancock's Second Corps. Ewell had aggressively met Warren's attack early in the day and then counterattacked. The day ended in a stalemate after the bloody brawl in the tangled undergrowth of the forest.⁸

The battle began again on May 6 in the early morning when Warren and Sedgewick on the Federal right pushed west on the Orange Turnpike, and Hancock on the left attacked down the Orange Plank Road.[9] Private William B. Greene from Raymond jotted in his diary a record of the action he saw around Todd's Tavern with Company G of the Second United States Sharpshooter Regiment: "May 6th finds me at an early hour engaging the enemy in deadly contest. This is my first battle & when I first started on the charge this morning I felt that I could fight & do anything for my bleeding country. But after I had got out the first time my patriotism had died & I thought of nothing but to keep clear of the enemy's bullets-zip, zip, zipping around me. We fought them until 2 PM, when they succeeded in flanking us & then away we went to the rear."[10]

The Confederates chased the sharpshooters back to their entrenchments. The marksmen jumped into their trenches, formed a line, and then poured several well-aimed volleys into the attacking Confederates. Even this was not enough to stop the tide of gray-clad soldiers. The sharpshooters retreated to a second line and there again turned and blasted the pursuing Confederates. "The enemy soon retreated in confusion," Private Greene related, "leaving many, in fact all, of their killed and wounded in our front."[11] Forty-four-year-old Private Joseph S. Floyd of Hudson was killed in the fighting. Corporal James M. Gilman of Tamworth and Sergeant Abner Colby of Manchester were captured; both were released in January 1865.[12]

"I have just been through a terrific battle almost equal to that of Fredericksburgh," Private Willard J. Templeton of the Eleventh New Hampshire told his parents the evening of May 6 from his camp about three miles from Chancellorsville and describing the actions of the Ninth Corps, particularly the Second Brigade. "Our brigade formed a line in front of 4 lines of the 3rd Div. And we all together charged on the rebels driving them half a mile over two lines of rifle pits. They fought desperately for the bullets were showered amongs us like hailstones during a shower. I was not scratched though the bullets were buzzing about me for three-fourths of an hour."[13] The Ninth Corps pushed the Confederates back but they regrouped and, as Templeton described, were "on our flank and in another minute we heard the bullets whizzing by us from that direction. We all commenced running back many were taken prisoners Col. Harriman was taken prisoner Lieut. Col. Collins killed two Captains, Clark and Dudley wounded."[14]

Colonel Walter Harriman of the Eleventh New Hampshire summarized the Federal attack: "At about one o'clock in the afternoon our brigade charged the enemy's lines.... We were in an oak wilderness, at the right of a plank road leading from Fredericksburg to Orange Court House. We carried two successive lines of the enemy's works by charging desperately upon them."[15] Harriman opined on why the attack collapsed: "While the Eleventh was gallantly fighting its way under the fiercest musketry fire that this war has known, our connections, both to the right and left, became broken, found ourselves without support, isolated from the rest of the division, and far in advance. A fresh brigade charged upon our left flank. The regiment retreated on a lively run and I was taken prisoner."[16] In addition to Harriman's capture, Lieutenant George Nelson Shepard of the Eleventh New Hampshire, recounted, "The lamented Collins [Moses N. Collins of Exeter], lieutenant colonel of the regiment falls mortally wounded by a musket ball through the head; Captain Clark [Joseph B. Clark of Manchester] is disabled by a gunshot wound in the arm; Lieutenant Currier [John Charles Currier of Derry] receives a severe wound in the face; scores of men hobble to the rear."[17] Captain Hollis O. Dudley of Manchester was also badly wounded, so command of the Eleventh went to Captain Sewell D. Tilton of Raymond. Private J. Lewis Chase of Company A was badly wounded in the face by a musket ball. The Eleventh New Hampshire lost nine men killed and thirty men wounded in the Battle of the Wilderness. Forty members of the regiment were captured, including Colonel Harriman. As he was led back over the same ground the brigade had fought over, Harriman saw the body of Captain Augustus Edgerly of the Ninth New Hampshire. Harriman remained a prisoner of war until his exchange in September 1864.[18] The Ninth and the Sixth New Hampshire regiments participated in the same attack as the Eleventh.

Brigadier General Simon Griffin, former commander of the Sixth New Hampshire, was in command of the Second Brigade and the only officer on horseback that day. Upon reaching the battle line, he dismounted and handed his horse over to an aide who, along with the horse, was soon killed. Griffin's overcoat had been shredded by bullets. Griffin could be proud of his former regiment. The Sixth New Hampshire made a spectacular bayonet charge on a line of Confederate works, capturing seven officers and one hundred men. Because of the woods and dense undergrowth, the lines did not advance evenly, and a gap opened long enough for the Confederates to mount the flank attack that shattered the Federal line. The Sixth New Hampshire lost forty-five men killed and wounded at the Wilderness. The Ninth New Hampshire suffered few casualties, but Colonel Herbert B. Titus had become sick, which left Major Chandler in command of the regiment.[19]

Thus far, the Battle of the Wilderness had been a struggle between the infantry; the artillery was ineffective in such a densely forested area. About two o'clock, Major General Hancock rode up to the First New Hampshire Light Battery, looking for its captain. He was sent to Captain Frederick Edgell, whom he immediately engaged in an earnest conversation. Hancock informed him that General James Longstreet was about to attack and that Edgell's battery would be needed to guard Plank Road. Hancock emphasized to Edgell that if the road was lost, they would be cut off and could not be resupplied. Hancock asked, "Now, captain, can you hold them in check?" Edgell's replied, "We shall try to do so." It would not be long before the battery would find out the answer.

A half hour later, a flood of Confederate troops poured down the road toward the Union breastworks, Edgell's men in battery only a few yards behind. Just as the Confederates approach the breastworks, the battery's supporting infantry rose and delivered a withering volley into the advancing enemy. Edgell's men fell back and cleared the front for the artillery. "Just as the rebels were mounting the breastworks twenty yards in our front, we fired with double charges of canister," Sergeant Cooper said, "just skimming the top of the breastwork they were coming over. This unexpected discharge from twelve cannon right in their teeth terribly disconcerted the advancing enemy, and though they tried it three separate times, and from as many different directions, still, the plank road, their coveted object, remained in our possession."[20]

The Battle of the Wilderness ended in a tactical draw but is considered a strategic victory for the North because Grant had not been stopped. Unlike the conclusions of previous battles, when the two armies would separate and not see another battle for several months, there was no respite for Lee. Although Grant had been terribly depressed by the results of the battle—over seventeen thousand Northern soldiers killed, wounded, or missing[21]—Grant picked himself up and immediately moved his army south, trying once more to gain Lee's right flank. The two armies would find each other again, sooner rather than later, around Spotsylvania Courthouse.

"We who had been engaged on the right of our lines, were now, after dark, drawn out from the front and passing in the rear of the lines were marched all night toward our left and moved up again into the line, to be followed the next night by those troops who we left on the right of our line," Sergeant Cooper said. "Thus he [Grant] was continually changing the troops from the right to the left of his line, and at the same time threatening Lee's right flank, and working around by the main road toward Richmond."[22]

Although the Army of the Potomac had been battered, it was not beaten, and the morale of the troops was still good. Second Lieutenant John E. Cram of the Eleventh New Hampshire was optimistic in his letter to his parents from the battlefield on May 7: "General Burnside is confident of success & I think we shall conquer them after a while. Burnside was riding along our lines most of the time of the fighting was going on & seemed as calm as though he had been in some hotel." Cram described the position and his surroundings: "Quite a lot of dead men are lying close by me that have not been taken off. The wounded are being taken from the field as fast as possible. Our line of battle is now in a piece of hard wood growth a great deal like our woods up near Fisk's Pasture."[23]

In Kittery, Maine, on May 11, Eliza Greene lamented the dreadful losses of the war to her cousin Private Greene, serving with the sharpshooters: "I see by the papers we have had one great Victory and I hope before another snow falls there will not be a rebel on the face of God's foot stool. How many poor Mothers,

Wifes and Sisters hearts have been broken since this Cruel War commenced? Oh I think it is dreadful. I hope Cousin Willie, you will be spared for your dear Mother's sake, for she has only one left without you." Private Greene's cousin was fortunate that she would not have to be concerned about her own sons, only aged five and two and safe at home in Maine.[24]

John W. Chase was going to school in Lowell when he found out that his brother Lewis had been terribly wounded at the Battle of the Wilderness and on May 12 immediately wrote to his sister Sarah: "It is with pain that I read Lewis Chase's name among the wounded soldiers and I know not how bad he was wounded. Suppose it is J. Lewis but it reads Lewis, goes without doubt it is our brother. Tell Mother it is no use to worry-as there many noble fellows all about as have fallen in the last great blow."[25]

Both armies spent May 8 and 9 maneuvering like two prizefighters for a favorable position. The skirmishing was continuous, but Lee eventually settled into positions roughly resembling a horseshoe around Spotsylvania. From left to right were the corps of First Corps Commander Richard Heron Anderson, Ewell, and Third Corps Commander Hill, the latter of whom was too sick for command after the Battle of the Wilderness and was temporarily replaced by Major General Jubal Early. Anderson commanded the First Corps after Longstreet was wounded several days earlier. Left to right in the Federal lines found General Ambrose Everett Burnside along the Fredericksburg road opposite Early, Warren, and Sedgewick near the center, and Hancock on the right, facing Anderson's Corps along the Po River.[26] Private Howard M. Hanson of the Ninth New Hampshire briefly jotted in his diary what occurred on May 9 just at the beginning of the battle: "Gen. Sedgwick killed."[27]

The First New Hampshire Light Battery was involved in a curious incident when the Second Corps was taking up positions along the Po River. Grant, Hancock, and General George Gordon Meade were looking across the Po River at a Confederate wagon train crossing their front. Someone suggested that the artillery should shell the wagons. Meade objected, saying that it would accomplish nothing. Others argued for it, and he consented.[28] "We could see the enemy's baggage trains moving along by the side of a piece of woods about a mile away," Sergeant Cooper of the First New Hampshire Light Battery explained. "We unlimbered and gave them a taste of three inch rifle shells, which startled their mules, upset their wagons and skedaddled their whole train in fine style."[29] The result was that it was a waste of ammunition, and it prematurely alerted the Confederates to Hancock's presence across the river. The rebels immediately brought up artillery and reenforcements to their side of the river.

The same New Hampshire units who had fought at the Battle of the Wilderness were about to go into a second major battle in less than a week minus many of their officers killed, wounded, and captured at the earlier battle. "Such a battle probably never was fought since the world began," Private Templeton of the Eleventh New Hampshire said of the Battle of the Wilderness.[30]

Sergeant Howard M. Hanson's brief entry in his diary set the tone for the day on May 10: "Some very hard fighting through the day at Spotsylvania Court House."[31] On the right flank, Hancock's Second Corps crossed the Po River and attacked a section of Anderson's First Corps. The First New Hampshire Light Battery was attached to Hancock's Corps. "We came into position in a ploughed field behind a small earthwork," explained Sergeant Cooper about the battery's position. "Here we had a very warm spot. Not a head could be shown above the protecting earthwork without being a mark for a bullet from a rebel sharp-shooter. . . . The battle waxed hotter and hotter until 7 P.M. The shells roared and screamed around us and the stream of lead seemed as though it were continuous."[32] Action along the Po River was hard on the battery that day. Not only was Cooper wounded but also Private Thomas C. Cheney of Manchester, Lieutenant William Chamberlin, also of Manchester, and Privates John Collins, Kitridge J. Smith, George E. Barnes, Smith G. Mooney, and Solomon M. Fairbanks. Everyone was taken to the rear, Sergeant Cooper said, and the position of the First New Hampshire along the Po "was maintained until the night of the 11th, when the corps was quietly withdrawn, and by daylight of the 12th were before the enemy's strong position at Spottsylvania."[33]

On the opposite flank of the Union army, Major General Burnside's Ninth Corps attacked down the Fredericksburg Road toward Spotsylvania Courthouse. Early's defenses were thin, and Burnside was able to make considerable gains against the weakly held lines and by nightfall was tantalizingly close to Spotsylvania Courthouse. The official historian of the Eleventh New Hampshire explained why the gains of the Second Brigade specifically and the Ninth Corps in general were not expanded: "This position was abandoned later in the day by order of Grant, notwithstanding the remonstrance of Burnside. The abandonment of this advanced position proved a mistake."[34] True, the order was given by Grant but only after Burnside had expressed concerns that he felt his right flank was not aligned with the Fifth Corps on the left. Neither realized how thin the Confederate defenses were just east of the courthouse. Lee, on seeing the threat to his right flank, returned to Early those troops who had been used earlier in the day on the Confederate left. The threat to the area around the courthouse was over. Burnside's timid assaults of the day luckily produced few casualties in the three New Hampshire regiments in the Second Brigade of the Ninth Corps.[35]

"Weds. May 11 not much fighting today," said Sergeant Hanson's diary entry, capturing the on-and-off character of the Spotsylvania campaign.[36]

Farther south in the Army of the James, Private Horace H. Adams of the Tenth New Hampshire told his brother about the fight he had gone through on May 9 several miles north of Petersburg at Swift Creek: "Our regiment had the toughest time the last two days. . . . After we advanced about 3 miles we met the Rebel pickets and drove them about a mile and kept advancing . . . during the day the Rebels made a Charge on marstins Brigade when they were repulsed. Losing 150 killed and 90 taken prisoner. . . . Kept up a Sharp fire Untill 11 o'clock at night when the Rebels made a charge on our Reg. We waited until they came within 50 yards. When we poured in a deadly fire which repulsed them. During the night they charged on our Reg. 4 times and got repulsed every time with great loss."[37] Second Lieutenant Stephen J. Wentworth of the Fourth New Hampshire wrote to his mother about Swift Creek, although the Fourth, involved in destroying the railroad, was not in the actual fighting: "An attack was made on the railroad. The telegraph wire was cut and some of the rails of the track was taken up. . . . More than a mile of track was torn up and the telegraph wire cut for several miles. We then continued the march for Petersburg. When within about four miles of the city, the Rebs made a strong stand and a sharp fight took place. . . . Our Regt. was on the battlefield but did not become engaged . . . soon we was on the road back to the camp we left the day before."[38]

The day was blistering hot, and during this attack, the Thirteenth New Hampshire was posted in the rear of the Tenth New Hampshire. During the night charges by the Confederates when the position of the Tenth along the creek began to deteriorate, an aide from headquarters rode up to Colonel Michael T. Donohoe and advised him to retreat. According to Private Adams, "The Col. Replied This Regiment don't retreat."[39]

The Tenth and Thirteenth held their positions until morning and then withdrew. Generals Quincy Gillmore and William F. Smith wanted to punch through to Petersburg, but Major General Ben Butler was content with ripping up the railroads in the area and then retiring. Butler was back in his original position on May 11. The action at Swift Creek marked the beginning of the sanguinary Drewry's Bluff campaign, a protracted battle that would last until May 19.[40]

The New Hampshire regiments in the fight were in two corps. In Major General Quincy Gillmore's Tenth Army Corps were the Third and Seventh New Hampshire in the Second Brigade of Brigadier General Alfred H. Terry's First Division and the Fourth New Hampshire in the First Brigade of Brigadier General John W. Turner's Second Division. In Major General William F. Smith's Eighteenth Army Corps were the Tenth and Thirteenth New Hampshire in the Second Brigade of Brigadier General William T. Brooks's First Division and the Second and Twelfth New Hampshire in the Second Brigade of Brigadier General Godfrey Weitzel's Second Division.[41]

May 11 had been warm, and the rains fell on and off all day. The fields around Spotsylvania Courthouse were quickly becoming a muddy mess, churned up by the constant movement of soldiers and the equipment of their armies.

Grant decided to stage a massive attack the next day and moved Hancock's Corps opposite the top of the Confederate salient. Hancock, along with Burnside's Ninth Corps, was to launch a coordinated attack at dawn May 12 against the Confederate center and right. The warm and humid night passed quietly except for the incessant calls of some nearby whippoorwills. Oddly, there was no picket firing along either of the lines, as if both sides knew that a fierce, earth-shattering battle was about to erupt, and they were taking what time they could to rest before the demands of battle would be put on them again.[42] In the part of the line occupied by the Sixth New Hampshire, everyone was sleeping except Sergeant Hiram Drown of Piermont. The twenty-six-year-old soldier from Company B hated the sounds of the whippoorwills. He complained to Captain Sam Adams that they were taunting him, and he could not sleep. Private Thomas Bradley chimed in, "I like to hear them, for they keep saying, 'Whip-you-will,' which means that we shall whip the Johnnies tomorrow, sure." Both Bradley and Drown survived the coming battle, but both were dead by October from wounds received at Cold Harbor and Bethesda Church, Virginia, respectively.[43]

In the dark of 4 A.M. on May 12, the attack commenced. The men of the Ninth Corps moved forward through the foggy mists with the Ninth New Hampshire in the advance as skirmishers. They groped their way through an open field, through some underbrush, and down into a ravine. By now the Confederates were aware that they were under attack, and the scattered popping of the muskets turned into one constant roar. The Ninth Corps was moving to the right in column by brigade with Griffin's brigade on the right. Burnside was to try to keep contact with Hancock's left flank as best he could, so Griffin kept shifting his brigade to maintain his alignment. As could be expected in the heat and noise of battle, this alignment could not be kept. Because of the incessant rains, many of the soldier's cartridges misfired or refused to fire altogether. Eventually a gap opened between the two corps,[44] and in the half-light of dawn, a regiment of dark-coated soldiers worked their way into the gap. They were just about to flank the Eleventh New Hampshire when they were recognized as Confederates. Captain Leander W. Cogswell turned his company to meet the Confederates and gave them a sharp volley. The Confederate threat quickly evaporated, and the Federal lines continued to move forward.[45] The gap, however, remained, and a serious counterattack was forming on Hancock's left. Major Chandler of the Ninth New Hampshire did what he could to bring his men more to the right to seal the breach, but the brigade's formation had fallen apart, and the New Hampshire Sixth, Ninth, and Eleventh were all engaging the enemy on a regimental level. The Confederates were again making their way around the line to flank the scattered New Hampshire units.[46]

"Thursday May 12th finds us again engaging the enemy," wrote Private Greene, serving in Company G Second United States Sharpshooters. "We made a flank movement from our old position on the Poe [Po] River last night and very quietly slipped five miles to the left, surprised the enemy in their works . . . & after a brief but deadly contest succeeded in driving the enemy from their entrenchments." What Greene saw in the trenches shocked him: "Never did I see so many men in one pile dead before. They lay four deep in some places. . . . I never saw bullets fly so as they did today. In the rear of the enemy's works there was a tree six inches through completely cut off by the leaden hail."[47]

The Ninth New Hampshire began to fall back, its flag riddled with over twenty bullet holes. When the national colors went down, Private Eugene Parsons of Lowell picked it up and held it high so the men could rally around it. As the Ninth fell back, Major Chandler was seriously wounded and taken to the rear in a blanket. Lieutenant Colonel Babbitt, in temporary command of another regiment, was also wounded. Lieutenant George Sylvester of Concord received a mortal wound. Lieutenant Charles Wilcox of Keene was captured and not regained until just before the end of the war. Corporal Elmer Bragg of the Ninth was seriously wounded and was left behind with the Confederates. Soon after the battle, he assured his parents that everything was fine: "I received a slight bayonet wound in the breast I hope to be well again soon."[48] Bragg died before the end of the summer. From a hospital bed in Fredericksburg on May 13, Major Chandler described his condition to his brother: "I was seriously wounded in the engagement of the Ninth near Spotsylvania C.H. [court house]. The ball entered my right thigh and passed directly through."[49] Several days later, Chandler told his mother the Ninth New Hampshire's status: "Our regiment suffered heavily. Col Titus has been absent sick with fever for ten days. Col Babbit was seriously wounded on Thursday. My wound though deep and severe is not called by the surgeons a dangerous one." Major Chandler survived his wound and the war and lived in Canterbury, New Hampshire, until his death in 1883.[50] Just after shooting a Confederate color-bearer in the seesaw battle, a musket ball smashed into the face of Private Alvin B. Williams of the Eleventh New Hampshire, killing him instantly.

The Eleventh New Hampshire was falling back as well. Color-bearer Daniel West of Chester had just been wounded when Second Lieutenant Cram of Raymond ran forward and grabbed the colors. He wanted to go forward again, but Captain Sewell D. Tilton, then in command of the Eleventh, shouted to him that they had to withdraw. Cram was rooted to the spot, and when the remainder of the men of the Eleventh saw him, they started to move forward again to the attack. Shortly after, both Tilton and Cram fell from serious wounds.[51]

An exploding shell killed Private Lewis E. Crowell of Company E, First United States Sharpshooters, as he was falling back. He was buried on the field by his brother Gilman Crowell and Sergeant David Wyatt. His body was eventually brought home to Hopkinton and reburied. Justifiably proud of its contribution

LIEUTENANT JOHN E. CRAM, *Eleventh New Hampshire, Company B. Cram was severely wounded at Spotsylvania on May 12, 1864, while leading a heroic charge against the Confederates. He settled in Raymond after the war. Photograph courtesy of NHVA*

to the war, the town of Hopkinton was immortalized in the poem *The Hopkinton Boys:* "Dear Hopkinton has done its part to keep our country great; she's been as true as any town in the Old Granite State."[52]

Casualties for the three New Hampshire regiments involved at the Battle of Spotsylvania amounted to over one hundred killed and five hundred wounded. Seventy men of the Ninth New Hampshire were captured. In the Eleventh six color-bearers were killed or wounded. Colonel Griffin, because of his heroic actions, was promoted to brigadier general. His diligence in protecting the left flank of the Second Corps allowed Hancock to go on and punch a hole in the Confederate defenses.[53]

Action continued around Spotsylvania Courthouse until after May 19, when Grant withdrew once more trying to get around Lee's right flank, and again the cost was high. In the days that Grant's army was engaged at Spotsylvania, he lost

12,632 killed or wounded. Coupled with the Wilderness, this came to almost 27,000 men in only two weeks of fighting, and the army had not yet arrived at Cold Harbor. Over 4,000 Federal soldiers had been taken prisoner during the spring campaign so far, while the Confederates had 4,000 men captured at the Battle of Spotsylvania alone. Confederate casualties were difficult to estimate, since they fought a mostly defensive battle. However, most sources agree that Lee lost 8,000 men in the savage fighting that went on for most of the day on May 12. Trying once again to out maneuver each other, both armies were now headed for the North Anna River.[54]

As the Battle of Spotsylvania reached its height on May 12, the Army of the James began to move out of its defensive works at Bermuda Hundred. Butler's intrepid army turned north and headed once again for the Richmond-Petersburg Turnpike. With Smith's Eighteenth Corps on the right and Gillmore's Tenth Corps on the left, Butler was at last launching his drive on Richmond. It was not long until just south of Richmond, Butler's army ran into a string of Confederate fortifications, running from west of the turnpike northeast to the James River. The Tenth Corps made contact with the outer ring of defenses first, and it was the luck of the Third New Hampshire to be the first regiment to open on May 13 the Battle of Drewry's Bluff.[55]

The Third New Hampshire was now under the command of Major James F. Randlett of Nashua. Acting commander of the regiment Lieutenant Colonel Josiah I. Plimpton was assigned temporarily to General Terry's headquarters. On the early morning of May 13, skirmishers of the Third New Hampshire attacked the Confederate defenses, just west of the turnpike. The New Hampshire men and the Tenth Corps under Gillmore made contact with the Confederate defenses, first hitting the lower left end of a diagonal set of fortifications that stretched off to the northeast. Smith's Eighteenth Corps reached the line on the right also, but this whole set of lines was only forward rifle pits. The Confederates quickly abandoned this position and withdrew into their second line, a string of heavy earthworks and redoubts.[56]

Instructed to move farther to the left so they could get around the flank of the Confederates, the Third New Hampshire crossed the railroad line, not expecting to run into the enemy until they got behind them. "We had scarcely stepped upon the bridge where we met the enemy outside of their works," Adjutant Elbridge J. Copp of the Third said. "Into a field and up a slope the charge was made with a yell; the rattle of musketry was now intense; our boys were dropping to the ground, killed and wounded, the zip and ping of the rifle ball in rapid succession, the crack of artillery and shells exploding, uniting with the shriek of those who were wounded were the unearthly sounds known only to men who have been through the battle."[57]

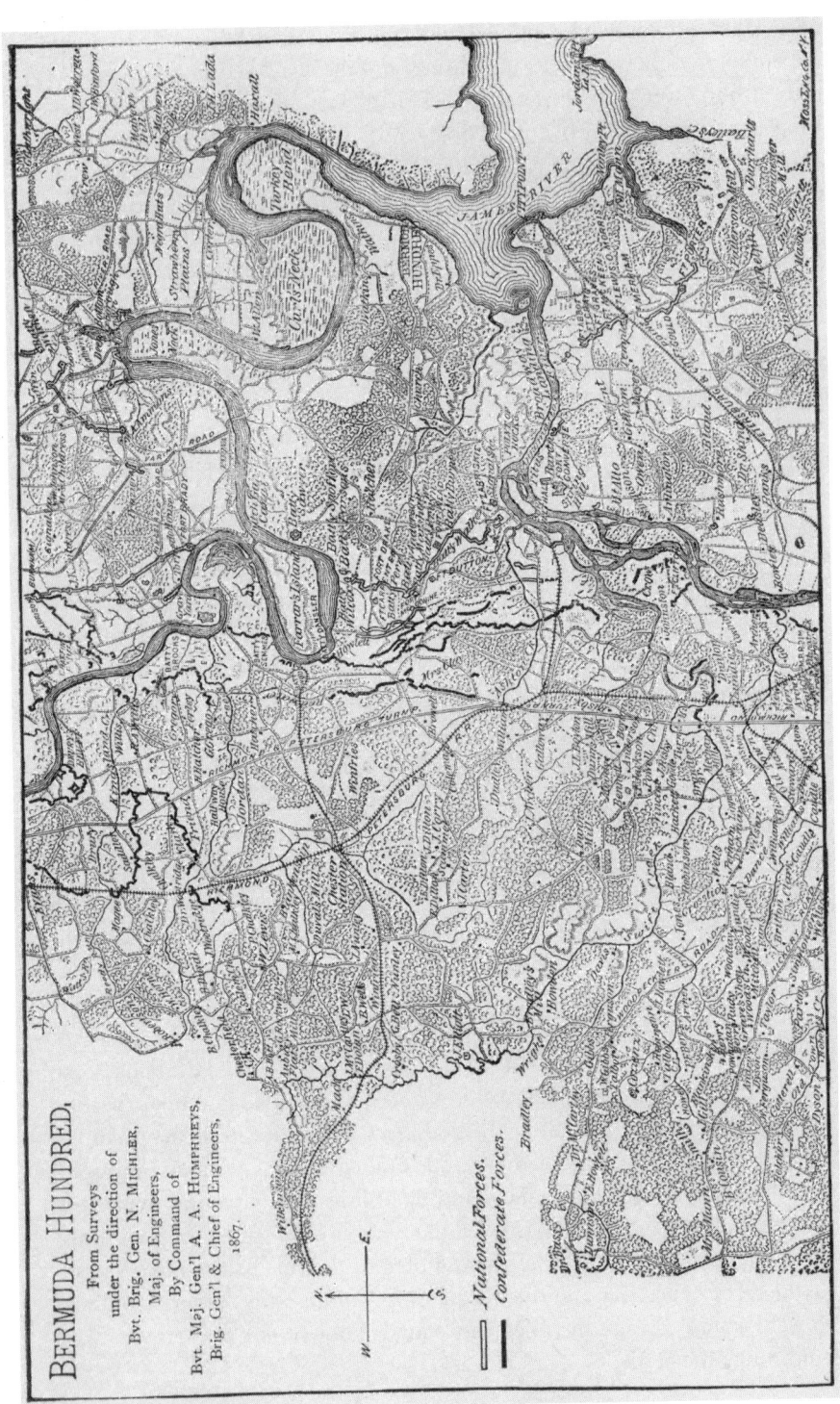

BERMUDA HUNDRED.

From Surveys
under the direction of
Bvt. Brig. Gen. N. Michler,
Maj. of Engineers,
By Command of
Bvt. Maj. Gen'l A. A. Humphreys,
Brig. Gen'l & Chief of Engineers,
1867.

National Forces.
Confederate Forces.

From Elbridge Copp, Reminiscences of the War of the Rebellion, 1911

"Marched six miles and charged on a battery our regiment lost 200 killed wd. & missing," succinctly wrote Private Alphonso Osborn of the Third.[58] Osborn did not exaggerate this figure, and had Terry's First Brigade not arrived in time, the Third New Hampshire would most likely have been destroyed. As it was, Captain Richard Ela of Concord lost his life instantly when a bullet shattered his skull, and Major Randlett, Adjutant Copp, and Lieutenant Charles Hazen were all wounded. Second Lieutenant Daniel Eldredge noted in his journal that he and Ela had shared a cup of coffee that morning, and Ela had said that he would never drink another cup.[59]

Adjutant Copp of the Third New Hampshire explained how he was wounded: "Forward we were charging under this hot fire from the entrenchments and the buildings. I was just getting over a fence ... when I felt the sting of a bullet. Looking, I saw that a ball had passed between the hilt of my sword and my hand taking off a piece of my riding glove and the flesh. . . . Thinking it was a close call, I was again hit by a rifle ball in the shoulder; the blow was as a heavy club and I fell to the ground."[60] Copp was removed from the battlefield and taken to Chesapeake Hospital in Hampton, where he recovered fully.[61]

The Confederates on the left retreated in the direction of their primary works near Fort Darling. The Union troops harassed them with artillery shells until they were out of range. Once again the skies opened over the already sodden Virginia countryside. The rain did not dampen the spirits of the men of the Third New Hampshire, for when they heard that they had driven an entire Confederate brigade, every cap came off and was thrown into the air amidst a hearty cheer. On the evening of May 13 at the Battle of Drewry's Bluff, Lieutenant Eldredge was detailed with others of the Third to venture out and retrieve the wounded. They made several trips, and on the last one, Eldredge had to decide whether to bring in a wounded Confederate soldier or the dead body of his friend Captain Ela. He opted to bring in the wounded Confederate, hoping that his life could be saved. Fortunately, he was able to bring in Ela's body the next day, and it was buried behind their lines.[62]

The Seventh New Hampshire, placed in a supporting role to the Third New Hampshire, did not suffer many casualties on May 13, but on the next day, the regiment suffered four dead when ordered to advance on a Confederate battery. The Third lost roughly the same number.[63]

On May 14, the Tenth Corps ventured out of the captured Confederate works and headed for the next line of fortifications. The railroad was crossed again and the men of the 3rd, Fourth, and 7th camped in an open field at nightfall. Occasional bullets from Confederate snipers zipped by, some missing, but some finding their marks. Second Lieutenant Daniel Eldredge related a story in his diary how fate often took over in such situations: "I was awakened by a comrade Corporal John W. Brown of Strafford, NH who had received a ball in his head, cutting a furrow across the back of it. I was in a reclining position at the time and facing the enemy. From the position which Brown occupied at the time and the fact that a small bush was cut off near my head, I concluded that the bullet must have passed between my hand and shoulder, my arm being bent and my head resting on my hand. I kept awake after that." Corporal Brown survived his wound and was discharged from the army that September.[64]

Private Elias A. Bryant of the Fourth New Hampshire also remembered that night and what happened the next day on Sunday May 15: "We passed the night in the open field. In the morning we began an advance under heavy musketry fire of the rebel lines and also of the guns in the fortifications on Drewry's Bluff. . . . The general direction of our movement was toward the northeast and we made the extreme front and center. We finally took position behind a fence and threw up the earth against it as a little protection. The men used for this their plates, dippers, pieces of board-anything which could be used to dig with."[65]

The digging was hard because it was raining again and the fields were a mass of clotted and churned up mud. The Fourth New Hampshire stayed in this position for the rest of the day, trading shots with the Confederates opposite them. Once again, New Hampshire soldiers were gradually being picked off by accurate sniper fire. Private Alanson W. Barney of Manchester was killed instantly by a sharpshooter's bullet.

Private Bryant and some other soldiers noticed that many of the shots were not coming straight from the Confederate line, but lengthwise down their line from a small woods. When Captain Jasper Wallace of Dover fell wounded, Colonel Bell was determined to flush out the snipers. He detailed a group of men to rush the trees, and they fired on the sharpshooter, causing him to fall out of the tree. He was shooting from a platform he had installed at the top. The Confederates emerged from the lines several times during the misty, rainy day but were repulsed each time.[66]

On May 15, Private Greene of the Second United States Sharpshooters was in action again around Spotsylvania Courthouse. He and several other sharpshooters were ordered out before dawn to a house very close to the Confederate lines. Greene picked a good spot by a window to set up his sniper's nest, and throughout the house, his comrades did the same. An hour later, Greene was peering out the window and saw men moving through the predawn mist. He was about to pick a target when he began counting them. Five men turned into ten, ten turned into twenty, and suddenly Greene was faced with not a Confederate patrol but a reconnaissance in force by half a Confederate company. He shouted to his mates that they needed to get out of there, but by the time he reached the ground floor, they were already gone. Greene made his way out of the house and was spotted by the advancing Confederates, who ordered him to halt. "They then fired at me but I made out to get to the woods before they could load again

& then I managed to keep the largest trees between me and them," the sharp-shooter related. "But they did not propose to lose me & gave pursuit & I guess I made use of my legs until I got to the breastworks."[67]

On May 16, New Hampshire troops in Smith's Eighteenth Corps unsuccessfully attacked the Confederate works. The always-opinionated Captain George F. Towle of the Fourth New Hampshire said about the Drewry's Bluff campaign, "Now it seems serious business is at last to begin. The skirmishing of the last three days is but the prelude to real and earnest work. Butler evidently means to attempt something but with two such corps commanders as Smith and Gillmore, jealous of each other and each equally opposed to their Chief it does not appear he may be very successful."[68]

Monday, May 16 was a crucial day for Ben Butler. He ordered a general attack to be made by both corps along the entire line. A dense fog shrouded the battle-field as the men moved forward to attack the Confederate forts. In a case of incredible bad luck, just as the Federal battle line came within three hundred yards of the forts, the sun burned through the fog, making the field and the men perfectly visible from the forts. Instantaneously, every gun in the forts went off, and the men immediately dove for cover. Some, like Sergeant Charles E. Colcord of the Fourth New Hampshire, didn't move fast enough. He received a mortal wound, and most of the color guard were killed or wounded. One flag bearer had both feet severed from an exploding shell.[69]

The Confederates again came out from their protected positions and attacked the vulnerable Union line of battle. In one of these mad rushes, Major Charles W. Sawyer of Dover was wounded in the shoulder. He was removed from the battlefield but died from infection in a hospital in Concord, New Hampshire.[70]

On the right side of the Union line, the men of the Second, Tenth, Twelfth, and Thirteenth New Hampshire were having an equally difficult time. On the morning of May 16, Weitzel's division was placed with the Twelfth New Hamp-shire on the extreme left near the turnpike and the Second in the middle. Dense fog also covered this part of the field when the action began. The Confederates chose to attack in the fog, and the men came screaming through the dense blan-ket. The day before, the Federals had strung telegraph wire between tree stumps in their front. The same tactic that worked so well at the Siege of Knoxville was used again with great effect. The Confederate attack was literally tripped up. The men came on like demons, and the men of the Second New Hampshire poured multiple volleys into them.[71]

One of the lamented casualties from the Second New Hampshire was Cap-tain James H. Platt of Manchester. Regimental Chaplain John Wesley Adams recounted the conversation he had with Platt the previous day: "We talked of home and friends with an interest such soldiers were wont to feel. As I was about to leave, he remarked, 'I have come safely through all the past, and I am going in once more to live or die. If anything happens to me I want you to look after me and inform my wife.'" Platt was killed the next day, and the chaplain kept his promise. His body was taken home to Manchester and buried in the Valley Cemetery.[72]

Losses in the Second and Twelfth New Hampshire were light, with six killed and forty-eight wounded. The battle in the fog had actually been merciful for the New Hampshire men in that part of the line. It had been much worse for the Third, Fourth, and Seventh New Hampshire regiments on the left side of the line. The Third lost 66 killed and 152 wounded, while the Fourth had 16 men killed and 125 wounded and missing. The Seventh, which was in a supporting role, sustained four battle deaths.[73]

Brigadier General Hiram Burnham had also ordered his men to wind wire around the stumps to their front. This defensive maneuver helped to break up the Confederate attack the next morning in front of the Tenth and Thirteenth New Hampshire. The Thirteenth fired off over fifty rounds per man into the foggy shroud, and the Tenth added to the effect with their oblique fire. The Tenth New Hampshire lost eight men killed and forty wounded while the Thirteenth lost the same number killed but only twenty wounded.[74] General Pierre Gustave Toutant Beauregard's overall offensive strategy at Drewry's Bluff and his attack on the Sixteenth with ten brigades against the Federals was enough to make Butler call off the campaign. Because of a perceived threat to his rear from Petersburg and the uncooperative spirit of his corps commanders, Butler withdrew to Bermuda Hundred and allowed himself to be pinned there by vastly inferior Confederate forces.[75] Of the 16,000 men in Butler's army, 390 fell dead on the battlefield, and there were 2,380 wounded and 1,390 missing, assumed captured. The Confederates suffered about half of Butler's casualties. Approximately 106 of the nearly 400 dead were from New Hampshire regiments.[76]

The official historian of the Thirteenth New Hampshire gave a picturesque summary of the Drewry's Bluff campaign: "While we are thus ringing the doorbell of Richmond, and then running for dear life, leaving our 'May Basket' hanging on the doorknob and filled with all our best camp gear—as children play at the game with flowers; Gen. Sheridan with his cavalry has made the entire circuit of Gen. Lee's army, sweeping around between the rebel host and Richmond. . . . For a number of days—precious days—we were five to one, at least, of all the men the rebels could muster."[77]

Surmising that the whole campaign was little more than a reconnaissance, Second Lieutenant Ephraim W. Ricker of the Twelfth New Hampshire wrote to his mother after the battle: "Since I last wrote you last this army here has been within 9 miles of Richmond. We were in line of battle 5 days-and each day exposed to the enemies fire more or less. I think it was simply a recconisance to draw the forces from Gen. Lee." Ricker went on to be a captain and survived the war.[78]

Thursday May 19 was officially the last day of the Spotsylvania Campaign. Lee was concerned that Grant might try to slip around his right flank again. Lee sent in Ewell's corps to confirm his suspicions. A sharp fight ensued with Grant's rear guard, and it became clear to Lee that Grant was moving to the right again. While the army was in motion, and there was a slight cessation of hostilities, the soldiers had a brief chance to write and visit friends. Most men of Company B of the Eleventh New Hampshire were from Raymond and Deerfield, and they received a surprise visitor in late May. Private William B. Greene wrote to his mother on May 20 about seeing his old friends: "I visited the 11th N.H.V. & saw J. D. Folsom, Sam Randall, Jo Small, Geo. Donall, Leonard Tilton & others. They appeared to be glad to see me. John Cram is wounded in the legs." Except for Cram who was wounded at Spotsylvania, the rest of Greene's friends were in good health and free of impairments. However, by the end of the war, Greene's friend Tilton had died at Andersonville.[79]

While Greene was visiting his friends, the Army of the James and the New Hampshire troops in it were still engaged with the Confederates. "Yesterday we had another fight with them," Second Lieutenant Stephen J. Wentworth of the Fourth New Hampshire wrote to his mother on May 21 from Foster's Plantation about the action. "The enemy charged before daylight and was driven back, but the second time they were successful and got possession of the rifle pits. . . . The loss of our Reg't in yesterday's fight was eleven men; two lieutenants wounded one mortally. . . . It seems to me that very poor Generalship has been displayed. It seems as though our Generals went to work in rather a blind manner."[80] Lieutenants William D. Stearns of Amherst and John W. Brewster of Portsmouth were both wounded on May 20 but survived.[81]

Private Elias A. Bryant of the Fourth New Hampshire had some scathing comments about the action on May 20: "Oh bad management! Anyone could see that our little force could not hold the position against the force to be seen but a few rods below. . . . Many were the curses which went against Gen. Benjamin F. Butler. . . . Company C have lost heavily, only twenty-five out of the whole company left, no officers."[82]

Lee still maintained a slight tactical advantage over Grant. By doing so, he could fight Grant on ground of his own choosing. He was able to get across the North Anna River and set up a strong defensive position with the Army of the Potomac at his heels. The Battle of the North Anna stretched for three days. The Federal army made numerous crossings, but because of the course of the river, the army was divided in three parts, and their attacks were committed piecemeal. Even though he was sick, Lee was able to meet these thrusts and repel them. On May 26, Grant withdrew once again trying to find Lee's right flank.[83]

Private Greene, in action again with the Second United States Sharpshooter Regiment, recorded in his diary about the fighting, in which both the Second and

First Regiments participated: "We overtook the enemy & found them strongly entrenched on both banks of the No. Annie [Anna] River. My Regt. with the First went on the skirmish line where we remained until about five o'clock PM when the order came for us to move forward. On we went & charged the works on the north side of the river & after a pretty hard fight we compelled them to skedadle. L. W. Crane of my Co was dangerously wounded just before the charge."[84] Private Luther W. Crane of Bethlehem, New Hampshire, was mortally wounded and died in a Washington hospital on June 18.[85]

Action along the North Anna escalated the next day with the crossing of the river by both Hancock's and Burnside's corps. Private Greene told how the fighting intensified: "Co. G & C were ordered across the river & as near the enemy's works as we could get. We went one by one, crawling on our hands & knees until we got within good shooting distance, then we dug our pits with our tin cups for shovels & our case knives for pick axes & when we got our pits dug we opened on them & the troops [Hancock's] commenced moving across the bridge. . . . We kept the bullets flying from our truth full rifles & they dare not show their heads above their works."[86]

Assistant Quartermaster Andrew H. Young of Dover wrote to his wife from Hancock's Second Corps headquarters at Hanover Junction. He expressed a guarded opinion about the campaign: "There has been no general fight for a week. We are working round towards the Chickahominy. Everything here is working as well as could be expected. Butler has got licked as might have been expected, we expect to unite with Butler in a few days, and then whether we go into Richmond will depend upon who has the biggest guns."[87]

Lee once again proved himself the master of maneuvering and gained the Chickahominy ahead of Grant on May 28. He then moved southeast toward Cold Harbor, where he stopped and prepared strong defensive lines. On May 28 Second Lieutenant John E. Cram of the Eleventh New Hampshire was getting used to his surroundings at the Lincoln Hospital in Washington. From there he wrote to his parents in great detail about his wound and the hospital surroundings: "I am getting along nicely now & my wound is doing first-rate though the ball has not been extracted yet & perhaps will not be. It entered my right leg about three inches above the knee nearly on the front of the leg the ball passing back but not through. The bone was not injured. It runs a great deal & does not pain me a great deal: the worst is to lay here on my back. I can not move it without help. . . . It is a hard looking sight to go through this hospital & see the wounds of every description. . . . New Hampshire men from the city came over to see me every few days & offer to get me anything I wish & bring to me."[88]

Private Albert Stearns of the Ninth New Hampshire sent a letter home also describing his wound, but, unlike Cram, he could not be evacuated to a hospital: "I was struck in the hand by a Minnie bullet which wounded every finger as well as my thumb and the palm of my hand. . . . As we are cut off from the rest of the world for a few days wounded men have to go wherever the army go until the communication is opened by the way of the York or James rivers. . . . Of course we can't get very good attention here on the march as we have been riding in ambulances every day and nearly every night since we were wounded."[89] Stearns made a full recovery from his wound and settled in West Lebanon, New Hampshire, after the war.[90]

The month of May 1864 marked both a beginning and an ending in the prosecution of the war. The month opened with Grant tenaciously battering away at Lee's army and attempting to gain his right flank. The storied generals dodged and jabbed at each other, producing several major battles that resulted in horrendous casualties. It was an ending because now Lee faced a general who would not give up. Grant refused to retreat after being continuously repulsed. Gone were the days when a battle would be fought, and both sides would retreat to lick their wounds before rejoining the battle in a few months. Now that the two armies warily regarded each other across the lines at Cold Harbor, a terrible new phase of the war was about to begin. The nightmare experience known as trench warfare would be visited on the Virginia countryside around Petersburg approximately fifty years before it would produce millions of casualties in World War I.

"My horror and indignation were great"

CHAPTER 10

June 1864 to July 1864

If two New Hampshire men aren't a match for the devil, we might as well give the country back to the Indians.

Stephen Vincent Benét, "The Devil and Daniel Webster," 1936

Toward the end of May 1864, the two opposing armies were building up once again to a serious clash of arms. Picket firing and skirmishing became fairly continuous by May 30. Confident that Major General Ben Butler was securely pinned at Bermuda Hundred, General Pierre Gustave Toutant Beauregard sent Major General Robert Hoke and his six-thousand-man division to the aid of Robert E. Lee. Sporadic fighting at Totopotomy on May 31 resulted in the death of two soldiers from the Ninth New Hampshire Regiment. Ulysses S. Grant also received reinforcements from the Bermuda Hundred area. Major General William F. Smith's Eighteenth Corps and part of Major General Quincy Gillmore's Tenth Corps rushed to help the overall commander of the armies.[1]

The important road hub at Cold Harbor became the center of attention as Grant edged ever closer to Richmond, Virginia. Grant ordered Major General Phil Sheridan and his cavalry to attack the village and hold it. On his arrival, Sheridan found the village already occupied by Southern cavalry and drove them away. He continued forward until he ran into a solid line of Confederate infantry and then withdrew. Alarmed by the Federal thrust, Lee ordered Lieutenant General Richard Heron Anderson to take Cold Harbor back on June 1.

The first day of June was hot and humid, the dust rising from the movement of so many men and their equipment. Precisely at dawn, Confederate forces under Anderson slammed into Sheridan's men, who were armed with their repeating rifles. Charging across an open field, the Southern troops were cut down by the score. The first opportunity to break through the Confederate lines was lost when General Horatio Wright's Sixth Corps delayed attacking until late in the afternoon. The delay was not his fault because he was supposed to wait for the arrival of Smith's Eighteenth Corps and attack in unison. Smith, working with bad maps and advice, took the wrong road and did not pull into the Cold

Harbor area until 4 P.M. On Smith's arrival, six Federal divisions, including the First Division under Brigadier General William T. Brooks, went directly into battle. In the Second Brigade of the First Division were the Tenth and Thirteenth New Hampshire regiments.[2]

In the short and sharp engagement that ensued, the Federals pushed forward and briefly held a section of the Confederate line until they were thrown back. In this attack the Tenth New Hampshire lost one man killed and one wounded. However, losses in the Thirteenth New Hampshire were much more severe. Twenty-two men from the Thirteenth died in the space of five minutes and forty-five were wounded, including Colonel Aaron Fletcher Stevens. Captains George Farr and Rufus Staniels were both severely wounded but survived the battle and the war.[3]

The battle at Cold Harbor on June 1 was overshadowed by the larger battle that occurred two days later and is usually given only a footnote in most historical treatments of the subject. However, to the men of the Tenth and Thirteenth New Hampshire, as well as the rest of the Sixth and Eighteenth Corps, it was a short but vicious engagement that resulted in the loss of many of their comrades. Overall losses for the first day in the Federal army amounted to 2,620 men.[4]

Grant concluded that a coordinated attack on June 2 could carry the Confederate lines. He ordered Major General Winfield Scott Hancock's depleted Second Corps on a forced march and intended to send it directly into battle on its arrival. Because of the heat and condition of the dusty roads, Hancock's weary men did not reach Cold Harbor until dawn on June 2 and were in no condition to do anything but rest. Grant rescheduled the attack until late in the afternoon. As the time of the attack approached, Grant saw the terrible condition of Hancock's men, who had been ravaged by the conflict at Spotsylvania and the increasing rain, and decided to postpone the attack until dawn on June 3. Lee's army was still not completely formed, but this newest delay would give him all the time he needed to dig in and produce a nearly impregnable set of works to face the attacking Federals.[5]

In anticipation of the attack scheduled for June 2, the men of the Tenth and Thirteenth New Hampshire moved up as close to the Confederate lines as they could. They were able to dig for themselves some serviceable rifle pits by using their bayonets, tin plates, and cups. Midway through their digging project, they drew the attention of the Confederates in the opposite line and came under a galling fire. Twenty-one-year-old Second Lieutenant Daniel W. Russell of the Tenth New Hampshire was killed instantly when a Confederate bullet shattered his skull.[6]

Once again, the Ninth Corps under General Ambrose Burnside was on the extreme right flank of the Federal line. In position just north of Bethesda Church, the men of the Sixth, Ninth, and Eleventh New Hampshire had already been under fire on the morning of June 1. Sergeant Charles C. Paige of the Eleventh New Hampshire recorded in his diary the danger of his position: "I am sitting just back of the rifle pits. Minie balls are whizzing over my head. Our guns are firing an occasional shell over our heads in the lines of the enemy. One of the shells burst over our heads and a piece fell three feet from me. The next one just went over our pits and exploded."[7]

On June 2, the Ninth Corps moved four miles closer to Bethesda Church in order to anchor itself more firmly to the right flank of General G. K. Warren's Fifth Corps. This movement drew the attention of the Confederates, and when the Eleventh New Hampshire moved out into a large field, they came under fire from the opposing picket line. The turning movement was completed by dark, and the Ninth Corps was completely in position in the Federal battle line.[8]

As New Hampshire troops moved to take their places in line in anticipation of the great battle ahead, Governor Joseph Albee Gilmore was delivering a speech on the State House lawn in Concord. Speaking of the state's soldiers in the field, Gilmore said, "If New Hampshire has few generals, she has many heroes. The names of some of her regiments are familiar as household words. . . . They have proved themselves firm as the granite of their native hills in resisting the shock of war; terrible as the lightning which plays about their summits."[9] On the evening of June 2, pelted by rain, those same soldiers were writing their names on small slips of paper and pinning them to their uniforms so they might be identified if they fell in battle the next day.[10]

For the attack scheduled for dawn on June 3, the Second, Sixth, and Eighteenth Corps were slated to deliver the heaviest blow. The Federal army had gathered over 108,000 men, and the Confederates faced them with about half that number. However, the Southern troops had the advantage of being in strong defensive positions.[11]

On the extreme left flank of Grant's army was the Second Corps under Hancock. The Fifth New Hampshire, now under the able command of Charles E. Hapgood of Amherst, was in a brigade in Brigadier General Francis Barlow's First Division. Facing Hapgood were the rugged veterans of A. P. Hill's Third Corps. Next in line was Wright's Sixth Corps, composed mostly of regiments from the Mid-Atlantic States. Wedged between Wright's corps and Warren's Fifth Corps was Smith's Eighteenth Corps. Positioned almost in the center of the line, Smith's Corps contained the men of the Second, Fourth, Tenth, Twelfth, and Thirteenth New Hampshire regiments spread out through its various divisions and brigades. Lieutenant General Jubal Early's Second Corps was opposite Smith. In Early's Corps was the division of Major General John Brown Gordon that had nearly been wiped out at the salient in Spotsylvania.

To the right of Warren was Burnside's Ninth Corps, which contained Simon Griffin's Second Brigade and the men of the Sixth, Ninth, and Eleventh New

Hampshire regiments. Although most of the attention of the coming battle focused on the center of the Union line, these New Hampshire troops would also see their share of action.[12]

The soldiers of both armies woke to another foggy and misty June morning in Virginia. At precisely 4:30 A.M., Federal bugles sounded the charge up and down the five-mile battle line. The men of Hancock's, Wright's, and Smith's corps who were to provide the main assault moved out sluggishly. Because of the irregularities of the ground between the two lines and the nearly arced formation of the Confederate defenses, the Union attack was in trouble nearly from the start. Advancing almost en echelon, each corps not only had to deal with fire coming from their front but also enfilading fire. After the battle each corps commander blamed the other for not providing adequate support. The attack quickly broke down to piecemeal actions at the brigade and sometimes the regimental level.[13]

In Hancock's Second Corps, the men of the Fifth New Hampshire were instructed not to fire a shot until they reached the Confederate lines. In his report Colonel Hapgood provided a general description of the Fifth New Hampshire in action: "At 4:30 A.M. June 3, the regiment, with the brigade, charged the enemy's works and carried them, capturing two guns and one hundred and twenty five prisoners, which were sent to the rear. I found the enemy had a second line, and as my losses, up to that time, had been very light, I moved up to attack the second line, and then ascertained that the other regiments of the brigade had not carried the enemy's works and that the Fifth Regiment was between the enemy's lines with no connection on either flank, and, immediately, on ascertaining that no supports were in sight, gave orders to withdraw."[14] Thomas L. Livermore of the Fifth New Hampshire provided a more detailed account of his regiment at Cold Harbor: "The regiment numbered about five hundred, and in fine order the line charged forward without delivering a shot, and, with a loss of about fifty men, carried the works in front."[15]

The situation worsened for the Fifth New Hampshire when Hapgood decided to attack the second Confederate line. The large number of prisoners netted in the first battle line was left there to be transported to the rear. When the Confederate prisoners saw the retreating Federal troops, Livermore said, "The rebels in the rear who had thrown down their arms now took them up and fired into the backs of our men. Colonel Hapgood now deemed the emergency such as to warrant his ordering the men to retreat each for himself and the line . . . broke for the rear."[16] As the men ran pell-mell for their lines, they reentered the first set of Confederate works. Confederate artillerists peppered the passing groups of men with canister. An exasperated Captain John S. Ricker of Milton saw this harassing fire as he passed. An unverified story went through the ranks that he mounted a gun pit and, spying one of the Confederate gunners, swung his sword down and chopped off his head.[17]

By the time the men of the Fifth made their way back to their lines, they had been shot at on all four sides. Losses in the Fifth New Hampshire were heavy: 46 dead and 170 wounded on the morning of June 3. Captain George F. Goodwin of Lebanon, Maine, was cut down in hand-to-hand fighting in the Confederate works. Lieutenant John W. Spaulding, twenty-eight, was shot in the lungs and would suffer complications from his wound until his death in September 1865. Colonel Edward E. Cross would have been proud of his brave boys had he been alive to see them in action at Cold Harbor.[18]

The First New Hampshire Light Battery, attached to Hancock's Second Corps, engaged in skirmishing along the whole route to Cold Harbor. They were involved in fighting along the Totopotomy and near Sheldon's Crossroads. At Cold Harbor, the battery was only lightly engaged and fortunately only lost two men wounded.[19]

Smith's Eighteenth Corps, occupying the center of the Union line, went forward with the divisions of Brooks and Brigadier General John H. Martindale. In the Second Brigade of the First Division, the Tenth New Hampshire rushed forward driving in the pickets of the opposing Confederate line. The first line of enemy works was reached, and carrying it, they continued on to the second line. In the space of five minutes, the Tenth New Hampshire had twenty men killed and fifty wounded. Born in Ireland, Lieutenant James Knott fell in battle for his adopted country. The younger brother of Colonel Michael T. Donohoe, Adjutant Joseph J. Donohoe was severely wounded in the charge. A newspaper correspondent on the field described the Tenth New Hampshire in action: "Troops never stood under a more hellish fire than was poured upon the Tenth New Hampshire on this day. Half of the trees were cut down by shells, and, falling upon the dead and wounded mangled their bodies in a horrid manner."[20]

Like many soldiers, Sergeant Silas T. Goodale of the Tenth New Hampshire kept a war diary. His entry for June 3, 1864 was, "Wounded at the battle of cold Harbor in the left shoulder Went to field hospital. Found Ward Randall there had the ball taken out of me. This is Sgt. Goodale's final entry!"[21] Although Sergeant Goodale was severely wounded in the shoulder, he did not die. He survived the war but died in a tragic drowning accident in Hooksett Falls in 1888.[22]

The Thirteenth New Hampshire, along with the remainder of the Second Brigade, was held in reserve and was not committed to the dawn attack. The regiment was still subjected to fire from the Confederate lines, and several men were wounded. Second Lieutenant George H. Taggard of Nashua received a severe wound but later recovered.[23]

Martindale's Second division went forward with Brooks, who was to advance and keep contact with the right flank of Warren's Fifth Corps. In front of Martindale's division was an open exposed plain, with the Confederate line four hundred yards away. The Second and Twelfth New Hampshire Regiments were in Martindale's second brigade commanded by Colonel Griffin A. Stedman. The attack began, and Martindale's division swept away the enemy pickets just as Brooks had done. Smith ordered a temporary halt to ascertain that Brooks was aligned properly. He wanted to wait until Warren's corps came alongside before resuming the advance. Hearing firing to the right, he assumed that Warren had arrived and ordered Brooks and Martindale forward. As the Second and Twelfth New Hampshire advanced, it became clear that Warren had not arrived, and the brigades of Martindale's division were swept by a murderous fire from both front and left.[24]

The Second New Hampshire sidled up close to the Confederate entrenchments and traded shots with the defending graybacks. The men dug into the ground the best they could just to have a small amount of cover. Private Addison C. Messenger of Stoddard, who had joined the Second New Hampshire as a recruit while the regiment was at Point Lookout, Maryland, was looked on with suspicion by the veterans and was probably considered to be as unworthy as the majority of recruits arriving there. Messenger may have tried to tell them that he had already done a tour of duty with the Sixteenth New Hampshire in Louisiana, but it was not remembered that he did. As the men of the Second New Hampshire clung to what little cover they had at Cold Harbor and exchanged occasional shots with the entrenched Confederates, Messenger kept standing up to load and fire. He did so as coolly as if he were on parade. The firing and loading went on in this fashion until Messenger was shot in the chest and fell to the ground dead. Any doubts about the courage of the young man from Stoddard were removed forever.[25]

In the space of only a few minutes, three captains in the Second New Hampshire were either killed or mortally wounded. Captain George W. Gordon of Allenstown died one hour after having the top of his head taken off by a shell. He had been in the regiment from the beginning and had sustained wounds at both Second Bull Run and Gettysburg. Captain William H. Smith sustained multiple gunshot wounds to the legs and died three days later at Fort Monroe. His body was taken home and laid to rest in Exeter. Captain Henry Hayward of Dover was lying down and firing, but a bullet still found him and hit him in the neck. He bled to death three hours later, and his body is buried on the battlefield.[26] Losses for the Second New Hampshire on June 3 were eight men killed, eight mortally wounded, and fifty-four others wounded. The regiment was able to leave the field in good order despite its losses.[27]

The Twelfth New Hampshire, also in Stedman's brigade, suffered grievous losses because of its position in the column. The Second had been positioned well to the rear, but the Twelfth was in the vanguard and was thus subjected to a withering and brutal fire from three sides. Sergeant John L. Piper of Barnstead, who received a serious wound in the charge at Cold Harbor, made this comment about the attack: "The men bent down as they pushed forward, as if trying, as they were, to breast a tempest, and the files of men went down like rows of blocks or bricks pushed over by striking against each other."[28]

The Twelfth New Hampshire went forward until it totally lost all unit cohesion. Seeking shelter in the trees with the remnants of the other regiments of the brigade, the Twelfth New Hampshire waited and then slowly made its way back to the Federal line.[29] Lieutenant Alonzo Jewett of Bristol was also severely wounded in the attack. He stated that the men of the Twelfth New Hampshire were falling "half a platoon almost at a time, like grain before the reaper or grass before the scythe."[30]

Captain Thomas E. Barker, when told to gather his regiment for another charge, stated in no uncertain terms that he would not lead his regiment in another attack even if Jesus Christ himself should order it. Barker had been against using the old Napoleonic tactic of attacking in column, and when he argued with a superior officer who told him that it was an effectual technique, Barker replied, "The most effectual way of murdering men, I agree, and there is the evidence of it." He pointed out to the field in front, covered with the dead and wounded of the brigade. The discussion was abruptly cut off when the superior officer received a serious wound to the shoulder and was removed. In less than thirty minutes, 63 men of the Twelfth New Hampshire were killed, and 114 were wounded.[31]

Earlier in the war when the Twelfth New Hampshire was in camp opposite Fredericksburg, a small group of soldiers got together to reminisce about their school days in Tilton. Lieutenant Joseph K. Whittier rose and proudly boasted, "Well, boys, I feel it in my bones that I am going to live to see this rebellion crushed. When I get home I am going to study law, and put out my shingle in some city and you will hear from me later." Whittier made it through all the earlier battles of the Twelfth and received only a slight wound at Gettysburg. The tall, twenty-one-year-old officer from Laconia died on the field at Cold Harbor after being wounded in the body by grape shot.[32]

On the extreme right of the Federal line near Bethesda Church, Brigadier General Simon Griffin led his Second Brigade containing the Sixth and Eleventh New Hampshire across an elevated plain in search of a Confederate battery that had been harassing his section of the line. The Ninth New Hampshire had been left behind to support the Federal artillery. Companies C and I of the Eleventh New Hampshire were on the right flank of this moving body of soldiers, and after going a quarter of a mile, they unwittingly passed in front of a Confederate brigade hidden in the woods.[33] Sergeant Charles C. Paige stated that the order for double-time was given: "Under the circumstances while running double quick I was struck by a minie ball in my left arm, four inches above the elbow, directly in front and center of the humerous bone, breaking it clean off. In this condition with my arm dangling a part of the time, and partly held by the fingers with the other hand, I ran forward some forty feet and laid down behind a stump."[34] Captain George Nelson Shepard of Epping received a painful but not life-threatening wound in the left hip.[35]

The Ninth Corps had been ordered to keep its place in the line and was not ordered to participate in the same attack as the other corps. It did, however, respond to situations such as the one in which the Eleventh New Hampshire engaged. Therefore, losses among the Sixth, Ninth, and Eleventh regiments were comparatively light. A total of twenty-six soldiers died from these three New Hampshire regiments during the entire Cold Harbor campaign.[36]

The Battle of Cold Harbor had been bad enough, but the days afterward were days that held untold horrors for the wounded left on the battlefield. Lieutenant Richard W. Musgrove of the Twelfth New Hampshire recorded in his book the details of this nightmare experience: "Our dead and wounded lay within two hundred yards of the enemy lines. Though the battle was over, there was no cessation of hostilities for five days, and during this time no assistance was rendered those unable to crawl from the field, except such as was given at night." Each night, soldiers from all the regiments would cautiously crawl out onto the battlefield and help those still living. A lucky few were dragged back and survived. A truce was eventually agreed on by Grant and Lee, but by then the hundreds of wounded soldiers who could have been helped were already dead.[37] From June 2 to June 15, the Fifth New Hampshire lost more men than any other infantry regiment during the Cold Harbor Campaign. Of the 577 men who stood ready for duty on June 2, 69 men were killed, and 162 were wounded by June 15. Overall, Federal losses for this same time period were 1,845 killed, 9,077 wounded, and 1,816 missing and assumed captured.[38]

Writing to his wife on June 6, Private James Howes of Portsmouth had time to collect his thoughts and relate his experiences in the recent battle as a member of the Tenth New Hampshire Regiment: "I fought a most terrific battle on the 3rd with what results I know not. . . . Our regiment was under fire all day in the most advanced position of any brigade and there within 150 yards and right in front of a strong rebel battery and breastworks. We stood for about two hours under one of the most galling fires imaginable, the hottest and most destructive by far that I have encountered since my enlistment." Howes explained the effect of concentrated firing on the field: "Shells pouring into us by tens and twenties at a time splitting trees no matter how big and knocking down and annihilating anything and everything that happened to stand in their way then again exploding killing men by scores with their scattered fragments and then to see the trees with their hundreds of branches snapping, bending and waving apparently in a most frantic manner as if possessed with animal life."[39]

Once again, the two armies had to cope with the terrible aftermath of battle. No one was more affected by this than the surgeons and medical staff. Referring to soldiers recently wounded at Cold Harbor, Nurse Sarah Low of Dover said, "They brought in more dreadful wounds yesterday and brought a great many dead. Some of the wounds are in dreadful condition. One arm was so mortified that the flesh dropped off and as many as a pint of maggots were got out. It is impossible to keep maggots from some wounds for they multiple in less than a minute. All knee joint wounds die unless the patient is strong enough to go through amputation."[40] Private Frederic A. Eldredge of the Fifth New Hampshire was studying medicine in Manchester when he received his draft notice in September 1863. Eldredge followed the fortunes of the Fifth New Hampshire until he was wounded at Cold Harbor on June 3. Lying on his cot, the young intern probably saw the pain and suffering of the wounded around him and made up his mind to continue his medical career. Eldredge was appointed assistant surgeon in the First New Hampshire Cavalry soon after he was wounded and accepted the post in October 1864.[41]

During the Battle of Cold Harbor, George R. Norris was resting comfortably in his bed in the house of his parents back in Epping, when a sharp knock on the door woke him. Two Portsmouth police officers had arrived to take him into custody. Norris, who had been drafted the previous summer, was scheduled to report to the First New Hampshire Cavalry that August. Having failed to do so, he was branded a deserter, and the authorities had finally caught up with him. Norris was taken to Portsmouth along with another deserter from Exeter. Soon after his arrival, Norris became visibly ill and upon being questioned admitted that he had taken poison a short time before. Norris was so determined not to go to war that he committed suicide.[42]

A story that appeared in the June 10 edition of the *Rochester Courier* chronicled the unfortunate experience of Lieutenant George S. Cobbs of the Second New Hampshire Cavalry. The Second New Hampshire was part of the overall rearguard that was covering the retreat of Major General Nathaniel B. Banks's army back down the Red River. The New Hampshire horsemen skirmished by day and rode all night to catch up to the army and were in a constant state of exhaustion. In one such skirmish, Lieutenant Cobbs was captured. He was being led to the rear when a small force of Union cavalry came to the rescue. Seeing that they were about to lose their prisoner, one of the Confederates drew his revolver and shot the thirty-five-year-old Cobbs. His last words were, "They have murdered me!" Tender hands from his regiment buried him along the banks of the Red River. Cobbs's body was later reburied in the Alexandria National Cemetery.[43] The constant running battles and skirmishes of the Red River campaign had been especially hard on the men of the Eighth New Hampshire Second New Hampshire Cavalry. The regiment had lost ninety-six men killed, wounded, and missing during the three-month campaign. After its arrival in Morganzia, Louisiana, the regiment was sent to New Orleans on its veteran furlough.[44]

Other items in the news that day were several paragraphs of praise for Brigadier General Gilman Marston and a letter from Colonel Walter Harriman of the Eleventh New Hampshire, who was still a prisoner in Lynchburg, Virginia. In his letter dated May 9, Harriman reported that he was "neither dead nor disheartened as a prisoner of war."[45]

As the Cold Harbor campaign neared its end, the Third New Hampshire in Gillmore's Tenth Corps was involved in another one of the Union's lost opportunities to end the war. The plan as it was devised in Butler's headquarters was that two columns were to go to Petersburg and capture it if possible. Brigadier General August Kautz was to threaten the Jerusalem Plank Road with his cavalry and artillery, while Gillmore's section of the Tenth Corps was to demonstrate from the City Point Road. It was agreed that if Kautz's raid was successful, Gillmore would then attack and capture Petersburg.[46] The Third New Hampshire set out on this expedition on June 8 and had a rough time getting to Petersburg. About one third of the journey was through dense woods, which broke up any hope of keeping a tight formation. Mud holes and blasted trees further impeded the march. The dense undergrowth tore the soldiers' clothes, and they had to spend the night of June 8 lying exposed on the ground. When Kautz's cavalry column arrived at Petersburg, it was able to enter the city without opposition. However, Gillmore's force did not attack simultaneously, and when it did attack, it ran into lightly held defensive positions. Companies of the Third New Hampshire were sent forward as skirmishers, and the remainder of the regiment was detailed to protect a battery. Also present was the Seventh New Hampshire, which was also only lightly engaged and suffered no losses.[47] Only one man from the Third New Hampshire lost his life in this expedition. Private George L. Jones of Milford had been wounded at Secessionville, at Drewry's Bluff, and now outside of Petersburg. Jones received a wound to the head that caused his death soon after.[48]

At noon Quincy Gillmore came forward in the line to observe the Confederate position. There are two stories describing what Gillmore did next. The first story is that Gillmore and his staff broke for lunch and, taking their meal in a nearby home, were led to believe by the woman of the house that Petersburg was heavily defended. On the woman's word alone, Gillmore called off the attack and returned to Bermuda Hundred. The other story is that after Gillmore observed the Confederate lines, he simply decided that the enemy defenses could not be carried and cancelled the expedition.[49]

Upon the return of Gillmore, a court of inquiry was held. Captain George F. Towle of the Fourth New Hampshire recalled the mood around Butler's headquarters: "Butler is much enraged with Gillmore at the result of the expedition.

Kautz and Hawley have been examined by him. Butler insists that Gillmore could have taken Petersburg on that day, and I believe Butler was right in so asserting."[50] The investigation revealed that Kautz had encountered weak resistance and that only a handful of militia was defending the city. A great opportunity to take Petersburg and to perhaps shorten the war was missed. Towle's brief entry for June 14 describes the fate of Quincy Gillmore: "Gillmore has been relieved from the command of the Tenth Corps by Gen. Butler and ordered to Fort Monroe."[51] Temporary command of the Tenth Corps was afterward given to Brigadier General Alfred H. Terry.

On June 11, the Twelfth New Hampshire was dispatched to White House Landing to rejoin the Eighteenth Corps. The regiment caught up with the corps on the June 15 just as it was heading out for a second assault on Petersburg. Butler's previous attack had alerted the Confederates to Grant's intentions, so by the time this second force reached Petersburg, the Confederates were dug in all along the line with strong works and fortifications. The nightmare of trench warfare was about to begin.[52]

The Fifth New Hampshire was in action in the lines at Petersburg from June 16 to June 18. The regiment had crossed the river at Harrison's landing and went into line of battle early on the Sixteenth. During the course of these hostilities, a fatal bullet that passed through the body of a soldier in front of him struck Colonel Charles Hapgood in the arm. Dr. William Child of the regiment removed the bullet on the field. Command of the regiment passed to Major James E. Larkin of Concord. The regiment lost sixteen men killed during this attack on the defenses at Petersburg.[53]

The Third and Seventh New Hampshire regiments were also in action on June 16. As Grant's army was filing into its battle line around Petersburg, the Tenth Corps was sent to discover if the Confederates had left their lines along the Richmond-Petersburg Turnpike to reinforce Beauregard at Petersburg. It was reported at dawn on June 16 that no movement could be seen in the Confederate lines, but orders were not given to venture out until midday. The men of the Third and Seventh moved cautiously across the large open field that separated the lines, and reaching the first set of works, they discovered them abandoned and continued on to the next line. The second line of defenses was also found abandoned, and with a heavy line of skirmishers out front, the main body of troops approached the turnpike.[54] Lieutenant Daniel Eldredge of the Third New Hampshire was with his regiment on their march when he spied what appeared to be a glove on the ground. It was in front of him so he tried to kick it out of the way. This is when he made a gruesome discovery: "My horror and indignation were great when I discovered the resemblance to a buckskin glove was no less than a human hand covered with dirt. The human hand belonged to a body, half buried, the toes, hands and hair of which were all visible."[55]

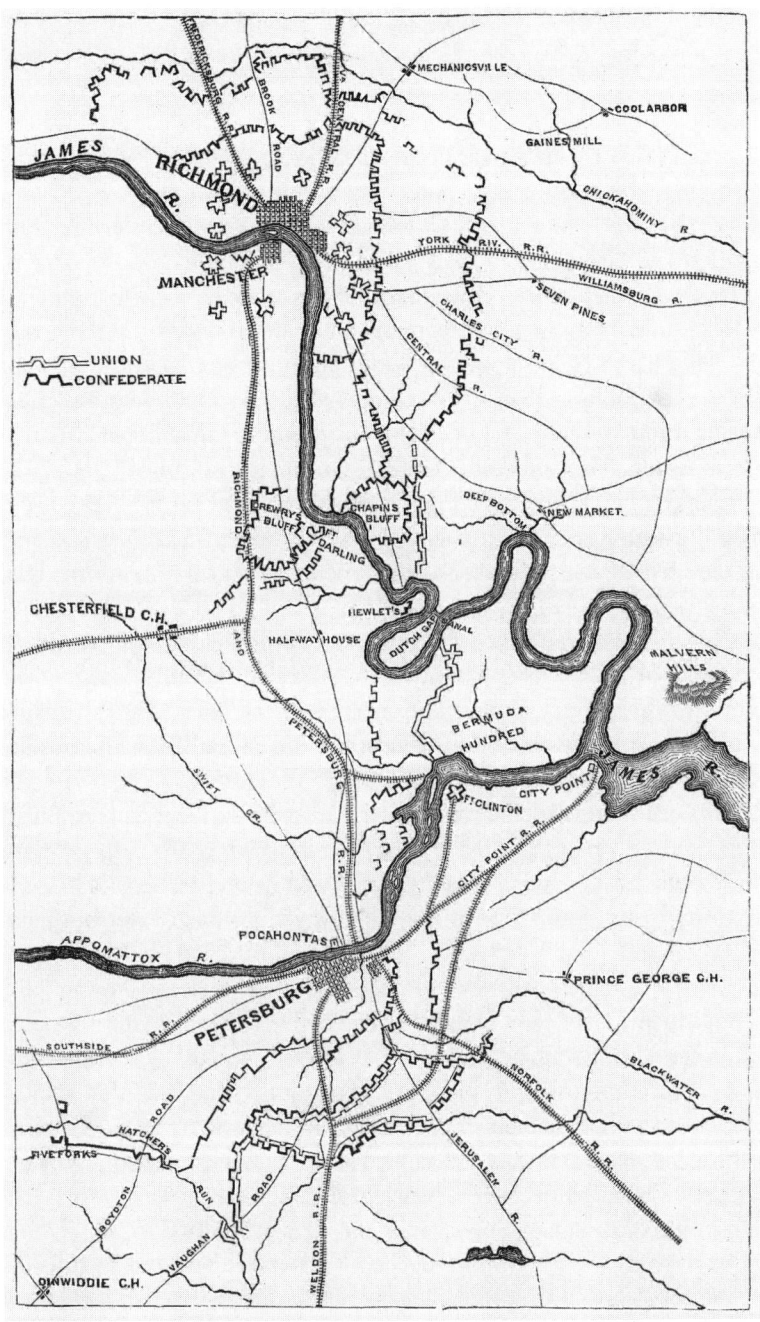

Richmond and Petersburg. From Daniel Eldredge, The Third New Hampshire and All about It, *1893*

At the Richmond-Petersburg Turnpike, the advancing Union force found the Confederates moving in large numbers south on it. The two forces discovered each other's presence simultaneously and immediately engaged in combat. It was ascertained that this force of Confederates belonged to Major General George Edward Pickett's division and were headed south to bolster the Petersburg defenses.[56] In the first contact, a large body of men rushed toward the Third New Hampshire. The two regiments on either side of the Third were armed with Spencer rifles, said Lieutenant Eldredge, who described the reception provided for the attacking Confederates: "Onward the rebels came expecting to annihilate the small force in sight, but they were repulsed by a few rounds from the seven-shooters."[57] The Third New Hampshire withdrew in good order and waited for the rest of the Federal force to come up. Before help could reach them, an unfortunate incident took place. The men of the Third New Hampshire realized that they were surrounded on three sides and were nervously awaiting the return of the skirmishers in their front. Someone saw the skirmishers running back toward the line, and assuming they had been routed, the unknown soldier shouted, "Retreat!" Suddenly large sections of the regiment started running for the rear. The officers tried to head off the stampede and were only successful when they drew their swords and threatened the runners with bodily harm. Fortunately, the men were returned to the main body of the regiment and order was restored in a short time.[58] In action near Ware Bottom Church, the Third New Hampshire lost fourteen killed and twenty wounded, while the Seventh New Hampshire sustained eight combat deaths.[59]

On June 15, the Tenth and Thirteenth New Hampshire Regiments in Burnham's brigade were part of a movement by Smith's Eighteenth Corps toward Petersburg. Their mission was to secure a foothold in preparation for the advance of Grant to the south side of the James River, north of Petersburg and south of Richmond. The New Hampshire men approached the defenses of Petersburg with the Thirteenth New Hampshire in front as skirmishers and the Tenth behind them. They soon reached a formidable five-gun battery situated on a bluff in their front. Battery Number Five, a defensive work with high parapets, was so named because of its place in a string of such batteries that formed a defensive ring around Petersburg.[60]

The Thirteenth New Hampshire occupied a ravine in front of and just below the battery and was not subject to the constant shelling as the troops to their left. Captains George Naylor Julian, Enoch Goss, and Nathan D. Stoodley got together and decided the only way to stop the shelling was to take the battery. The three bold captains rose from the trench with twelve enlisted men. They scrambled up the hill and captured the battery and one hundred prisoners.[61] The Thirteenth New Hampshire suffered thirteen killed and forty wounded in action around Battery Five. One of the wounded was the future historian of the Thirteenth

Second Lieutenant
S. Millett Thompson, *Thirteenth New Hampshire, Company E. Thompson sustained a serious wound fighting at Battery Five, Petersburg, Virginia, on June 15, 1864. He later became the regiment's official historian. Photograph courtesy of NHVA*

New Hampshire, Lieutenant S. Millet Thompson, who explained why his personal narrative abruptly stopped: "The writer must here—and most reluctantly for he desired very much to see the war through with the Thirteenth—drop the personal part of the narrative . . . while he goes to a military Hospital . . . with a bullet hole through a badly smashed ankle."[62] Captain Elisha E. Dodge of Rollinsford, commanding Company B of the Thirteenth New Hampshire, told a friend, "When you hear that Company B has broken and retreated or acted badly in battle, you may know I am dead."[63] In the advance to the Confederate line, Captain Dodge, waving his sword to rally the men, drew the attention of Confederate artillerists and was wounded in the chest and leg by shrapnel. He died two weeks later of blood poisoning after refusing to grant the surgeons permission to amputate his leg.[64]

The day after Battery Five had been captured, some Confederates were observed in a ravine one hundred yards behind the battery. Three companies of the Tenth New Hampshire were detailed to clean out the infiltrators, who were intent on recapturing the battery. Irish-born Captain James Madden commanded the fifty-four men of the Tenth New Hampshire who were selected for the detail. The Confederates were overwhelmed in the ravine, and fifty of them surrendered but not without a fight. Three men from the Tenth New Hampshire were killed and six wounded in the action. Among the slain was the twenty-nine-year-old Irish captain from Manchester.[65]

Hail to the Kearsarge, castle of oak, and pride of the heaving sea!
Hail to her guns, whose thunder awoke the waves,
and startled with lightning stroke, the nations that should be free![66]

Captain John Ancrum Winslow had been looking for the CSS *Alabama* for over a year. It appeared that the elusive Confederate commerce raider would never be found. On Sunday morning June 12, 1864, he was walking the deck of his ship, the USS *Kearsarge*, anchored in the Scheldt River not far from Vlissingen, The Netherlands. An emergency telegram from William L. Dayton, the American minister to France, was handed to Winslow—the previous day, the *Alabama,* after twenty-two months at sea, had sailed into the neutral, French seaport of Cherbourg for badly needed repairs. A quick look at the charts showed Winslow that his quarry was three hundred miles away. He immediately had a gun fired to summon the crew back to the ship. The *Kearsarge* got underway that morning, and the crew immediately readied the ship for battle. Two days later, the *Kearsarge* arrived off the eastern approach to Cherbourg. Winslow entered the harbor and steamed right by the *Alabama* without attacking, throwing down the gauntlet to his one-time friend and messmate Captain Raphael Semmes. The *Kearsarge* left the harbor and took up station just outside the harbor mouth and waited for the *Alabama* to come out. Semmes knew that he had to fight, but after twenty-two months at sea, his ship was not fit to go into combat. The *Kearsarge* was primed and at its peak; chains were strung over her sides to protect the flanks of the ship and deflect solid shot. Five days passed, but Winslow knew Semmes would come out eventually.[67]

At 10:20 A.M., June 19, as Captain Winslow was about to begin divine services for the crew, a crew member shouted, "She's coming out, sir!" The drums beat to general quarters, and Winslow brought the *Kearsarge* about and headed out to sea. Newington resident and landsman aboard the *Kearsarge* Martin Hoyt detailed the sea battle.

> The engagement commenced shortly before 11 and lasted until 12. The *Kearsarge* did not reply until the *Alabama* had fired three broadsides; the *Kearsarge* meanwhile steaming directly for her. When the *Kearsarge* got in favorable range, the 11 inch shells immediately got in their work and soon crippled the *Alabama.* The gunnery of the men on the *Alabama* was very rapid and reckless. They fired some 270 shots, while the *Kearsarge* fired about 170. I was a member of the 11 inch gun crew on the quarterdeck. Our gun captain was William Smith, an exceptionally cool-headed man. I believe that the way he handled this gun was greatly instrumental in sinking the *Alabama.* The most of the casualties of the fight on the *Kearsarge* occurred at this gun. Quarter gunner Dempsey had an arm shot off at the shoulder. McBeath was wounded in the

leg and William Gowan was shot in the thigh and died in the hospital at Cherbourg. The latter stood next to me at the time he was wounded. An eight inch shell lodged in the rudder post of the *Kearsarge* but which did not explode.[68]

According to Hoyt's account, shortly before the surrender of the *Alabama,* the ship made a vain attempt to get back within the three-mile limit of French waters. The *Kearsarge* blocked her way, and it was then that Semmes decided to surrender his ship. The English yacht *Deerhound* rescued Captain Semmes, twelve officers, and twenty-seven men. Many of the *Alabama*'s valuables had already been taken off and placed aboard the *Deerhound.*

"The *Alabama* had ten men killed and wounded in the engagement," Hoyt recalled about the battle. "Our boats rescued some 67 men and its officers while French fishing boats picked up the remainder of the *Alabama* crew."[69] Other sources show the losses for the two ships were one dead and three wounded for the *Kearsarge* and nine dead and twenty-one wounded aboard the *Alabama.*[70]

This sea battle became the subject of scores of paintings during and after the war. The French artist Édouard Manet, who witnessed the battle, painted it soon after. A painting of this classic naval duel hangs in the Langdon Public Library in Newington, New Hampshire. Produced in 1884 by William P. Stubbs, it was owned by Hoyt and donated to the library two years before his death in 1918.

Two days after these ships fought off the coast of France, the First New Hampshire Cavalry was involved in what became known as Wilson's Raid. Early on June 21, the New Hampshire horsemen rode south out of Petersburg, Virginia, down the Jerusalem Plank Road, where troopers under General Kautz met them. All five thousand cavalrymen were under the command of Major General James Wilson. His mission was to operate with Kautz destroying rails on the Southside Railroad and to go as far west as Burkeville.[71] On the first day the entire command rode fifty-four miles with ripped-up rails and burning bridges in their path. On the next day, the force encountered opposition from Confederate cavalry under Fitz-Hugh Lee, who attacked with such violence that four companies of the First New Hampshire became separated from the rest of the force. Companies A, B, and C of the First quickly dismounted and counterattacked, thus allowing the separated units to rejoin the main body. The Confederates lost 150 men killed and wounded on this day of fighting.

The combined forces of Kautz and Wilson regrouped and started fighting their way east toward the Union lines around Petersburg. Wilson returned on July 1 minus fifteen hundred men and twelve guns, but they had severely disrupted Lee's lines of transportation and communication west of Petersburg. Most of the Union casualties were men caught behind the lines and captured.

One man of the First New Hampshire was killed near Reams's Station on June 29, and seventy Confederate soldiers became prisoners of war.[72]

Just as the New Hampshire cavalry rode out to start its raid, companies F and G of the Second United States Sharpshooters were engaged in early fighting around the Weldon Railroad. Company F was acting as an advanced guard and became involved in a firefight with some Confederates who were in position in a nearby wood. The firing became intense, and the sharpshooters began to withdraw. As the green-coated riflemen backed away, a musket ball struck Sergeant Julian P. Dodge in the face just below his nose. He whirled around and fell. The Confederate who shot him was observed in the act and was quickly gunned down by Dodge's companions. To his sister Eliza on July 2, Sergeant Solomon Dodge of the Eleventh New Hampshire wrote, "I have some sad tidings for you, sad for us all, for it is concerning our dear brother Julian. Yesterday, a messenger from the 2nd U.S.S.S. telling me that Julian was reported killed last week."[73]

Reams of paper have been used to describe the conditions of trench warfare around Petersburg from July 1864 to April 1865. The short description by Private Elias A. Bryant of the Fourth New Hampshire captures the elements of this maddening form of conflict: "Hot day. We are in the trench today. Potter of Company D killed. A bullet passed through his arm and side. I remember him as a wild and reckless fellow. One man in Company F was knocked down by the wind of a shell, which burst after passing him. One piece came down near me where I was cooking."[74] The Company F soldier was twenty-one-year-old Private Frank L. Potter of Manchester. Bryant's entries in his diary tell the essence of this type of warfare. Each day he mentions the weather, whether it was his company's day to be in the forward trench, and usually reports one or two men were killed or wounded by opposing sharpshooters. On July 10, 1864, Lieutenant George E. Upton of Company G Sixth New Hampshire wrote about the trenches at Petersburg, "We are in the second line of intrenchments today, consequently not quite so much exposed as when we are to the extreme point, yet there is a danger anywhere around here when one gets above the ground. I am now occupying a hole that is in dimensions about six feet by three feet in depth. . . . The weather continues about the same as when I last wrote, dry, hot and awfull dusty."[75] "We have to do picket duty every other day two days on and one day off," Corporal Horace H. Adams of the Tenth New Hampshire wrote to his brother in Portsmouth. "Sharpshooting is made Easy and woe to the man that exposes his head 2 inches above the breastworks, for he is Sure to get it pluged. Since I wrote to mother we have lost one man from our Company, while on Picket. Shot Dead."[76] Major Phin Bixby of the Sixth New Hampshire recorded in his diary, "When I arose on the morning of the 14th [July] little did I realize what a day may bring forth. After breakfast I went out to the fort which the 2nd [New Hampshire Regiment] and my Regt. were building. Had been there but a short time when I was shot through the left shoulder by a Rebel Sharpshooter. My good fortune followed me. . . . for although the wound is severe it is not dangerous."[77] Lieutenant Colonel Henry Pearson did not have the same good fortune following him in May at the North Anna River. Pearson, an Exeter resident, was also was hit by a sharpshooter's bullet, but instead of the ball passing cleanly and completely through his shoulder, it slammed into his forehead, killing him instantly.[78] Bixby was away from the regiment for only three months but was appointed lieutenant colonel later in July to replace Henry Pearson. Another man who fell from a sharpshooter's bullet was the chaplain of the Twelfth New Hampshire, Thomas L. Ambrose of Ossipee. Ambrose, who had been captured at Chancellorsville, had been regained from the missing and was ministering to the sick in the front lines at Petersburg when he fell on July 24. By the summer of 1864, the Twelfth New Hampshire had been reduced by battle deaths and disease to a mere 112 men.[79]

To relieve Union pressure on his Petersburg lines, Lee detached Jubal Early's Corps and sent it to the Shenandoah Valley. Early, in his own hometown of Lynchburg, defeated Major General David Hunter on June 18 and began to move down the valley with his small army of ten thousand men. They crossed the Potomac, fought at Monocacy on July 9, and by July 11 were at the outskirts of Washington, D.C., itself.[80] "The great point of interest is now Washington and vicinity," wrote Dr. William Child of the Fifth New Hampshire on July 15 to his wife. "We have no communication with the North except by water. What the result will I can not tell—or whether the rebel expedition is a mere raid or not. From all I can learn in the papers we shall be much annoyed by them—even if we do not lose Washington."[81]

"We have been having quite a time with the rebs here," Private J. Lewis Chase of the Eleventh New Hampshire wrote from his Washington hospital bed to his parents about the excitement in the nation's capital. "I suppose they came in within four miles of the city and attacked the forts but did not make much out of the offer—they were just to days to late if they had made the attack on Saturday instead of Monday they could have taken the city without much trouble we had no troops here of any account but Grant got wind of it and sent the sixth corps they arrived just in season to save the city."[82]

An important point that Private Chase did not mention was the brave delaying action that was fought by Major General Lew Wallace at the Battle of Monocacy on July 9. The extra days allowed Grant time to shuttle Horatio Wright's Sixth Corps to Washington in time to bolster its defenses.[83]

While Private Chase was recuperating in the Stanton Hospital in Washington, his colonel, Walter Harriman, was permitted by his Confederate captors to receive his first letter since being taken prisoner at the Wilderness in May. Since Harriman's last communication that he was being held in Lynchburg, the Confederate authorities moved him to North Carolina, to Savannah, and finally to

Charleston, South Carolina. Harriman's journal entry for June 19 describes what was being done: "We are 'out of jail' but not out of the 'hotbed.' Yesterday they moved us from the prison where we had been about a week, and brought us into the burnt and 'shelled district,' where we are now occupying a three-story wooden building that was once a private residence. The two-hundred-pound shells from our guns are whizzing into this part of city once in fifteen minutes day and night." Harriman said the entire population in that part of the town had long since been evacuated. The Federal prisoners were being held their obviously as human shields to deter further bombardment of the city.[84] Harriman was exchanged on August 3 after the Confederates discovered that fifty of their officers would be put in harm's way on Morris Island. The New Hampshire officer had been held in the lower part of the city nearly seven weeks and, miraculously, the building he was housed in survived intact.[85] Harriman rejoined the Eleventh New Hampshire for a brief time and then went home to New Hampshire to campaign for Abraham Lincoln's reelection. Near the end of the war, he briefly became a brigade commander and in 1867 governor of the state. The highly esteemed soldier-politician of the Eleventh New Hampshire died in Concord in 1884 and is buried in his hometown of Warner.[86]

"They seemed to be all about us"

CHAPTER II

July 1864 to September 1864

Then gather 'round my comrades and hear a soldier tell
how full of honor was the day when every man did well.

Martin Farquar Tupper, "Waterloo,"
Complete Poetical Works

In order to replenish the thinning ranks of the Union army, President Abraham Lincoln issued a call for an additional 500,000 men on July 18, 1864. As a result, the state of New Hampshire formed the last regiment to be sent into the field during the Civil War—the Eighteenth New Hampshire Volunteer Regiment, with Charles H. Bell of Exeter commissioned as its colonel and James W. Carr of Manchester its lieutenant colonel. These two officers immediately started to recruit soldiers with the hope that it would be an all-volunteer unit.[1]

Major General William F. Smith was relieved of his command of the Eighteenth Corps in mid-July because of dissatisfaction with his handling of the attacks on Petersburg the end of June. Temporary command of the corps went to Brigadier General John Henry Martindale. Major General Ben Butler's two corps commanders have been much maligned over their noncooperation with their commander, but the common soldier had a different view. Corporal Horace H. Adams of the Tenth New Hampshire told his brother, "Baldy Smith our Corp Commander has been relieved The men feel sorry to lose him he was a Good officer and knowed how to take the Johnnies, by Surprise."[2]

While generally assumed that unit cohesion in both armies was based on loyalty to the regiment and although this was true to an extent, far more credence can be given to loyalty to one's town or company that constituted the basis for cohesion. Most men in a company were raised on the town level, so everyone grew up with or at least knew everyone else in the company. A good example of this is Company A of the Eleventh New Hampshire, a company of one hundred men formed entirely from the towns of Epping, South Newmarket, and Fremont, New Hampshire. Indicative of this camaraderie and town identification is a letter by Private William B. Greene of Raymond to his brother on July 25, 1864:

"I see G. P. Sargeant occasionally. Saw Charley Dodge the other day & expect soon to see the Raymond boys in the 10th N.H. Vol. S. D. Tilton is in command of the NH 11th at present, Col Harriman being a prisoner at Charleston, S.C."[3]

For General Robert E. Lee, it was a matter of numbers, and for Lieutenant General Ulysses G. Grant, it was a matter of time. Neither commander wanted the war to stagnate, and both sought to outmaneuver the other. Lee was well aware that trench warfare meant attrition of the few soldiers he could put into his defensive lines around Petersburg. Positive news was needed from the battlefront soon, or the president of the United States stood little chance of being reelected. The shortest distance between the two armies was six hundred yards, and the Ninth Corps of the Union army was in the trenches in this area. The Sixth, Ninth, and Eleventh New Hampshire regiments, all part of the Ninth Corps, were in this part of the line, which was to be the location of one of the most fantastic yet tragic episodes of the war.

While the troops welcomed this respite from the huge grinding battles they had participated in over the last three months, Grant was conferring with Major General George Gordon Meade on where the best place would be to launch a general attack. Then came a suggestion from an unlikely quarter. Another regiment in the Ninth Corps was the Forty-eighth Pennsylvania, tough and battle-hardened coal miners from northeast Pennsylvania. Their lieutenant colonel, Henry Pleasants, proposed a radical idea and one that had been used with some effect at Vicksburg. Pleasants suggested to his corps commander, Ambrose Burnside, that the corps dig a mine under the Confederate fortifications, pack it with powder, and blow it up. Then they would have a clear road not only to Petersburg but probably to Richmond as well. Burnside liked the idea, Meade did not, and Grant eventually approved the plan but refused to offer Pleasants the assistance of the army engineers.[4]

Work on the mine began June 25 and ended on July 23. Captured Confederate prisoners admitted that they knew the Federals were digging but did not know where. Pleasants supervised the construction of the mine in the shape of a T under the Confederate fortifications. The main gallery of the mine was 510 feet long, and each arm was 50 feet long. Colonel Pleasants needed twelve thousand pounds of powder to make the necessary breach in the line. He was given only eight thousand pounds and no proper mining tools to do the job. Pleasants had to improvise everything he needed to complete the project.[5] The explosion of the mine was to be the prelude to a general assault by Burnside's Ninth Corps troops. The former army commander wanted to be sure that everything went right for him this time and ordered Brigadier General Edward Ferraro's Fourth Division to train for this kind of assault. By the time the mine was done, the black troops knew their jobs and what was expected of them. Then fate intervened. An order from Meade forbade Burnside to use the black troops as a vanguard and told him to choose another division to lead the assault. The duty to lead the assault should have fallen to Brigadier General Robert B. Potter's Second Division because it was the one with the most experience. Instead, Burnside allowed fate to decide—the three division commanders drew straws. First Division Commander Brigadier General James Ledlie picked the short straw. A worse selection could not have been made. Ledlie was a known drunk and not one to be seen leading his poorly disciplined men in battle. The New Hampshire men of Potter's division would be in the second wave to attack just behind Ledlie's troops.[6]

The mine was ready, and the fuses were laid on July 27. Everyone knew that something "big" was going to happen in this part of the line, and activity increased in the days preceding the explosion. "Thursday July 28th, 1864," Sergeant Howard M. Hanson of the Ninth New Hampshire recorded in his diary about the heightened activity. "All was still and quiet until an artillery Fight wich continued until near Midnight our guns setting fire to Petersburg."[7] Detonation of the mine was scheduled for 3:30 A.M. on July 30. The anticipation is evident in Hanson's next entry: "Friday July 29th, 1864: Went to bed but not to sleep much as it was expected that we should make an advance and blow up that Fort in the morning."[8]

At the appointed time on Saturday morning, the fuses were lit. Troops of the First Division were poised and ready for the attack, but Brigadier General Ledlie was nowhere to be seen. The time for the detonation came and went without the expected explosion. Two intrepid soldiers from the Forty-eighth Pennsylvania volunteered to go into the mine to determine why the detonation had not occurred. They soon returned after resplicing and relighting the fuse. At 4:44 A.M. the mine exploded. The earth shook, heaved, and the blast hurled tons of dirt, equipment, and people into the air. The blast created a crater 200 feet long, 90 feet wide, and 25 deep. Seconds later, the things hurled upwards by the blast all came raining down. Body parts, animals, muskets, and stones came back down to bury the stunned Confederates who survived the initial explosion. Over 270 South Carolinians in the immediate area were killed or wounded in the blast.[9]

Sergeant Hanson of the Ninth New Hampshire recalled the action that morning: "At just 4 o'clock the Fort went up and our artillery opened on the rebels and our brigade advanced the firing was awful heavy and continued until after Noon."[10] The men of Ledlie's division went forward and tumbled down into the crater, and without leadership, the confused and frightened soldiers milled around in the crater, not sure of what to do next. Potter's division was coming into the battle just to the right of them.

Brigadier General Simon G. Griffin's Second Brigade went forward. The New Hampshire regiments in his brigade could muster only six hundred rifles. Because of the terrible casualties since May, captains were now in command of

Griffin's regiments. Captain Robert L. Ela of Concord commanded the Sixth New Hampshire, Captain John B. Cooper of Newport commanded the Ninth, and Captain Sewell D. Tilton commanded the Eleventh until he was wounded early in the battle. Command of the Eleventh then passed to Captain Arthur C. Locke of Epsom.[11]

The Confederates recovered quickly from the mine explosion and turned their cannon and muskets on the helpless men trapped in the crater. The men of the Sixth New Hampshire breached the Confederate line and immediately engaged in hand-to-hand combat with the enemy in their trenches. General Griffin tried to rally the men in his vicinity to push on and take their objective, which was Cemetery Hill. Bullets tore through his uniform, but he was unhurt. Griffin was unsuccessful in trying to move the mass of men forward. Each minute that was lost trying to rally the men in the crater gave the Confederates more time to recover from the blast. The firing from the front and sides became too much, and the attack failed.[12]

The Sixth New Hampshire put forth a valiant effort to carry out its orders but the Confederates inflicted heavy casualties. The regiment lost nine dead and forty-three wounded. Sergeant Major Abraham Cohn, in the act of delivering orders to several Ninth Corps generals, received a serious wound in the shoulder. Cohn, who was born in Prussia, was given the Medal of Honor for conspicuous bravery at the Battle of the Wilderness.[13]

When the men of the Ninth New Hampshire went forward, they were able to gain the ruins of the Confederate fort quickly and plant their colors on what was left of the parapet. The colors fell twice but were twice regained. Sergeant Leander A. Wilkins of Northumberland would win a Medal of Honor for his actions at the mine explosion. A Confederate soldier had taken the flag of the Twenty-first Massachusetts Infantry until Wilkins accosted him and took it from him. It was later returned to the Bay Staters, and a grateful Congress honored Wilkins.[14]

When the Ninth New Hampshire breached the line, Sergeant Newell T. Dutton of Claremont described, "Our colors were first over the line. Red Parsons the other color bearer was mortally wounded before we reached it. The fort was one mass of ruins. Debris of all kinds was everywhere. Mangled bodies were lying around. Some were half-buried while several Johnnies were trying to extricate themselves from the dirt. We immediately charged down into the pits and took a number of prisoners. The Johnnies were pouring a flanking fire into us, not two rods distant. It was a terrible scene."[15]

There were many stories of personal courage and bravery at the Battle of the Crater. Sergeant Charles J. Simons of Exeter became detached from the rest of the battle but continued to fight his own private war. He was surrounded by Confederates but personally engaged each one. He shot one soldier, then wheeled around, and bayoneted another. Just as he was about to attack a third soldier, he was hit with the butt of a musket. Simons was dragged into a nearby bombproof as a prisoner. The Confederates, except for those in the bombproof, soon retreated from this area, and Simons was successful in convincing the Confederates in the bombproof to surrender to him. Simons's comrades in the Ninth were surprised to see the twenty-one-year-old-lad coming back to the Federal line with five Confederate prisoners in tow.[16] Captain Andrew J. Hough of Dover had been so seriously wounded that his Confederate captors began digging a grave for him. He made a miraculous recovery and was later exchanged.[17]

By this time the crater had become so full of screaming and fighting men that no forward progress could be made. There were no lines, and vicious personal combat took place everywhere in and around the crater. Both sides took prisoners, flags, and lives until the soldiers disengaged later in the afternoon. Casualties in the Ninth New Hampshire were appalling. The regiment lost almost fifty per cent of its strength at the crater: sixty-nine men wounded or captured and twenty-three dead on July 30.[18]

Just as the Eleventh New Hampshire rushed forward, Captain Tilton received a serious wound that knocked him out of the battle and the war. Captain Locke took the men forward into the destroyed Confederate works. Sergeant Lewis Childs of Warner carried the national flag at the Battle of the Crater. The colors of this regiment were also lost and regained twice (finally, they were ripped in two and saved).[19] In the midst of the confused fighting at the crater, Childs soon found himself surrounded. The following is Childs' account of how he saved the colors of the Eleventh New Hampshire: "They seemed to be all about us and we were obliged to fight hand to hand. A big fellow near me shouted 'Surrender the colors or I'll put a ball through you!' 'I'll never surrender!' I returned and the rebel fired. The ball passed through my blouse under the left arm leaving me unharmed but killing another man close by. The rebel then turned the butt of his gun, but I gave him a blow back of the ear which brought him to his knees and freed me from further trouble from him. But there were plenty of others and another big fellow grabbed me by the collar and took the colors. With the aid of my guards and by using my fists to good advantage, I succeeded in retaking them." All the men around Childs had been shot or bayoneted. Childs shoved what was left of the flag into his shirt and tried to make his way back to the Federal line. He was intercepted by three Confederate soldiers who took him prisoner and started him back to their line. Childs feigned exhaustion and said they would have to carry him. The graybacks carried Childs a short distance and then put him down to rest. He saw an opportunity and kicked one of his captors and knocked the other one down. In a second Childs was up and running. "I heard them shout, 'Halt or we'll shoot!' but kept dodging first to one side then the other to prevent their taking accurate aim. The balls were whizzing in all directions both from the rebel and Union lines. A ball coming from our lines hit me in the leg, partly shattering the bone. I scarcely noticed it but kept on until I reached our lines, when I fell and the boys in my company dragged me back to comparative safety." Childs survived both his wound and the war.[20]

In the action described by Childs, one of the men who fought over the flag was Private Willard J. Templeton of Hillsboro. Templeton received a mortal wound and died the same day. Private Henry W. Rowe of Candia was wounded severely at the crater but survived. Rowe was another member of the Eleventh New Hampshire who would be awarded a Medal of Honor for bravery in the Siege of Petersburg.[21] The Eleventh New Hampshire walked off the field after the Battle of the Crater with only sixty men. The regiment lost twenty-two dead and forty wounded or captured.[22]

In concert with the attack of the Ninth Corps at the crater, the Tenth Corps just to Burnside's right made an unsuccessful attack on the Confederate lines. The Fourth New Hampshire was in the Third Brigade of Brigadier General John W. Turner's division of the Tenth Corps and was involved in the assault. Colonel Louis Bell had been elevated to the command of the Third Brigade, and Captain Joseph M. Clough of New London led the attack on July 30. Principal Musician Elias A. Bryant recorded the Fourth's role in the attack and his own wounding: "About three o'clock we moved up to the front and lay till half past four, when the fort was blown up, and we opened on the rebels with artillery very heavy. We moved up a piece and supported the charging column, then moved back again and lay by the fort. I was struck while charging across the field. Laid about half an hour and was taken down to a wood and after probing the wound they put me in an ambulance as quick as they could get one. As we ran down the hill I was struck. It struck my right thigh in the upper third of the bone just as, in the act of running, I was throwing the limb forward." Bryant was carried away to a field hospital. When he was brought into the hospital tent, the surgeon said, "Take him right out and lay him on the table." Bryant knew that his wound was severe, and what was probably going to happen next. He asked for chloroform, and the attendant placed a rag saturated with the chemical over Bryant's face. The doctor removed Bryant's boot and examined the wound. "It is a hard case, isn't it? It has to come off close to the body." Bryant related the experience of having his leg amputated: "There immediately followed a terrible shock of pain. The feeling was as if a wire had been thrust up through every line of my body. It was like a flash of lightning, then I became entirely unconscious and knew nothing more until I opened my eyes, as if from sleep, as I found myself on a bed in the hospital. The moment my hand touched the bandages the full sense of my loss came over me, but it was only for a minute. I made up my mind that I had to make the best of it."[23] Bryant was lucky because he survived the loss of his leg and did not succumb to infection.

During the attack, Captain Clough was seriously wounded, and command of the regiment passed to Captain Francis W. Parker of Manchester. The regimental flag and staff were riddled with bullets during the fierce enfilading fire the regiment sustained in the attack. The losses of the Fourth New Hampshire were thirteen killed and thirty-seven wounded. Around 4 P.M., the attack was deemed a failure, and the men started to make their way back to their lines.[24]

Overall losses for the Union army at the Battle of the Crater were 3,798 men killed, wounded, or missing. Sixty-seven men from New Hampshire who watched in awe and excitement as the mine was detonated died in the futile assault that followed. After the battle generals and politicians scrambled to assign blame for the failure of the enterprise. Lengthy inquiries and proceedings followed the Battle of the Crater, resulting in Major General Ambrose Burnside being found guilty, relieved of command, and not given a new one. The ever-faithful soldiers of the Ninth Corps, the New Hampshire men included, felt the blame rested elsewhere.[25]

From Stanton Hospital in Washington, Private J. Lewis Chase of the Eleventh New Hampshire wrote to his brother John about various matters, including the draft and the recent battle near Petersburg. Not in possession of all the information, Chase asked, "What do you think of Gen. Grant's operations it seems that he has not forgot his old tricks the paper states that he blew one entir regt into the air and Sixteen guns it was done in front of the 9th & 18th Corps. I think we shall get more news from there soon."[26]

Former commander of the Fourth New Hampshire Colonel Louis Bell was tired. He applied for a furlough so he could go home to Chester to see his wife, Molly. Bell told her that the most trying parts of the service were not necessarily the battles, but "the constant anxiety and watchfulness required at the front, want of sleep, and weary care—the force I have commanded has done more fighting during this time than any other part of the army—of those under my command since May 1st near fifteen hundred have been killed and wounded. About as many as the whole population of Chester, men, women and children." Bell asked the same question that many exhausted soldiers were asking themselves by the summer of 1864: "I wonder if this war will ever end? I sometimes doubt it but I can not believe that God will permit us to be finally defeated."[27]

During the fighting around Petersburg, two Confederate battle flags were captured by men of the Thirteenth New Hampshire. Sergeant James R. Morrison and Corporal Peter Mitchell, both of Portsmouth, gave the flags to Colonel Aaron Fletcher Stevens to be shipped back to New Hampshire. Colonel Stevens sent the flags to Governor Gilmore. In the accompanying letter, the colonel said, "These trophies are entrusted to your care as mementoes of the gallantry of the young men who took them with the request in their behalf that they be retained

CAPTAIN GEORGE HAMILTON
PERKINS, *United States Navy.*
Perkins retired from the navy in
1891 after a long and storied
career. He commanded a ship
in the Battle of Mobile Bay on
August 5, 1864. Photograph
courtesy of NHVA

in the custody of the executive of New Hampshire until the men who captured them shall indicate some other disposition of these memorials of NH gallantry and success."[28]

On the morning of August 5, 1864, Admiral David Farragut with his fleet of eighteen ships entered the bay at Mobile, Alabama. Farragut was expecting heavy resistance, and it came in the form of two stoutly defended forts and the appearance of the heavy ironclad CSS *Tennessee.* Shortly after Farragut's entry into the bay, the battle became a wild melee of exploding shells and burning ships.[29]

"We had a desperate fight on the morning of the 5th," wrote George Hamilton Perkins of Hopkinton, commander of the ironclad USS *Chickasaw,* wrote on August 8. "No one was hurt on board my vessel, but the squadron lost a good many. Captain Craven of the *Tecumseh* was blown up by a torpedo just ahead of me."[30]

It was after the USS *Tecumseh* exploded and sank that Admiral Farragut shouted his famous order, "Damn the torpedoes, full steam ahead!" (The weapons called torpedoes at that time were floating mines sewn in the bay across the path of the attacking ships.)[31] After Farragut's famous order, his flagship, USS *Hartford,* led the way past forts. The *Tennessee* appeared and was rammed three times by Federal ships. Because of defective fuses, the *Tennessee* had difficulty returning fire and was then showered with shells when the remainder of the Federal fleet came up. The Confederate ship surrendered soon after, and three days later Mobile Bay itself, along with its forts, was surrendered as well.

"I had a hard fight with the rebel ram *Tennessee* and have been highly complimented by the Admiral and other old officers, for the part I took in the engagement," Perkins continued his description of the engagement. "I have been fighting forts every day since, and Fort Gaines surrendered this morning. I shelled Fort Powell, the afternoon of the 5th, and during the night the rebels blew it up. . . . The other ironclad are more or less disabled. . . . I must tell you that I have the credit of taking the rebel ram *Tennessee* and of wounding Admiral [Franklin] Buchanan."[32] Of the 3,000 Federal sailors engaged in the Battle of Mobile Bay, over 300 became casualties, including the 93 men who lost their lives when the *Tecumseh* went down. The crew of the *Tennessee* suffered the loss of 2 dead, 9 wounded, and 280 captured, including Admiral Buchanan.[33] Perkins stayed in the navy even after the war, was promoted to a full captain in 1882, and retired from the navy in 1891. He moved to Boston. Today there is a fine memorial to him behind the New Hampshire State House.[34]

General Ulysses S. Grant suspected that Robert E. Lee might have stripped his line of troops just south of Richmond to bolster his defenses around Petersburg. Therefore, on August 13 Grant ordered the Tenth Corps under Major General David B. Birney and the Second Corps under Major General Winfield Scott Hancock to move on Richmond. The James River was crossed at Jones's Neck, and the Tenth Corps marched to Deep Bottom and advanced to the front. The Third New Hampshire was posted on the far left of the line and engaged in light skirmishing at dawn on August 14. The remainder of the day was spent adjusting the lines. Lieutenant Colonel Josiah I. Plimpton was ordered to keep the Third New Hampshire in readiness in the event of a Confederate attack.[35]

It had been discovered that resistance in their front would be stiffer than they expected because of the presence of two Confederate divisions: troops under Brigadier General William Mahone and a significant cavalry force under Brigadier General W. H. F. Lee. There were troop movements and light skirmishing throughout the day of August 15. That night, the men of the Third and Seventh New Hampshire regiments of Hawley's brigade bedded down at Fussel's Mills near the old Malvern Hill battlefield.[36] Adjutant Elbridge J. Copp and Lieutenant Colonel Josiah I. Plimpton discussed the battle they were sure was coming on the next day. "Adjutant," Plimpton said, "this is my last night on earth, tomorrow we shall go into the fight and I shall not come out of it." Copp dismissed the comment because Plimpton had had that feeling several times, and nothing had happened.[37]

On the morning of August 16, Grant rode by the troops for a casual inspection. Lieutenant Daniel Eldredge of the Third New Hampshire said of Grant, who passed by him: "Grant is not prepossessing of any means and at least he was not so at that time, having on a soldier's blouse, a slouched hat without cord or ornament and a very cheap strap which came over in front as though the blouse pocket had been filled with apples. His horse being quite small, the General did not attract the attention that his companion, Gen. Hancock did, he being a large, powerful man."[38] After a brief meeting between Grant and Hancock, the battle line moved forward. A dense forest was encountered almost immediately, and the men had been marched and countermarched so many times no one was sure where they were going. It seemed to the men of the Third and Seventh New Hampshire that they were being fired on from all sides. The tangled undergrowth and briars tore at their faces and uniforms. Fighting had thus far been sporadic, and, finally, the brigade made some progress when they came upon some abandoned rifle pits. The soldiers felt the barrels of the discarded muskets, which were still warm. The line continued forward, and a large clearing could be seen ahead.

The men spilled out into the clearing and were immediately confronted by another set of fortifications. The Federal lines were reformed, and the Confederate works was attacked but not carried. The men retired out of the field and back to the first set of abandoned works. The Confederates launched three desperate counterattacks, all repulsed from this first line. What happened while the Third and Seventh New Hampshire regiments were in the open field is of the most concern. The Third New Hampshire, at the time of this battle, was armed with Spencer rifles and was able to keep up a lively fire against the main Confederate works. The day was hot, and many of the men had removed their coats and outer clothing. Lieutenant Eldredge had removed his blouse and folded it over his arm. "The bullet struck nearly at a right angle with my body, passing through my blouse and shirt sleeve then entering my forearm near the elbow, passed obliquely through the arm between the bones, fracturing both ulna and radius, making its exit halfway between elbow and wrist." The bullet, after leaving Eldredge's arm, smashed into his chest, but luckily the blouse and vest folded across his arm and a memorandum book that he kept in his left breast pocket stopped the bullet.[39]

Eldredge started making his way back to the first line and met Lieutenant Colonel Plimpton along the way. Plimpton stopped what he was doing and helped Eldredge bandage his arm and sent him on his way to the rear. Adjutant Copp was also present and after Eldredge left, continued to confer with Plimpton near the regimental colors when he, too, was hit by a bullet. Copp said, "Opening my eyes in a dazed and benumbed condition, I found myself lying on the ground, with the rattle and crash of musketry, the explosion of shells and the shrieking of wounded men around me." Copp had been hit by a bullet that passed through his ribs, punctured his liver, and exited out his back. Copp's was considered a serious wound, but he made a full recovery.[40]

Josiah I. Plimpton, however, was another story. A shower of bullets hit where Copp and Plimpton were standing, and just as Copp went down from his wound, Plimpton was killed instantly when a ball struck him in the chest and penetrated his heart. Also standing in the position was Lieutenant Simon Nudd Lamprey of Hampton, who received a musket wound to the body and died the next day.[41]

Captain Arlon S. Atherton of Richmond, New Hampshire, was seriously wounded in the lung and was left on the field when the Confederates counter-attacked and pushed the Third New Hampshire back. As the Federal wounded were being taken off the field, Atherton made a Masonic sign with his hands. A nearby Confederate surgeon was soon at his side. Atherton's mouth and throat were filled with blood, and he would have died had the quick-thinking surgeon not washed out his mouth and throat with water. The surgeon took Atherton under his immediate care, and, though a prisoner, Atherton survived and was exchanged the next month.[42]

Lieutenant Eldredge had been taken to the rear to Federal field hospital and was waiting to be treated. He asked to be evacuated immediately to the hospital ship docked in river. He was refused by several orderlies who informed him that he had to pass through the care of the surgeons first. Although he could not see them being performed, Eldredge could hear amputations being done in the next room. He resolved that he wanted better care for his arm and made a Masonic sign. Soon, a complete stranger came to his bedside. Eldredge requested that he be removed to the hospital ship, and the man disappeared for a few moments. He returned with a clean stretcher and several helpers. Eldredge was removed to the ship, and his arm was saved.[43]

The total losses for the Third New Hampshire were twenty-two men killed and seventy-one wounded. The regiment started the day with only two hundred men. By the end of the day, the regiment had lost nearly half its strength, its colonel, and many officers who had been killed or wounded. Very little was gained from the battle itself.[44]

The Seventh New Hampshire that was brigaded with the Third was also a badly depleted regiment. When it arrived at Deep Bottom, less than three hundred men were fit for duty. The Seventh New Hampshire, now under the command of Lieutenant Colonel Thomas A. Henderson of Dover, was ordered to man the first set of works taken from the Confederates. As they were preparing their position, they saw the battered remnants of the regiments who had tried to take the second set of works and failed. One in three men who attacked the first set of works became a casualty; the men of the Seventh knew what was in store for them. The Confederates launched two fierce counterattacks against their first line. Both of these, with the help of the Seventh New Hampshire, were repulsed. The official historian of the Seventh New Hampshire relates a sad story: "It was during one of these assaults that Lieut. Col. Thomas A. Henderson fell, struck in the hip by a rifle-ball, from which wound he died in about four hours, having literally bled to death, falling while faithfully performing the duties of his office."[45] The Seventh New Hampshire, along with the rest of the brigade, withdrew even from these trenches to a safer position to the rear. Command of the regiment passed to Captain Augustus W. Rollins of Rollinsford, who was promoted to lieutenant colonel in September 1864. At Deep Bottom, the Seventh New Hampshire suffered the loss of four men killed and twelve wounded.[46]

Just before dawn on August 16, 1864, Lieutenant Stephen J. Wentworth of Somersworth was leading a company of the Fourth New Hampshire as skirmishers at Deep Bottom when they ran into a Confederate picket line. A spirited firefight broke out in which Wentworth was shot and killed instantly.[47] That morning, the Fourth New Hampshire made it to the large open field at Deep Bottom but was also pushed back to the first set of Confederate works. The enemy counterattacks nearly engulfed the regiment, and the men were engaged in a ferocious, fighting withdrawal.

The Fourth New Hampshire was in the First Brigade commanded by Colonel Thomas O. Osborn. Osborn was wounded and knocked out of the action early, and command of the brigade went to a major of a New York regiment. When this man was shot in the leg, brigade command then went to Captain Francis W. Parker of Manchester, who held this command for only a short time, when he was disabled by a severe wound to the neck. With such attrition among the officers, it became prudent to withdraw the men, and the Fourth retreated along with the other brigades of Brigadier General Robert S. Foster's First Division. At the end of the battle, only one captain in the Fourth New Hampshire was left, and he assumed command of the regiment. Captain Isaac W. Hobbs of Great Falls was still suffering from the wound he received outside of Petersburg on July 18, but he dutifully accepted his responsibility until he was discharged in November 1864.[48]

The unsuccessful attack at Deep Bottom was probably the bloodiest and most useless battle fought by the Fourth New Hampshire. In it the regiment lost eleven men killed and forty-five wounded. Each side brought about twenty thousand men to the battle, but because the Confederates were fighting mostly from prepared positions, their losses were decidedly less than the Federals. The men in blue lost 2,899 men killed, wounded or missing, assumed captured.[49]

By the fall of 1864, many of the New Hampshire regiments that had been through so many sanguinary battles were in real danger of passing out of existence. Now, the Third New Hampshire was about to be further depleted by the loss of 271 veterans. These losses did not come from bullets or shells but from the expiration of their enlistments. After these men went home, the Third New

Hampshire was left with only 165 men fit for duty. After the grinding battles of the summer campaign, along with the constant exposure of life in the trenches, two hundred men were on the sick list.[50]

The Battle of Deep Bottom represented Grant's attempt to extend his lines to the north, and on August 18, he ordered Warren's Fifth Corps to strike the Weldon Railroad and try to push the lines farther south and west. The operation was a success, and the Federals assumed control of the railroad but at the cost of 544 killed and wounded the first day and 382 killed and wounded the second day. More than twenty-five hundred soldiers were captured when one entire Federal division crumbled under the fierce Confederate counterattacks. New Hampshire losses in this battle were minimal.[51]

New Hampshire regiments not involved in the Battle of Deep Bottom lost twenty-two men in the month of August around Petersburg. Most affected were the Tenth New Hampshire, losing five men, and the First New Hampshire Cavalry, losing five in action near Kearneysville.[52]

Twenty-three-year-old Private Christopher Hoyt of the Fourteenth New Hampshire wrote to his brother and sister on August 25 about his poor health and the hard marches. Camping about four miles from Harpers Ferry, Hoyt, already bitter about the war, related his opinions: "I hope they will go clean to New Hampshire you may fight them for ten years and then you can not lick them out and it is no use to fight. I hope they will get a new president this fall either have it better or worse the dam Generals will straddle their Horces and then you have got to march. I have run all that I want to in this war."[53] Despite his poor health, Hoyt lived through the battles at Opequan Creek and Cedar Creek. He also lived to see the outcome of the election that fall. Unfortunately, Hoyt's health deteriorated further, and he died of disease in December 1864.[54]

At its convention in Chicago, Illinois, at the end of August, the Democratic Party was looking for a candidate who could beat Lincoln in the coming election in November, and the man chosen Major General George B. McClellan. Former president Franklin Pierce received some nominations but withdrew his name from the running. President Lincoln had already been renominated by his party at the Republican convention in early June.[55]

The reenlisted men of the Eighth New Hampshire were at home enjoying their furloughs, but several of them managed to get into some trouble, and one was even held for murder. Seven privates and a lieutenant of the Eighth were riding the train from Manchester to Concord, assuming that because they were veterans, they would not have to pay for their fares. The conductor, George Clough, insisted that they pay for their ride, and they began to verbally abuse him. Clough had had enough. He managed to get the other passengers out of that car, and he locked both doors, confining the nonpaying offenders. Realizing that they had been locked in, the disgruntled soldiers began smashing furniture and windows.

Clough telegraphed ahead to Concord so the police would be waiting, and at Concord, the rioting soldiers were taken into custody by City Marshal Pickering and locked up. Pickering was in no mood for soldier pranks, and he exacted the correct fare plus cost for damages from some of the soldiers; the rest he left behind bars. A sadder incident occurred the next day involving soldiers on furlough from the Eighth New Hampshire. Privates David Parks, James Hazzard (also known as James Coburn), and several other men went to the train station to meet some friends when they spied some stacked arms on the platform belonging to the Veteran's Reserve Corps. Hazzard was one of the privates involved in the vandalism on the train the previous day and apparently was still feeling devilish, because he picked up one of the muskets and started to recklessly go through the manual of arms. George E. Sheldon of Hancock was on the same platform waiting for the train to take him home. He had just successfully arranged for and paid for a substitute and was going home free from the onus of military service.

The musket that Private Hazzard was so carelessly handling went off. The rifle was loaded with buckshot and a ball. The ball struck Private Parks in the arm and passed through and struck another man waiting on the platform. The buckshot hit Sheldon, and he collapsed on the platform. People rushed up to help and took the wounded men to a nearby doctor's office. Sheldon stayed in the doctor's office, suffering from his wound until his death four days later. Private Hazzard (aka Coburn) was taken into custody. A simple soldier's prank had turned into a case of murder. Hazzard was discharged from the Eighth New Hampshire, effective as of the date of the incident. The Manchester native was apparently acquitted or only mildly punished because he is listed as having a postwar address in Lowell, Massachusetts.[56]

In late August, Dr. James H. Crombie of Derry accepted an appointment at the Officer's General Hospital at Fortress Monroe. On his way there, he stopped to look in on his friend and fellow Francestown resident Elias A. Bryant of the Fourth New Hampshire. He found Bryant doing well in a hospital in Hampton, Virginia, recovering from the amputation of his leg.

One of Crombie's first patients when he arrived at Fort Monroe was Sergeant George Nelson Wheeler of the Tenth New Hampshire. Wheeler, a native of Amherst, had already had one tour of duty with the Third New Hampshire and just signed up with the Tenth that summer. Now Sergeant Wheeler was in the hospital dying from malarial fever. As Wheeler's life slipped away from him on August 23, Dr. Crombie asked him if he had anything he wanted him to tell his folks. Wheeler's short reply was, "I wish them all well." Dr. Crombie was pleased to report that another patient of his in the Tenth New Hampshire, Corporal Frank Mace, also of Amherst, would survive. Though born in Francestown, after the war Dr. Crombie settled in Derry and lived there until his death in 1884.[57]

On September 2, 1864, Atlanta fell, and so did the chances for George B. McClellan to succeed Abraham Lincoln as president. The long-sought victory in the east had finally been realized and thus guaranteed Lincoln a second term in the White House. Major General Phil Sheridan's army began to regroup in the Shenandoah Valley near Winchester. "Little Phil's" belligerent movements in the lower valley would have ominous consequences for the men of the Fourteenth New Hampshire regiment.[58]

Colonel Robert Wilson of the Fourteenth New Hampshire had suffered enough. On September 6, he was discharged from his duties because of chronic diarrhea, diphtheria, and rheumatism. The fifty-three-year-old colonel from Keene returned to New Hampshire but after a brief term in the New Hampshire Legislature died at his home in 1870.[59] Sergeant John Henry Jenks of the Fourteenth New Hampshire was sympathetic to his fellow Keene resident. On September 10, Jenks wrote to his wife about Wilson's departure from their camp near Berryville, Virginia: "Col. Wilson left for home yesterday morning quite early. It was a very sudden move, the reason for which I don't yet understand. A little more than a week ago he sent in a request to be discharged which was granted. He was a father to the Regt, looking after the interest of the boys better than most Colonels. For his sake I am glad he is out of it. . . . Major [Alexander] Gardiner is now in command of the Regt. I should not be surprised if he were appointed Colonel."[60] Gardiner of Claremont, appointed major in September 1863, was appointed Colonel on September 18, 1864. As Colonel Gardiner was being mustered in, he was handed orders that directed him and the Fourteenth New Hampshire to leave Berryville and march toward Winchester.[61]

The mobilization of the Fourteenth New Hampshire was in response to a series of events that began on September 16. Confederate Lieutenant General Jubal A. Early was convinced that Sheridan's mission was simply to tie down Early's forces in the Shenandoah Valley and not attack him. Sheridan was under orders not to move until Early sent back the reinforcements that Lee had loaned to him for his summer campaign. Early sent Kershaw's division toward Martinsburg to divine Sheridan's intentions.

Early had also discovered from informants in Winchester that Grant was in the area to meet with Sheridan. He decided to strike at Sheridan before Sheridan could strike him. Grant went to see Sheridan to give him his orders but instead approved Sheridan's bold plan to move around Early and prevent him from making the kind of maneuver back up the valley that his former commander Stonewall Jackson had executed with such skill and daring. Sheridan instead would strike Early first by hitting his men at Winchester, then defeat the force in the Martinsburg area. It was with this intent that his army moved toward Opequan Creek and Winchester only five miles beyond.[62]

On September 19, the men of the Fourteenth New Hampshire of Brigadier General Henry W. Birge's First Brigade were awakened at one o'clock in the morning. They had a quick cup of coffee and then fell into ranks. The men moved out across the fields and eventually folded in with the rest of Brigadier General Cuvier Grover's Second Division that then joined the other divisions of Major General William Emory's Nineteen Corps. The entire Corps headed for Winchester down the Berryville Pike.[63]

The Fourteenth New Hampshire kept to the right hand side of the road until they arrived at the Opequan Creek ford. Traffic at the ford was snarled because the wagons of the Sixth Corps directly in their front blocked the way of the Nineteenth Corps, thus putting them two hours behind. This delay allowed Early to concentrate his army just east of Winchester and dictate that the battle would be fought on ground that he selected between Winchester and Opequan Creek.

After crossing the creek at 7 A.M., the men of the Fourteenth New Hampshire were visibly shaken by what they saw. They had not yet seen combat, and now they were viewing the grim residue of battle. Lined all along the Berryville Pike were the dead and wounded from the cavalry fight earlier that morning. At 10 A.M., the Fourteenth arrived within three miles of Winchester. The Nineteen Corps was then formed into four lines, with the First Brigade of the Second Division occupying the front line. The Fourteenth New Hampshire received the honor of being the last regiment on the right side of the line. In this position they were about five hundred yards on the right hand side of the Berryville Pike. The Sixth Corps was anchored securely on the left flank of the Nineteenth Corps and was astride and to the left of the pike. The men then rested while the senior officers, including Sheridan, made adjustments to the lines. This took almost two hours, and the men of the Fourteenth munched on the contents of their haversacks just short of the tree line, where they halted.

Colonel Gardiner sent Company G of the Fourteenth forward into the woods as skirmishers, who maintained good order through the woods until the familiar pop-crack-pop was heard from picket and skirmish firing. The first line, which consisted of the First and Third Brigades, went forward, followed by the second line composed of the Second and Fourth Brigades. Again, the lines maintained good order as they traversed the woods. At the edge of the forest, the line was redressed, and the first lines stepped out into a large open field. It was Sheridan's original order that, in order to maintain proper alignment with the Sixth Corps on the left and the advancing lines to their rear, the first line should only go a short distance into the field and then lie down. The field was approximately eight hundred yards long and perfectly level until it sloped upward into the next tree line.

The First and Third Brigades moved out into the coverless field. The men of the Fourteenth immediately came under fire that was random until they reached

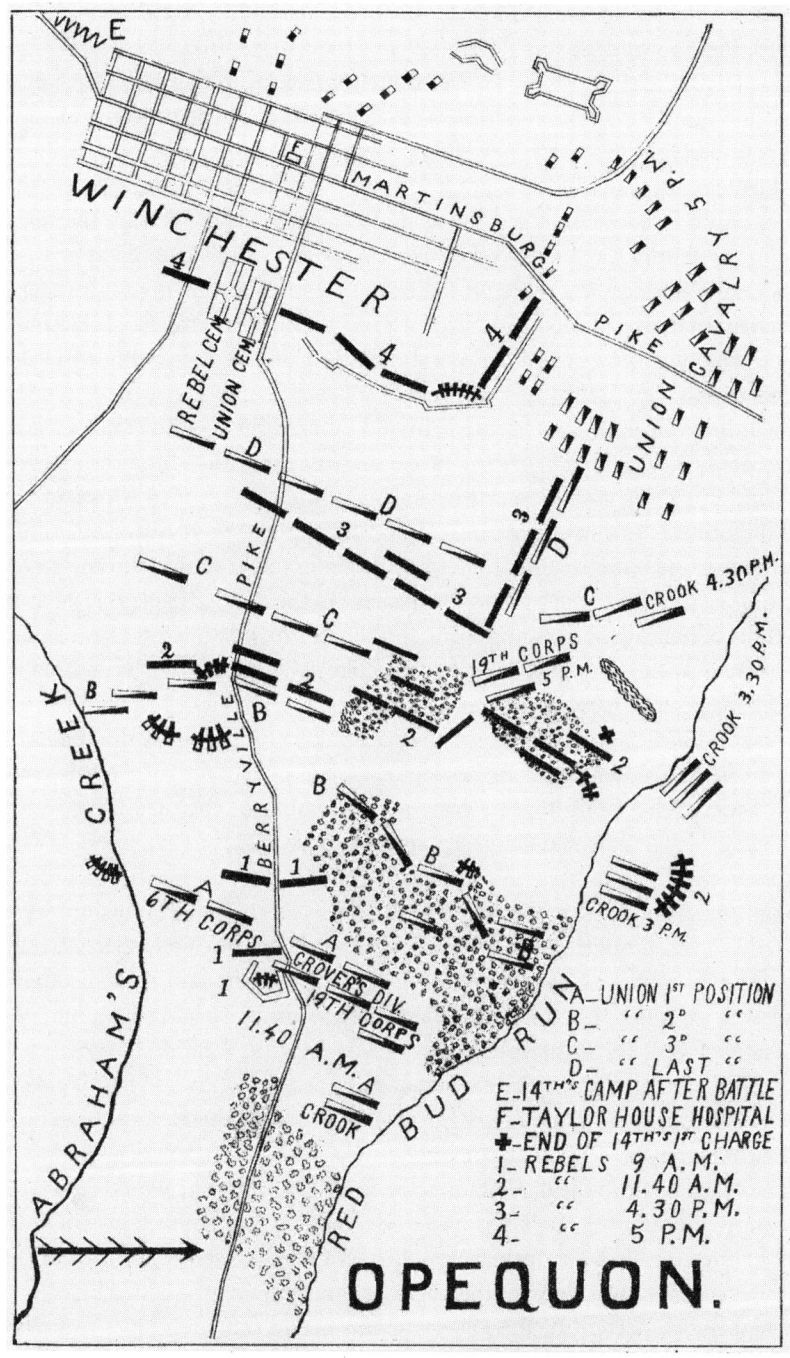

From F. H. Buffum, A Memorial of the Great Rebellion, *1882*

the middle of the field when the order to charge was given. As the men rushed forward, their alignment was disrupted, and they started to receive heavy fire from both front and sides. The Fourteenth New Hampshire periodically halted to fire and started to take horrendous casualties. The color-bearer, Corporal Charles A. Ball of Winchester, New Hampshire, was wounded and died a month later. Lieutenant John W. Sturtevant had been wounded earlier during the skirmishing, only to come back and be wounded a second time during the main phase of the battle. Captains William H. Fosgate and William A. Chaffin were both killed in the exposed center of the field. Four men advancing in Company F were simultaneously shot and all died except Corporal Francis H. Buffum, who survived his wounds and the war and later became the official historian of the Fourteenth New Hampshire Regiment.

The lines eventually crossed the field and entered the second set of woods, where fierce hand-to-hand fighting broke out. All formations lost their alignment, and it was discovered that the first line of the Nineteenth Corps had become disconnected from the Sixth Corps on the left and their supporting lines to the rear. These lines became lost and confused in the heat of battle and never came to the support of the advanced brigades. As the men struggled in the forest, artillery shells came crashing through the trees from a nearby Confederate battery. By now the Union advance had completely fallen apart. Men started to fall back in groups, many being captured as the Confederates of Major General John Brown Gordon's counterattack enveloped them. Standing in the center of the open field, Colonel Gardiner desperately tried to rally the men of his regiment. It was at that point that he was mortally wounded (he died three weeks later). Gardiner was succeeded by Captain Theodore Ripley of Winchester, New Hampshire.

Total casualties for the first battle of the Fourteenth New Hampshire were horrifying. Even though they had never seen battle before September 19, they went into the fight with only 450 men. Fifty-four officers and men died, and ninety were wounded. In downtown Winchester, Virginia, a beautiful monument to the fallen members of the Fourteenth New Hampshire Regiment was erected in the National Cemetery, an immaculately groomed cemetery and a fitting resting place for the heroic men of New Hampshire who gave their lives at the Third Battle of Winchester.[64]

In New Hampshire the last infantry regiment that the state would raise was being mustered. During the latter half of September, Companies A through E of the Eighteenth New Hampshire were brought into the service of the United States. Recruitment was slow for this regiment, but it was totally filled by volunteers. Eighty-five percent of the 978 men who would serve with this regiment were from New Hampshire. About seventy-five percent of the men enlisted for one year, and the remainder for three. Each man who joined the regiment

Captain George W. Towle,
*Tenth New Hampshire, Company D. Father of George F.
Towle of the Fourth New
Hampshire, Towle was a crusty
old fighter who inspired the
men of his company and regiment. Photograph courtesy
of NHVA*

received a federal bounty payment of $33.00 and a state bounty of $100.00. The men of the Eighteenth Regiment came from all walks of life: 375 farmers, 343 mechanics or craftsmen, 75 laborers, and the rest a variety of professions. The majority were five feet eight inches tall, and 170 of them were eighteen or younger. The average age in the Eighteenth New Hampshire was 25.[65] The Eighteenth New Hampshire was formed with a core of highly experienced officers. Thirty-one of its thirty-nine officers had previous service in another regiment. In the ranks 140 had been members in another regiment and had already done one tour of duty.[66]

The last three days in September 1864 were days of intense fighting for New Hampshire troops involved in Federal attacks southeast of Richmond and southwest of Petersburg. The Tenth and Thirteenth New Hampshire regiments participated in the Battle of Fort Harrison, or Chaffin's Farm, just south of Richmond, while the Sixth, Ninth, and Eleventh New Hampshire Regiments took part in the Battle of Pegram Farm, otherwise known as Poplar Springs Church, south of Petersburg. The Fourth New Hampshire was involved in fighting at New Market Heights, just down the road from Fort Harrison. The remaining New Hampshire regiments in the Petersburg-Richmond area were either still in the trenches or involved in harassing raids against the Confederates.[67] The men of the Tenth New Hampshire probably viewed it as a mixed blessing when they arrived at Aiken's Landing on September 28 and received 150 new Spencer rifles. This meant that the firepower of the then two-hundred-man regiment would be greatly enhanced. Unfortunately, it also meant that Colonel Michael T. Donohoe would be taking his diminutive regiment into combat again.[68]

The next morning the Eighteenth Corps under Major General Edward O. Ord and the Tenth Corps under Birney crossed the James River to make a two-pronged attack and then move on Richmond. Grant ordered this attack because he also wanted to prevent any more reinforcements going to Early's army in the Shenandoah Valley.[69] The Thirteenth and Tenth New Hampshire regiments were in this attack in the First and Second brigades, respectively. Colonel Stevens of the Thirteenth had personal command of the First Brigade; Brigadier Hiram Burnham commanded the Second Brigade.[70]

Action for the Tenth New Hampshire came much quicker than expected. At dawn on September 29, the Tenth New Hampshire along with the 118th New York formed a skirmish line and advanced. The enemy's line was encountered, and the effective fire from the Spencer rifles pushed the Confederates back. Colonel Donohoe's horse was shot out from under him while he was commanding the skirmish line. The Confederates were pushed back about three miles until they gained the safety of their works at Fort Harrison. A short time later, the First Division came up and immediately went into battle. The eight cannons in the fort and the fourteen surrounding it greeted the oncoming Yankees with a storm of iron. Large gaps opened in the Union lines as the advancing troops were swept with canister and accurate musket fire. The parapet was gained quickly, and the Federals turned the guns around and began firing them at their former owners. Brigadier General Burnham was killed while he was personally working one of the cannons.[71]

The Thirteenth New Hampshire also rushed the fort with its 187 rifles. There was no time for firing, so the order was to charge the fort with bayonets only. The men of the Thirteenth later used their bayonets to scale the fort's sheer walls. Others, to gain entry to the fort, stood on each other's shoulders or boosted one another up and over the walls with cupped hands. The men's faces were blackened from the discharge of muskets at nearly point blank range. The fort was taken by 8 A.M., and the new occupiers immediately started preparations for a counterattack.[72]

The Federal skirmish lines with Spencer rifles were deployed again in order to pursue the fleeing Confederates and prevent them from reforming. It was during this action that Colonel Donohoe was severely wounded. Colonel Stevens also fell wounded lay on the ground in front of the fort as the Thirteenth New Hampshire and the rest of his brigade traversed the open field in front of the fort. When it was secured, Colonel Stevens then was recovered. The first day of fighting had been costly for these two regiments. The Thirteenth New Hampshire lost fifteen killed, and the Tenth lost nine.[73] While scaling the parapet of

Fort Harrison, Private James Brady of the Tenth New Hampshire, a substitute from the town of Kingston, captured a Confederate flag. For bravery in action, Brady was awarded a Medal of Honor.[74]

The night was a sleepless one for the new defenders of Fort Harrison, the New Hampshire men kept busy all night erecting breastworks in the back of the fort. With the coming of day, the Confederates did not wait long to mount their counterattack with A fierce bombardment of the fort commencing at dawn. The Confederate skirmishers drove in the Federal picket line and made ready to storm the fort. The Tenth New Hampshire and any other unit possessing Spencer rifles were evenly distributed along the fort walls. This time their job was to repel the attack that they all knew was coming. The lines of the grayback troops soon appeared, and then wave after wave charged upon the fort. The repeating rifles performed their deadly work, and the Confederates under General Richard Heron Anderson fell in droves.[75] Before long, the Confederate attack collapsed, and again the Tenth and Thirteenth New Hampshire were detailed to pursue the attackers. The two undersized regiments from New Hampshire brought in over five hundred prisoners; roughly twice their number.

More casualties were sustained on the second day of fighting. With the diminished size of these regiments, these were losses that they could ill-afford. The total numbers lost at Fort Harrison for the two days were twenty-three killed and fifty-eight wounded for the Thirteenth New Hampshire and eleven killed and twenty-three wounded for the Tenth. These losses reduced the Thirteenth to about 100 men and the Tenth to about 150. After Colonel Donohoe was wounded, command of the Tenth New Hampshire briefly passed to Captain John Caswell of Manchester, but when he was killed soon after, command went to Captain Timothy B. Crowley of Nashua.[76]

For his part in unmasking a possible Confederate spy, Lieutenant Charles H. Curtis of the Thirteenth New Hampshire received a letter from Brigade Commander Joseph H. Potter on behalf of Major General Ben Butler on October 16, thanking him. An individual by the name of Kidder came into the Union lines in a major's uniform, stating that he was looking for a particular soldier who had been a casualty at Fort Harrison. Curtis carefully observed while the man made notes of all the gun placements in the Union lines. Curtis reported the suspicious officer, and the man was arrested. From Potter's letter it can be deduced that the officer was probably a spy. It was not long thereafter that Curtis was appointed captain.[77]

The Fourth New Hampshire was about to go into combat on September 29 with only forty men, their scant number the result of the expiration of enlistments in September and Lieutenant Colonel Drew and 174 men not reenlisting. Although many of the men of the regiment did, not many were fit for duty in the end of September.[78]

The Tenth Corps under Birney moved down the New Market Road. After sweeping aside token resistance, the divisions under Birney encountered an earthwork fort where the Confederates were strongly posted. Captain George F. Towle of the Fourth New Hampshire described the action: "Foster's Division advancing up the New Market Road came upon the prolongation of their works. An enclosed work on the left of the road called 'Fort Gilmer' barred further progress.... The work appeared deserted and all was silent. We thought perhaps that it was evacuated. Finally as we gathered together in a group under an apple tree they opened on us with a furious artillery fire. Foster's division was then ordered to assault. The assault was repulsed and our loss severe." Both the Fourth and Seventh New Hampshire Regiments participated in this bloody and futile attack. On September 29, Union forces were successful in capturing Fort Harrison but not Fort Gilmer. The Fourth New Hampshire lost eight men killed in this engagement.[79]

To the south of Petersburg, the Sixth, Ninth, and Eleventh New Hampshire regiments were preparing for what would be their last major battle. Since the debacle of the Mine Explosion in July, command of the Ninth Corps passed to Major General John G. Parke. With his corps Parke was to join the Second and Fifth Corps in a thrust beyond Hatcher's Run. Although this attack would also be a failure, it resulted in the further stretching of Lee's already undermanned lines to the southwest of Petersburg.[80]

The Ninth Corps became heavily engaged at Poplar Springs Church (or Pegram Farm) on September 30. The average strength of these three New Hampshire regiments was about two hundred each, and they could ill afford any more casualties. However, without question or pause, when the bugles blew, they marched once more into battle.[81] Captain Arthur C. Locke led the Eleventh New Hampshire forward to make contact with the main line of the Confederates along the South Side Railroad. When they found the Rebels, the Eleventh was thrown back in a bloody repulse. Captain Locke was wounded, as well as Captains John C. Currier and J. Leroy Bell. Captain George Nelson Shepard assumed command of the decimated regiment. Their losses were twelve killed and seventy wounded. The Sixth and Ninth New Hampshire fared no better. Losses in the Sixth New Hampshire were eleven killed and eighty wounded, and the Ninth suffered nineteen battle deaths and ninety wounded. These New Hampshire regiments, like the Tenth and Thirteenth, were now in some cases down to only sixty men fit for duty. At the start of the war they could hardly have been mustered in as a full company, let alone a regiment.[82]

Sergeant Charles P. Chamberlin of the Eleventh New Hampshire was captured at Poplar Springs Church on September 30. He was taken first to Richmond and then to the prisoner camp at Salisbury, North Carolina, which had been made from an old cotton factory. It was adequate at the beginning of the war, but as the war progressed, conditions became worse. By the time Sergeant Chamberlin arrived, prisoners were crammed into insufficient quarters, and many had to live outside in tents. By the end of 1864, over thirty-seven hundred men had already died from scurvy, dysentery, and exposure. Chamberlin commented on his experiences in an 1886 newspaper article: "I was suffering from scurvy and in so feeble a condition that I was unable to obtain from the hospital books and records the exact number of deaths when we left but know that the deaths from January to February [1865] averaged forty or fifty per day so that in the short space of four and a half months nearly 6,000 had been drawn out on the dead cart."[83] The Eleventh New Hampshire lost twenty-four men dead in Confederate prisons.[84] Sergeant Charles P. Chamberlin was one of the lucky ones.

"God only knows what is in store for me"

CHAPTER 12

September 1864 to December 1864

I hope I shall never be called to pass through another such terrible battle as the Battle of Winchester.

Sergeant John Henry Jenks, Fourteenth
New Hampshire Regiment, letter

New Hampshire soldiers in the field were constantly trying to understand why they never received as many letters from home as they themselves wrote to their loved ones. Sergeant John Henry Jenks of the Fourteenth New Hampshire mentioned a reason in a letter to his wife from camp at Harrisonburg, Virginia, on October 1, 1864: "I expect one of your letters was captured by the Rebs, as I hear Mosby's gang captured our mail from Harpers Ferry to this place." In the last part of his letter, Jenks was still feeling the effects of the recent battle at Winchester: "I hope I shall never be called to pass through another such terrible battle as the Battle of Winchester. But God only knows what is in store for me. I mean to do my duty faithfully trusting in Him for safety. You don't know how anxious I have been about you for the last month. I am thankful you will not be left without something to help support you should I be taken away."[1]

Sergeant Jenks was not being melodramatic in his concerns. The soldiers in the field knew very well that death was everywhere, and they did not know when or where it would strike a man down. An example of this was Private Frank Wadleigh of the Fifth New Hampshire. The eighteen-year-old substitute from Kensingston had been mustered into the Fifth in August 1864. Wadleigh was doing simple sentry duty outside Petersburg so he had no particular feelings of dread on October 5. Deciding to have a smoke, he reached into his coat and took out his pipe and tobacco. He carefully tamped down the tobacco so as not to lose one precious bit. He put the pipe in his mouth and was about to light it when a Confederate sharpshooter killed him with one bullet.[2]

To say that tobacco was important to the average soldier is to underestimate the role it played in their lives. Corporal Jacob F. Chandler of the Eighth New Hampshire extolled the virtues of tobacco in a letter home: "After eating naturally

follows the pipe, that sweet solace in the lazy or tired hour; that soothing influence in a mad, melancholy or suffering hour; that finder and retainer of friends;
that acquaintance maker and holder; that which enlivens and gives point to conversation; which makes the plodding of the day endurable and the restful night
glorious."[3]

On October 1st, while Sergeant Jenks was writing his letter from Harrisonburg, Virginia, the men of the Seventh New Hampshire were involved in a reconnaissance just outside of Richmond. The morning was foggy, and the men could
not see much of the city, although they could plainly hear the church bells ringing out their warning that the Yankees were in the vicinity. As the Seventh New
Hampshire moved through a stand of woods, Sergeant George Corson of Nashua
looked down and noticed that his shoelace was untied. He fell out of line briefly
to tie his shoe. He put his left foot up on a stump to lace up the shoe when a
cannon shell came bounding through the woods. It bounced several times and
sheared Corson's left foot cleanly from his leg. The Seventh New Hampshire had
stumbled onto one of the many Confederate strong points just outside the city.
In the ensuing action, Private John Brown lost an arm, and Sergeant Charles B.
Wallace was severely wounded but survived. The regiment lost six wounded;
eleven men of the regiment were captured in the woods but were all regained
except Cyrus G. Caverly and Augustus Green, who died in the Confederate prison
camp at Salisbury, North Carolina. Sergeants George P. Dow and George F. Robie
were awarded Medals of Honor for conspicuous bravery during this action.[4]

The Third New Hampshire was also in action during the first week in October. On and off rain showers made the campaign difficult, but there were also
several days of dry weather when the men could dry themselves and their equipment. In several short and sharp clashes with the Confederates along the Darby-
town Road outside Richmond, the Third New Hampshire suffered the loss of
thirteen men killed during the month.[5]

By the end of the first week in October, Major General Phil Sheridan determined that Lieutenant General Jubal A. Early was not in the area of Harrisonburg and thus decided to move closer to his base of supply at Winchester by
starting his army back down the Shenandoah Valley toward that city. On October 10, he arrived outside of Winchester along the banks of Cedar Creek and
began fortifying. In Sheridan's transit from the middle valley, he lightly skirmished with Confederate cavalry and was harassed by a small Confederate force
near Fisher's Hill.[6]

Captain Theodore Ripley of the Fourteenth New Hampshire had been placed
in command of the regiment after he had been detached from Brigadier General
Henry W. Birge's staff. On the morning of October 19, the Fourteenth New
Hampshire and the Nineteenth Corps were posted about nine hundred yards to
the right of the Valley Pike. This was about an equal distance from Belle Grove

Plantation where Sheridan had his headquarters. The Fourteenth was positioned in some heavy breastworks on the right of the Nineteenth Corps. A thick belt of woods was to their front and Cedar Creek itself beyond that.[7]

Early knew of Sheridan's absence, but what he did not know was that Sheridan was on his return trip to the army and was as close as Winchester. Early had to either attack or withdraw for want of supplies. From the top of Massanutten Mountain, he and Major General John Brown Gordon surveyed the Union camps sprawled in their front. Early decided to attack. He ordered Gordon to attack the Federal right flank, Kershaw to attack Wright's Sixth Corps in front, and Wharton to slam into the front of the Nineteenth Corps.[8] When the Battle of Cedar Creek began in the early morning of October 19, the veteran divisions of Gordon's Second Corps would attack the Fourteenth New Hampshire's position. These tough veterans were commanded by Major Generals Robert Rodes and Stephen Ramseur. In Gordon's Second Corps were the remnants of the Stonewall Brigade, combat-tested Virginians would be once again thrown into the breach.[9]

During the night of October 18, the troops under General Early moved down from the mountain to their jump-off positions. Some of their activities were observed in the Union camp, but they were not expecting the Confederates to attack. Even though Early's surprise attack would be mostly effective, one division of the Nineteenth Corps was detailed to move out that morning to investigate the Confederate movements. The Fourteenth New Hampshire was to be a part of this reconnaissance.[10]

No sooner had Captain Ripley reported that the Fourteenth New Hampshire was ready to move out than he heard the scattered popping of muskets off to his left. As the noise of battle swelled, Ripley knew that this was a general attack and that the men who had not been scheduled for the reconnaissance would probably be surprised either in their tents or while cooking breakfast. This is exactly what was transpiring in front of the Eighth Corps and the part of the Nineteenth Corps. The remainder of the Nineteenth Corps and the Fourteenth New Hampshire braced themselves for the tidal wave of gray that was nearly upon them. The strongpoint of the Confederate attack fell directly on the Nineteenth Corps, and its ranks were shattered. The Fourteenth New Hampshire, along with the other regiments of the brigade and corps, were obliged to fall back, but they made the Confederates pay for every yard of ground gained. The sun was just rising, and the Southern army under Early had pushed the Federals back nearly two miles northwest of Middleton.[11]

When Sheridan heard the booming of the artillery at first light, he set off from Winchester south on the Valley Pike at breakneck speed. He arrived in the Cedar Creek area around 10:30 A.M. and immediately began to reform his disorganized army for a counterattack. Instead of pressing their advantage after the attack, the Confederates stopped to loot the Federal camps. This action, along with a continuous artillery bombardment of the Confederates, allowed Sheridan adequate time to realign his three corps.[12] After reforming his army north of Middleton, Sheridan counterattacked at 3:00 P.M. He not only pushed the Confederates back, he retook the ground lost that morning and more. The Federal cavalry pursued Early's broken ranks back to Fisher's Hill, capturing almost two thousand prisoners and an enormous amount of discarded muskets and equipment.[13]

The Fourteenth New Hampshire lost twelve killed and fifty-five wounded. Among the slain was Sergeant John Henry Jenks, who is buried in the National Cemetery in Winchester, Virginia.[14] Captain Theodore Ripley was captured, and command of the regiment fell to Captain Oliver Marston of Sandwich. Captain Ripley was regained in March 1865 from a Confederate prison in Danville, North Carolina, and appointed colonel in that month but not mustered in. After the war Ripley chose to live in Georgia just outside of Statesboro. On the evening of July 23, 1866, masked horsemen rode into his front yard and demanded that he come out. When Ripley emerged from his house and confronted them, he was shot to death.[15]

The Battle of Cedar Creek was the last big battle fought in the Shenandoah Valley. The Daughter of the Stars would remain in Federal control. The Fourteenth New Hampshire stayed in the Shenandoah Valley until January 1865. The regiment was transferred to Savannah, Georgia, where it performed garrison duty at Fort Pulaski until the end of the war.[16]

Corporal Horace H. Adams of the Tenth New Hampshire wrote to his brother in Portsmouth about his term of enlistment that had expired: "I raised my hand to serve the United States 3 years unless sooner Shot, only one year more and then I can say I am a free man. I am Still Corporal. We have only four corporals for duty in our Company. We have had Six men that have died from wounds two of them was shot dead. They died nobly fighting for there Country."[17]

In the end of October 1864, General Grant again increased pressure on the Confederate lines with another two-pronged attack. This time the main thrust was to be south of Petersburg, and the men of the Tenth and Eighteenth Corps were to make a demonstration north of the James River in order to occupy those Southern forces still near Richmond.[18] The Eighteenth Army Corps advanced toward the old Fair Oaks battleground, with the Tenth New Hampshire and the 118th New York Regiments out front as skirmishers. The Confederate skirmishers were soon encountered and driven back to their fortifications. The Tenth New Hampshire and the remainder of the Second Brigade charged the Confederate strongpoint and ran into a virtual hailstorm of shells and musket fire. The Federal attack ground to a halt, and the men of the Tenth were unable to reach the rebel works. They had to lie down and wait for nightfall in order to retreat.

The Thirteenth New Hampshire was only marginally engaged at Fair Oaks so suffered only a small number of casualties.[19] It was a different story for the battered and bloody men of the Tenth New Hampshire. While the regiment was pinned down just outside of the Confederate works, the rebels came pouring over the edge of the hill. Eight officers of the Tenth were captured. The colors of the regiment were quickly removed from their staffs to avoid capture. The state flag was torn up, and Sergeant John H. Durgin of Wilmot wrapped the national flag around his body. Unfortunately, before he could make his escape, he was captured. Durgin died in the Salisbury prison in January 1865.[20] Captain Enoch W. Goss of the Thirteenth New Hampshire was killed in the skirmish line.[21] Captain Crowley, who was in command of the Tenth New Hampshire, was wounded.[22] Finally, Corporal Adams of Portsmouth received a mortal wound during the charge and would suffer from the effects of his wound until his death on November 9, 1864. The body of the Company G corporal was brought home and buried in Portsmouth.[23] The Tenth New Hampshire lost a total of six killed and sixty-eight wounded or captured. Two days later, the Tenth New Hampshire was under the command of a second lieutenant.[24] The demonstration made by the Tenth and Eighteenth Corps resulted in the loss of eleven hundred men killed wounded or missing. Grant's main effort south of Petersburg met heavy resistance near Hatcher's Run. Lack of cooperation between Second Corps Commander Major General Winfield Scott Hancock and General Joseph Warren resulted in the repulse of the Federal assault and the tally of twelve hundred casualties. The Southside Railroad and its environs remained in Confederate control.[25]

November 1864 arrived, and with it came the presidential election that everyone, both North and South, had been anticipating. For the first time the standing armies would be allowed to participate in the election. Although a convention was approved by the people of New Hampshire to consider in 1865 changing the constitution, the state supreme court had already decided that it was constitutional for soldiers to vote while they were out of state and serving in the field. Now, not only was there electioneering at home in the towns and cities of New Hampshire but also in the camps of the armies.[26]

The nominees of the Republican Party were Abraham Lincoln for president and Andrew Johnson of Tennessee for vice president. The current vice president, Hannibal Hamlin of Maine, was dropped in favor of Johnson in the hope of attracting more votes from the Midwest. Because of a scandal and machinations by his political enemies, Senator John Parker Hale had been voted out and replaced by Aaron H. Cragin. To soothe Hale's battered ego, Lincoln made him minister to Spain, although Hale had desired the appointment to France.[27] During the first week of November, electioneering was reaching a fever pitch in New Hampshire. Future governor of New Hampshire, then Secretary of State

Benjamin F. Prescott, released an instructional broadside from his office to the heads of Republican Committees in the state. At the top of the page, CAUTION was printed twice in bold, black letters. Never referring in the broadside to the opposition as Democrats, it only referred to them as "Copperheads." One of the instructions read, "In the close towns, the copperheads will make a desperate effort to elect their Representatives and there is where they are now making their greatest effort. The greatest care should be exercised in these towns in guarding every point." A list of suggestions followed, and perhaps the most shocking one instructed party workers, "If there is any man in your neighborhood who is a little uncertain, have a man visit him constantly and talk with him and furnish him facts and the proper kind of reading matter, to disabuse his mind of copperhead misrepresentations."[28] On November 8, Lincoln was reelected with 2,330,552 votes to McClellan's 494,567. In the electoral vote, Lincoln garnered 212 and McClellan only 21. McClellan carried only Delaware, Kentucky, and New Jersey. The state of New York went to the Lincoln camp only by the slimmest of majorities.[29]

Lincoln carried the state of New Hampshire but not by a landslide. The Republican president received 36,600 votes to McClellan's 33,034. Studying the returns from Rockingham County alone is instructive. From the figures it appears that Lincoln carried the large towns and cities while McClellan carried the majorities in the small towns. The towns of Exeter, Hampton, Londonderry, and Portsmouth all went to Lincoln, while many small towns surrounding them like Epping, Kingston, Nottingham, and Raymond reported majorities for McClellan.[30] One reason why the towns voted as they did could have been the size of the towns themselves. The smaller towns like Fremont, North Hampton, and Newton tended to be closely knit communities where everyone knew each other or was related, and if such a town lost a number of its sons and fathers in battle, its war-weary residents would be more likely to vote for a change in administration. The larger towns like Salem, Newmarket, and Deerfield also lost residents in the war but had a larger, perhaps less-cohesive population and therefore supported Lincoln.

The majority of military votes went to Lincoln, with 116,887 to McClellan's 33,748. This majority held also for New Hampshire troops in the field. Lincoln received 2,066 votes, and McClellan received 690. One of the New Hampshire regiments that did not give Lincoln a majority of their votes was the Eighth New Hampshire regiment. New Hampshire historian Mather Cleveland explains that this was because the regiment felt abandoned and that they blamed the administration for their losses from disease in Louisiana and the failure of Banks's Red River Campaign. The Tenth New Hampshire gave McClellan the majority of their votes, supposedly because they were composed mostly of Irish Democrats from Manchester.[31] The Third New Hampshire was the only New Hampshire regiment who did not get the chance to vote in the election, because the men were held in reserve on Staten Island in the event of trouble on Election Day in New York City. The election proceeded quietly, and their services were not needed.[32]

With Lincoln's reelection and the Federal victory only a matter of time, issues such as the final abolition of slavery, reconstruction, and the readmittance of the Southern states were all questions coming to the forefront of discussions in Washington and throughout the North. Desertions, however, were at their highest rate in the Union armies since the draft went into effect in July 1863. According to historian Ella Lonn in *Desertion during the Civil War,* 3,648 men deserted from New Hampshire regiments during the war because of the unbearable hardships the men had to endure; going for long periods of time without proper food, clothing, or medical care; inadequate arms and ammunition; and finally, in the case of foreign soldiers, a profound interest in gaining as much bounty money as possible without serving one day in the ranks.[33] The Adjutant General's Report for the State of New Hampshire lists 4,766 men deserted, a figure that is quite at variance with the Lonn figure. Some of the figures used by the Adjutant General require elaboration. The Seventeenth New Hampshire was never mustered into service, and the First New Hampshire Regiment, a ninety-day regiment, had only seven desertions. An examination of the three-year units shows the First New Hampshire Light Battery had the fewest desertions, with only nine men leaving. The New Hampshire regiment with the highest number of desertions was the Sixth New Hampshire with 654, followed by the First New Hampshire Cavalry, with 569.[34] The Fourth New Hampshire, in the service of the United States from September 1861 to August 1865, had only 152 men desert. The unit served in Florida, South Carolina, and Virginia and was in a number of major and minor actions. The regimental historian, however, felt compelled to print the names of the deserters in the regimental history saying, "They disgraced the regiment and state that sent them to keep company with good soldiers."[35]

In *The History of Warner, New Hampshire,* Colonel Walter Harriman, colonel of the Eleventh New Hampshire and future governor of the state, describes his regiment's experience with deserters: "Even the doors of jails and prisons were opened, in certain cases and the inmates were granted immunity from punishment on enlisting as soldiers. Of such recruits, 625 were sent forward to fill the depleted ranks of the 11th NH regiment but only 240 of them ever reached the regiment at all."[36]

In addition to a list of names of deserters, the official history of the Third New Hampshire details descriptions of court-martial proceedings and executions. One of the more bizarre cases involved a deserter who was tried and sentenced to be shot. It is not recorded whether the prisoner, James F. Brown, moved, or the firing squad flinched, but the first volley did not kill him. Lieutenant John H. Hitchcock ordered a second volley. This also failed to kill the prisoner. Clearly frustrated that the prisoner refused to die, Lieutenant Hitchcock ordered Private Alphonso Osborn out of line and told him to kill the prisoner. Osborn approached Brown and shot him to death at close range.[37]

After the war, the consequences of desertion even in far away places continued to affect New Hampshire. Because of the proximity of Canada, deserters started returning to the United States through Vermont, New Hampshire, and Maine. Groups of deserters were seen crowding into small towns and villages in New Hampshire as early as May 1865. Naturally, there was trouble between these "disloyal" individuals and the veterans who had legitimately served their state. In many states no provision had been made for the punishment of returned deserters after the war was concluded, so many of them stepped back into their roles of civilians but not without being followed by the angry glazes of their one-time friends and neighbors.[38]

If possible, Christmas in the warring armies in 1864 was even bleaker than the previous year. Besides doing their regular duties for a Sunday, the men of the Thirteenth New Hampshire made their Christmas special. In addition to having foot races, a greased pole climb, and a mock review, the soldiers purchased a plum pudding from a sutler, but the pudding was hard and stale. The men tried to improve it by pouring a flask of brandy over it and even igniting it. Even so, the men said that "they could not remove the taste of that pudding out of their mouths for a month; and the sutler has no further market. The pudding was old, mouldy, and had soured."[39] President Lincoln received a most welcome Christmas present after having to endure an agonizing year of political uncertainty. General William Tecumseh Sherman telegraphed Lincoln on December 22 that he was giving him the occupied city of Savannah, Georgia, as a present.[40]

The last major Southern port to keep blockade-runners in business was Wilmington, North Carolina. The formidable fort at its entrance was destined to be one of the last major campaigns involving New Hampshire troops. The fort was bombarded on Christmas Eve but with little effect. Attempted landings north of the fort failed on Christmas Day and resulted in high casualties for the Federals. Much to the chagrin of Major General Ben Butler, the landing force had to be hastily evacuated when Confederate reinforcements appeared. Butler's inept handling of the expedition resulted in his being relieved of command by General Grant. The men in the Third, Fourth, and Seventh New Hampshire regiments were standing by and would be utilized in the next attempt on Fort Fisher, which was about two weeks away.[41]

The year of 1864 had seen the loss of many men from New Hampshire. Commenting on the loss of his brother Sergeant Julian P. Dodge the last summer, Sergeant Solomon Dodge of the Eleventh New Hampshire wrote to his sister, "It will be very sad indeed for me to visit home now that it is known that our dear brother is dead. It is hard indeed to part with such a dear brother but we must remember that his life was given in the defence of those Glorious old Stars and Stripes that now and ever shall flote in triumph over the best Government that ever existed on the face of the Earth."[42]

"They looked like living skeletons"

CHAPTER 13

January 1865 to March 1865

Up in the mountains of New Hampshire God Almighty
has hung out a sign to show that there he makes men.

Daniel Webster, quoted in Benjamin Willey,
Incidents in White Mountain History

Private John R. Downs of the Fifth New Hampshire was a devout Christian. He ended every entry in his diary with a Bible verse and an inspirational message. Downs was recuperating from wounds in a Washington hospital and was eagerly awaiting transfer back to New Hampshire. As is apparent from his diary entry, he was unhappy with his stay in the hospital: "No news about going home yet, my health is about the same as usual. Our living is very poor and it is lonely here in the hospital. Our bread is sower about half the time, our tea and coffee is cold and like dish water. The cups black and rusty, the plates the same half the time."[1] On January 10, Downs reported that inmates were stealing clothes and selling them to get money for whiskey. In mid-February, Downs discovered that he was to be transferred to Webster U.S. Hospital in Manchester, New Hampshire, and concluded his diary with a long poem about the Fifth New Hampshire and this typical soldier's prayer: "Hope the war will end soon so that I with others can go home to stay. I love home. May the god of battles nerve us all to the work and crush the rebelyan this summer."[2]

Several Confederate armies were still in the field, and functional seaports were still in Southern hands. The Union could not be crowned with victory until those armies and ports were either vanquished or surrendered. In January 1865 neither of those possibilities appeared likely. Major General Ben Butler had failed in his attack on Fort Fisher in December, and now a second attempt was to be made in mid-January under Major General Alfred H. Terry. Unlike Butler's debacle, Terry's amphibious landing was a tactical masterpiece with all of the attacking parties fully coordinated.[3]

Located on the southern end of a long peninsula and on the eastern side of the entrance to the Cape Fear River, Fort Fisher was the guardian of the approaches to Wilmington, North Carolina. The fort itself was a long and formidable set of earthworks that resembled a giant letter L. Fort Buchanan was at the peninsula's tip, and Mound Battery was located just south of Fort Fisher's landward side. Along the entire length of the fort was a series of traverses that protected each individual earthwork making them in affect mini-forts strung together.[4] The length of the fort facing seaward was almost one half mile, and the side facing land was a thousand feet. Strong bombproofs inside the fort protected the garrison against the inevitable bombardment they would be facing. Commanded by Colonel William Lamb, Fort Fisher boasted a garrison of eighteen men, mostly North Carolinians, and forty-seven heavy cannons. Numbered among the cannons were fifteen Columbiads as well as one English-made 150-pounder Armstrong gun.[5]

Facing Fort Fisher on this second attempt to capture it was another vast armada of ships and men. The naval and marines forces were under the command of Admiral David Porter aboard his flagship, the *Malvern*. Including Porter's ship, the Federal armada contained forty-four ships. The total number of Federal troops in this second invasion was eight thousand, including the Third, Fourth, and Seventh New Hampshire regiments. Brigadier General Adelbert Ames commanded the Second Division of the newly formed Twenty-fourth Corps. In his division were three brigades commanded by Brigadier General Newton M. Curtis, Colonel Galusha Pennypacker, and Colonel Louis Bell. At the time of the attack on Fort Fisher, the Fourth New Hampshire was in Bell's brigade and was commanded by Captain John H. Roberts of Dover. In a separate, attached brigade commanded by Colonel Joseph C. Abbott were the Seventh New Hampshire, commanded by Lieutenant Colonel Augustus Rollins of Rollinsford, and the Third New Hampshire, commanded by Captain William Trickey of Wolfeboro.[6]

The Federal troop transports left the Bermuda Hundred area on January 3 and met the remainder of the fleet off Beaufort, North Carolina. On the morning of the January 12, the monitors and gunboats led the way south, followed by the landing force. The troops were landed the next morning about five miles north of Fort Fisher. They were now between the fort and the five thousand Confederates of Major General Robert F. Hoke. Abbott's brigade was detailed to hold the line in case this force decided to attack Terry's landing party from behind.[7]

Much of the morning of January 15 was taken up with Terry personally positioning the troops for the attack against the fort. The First Brigade under Curtis was finally moved out of the trees about 3 P.M. to about four hundred yards from the fort. The men hastily dug trenches with whatever equipment they had. They drew the immediate attention of the gunners in the fort, and shells soon began to drop in the ranks of the New York regiments.[8] The Federal fleet, anchored offshore, responded at once with its own bombardment and sent

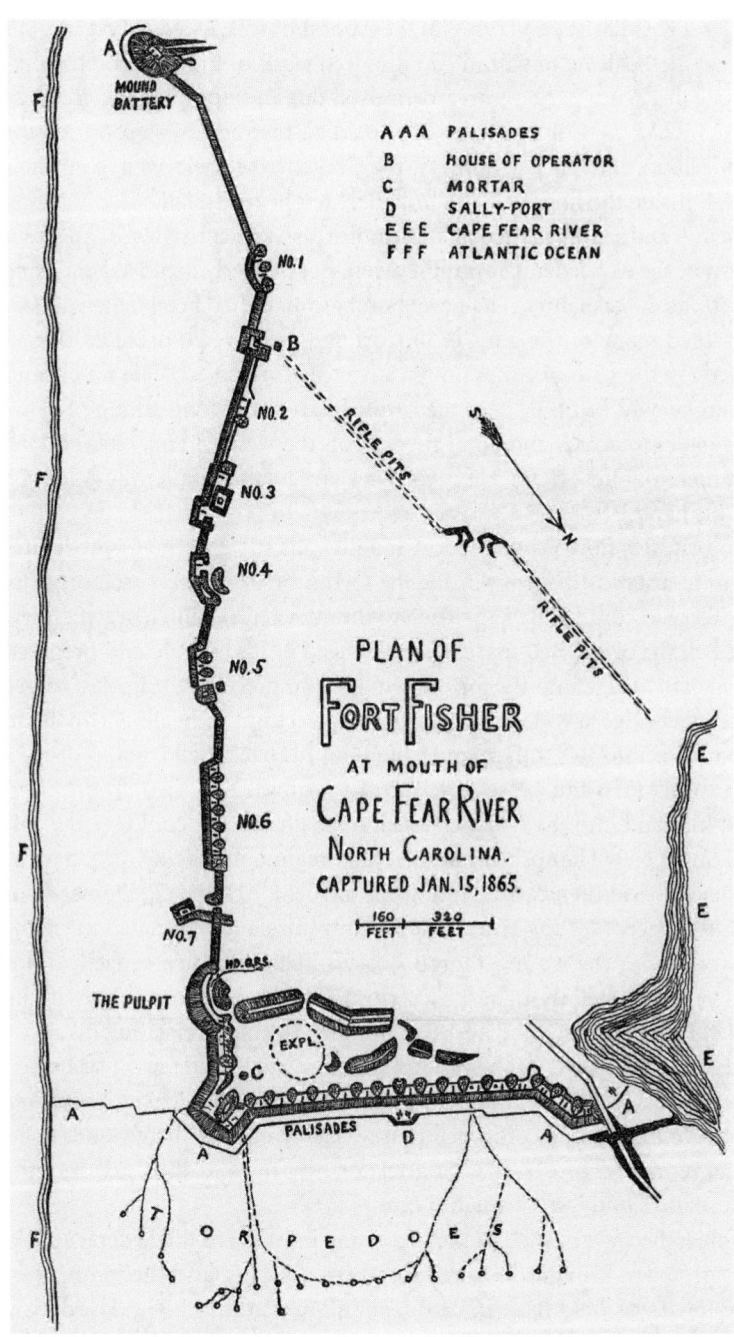

From Henry W. Little, Seventh Regiment New Hampshire Volunteers in the War of the Rebellion, *1896*

the Confederate artillerists scurrying to their bombproofs. Curtis's brigade was moved up again, this time to within two hundred yards of the fort, and the digging began again. Pennypacker's brigade moved out and occupied the trenches just vacated by Curtis. Colonel Louis Bell readied his men to step out of the woods and follow Pennypacker. Some of the Confederate shells went over their mark and fell inside the lines of Bell's brigade, Men began to fall.[9]

The marines and sailors landed near the northeast corner of the fort and kept the attention of the Confederates, but they were not properly deployed and were repulsed with heavy casualties. The naval bombardment had been beneficial because it disabled many of the guns in the fort and destroyed a number of land mines directly in the path of Ames's three advancing brigades.[10] The sailors and marines paid heavily, but they kept the Confederates busy long enough for the first two brigades to attack and enter the fort on the western end. Colonel Bell readied his men to follow them. He paced back and forth impatiently, holding a ramrod in his hand.[11]

The two brigades now inside the fort fought valiantly, but the Confederates fought them to a standstill. From inside the fort, Ames sent a dispatch urgently requesting Terry to commit Bell's brigade to the attack. Captain George F. Towle ran to give Bell the order. Bell marched at the head of his brigade and prepared to cross the small bridge into the fort to help the two preceding brigades. Just as Bell reached the bridge, a volley of musketry erupted from the walls above them. A bullet slammed into Bell's chest and exited out his back. Bell tried to dismiss the wound to his men but he soon fell to the ground. The men around him rushed past him and into the fort. Bell asked to be lifted so he could see the colors of the Fourth New Hampshire and his other regiments waving on the parapet. This they did and then carried him from the field.[12] Dr. David Dearborn of Weare was the surgeon of the Fourth New Hampshire and was called to examine Bell's wound. "Is the wound mortal?" asked Bell. Dearborn replied, "I am fearful it is Colonel." Bell thought for a second. "I thought as much myself," he said. Colonel Louis Bell died the next day from his wounds, repeating his wife's name until he expired. Bell's body was brought home to Chester and was buried on a cold winter day next to his father Samuel. Bell's six-week-old son, Louis, was baptized next to his father's coffin before it was lowered into the ground. Bell's wife, Mollie, remained prostrate with grief for months and died just months after her husband's body was brought home.[13]

One by one, the traverses fell to the increasing pressure of the Federal attack. Abbott's brigade was brought in to reinforce the attackers, and the remnant of the marine force was held back in case Hoke should attack.[14] The Third New Hampshire was committed to the attack and relieved the shattered brigades under Ames. The fighting was continuous as each traverse had to be taken by bitter hand-to-hand fighting. Night was approaching, and an exhausted Ames urged

Terry to break off and hold their ground until dawn. Terry disagreed. The Confederates had to be as tired as they were, and he ordered in Abbott's brigade to continue fighting. The men of the Third New Hampshire rushed forward and carried several more traverses. The Confederate resistance finally broke down around 10 P.M., and the remainder of the garrison was surrendered. Colonel Lamb, the garrison commander, was badly wounded in the fighting.[15]

The Federal force sustained 955 casualties in the attack. The Confederates lost 500 men, and the United States Navy and Marines suffered over 600 casualties, mostly among the marine landing force.[16] Casualties for the three New Hampshire regiments involved in the Battle of Fort Fisher were surprising light for such a vicious battle. Each of the regiments lost two dead and fifty wounded. Today Fort Fisher is a beautiful park run by the state of North Carolina. Sadly, since the war, over half of the fort and its traverses have been washed out to sea.

The day after the capture of Fort Fisher, an accident occurred that resulted in the death of several New Hampshire soldiers, which Captain Towle recorded: "While we were loitering after breakfast, we heard a loud explosion toward Fort Fisher. It was about 8 o'clock. A deep and smothered shock and an immense volume of earth thrown into the air. The main magazine had blown up. Bell's brigade was in bivouac around it. About 100 men were buried, were to be dug out, also 30 Confederates wounded. After a full inquiry we decided it to be an accident. The marines after the fight had returned to plunder. It was supposed that a match lighted had been thrown into some loose powder."[17] Two men from the Third New Hampshire died in the blast caused by drunken sailors in the magazine. The inebriated salts carelessly detonated thirteen thousand pounds of gunpowder and caused the deaths of twenty-five Federal soldiers and the wounding of sixty-six.[18]

By January 1865 the prisoner-exchange system had completely broken down, leaving hundreds of New Hampshire soldiers to languish in Confederate prison camps. Sources differ on an exact number but generally agree that about 400 New Hampshire men died in Southern prisons. Of that number, 144 men died at the infamous Andersonville Prison in Georgia. The number-one killer of New Hampshire soldiers at Andersonville was diarrhea brought on by malnutrition, bad water, and unsanitary conditions. Scorbutus, or scurvy, claimed the lives of forty-five men from New Hampshire, and dysentery claimed twelve. Twenty-one men died of a variety of causes, such as, bronchitis, pneumonia, and gangrene.[19] Most of the New Hampshire regiments were represented among the inmates at Andersonville, but it was the Seventh New Hampshire that lost the most men—forty-three. The First New Hampshire Cavalry, the Fourth New Hampshire, and the Ninth had the highest totals after that.[20]

"I saw at the landing one day a party of Union soldiers from Andersonville," Private Hale Chadwick of the Eighteenth New Hampshire said. "They looked like living skeletons, just bundles of rags and bones; men that went out in perfect health, weighing one hundred and fifty to two hundred pounds, reduced by starvation and disease to less than one hundred. Some had to be taken up and carried on board the boat, a sad sight truly."[21]

New Hampshire troops were also housed at the prisons at Salisbury, North Carolina, Florence, South Carolina, and Libby Prison in Richmond. Scores of fascinating stories describe the appalling conditions of these camps. Lieutenant Colonel Benjamin T. Hutchins of the First New Hampshire Cavalry left a particularly vivid account of Libby Prison. Hutchins, a native of Concord, was selected by the Confederate authorities to distribute blankets to Federal prisoners in Richmond and on January 1, 1865, was given a thousand blankets to give to the nearly three thousand prisoners. He received more blankets later, but they were still not enough. "We issued to men who had just arrived from Western Virginia ninety-two blankets; and here I must say that among all the prisoners whom I have yet seen these are the most destitute. None had blankets or overcoats. In most cases their hats and coats had been taken from them, and but very few had boots or shoes on their feet."[22]

Andrew W. Whidden of Portsmouth had joined the army at eighteen against his widowed mother's wishes. The twenty-one-year-old enlisted in Company G Tenth New Hampshire, commanded by Captain Towle of the same city. At the Battle of Fair Oaks on October 27, 1864, Private Whidden could have retreated with the rest of his regiment when they were called to do so, but he stayed behind to comfort a mortally wounded comrade. An hour passed and Whidden's friend died, but Whidden had been surrounded by Confederates and was taken prisoner, taken to Libby Prison in Richmond, and then transported to Salisbury Prison. By early November 1864, the prison was already overcrowded, so the new arrivals were simply kept outside with no shelter. The elements soon took their toll, and Whidden died January 27, 1865. He is remembered with a gravestone in the Harmony Grove Cemetery in Portsmouth.[23] At the Florence, South Carolina, prison camp, two other New Hampshire men died, Private Horace J. Hall of Exeter and Private Albert S. Flint of Wilton, who are buried in the National Cemetery nearby.[24]

The beginning of February 1865 was cold and rainy in Virginia. Ulysses S. Grant decided to hit the Confederates again and try to stop the flow of supplies coming to Petersburg over the Weldon Railroad. He dispatched the Second and Fifth Corps, and they were in a sharp fight at Hatcher's Run. The Eighteenth New Hampshire was sent to the Petersburg trenches to replace the troops that had been used in the attack. The regiment was at the mercy of the elements and Confederate artillery fire until they were withdrawn and taken back to City Point about February 15.[25]

Desertion was still a problem in the Army of the Potomac that winter. The first and the last execution of a soldier in the Twelfth New Hampshire occurred on February 9. Private Joseph Sharp, a recruit from Manchester, had joined the Twelfth New Hampshire when the regiment was at Point Lookout, Maryland, but at the Battle of Cold Harbor, he deserted and went north. Sharp took a bounty and enlisted in the Fifth Maryland. Luck was not with Sharp because the Fifth later was brigaded with the Twelfth. It was not long until one of Sharp's acquaintances in Company A recognized him and reported his presence in the Maryland regiment to Colonel Thomas E. Barker. The Maryland colonel at first refused to help Barker in the apprehension of Sharp but later acquiesced. When confronted, Sharp denied the entire story, but when he was told that he would stand before his former company mates, he broke down and confessed his identity. Colonel Barker stated that if Sharp had stopped there, he could probably have had him convicted and slated to receive only minor punishment. Instead, Sharp confessed to being a bounty jumper and therefore sealed his fate. Sharp faced the firing squad on February 9 and became the only soldier in the Twelfth New Hampshire shot for desertion.[26]

The Third New Hampshire was all packed up and ready to go, fully expecting that they would be marching into and occupying Wilmington, North Carolina. February 10 had been windy but pleasant, and the following day, the regiment set out as part of a large force. Resistance was encountered at Half Moon Battery, but the regiment overran the line that was manned by the Seventeenth North Carolina. The Third New Hampshire lost two men killed and several wounded in this engagement. Because of the unknown quantity of Hoke's force in front of them, the entire force, along with the Third and Fourth New Hampshire, was withdrawn at nightfall to their original rifle pits on the coast near Fort Fisher.[27]

The State of New Hampshire furnished several units of heavy artillery that served at Fort Constitution in Portsmouth and the forts that encircled Washington. Company A was formed on July 1863, and served first in New Hampshire and then performed garrison duty in Washington until September 1864. It returned to Portsmouth and finished out its service there being mustered out in September 1865.[28] A second company of heavy artillery, formed in September 1863, served at Fort McClary at Kittery Point. The service of this company was nearly identical to the first company. These companies became companies A and B respectively when the First Regiment New Hampshire Volunteer Heavy Artillery was formed in September 1864. The full regiment served in both Portsmouth and Washington and was mustered out in June 1865.[29]

Duty in these heavy artillery units was less arduous than that performed by their brothers in the trenches, so soldiers in these units had plenty of time for correspondence. Corporal Gideon Gilman of Ossipee wrote many letters full of opinions to his friends and family back home. Writing from Fort Kearny to one such friend, Gilman said, "There will be in all probability a big fight some where and How this thing is played out where that battle is to be is not known and whether at all will depend on circumstances if Sherman gets hold of old Beauregard I think that he will shake the fight pretty much all out of the rebs." Gilman also remarked on the large number of Confederates who were surrendering every day: "Their soldiers coming into Washington every day from two to three hundred at a time and take the oath of allegience. I saw a few days ago 150 of them and a more motley crew you never saw some in gray, some in blue some nearly naked in only blue shirts." Gilman, like most of those that served in the heavy artillery, survived his term of service.[30]

From the trenches at Petersburg, Private Edmund K. Brown of the Sixth New Hampshire wrote to his wife in February, and it is apparent that all the dangers and misery were still with the Union soldiers, despite the increasing talk of peace: "Last night because of the picket line had been on for 24 hours one man in the 9th N.H. was shot in the leg and during the 12 hours of night, that I was there more than 100 bulletts came over and circld my head, but there was none that came near enough to me so that I got hit but I came very nearly to it. Thank God I am yet safe and well with the exception of my having the Diaree bug and I'm first there most of time." Brown died of disease in July just one week before the Sixth New Hampshire was mustered out of service.[31]

The threats to General Robert E. Lee and his army were mounting as February turned to March. The end of the war appeared to be in sight. As Gilman indicates, there was still some uncertainty as to how long it would take to wrap things up. Lee's lines around Petersburg were rapidly becoming untenable, and if he chose to abandon those lines in favor of an escape march to the west, then Richmond's fate was certainly sealed. General William Tecumseh Sherman was making a brisk march through North Carolina and, except for a brief halt to fight the battles of Aversboro and Bentonville, his army was barreling towards Lee's rear. Wilmington was about to be occupied, and that force would most likely be coming north as well.[32]

By March 1865 the previous year's fighting and the expiration of enlistments had seriously depleted many of the New Hampshire regiments. The Fourth and Fifth New Hampshire were mere shells, not even remotely resemble the regiments that marched off to war three years before. Colonel Louis Bell had been killed at the Battle of Fort Fisher, and the Fourth New Hampshire awaited the appointment of a new colonel; Captain William Badger was named colonel of the Fourth New Hampshire in February but never mustered in. Aside from being unpopular with Captain Towle of the Fourth New Hampshire and others, the captain explained why Badger was not mustered, "The regiment did not have the authorized number of men to legally have a colonel mustered without an order from the corps commander. This, of, course, General Terry would not give and the regiment went home without a Colonel."[33] The Fifth New Hampshire also had the same troubles with its quota of men. Because the Fifth was under-strength, during the winter it became known as the Fifth New Hampshire Battalion, with only eight companies. Even with the addition of a company of New Hampshire Sharpshooters, it was still not enough. This new organization was under the command of Captain Welcome A. Crafts. Richard Cross, the brother of Colonel Edward Everett Cross, would have been colonel, but again there were not enough men for him to be mustered into that position.[34]

Although the size of the regiments had dwindled, their living conditions had improved thanks in part to the work of the Christian Commission. John M. Davis wrote to the *Portsmouth Journal* on Saturday March 4 about the New Hampshire soldiers he visited. "I spent my time at the front, with the 24th Army Corps-Army of the James. There were four New Hampshire regiments, the Second, Tenth, Twelfth and Thirteenth, in this Corps which I visited. The soldiers live in little stockade houses made of rough logs and covered with mud. The roofs are made of canvas cloth. They sleep upon the ground or upon poles covered with their rubber blanket and overcoat; and they do not remove their clothes. They are in good spirits and would like the rebels to attack them in their works. They complain some of their rations, and in some cases I think they do not have enough to eat, though they are looking rugged. They have not been paid for six months and would be destitute of many things which the Christian Commission gives them." Davis said he and others of his group passed out books, testaments, writing paper, comfort bags, and many other items to the soldiers.[35]

The state Republican convention, held in January, unanimously nominated Manchester mayor Frederick Smyth for the office of governor. The Candia resident won the governor's seat in March, beating Democrat Edward W. Harrington by six thousand votes. Smyth had gained recognition as president of the State Republican Convention in Manchester in 1860 when he introduced Abraham Lincoln as the next president of the United States. Smyth, who assumed his office in June 1865, would welcome the New Hampshire boys when they came home from the war.[36]

In January 1865 Congress passed the Thirteenth Amendment, which abolished slavery. It was ratified and became part of the Constitution in December of that year. As Lincoln was about to experience his second inauguration, the talk in Washington was becoming more focused on postwar America and how the government would handle the reconstruction issue. More New Hampshire soldiers would be killed and wounded before the issues could be decided.

Abraham Lincoln wanted to bring the soldiers home. As he delivered his second inaugural address on March 4, famous for his words "with malice toward none," Lincoln asked the country to "strive on to finish the work we are in; to bind up the nation's wounds; to care for him who shall have borne the battle, and for his widow and his orphan."[37] Despite Lincoln's words of hope and encouragement, the war went on. Sherman was surprised at Aversboro and Bentonville in mid-March but prevailed over the valiant but hopelessly outnumbered forces of Lieutenant General William Hardee and General Joe Johnston.[38]

Captain Towle of the Fourth New Hampshire confided an amusing story to his journal on March 20 about Sherman: "He remarked that he got a good many letters from ladies asking for a lock of his hair and that he would have none left if he gave to all. 'So,' he says, 'When I get a letter, I just chop off a piece of this fellow's [red hair, belonging to his orderly] and it goes all right.' They never knew the difference. The orderly hair was the same red shade as Sherman's."[39]

Lee wanted to help Johnston in his conflict with Sherman by sending him reinforcements. The only way he could do this was to relieve the ever-increasing pressure that Grant was applying against the Confederate lines at Petersburg. Confederate president Jefferson Davis approved Lee's plan for an offensive action. If successful, perhaps it would cause Grant to withdraw his lines in order to protect City Point.[40]

At 4:15 A.M. on March 25, Major General John Brown Gordon sent three handpicked brigades against the Federal position at Fort Stedman, located only 150 yards from the Confederate lines. The surprise was complete, and the bluecoats were thrown out of the fort. The Confederate force went beyond the fort but could not consolidate their gains before Major General John F. Hartranft's Ninth Corps mounted a massive counterattack. The entire battle was over by 8:00 A.M. The Confederates suffered nearly four thousand casualties, mostly men captured when the Federals retook the fort. The Northern soldiers lost about a thousand men killed or wounded. Among those thousand soldiers were three men from the Fifth New Hampshire who had been killed.[41] The Eighteenth New Hampshire was marginally involved in the Battle of Fort Stedman. The regiment had been detailed to cover the Eleventh Massachusetts Battery as it shelled the advancing Confederates.[42]

Private Frank P. Harriman of Company E related an embarrassing personal story that occurred just as the Confederates attacked on March 25. In the darkness and confusion, Harriman put on his boots without realizing that a sword belt strap was underneath his foot inside the boot. When all the soldiers made a mad dash for the front, Captain William A. Gile of Franklin grabbed his sword belt and started running. When he started for the door, Harriman said, "One of my legs jerked suddenly into the air. Captain Gile, a man of two hundred pounds, had gone the length of his rope, wildly rushing for the head of his company, and I, over six feet tall, with one leg outstretched, and my foot as high as the Captain's head." Despite the intense stress of the situation, both men sat down laughing while Harriman removed his boot to free the captain's captive sword belt. They then ran to take their positions in the line.[43]

On the night of March 29, the Confederates made another attempt at taking Fort Stedman that also failed. During this battle, the Eighteenth New Hampshire suffered its first losses. Major William Brown of Concord was killed when he was hit in the head by a musket ball and Lieutenant Colonel Joseph M. Clough was badly wounded in the face by a bursting shell. Private Daniel A. Webster of Fremont was killed when he was struck in the head by a shell fragment.[44] Private Chadwick of Webster remembered that there were "so many pieces of artillery being in action, with the musketry fire, the report of a single gun at times could not be distinguished. Our musketry fire, the guns of Stedman, Haskell, Batteries Nos. 10, 11, and 12, with the fire from the forts in the rear. This was something no body of men no matter how brave, could face without being annihilated."[45]

While the Eighteenth New Hampshire was involved at Fort Stedman on the March 29 and 30, the Fifth New Hampshire was off with the Second Corps on another raid crossing Hatcher's Run. Torrential rains halted the advance of the Fifth in the area of Dinwiddie Courthouse. The next day, Major General George Edward Pickett's force of nineteen thousand infantry and cavalry fell on the left flank as it moved toward Five Forks. The sudden attack pushed the Second and Fifth Corps back to the Dinwiddie area. This action was considered as part of the Appomattox campaign and was but one brief episode in the final act of the war. The Fifth New Hampshire suffered only minor casualties in this engagement. Even though the end of the war was just around the corner, this famous regiment would be involved in two more serious battles.[46]

"Soldiers scarred by many a battle . . . wept aloud"

No more shall the war-cry sever, or the winding rivers be red,
they banish our anger forever, when they laurel the graves of our dead.
Under the sod and the dew, waiting the judgment day;
love and tears for the blue, tears and love for the gray.

> Francis Miles Finch, "The Blue and the Gray,"
> *The History of Rockingham and Strafford Counties*

The failure of Major General John Brown Gordon's attack at Fort Stedman and the Federal probe at Dinwiddie Courthouse convinced Robert E. Lee that if he was to save the remnants of his army, he must withdraw. This meant the loss of Petersburg as well as Richmond itself. There was a slim possibility that if he could outrun Ulysses S. Grant, Lee could link up with General Joe Johnston's army in North Carolina and continue the struggle from there. By April 1, 1865, it became apparent to Lee that he had to leave. At dawn on April 2, the Federals renewed their assaults all along the Petersburg line and broke through at several points. On April 3, the Federal army entered Richmond. Who entered the city first? This has been a subject of controversy since the city fell, even to the present day. There are literally a dozen claims from different regiments from as many states that they were the first.

Among New Hampshire regiments the Tenth, Twelfth, and Thirteenth all lay claim to being the first to enter Richmond. The reality was that when the lines around the city were found to be abandoned, it became a mad dash to see who could be first to reach the capitol. The controversy splits in half when claims were also made as to who raised the first Federal flag over Richmond on April 3. Of the New Hampshire regiments claiming to be the first into Richmond, the Thirteenth New Hampshire presented the strongest case, which included a letter from Brigadier General Charles Devens to Governor Frederick Smyth. Devens, a native of Massachusetts had every reason to back the claim of the Fortieth Massachusetts that they were first. He instead stood by the following letter at the time and for many years afterward:

Headquarters Third Division
Twenty-Fourth Army Corps
Near Richmond, Va. June 22, 1865

To His Excellency, Frederic Smyth,
Governor of New Hampshire:

Governor—The Thirteenth New Hampshire Regiment was the first regiment of
the army whose colors were brought into the city of Richmond on the morning
of April 3, 1865. I am, governor, very respectfully,

Your obedient servant,
Charles Devens
Brigadier and Brevet Major General, U.S. Volunteers Commanding[1]

The race to Amelia Courthouse in Virginia was on. The two armies moved in
parallel lines. The Confederates won the race and arrived at Amelia Courthouse
on April 5 but were disheartened and discouraged to find that the much-needed
supplies had not arrived by rail as promised. Lee's army lingered in the area
around the Richmond and Danville Railroad, but they could see the Union Fifth
Corps quickly advancing on them. On the morning of the April 6, Lee saw the
Federal Second, Fifth, and Sixth Corps arrayed against him and attempting an
enveloping maneuver. The Union corps commanders were trying to get around
and behind Lee while he tried to slip around their left flank.[2]

The Confederates were still on the run but halted several times to put up a
fight. Each time the Confederate army was whittled down a little more. One of
the more severe conflicts occurred at Sayler's Creek. The Second Corps alone
captured fifteen hundred prisoners and scores of wagons full of wounded soldiers. In these running fights, the Fifth New Hampshire lost twenty-three men
killed and wounded, but the fighting was still not over with end of April 6.[3] The
Second Corps was now literally on top of Lee's army and caught a large portion
of it crossing High Bridge. Major General Francis C. Barlow's division rushed to
the bridge and scattered the Confederates who were in the process of destroying
it. Colonel Thomas L. Livermore, although not able to fight with his own Eighteenth New Hampshire, was on the staff of the Second Corps and found himself
leading a detachment against the bridge to prevent its destruction. Livermore
not only tried to put out the fire that had started on the bridge but was also
engaged in hand-to-hand combat with the Confederates who were trying to
hasten the fire's progress. Livermore and his men succeeded in putting out the
fires at High Bridge, and the Second Corps was off again in pursuit of the rear
of the Army of Northern Virginia. The Fifth New Hampshire was involved the
entire day in running skirmishes with the Confederates. A portion of Lee's army
was entrenched near Farmville, Virginia, and the Fifth, advancing toward this

position, became locked in mortal combat with the men of Brigadier General William Mahone's division. Every time the Fifth tried to advance, Mahone's men poured a heavy fire into them. The advance continued, and by the time the Fifth reached the works of the Confederates, they were too weak to resist the rebels' violent counterattack. The colors and color-bearers were captured, and many of the officers killed or wounded. The Fifth New Hampshire lost twenty-two dead in this, their final battle. Luckily, the colors of the Fifth New Hampshire and those men captured with them were quickly recovered in the following days. April 9 brought news of the surrender of Lee's army. The Bloody Fifth was the last New Hampshire regiment to see action in the Civil War.[4]

Private J. Lewis Chase recovered from the wound that he received at the Battle of the Wilderness and was in camp with the Eleventh New Hampshire about thirty miles east of Appomattox Courthouse. Writing to his parents on April 10, he described the entrance of the army into Richmond, "Last Monday morning we immediately broke camp and marched into the city it was a hard looking sight to see the dead in front of the rebel works the greater part our men." Chase excitedly gave his parents the news that had just broken in the Federal camp: "News has just come that Gen Lee has surrendered with 30,000 it is official so you can rely on it well bully for that there the boys are cheering for the good news it is official from Gen Grant the bands are playing the drums are beating and the men are cheering I can not write more now you will read it all in the papers THE WAR IS OVER."[5]

News flashed across the telegraph wires all over the North. Third New Hampshire adjutant Elbridge J. Copp was still at home in Nashua, recuperating from wounds he received at the Battle of Deep Bottom. He was in the town bookstore when a telegram arrived from Boston that Lee had surrendered. Copp was sure that he was the only one in town that had heard the news. He hurried over to the store where he had been folding newspapers when the war began. He looked under the counter and pulled out a fourteen-inch-long cannon that he had used for Fourth of July celebrations before the war. He took the cannon out onto the main street of Nashua, packed it full of powder, and touched it off. The detonation shattered the storefront window, and Copp yelled, "Lee has surrendered!" He loaded the cannon and fired it off again, the entire time shouting, "Lee has surrendered!" at the top of his lungs. It wasn't long until Copp had attracted a small crowd, and he was all too happy to impart the good news that then quickly spread through Nashua.[6]

Celebration and adulation over the end of the war lasted exactly five days, until it was brought to an abrupt halt by the worst of all tragedies. President Abraham Lincoln was fatally shot on the night of April 14, Good Friday.

Two men from New Hampshire saw Lincoln on the last day of his life. Senator John Parker Hale had seen many changes in the course of his political career.

Hale had agitated against the annexation of Texas back in 1845. More recently, he had lost his U.S. Senate seat after ten years and was faced with being out of a job. Waiting for the president on April 14, Hale knew his future was secure. He had coveted the position of minister to France but it was felt he was not qualified enough for the position. He was instead given the position of minister to Spain. Hale had come to Washington to receive his final instructions before leaving for Madrid and had stopped to see Lincoln. When Hale was admitted to see the president, the two men who had disagreed on many subjects engaged in polite conversation. On this afternoon of April 14, Lincoln asked Hale to keep in touch and to keep him posted on any developments. The near end of the war made the atmosphere a cordial one. After their discussion was concluded, Hale left to prepare his family for Spain.[7] Lincoln probably breathed a sigh of relief. Being rid of Hale meant that there would be one less radical to oppose his reconstruction policies.

That evening Lincoln attended the play at Ford's Theater and was shot by John Wilkes Booth. Surgeon William Child of the Fifth New Hampshire Regiment attended Ford's Theater that evening as well. After the evening was over, he penned a letter to his wife immediately: "This night I have seen the murder of the President of the United States. Just at the close of an interesting scene a sharp quick report of a pistol was heard and instantly a man jumped from the box, in which was the President, to the stage—and rushing across the stage made his escape. The assassin exclaimed as he leaped 'Sic Semper Tyrannis'—Thus always to tyrants. It seems all a dream—a wild dream. I cannot realize it although I know I saw it only an hour ago."[8] Lincoln died at 7:20 the morning of April 15. The shock to the country was immediate. Daniel Eldredge of the Third New Hampshire wrote, "Strong men wept in the street like children."[9] Captain Ira M. Barton of the First New Hampshire Heavy Artillery stated, "Soldiers scarred by many a battle—armless, with legs gone—wept aloud—old men as well as young men were sobbing as of a broken heart."[10] On the evening of April 15, a delegation of citizens called on former president Franklin Pierce at his Concord home for some encouraging words. According to Daniel Eldredge, Pierce "made quite a Union speech although everyone present knew that every word he uttered was a false expression of his views."[11]

On April 18, Concord Mayor Moses Humphrey announced that the following day would be a day of mourning for the fallen president. A broadside appeared in the streets of Concord.

To the Citizens of Concord
Funeral of President Lincoln
In accordance with the terms of a proclamation issued by His Excellency, the
Governor of New Hampshire urging people of our state to observe the day set

apart for the funeral obsequies of our late lamented Chief Magistrate by a
general suspension of business and by quietly assembling in their accustomed
houses of worship for humble and devout prayer, I give notice that the bells
of several churches in this city will be tolled and minute guns fired from 11 to
12 o'clock of Wednesday the 19th instant and that the North Congregational
Church, the Episcopal Church, the Unitarian Church and the South Congregational Church will be opened for public prayer and other appropriate services
at noon on that day. The schools and public offices will be closed from 11 to 3
o'clock and I would urge upon the patriotic and devoted citizens of Concord
to suspend all business and labor between those hours and heartily unite in
observance of the solemn services of the day. I am confident that the profound
gloom and deep anxiety which oppresses every heart demand the consecration
of the hours, during which the last sad rites of affection and respect are paid to
ABRAHAM LINCOLN, to God and to our country and will guarantee the suitable
observance of the day.[12]

In Portsmouth, Mayor John H. Bailey also made a call for a public memorial
service, and on the following Monday, a speaker's stand draped in black was
placed in front of the Atheneum. Thousands of citizens in attendance on that
day heard speeches by former governor Ichabod Goodwin and were treated to
songs played by the Portsmouth Cornet Band.[13]

In Washington the body of the late president was prepared for burial by Benjamin Brown French, a Chester, New Hampshire, resident. French, from one of
the leading political families of the state, enjoyed several Federal positions, including the chief marshal of Lincoln's inaugural parade, commissioner of public buildings, and a clerk in the United States Treasury. Now he had been put in
charge of making all the funeral arrangements for the president. French directed
the decoration of the Capitol, instructing that it be decorated with black mourning cloth. He also designed and supervised the construction of the catafalque
that Lincoln's coffin rested upon, as well as the construction of the coffin itself
in which the president would be lying in state.[14]

Nurse Sarah Low and her friends tried to view the president's body on April
18, but the crowds were too great. On April 19, Low said, "We watched Lincoln's
funeral procession to the Capitol at 2. It was very solemn and many persons
were overcome." On April 20, she and her friends tried again to view the remains
of the president. This time they were successful. "There was a long procession
waiting to go in which moved a step or two and then stopped, and so on. It was
a very impressive sight in the Rotunda, in the dim light as we entered we saw on
one side a line of officers sitting in full and brilliant uniform. In the center was
the coffin, and officer standing at the head and foot. The flowers on the coffin
that had been beautiful the day before were faded and it seemed forlorn that

they had not been replaced by fresh ones. Lincoln's face looked very thin and shrunken, the face was dark and it seemed to me that he looked like a murdered man."[15] Andrew Young, Low's friend from Dover, was also in attendance at the funeral. He wrote to his wife his opinion of the late president, "It will be long before we see another man like President Lincoln so strong so wise and determined at the same time so kindly and genial. He seemed to yield to everybody yet was as true to the principles which have characterized his administration as the needle to the pole."[16]

The ramifications and possible repercussions of the death of Lincoln were not lost on anyone at the time. Soldiers in the field probably had the best feel for what would most likely happen next. Lieutenant Solomon Dodge of the Eleventh New Hampshire described his feelings to his sister on April 22, 1865: "The assassination of Lincoln seemed to create a dead silence over everything and everybody. How sad that he should be stricken down just at this time when the day was just beginning to dawn on our beloved country. Many of the paroled prisoners seem to feel very bad about it they seem to think that they will be worse off under the rule of Johnson than Lincoln." Dodge told them about a curious but highly symbolic gift he was sending home: "I have a bit of a relic picked up on the battlefield at Petersburg on April 2nd, 1865, which I will send to Robert. It is a Rebel and a Yankey bullet which met and were sealed together in one solid Union, an emblem of what our Country will be when this war is closed."[17]

Lincoln's funeral train left Washington on its way to the president's final resting place in Springfield, Illinois. Colonel Walter Harriman, writing of the entire bittersweet experience of April 1865, stated, "But now there was sorrow in hearts where joy had been; for the great Emancipator, now, too, the great Martyr, was even then going to his long home, borne thither in funeral procession traversing half the land, with the hearts of his bereaved countrymen in mourning convoy."[18]

The war was finally over, but it felt like something was missing. The war that everyone thought would be over in a month had dragged on for four agonizing years. For many it seemed that the country had always been at war. The realization that the war was finished was manifest both in the movement of Union troops to Washington for a great parade and in the lonely, destitute Confederate soldier making his way back home to a bleak and uncertain future. The Fourteenth New Hampshire had been assigned to garrison duty at Fort Pulaski in Savannah, Georgia, and would not be participating in the Grand Review.[19] A small detail of men from the Fourteenth New Hampshire was on hand at Fort Sumter when General Robert Anderson returned to the fort that he had to surrender at the start of the war. The men cheered as he ran the Stars and Stripes up the pole, and the original flag snapped crisply in the breeze. There was some trouble with paroled Confederate soldiers in Augusta, and the Fourteenth New Hampshire was brought up to Savannah to restore order. While they were patrolling the streets, the men were treated to a historic sight. Down Washington Street came a group of carriages carrying the recently captured leaders of the Confederate government. As Jefferson Davis passed, the soldiers were quiet, but a number of the Confederates who lined the streets jeered and shouted at the deposed leader.[20]

For two days, the Grand Review of the armies took place. On May 23, it was the Army of the Potomac, and on May 24, it was Sherman's army of the West. From the Capitol and all along Pennsylvania Avenue, thousands of people crammed in to witness the spectacle. Adjutant Elbridge J. Copp returned to Washington just in time for the parade and had a choice position near the White House reviewing stand. Copp recorded the dignitaries in the reviewing stand were: President Andrew Johnson, Grant, Secretary of War Edwin Stanton, General William Tecumseh Sherman, Secretary of the Navy Gideon Welles, and a host of senators, judges, and representatives. The days before the parade had been rainy, but on the morning of the parade, it had been clear and cool. At precisely 9 A.M., the Army of the Potomac appeared, with General George Gordon Meade at its head, and marched from its camp just east of the Capitol, around the building itself, and down Pennsylvania Avenue.[21] The army paraded past the White House with all its tattered and torn flags flying. Young wrote to his wife Susan in Dover, "Near two hundred thousand men in our army—all veterans— is what we will not see again in an age. They were twelve hours passing and marched in columns of companies—(there is a whole company abreast) and well closed up, they would reach from Dover to Concord." Young stated that the crowds were continuously pressing against the reviewing stand to get a look at Grant. "The soldiery could not stand a minute before them—they wanted to see Genl. Grant—Genl. Grant would stand up so they could see which he was. Then Sherman—then the President then Stanton and Howard."[22]

"It was the grandest spectacle of the kind ever witnessed in this country," Colonel Walter Harriman said about the parade. "It is confidently believed that in soldier-like bearing and general appearance no corps eclipsed the Ninth and no troops, those of that brigade from New Hampshire."[23]

After the Grand Review was over, the Fifth New Hampshire participated in an awe-inspiring event not witnessed by the masses. Dr. Child recorded in the official history of the Fifth New Hampshire: "On the 25th camp was quiet during the day. At night there was a general illumination. All the troops were on parade; each man had lighted a candle in the muzzle of his musket. As the men marched to and fro, countermarched, formed in squares, massed, deployed, assembled, the effect was beautiful."[24]

Bringing the Boys Home

CHAPTER 15

May 1865 and Beyond

The War is o-ar they'll fight no more and be not sent back again.
To muster out and pay them up and send them to their home.
I want to be discharged with them and share their honors too;
for I have neer disobeyed, one order that I knew.

The Poetry of John R. Downs

The mustering out of New Hampshire soldiers actually began eight months before the end of the war. Veterans of the First United States Sharpshooters were mustered out of the service of the United States on September 8, 1864. Those who reenlisted were folded into the ranks of the Second United States Sharpshooters. Veterans in the Second United States Sharpshooters were mustered out in November and December but fought at Hatcher's Run in February 1865, six days after the unit had been officially disbanded. Those veterans from New Hampshire who had reenlisted were formed into a loose company and attached to the understrength Fifth New Hampshire Regiment.[1]

The record of the three companies of New Hampshire sharpshooters is enviable. These companies participated in over thirty-five battles with thirty-seven killed in battle and twenty-nine dying of disease. Only thirteen men from the three companies deserted.[2] One of those men was Private William B. Greene of Raymond, New Hampshire. He deserted and spent some time in Wisconsin, but returned, serving with distinction until the end of the war. The war left him a wasted man. A bout of typhoid fever limited his abilities. Greene took up shoemaking in Haverhill, New Hampshire, until his "traveling bone" acted up again, and he sought his fortune in the West. Greene began to make some progress in his business in Dunlap, Kansas, until he was badly injured when his horse bolted, and he was thrown from his carriage. Thirty-five-year-old Willie died from this fall on March 21, 1879, and was brought home to Raymond for burial.[3]

Men who had never laid eyes on the granite hills or forests of New Hampshire served in her companies and regiments. Private Daniel Buckingham, originally from Ohio, deserted from his unit, which was stationed in California. He came east looking for action and enlisted in Company F Second United States Sharpshooters. Buckingham was severely wounded on the third day at Gettysburg and died of disease five months later. Private Sexton W. Williams, a friend and traveling companion of Buckingham and from Kentucky, enlisted along with Buckingham and served in Company F. Williams was twice wounded during the Siege of Petersburg and died of his wounds on August 4, 1864.[4] Possibly one of the last New Hampshire Sharpshooters to die in the war was not born in New Hampshire. Private Christian Frederic Meyer was born in Germany but lived in Kingston, New Hampshire. The twenty-five-year-old Meyer enlisted in October 1861 and died for his adopted state and country on February 5, 1865, at Hatcher's Run, Virginia.[5]

The first three-year regiment mustered out was the Eleventh New Hampshire under Colonel Walter Harriman. The ceremony was performed on June 4, 1865, in Alexandria, Virginia. The veterans who had reenlisted were transferred to the Sixth New Hampshire. The regiment, along with the original band it had brought from New Hampshire, boarded trains on June 5 in Washington and arrived on the afternoon of June 7 in Concord.[6] A huge crowd was on hand downtown, and former governor Joseph Gilmore officially received the regiment. Barely 360 men were left from the over 1,000-man regiment that had left the state three years before. It was a scene that would be repeated several times in the following months. Gilmore greeted Colonel Harriman, who said, "We have seen the Rebellion overthrown, and the Federal authority vindicated to the extremist limits of our country." Referring to the Eleventh New Hampshire, Harriman passed his hand over the gathering, "Seven hundred of our original number, discharged, disabled, deceased are with us no more."[7] The Eleventh New Hampshire participated in the inauguration ceremony of Governor Frederick Smyth on the next day, and on June 10, the regiment was paid and officially discharged.[8] At this time Smyth stated, "There is no apparent reason why New Hampshire should come out of this war impoverished by her loyalty and Georgia escape payment for her treason."[9] To many contemporary Americans, this statement seems shocking, especially since the state of Georgia had endured a tremendous amount of suffering and misery during the war. Such statements, however, were commonplace during Reconstruction.

Private J. Lewis Chase came home with the Eleventh New Hampshire and after his discharge returned to South Newmarket, now Newfields. On January 18, 1884, Chase and his wife Ida were aboard the liner *City of Columbus* as it steamed south from Boston to Savannah. About four in the morning, the ship crashed on the rocks off Martha's Vineyard. The ship stayed afloat for only five minutes after hitting the reef. Her hull torn open, the *City of Columbus* sank, drowning one hundred passengers and crew, including Chase and his wife. There is a cenotaph in honor of "Lewis," as he was known, and his wife in the well-kept cemetery in Newfields. The stone is lovingly decorated every Memorial Day by Chase family descendants and others.[10]

Captain George Nelson Shepard, also of the Eleventh New Hampshire, became the postmaster in West Epping after the war and married Rowena Thyng. It is an Epping legend that before the war, Rowena was being courted by the poet John Greenleaf Whittier, and the two carved their initials in a large oak tree on Red Oak Hill in Epping. Shepard was also instrumental in helping many of the veterans of the Eleventh obtain their pensions after the war.[11]

The next unit to be mustered out was the First New Hampshire Light Battery, which had been folded into the First New Hampshire Heavy Artillery but was called upon frequently for detached duty. The battery was mustered out in a public ceremony in Concord on June 9, 1865. Captain Frederick Edgell, who had given his name to the battery, was promoted to major in January 1865, and was transferred to the First New Hampshire Heavy Artillery. Edgell died in Georgetown, Massachusetts, in 1877. During the course of the war, the battery had over 150, with nearly 100 casualties either killed, wounded, or dying of disease.[12] The narrator of a large part of the First New Hampshire Light Battery's story, Sergeant Samuel Cooper, died in Manchester in December 1891. Private Thomas C. Cheney, who had been wounded in action at the Po River in May 1864, was mustered out in September 1864 and moved to Boston. Captain George A. Gerrish was captured during the Second Bull Run campaign, exchanged, and then was wounded at Fredericksburg. He was discharged on a disability several months later and died in Portsmouth in September 1866 from the effects of his wound.[13]

Less than two hundred men of the Ninth New Hampshire were on hand in the State House yard to turn in their flags to Governor Smyth. The regiment had been mustered out in Alexandria, Virginia, on June 10; they were back in Concord on the June 13 and were treated to a banquet at the Eagle Hotel. On June 14, the regiment, its arms stacked, was now watching Colonel Herbert B. Titus hand over its colors. It seemed impossible to believe that their experience as soldiers was almost over. Speeches by the governor and Senator John Parker Hale followed, and then the regiment men were dismissed for the day. The following day, the men of the Ninth were paid off, and the regiment was no more. The officers held several congratulatory dinners; then they, too, parted company.[14]

When the war started, Colonel Titus was a schoolteacher, and when it finished, he was a brevet brigadier general. He was wounded in action at Antietam and was promoted to colonel when Colonel Fellows resigned in November 1862. After the war Titus bought a large parcel of land in Virginia and practiced law in New York City. The former colonel of the Ninth New Hampshire died in 1905 and was buried in Chesterfield, New Hampshire.[15]

The letters and papers of Adjutant and Major George Henry Chandler provided much of the source material used in telling the story of the Ninth New

Hampshire. Chandler was wounded at the Battle of Spotsylvania, and the Concord native finished the war as a lieutenant colonel. When the war was over, Chandler resumed his legal studies at Harvard and received his law degree in 1867. Chandler moved to Baltimore and pursued a successful career there until his death in 1883, when he was then brought back home to Concord.[16]

The first six companies of the Eighteenth New Hampshire regiment were mustered out on June 10, 1865, in Washington, D.C. Those men who signed on for three years were transferred to Company G, which then served until July when they were officially mustered out. This last New Hampshire regiment formed during the war suffered three battle deaths and thirty-four men dying of disease. Because of mustering difficulties, Colonel Thomas L. Livermore was in charge of the regiment for only a few weeks at the end of the war.

The man in command of the Eighteenth New Hampshire for the majority of its existence was Lieutenant Colonel Joseph M. Clough of New London. Clough was a veteran of both the First and Fourth New Hampshire regiments. He was wounded in the Battle of Fort Stedman in March 1865 and became a brevet brigadier general by the end of the war. Clough resided in the town of New London after the war.[17]

On June 21, 1865, the Tenth, Twelfth, and Thirteenth New Hampshire regiments were all mustered out of the service of the United States in Richmond, Virginia. These three regiments departed Virginia as a provisional brigade under Colonel Michael T. Donohoe of the Tenth New Hampshire. Their journey home was not without incident. A number of the men procured a quantity of alcohol in Jersey City and proceeded to have a goin'-home party on their way to Boston. On the ride to Concord, their train derailed near Hooksett, which resulted in the injury of several soldiers.[18] The previous day the men of all three regiments had paraded their numbers in downtown Nashua. In 1862 these same regiments had left New Hampshire with three thousand men. On June 26, 1865, they numbered barely five hundred. After a short stop in Manchester at noon on June 27, the brigade set off on the final leg of its journey to Concord, arriving in that city at 7 P.M. A crowd of citizens and veterans met the train. All three regiments turned in their arms and their flags on June 28 to Governor Smyth. Following this ceremony, the men stayed on duty at Camp Substitute until July, when they were paid off, and their regiments passed out of existence.[19]

Colonel Donohoe finished the war as a brevet brigadier general and assumed a position with the Concord Railroad. He was a member of the Third New Hampshire and was wounded at the Battle of Fort Harrison in September 1864. While Donohoe was in command of the Tenth New Hampshire in Virginia, he received a telegram from his wife, who had just given birth, that she had a "new recruit for the 10th New Hampshire." The quick-witted Donohoe replied, "Muster him in and set him to work on the breastworks." Donohoe was frequently at reunions of his own and other New Hampshire regiments held in the Lakes Region of the state for many years after the war.[20]

Colonel Joseph H. Potter of the Twelfth New Hampshire was captured at the Battle of Chancellorsville and exchanged four months later. He was in command of a brigade of the Eleventh Corps and Twenty-fourth Corps. He finished the war as a brigadier general and joined the postwar army as a colonel. Potter retired from the regular army as a brigadier general in 1886 and died in Columbus, Ohio, in 1891. The Twelfth's official history recorded, "While he [Potter] had not the fecund brain or the tongue of a Whipple or Harriman, nor the daring energy of a Cross, it will, nevertheless, be hard to make some of the survivors of his regiment believe that he did not know his business."[21]

Severely wounded at Chancellorsville, Lieutenant Colonel George D. Savage survived the war and lived in Alton until his death in 1883. Savage provided in his will that if he preceded his warhorse Tom in death, when the animal passed away, it was to be buried in the cemetery with him. The horse died two years later and was buried in the Riverside Cemetery in Alton with his old master.[22]

Thomas Erskine Barker, a captain in the Twelfth New Hampshire, was also wounded at Chancellorsville. He was promoted to lieutenant colonel in 1864 and was a full colonel by the end of the war. He died in 1896 and is buried in Malden, Massachusetts.[23]

Colonel Aaron Fletcher Stevens of the Thirteenth New Hampshire began the war as a major in the First New Hampshire Regiment. He was in command of a brigade when he fell wounded at the Battle of Fort Harrison in September 1864. Stevens finished the war as a brevet brigadier general and ran successfully for the New Hampshire legislature in 1866. Stevens died in his lifelong home in Nashua in 1887.[24]

The Fifth New Hampshire was also mustered out June 28 in Alexandria, Virginia. Three days before, Dr. William Child had written to his wife, "It is now very certain that our Regt. will leave here for New Hampshire as soon as next Friday. I hope it will not be long before we shall meet in our own home."[25] When Child's regiment came home, the men performed the same ritual of turning in their torn colors to the governor. Child went back to his private medical practice in Bath. He died in his daughter's home in 1918 and is buried in Bath Village Cemetery.[26]

Thomas L. Livermore spent the majority of his service with the Fifth New Hampshire, although he started the war in the First New Hampshire and became a sergeant in the Fifth New Hampshire in the fall of 1861. He was wounded at White Oak Swamp and ascended to the rank of major. He accepted the colonelcy of the Eighteenth New Hampshire but was not mustered into that regiment until the end of the war. He served on the staff of the Second Corps during the closing phase of the war. Livermore is probably best known for his *Numbers and*

Losses in the Civil War in America 1861–1865. He was also the regimental historian for the Eighteenth New Hampshire. After the war Livermore was Boston Park Commissioner from 1889 to 1893. Livermore died in Boston in 1918 but was brought home to Milford, New Hampshire for burial.[27]

The Fifth New Hampshire had 2,119 men serve in its ranks. Of that number, 282 men were killed in battle, 756 were wounded, and 178 died of disease, giving the regiment a casualty rate of over 57 percent. Because of length of service, number of engagements, and number of men who served, the Fifth had the highest casualty rate of any New Hampshire regiment and perhaps of any in the Union Army.[28] The Fifth New Hampshire performed well under Colonel Edward Everett Cross, but the history of this brave regiment did not end with his death at Gettysburg. The greatest loss for the Fifth New Hampshire occurred at Cold Harbor when Colonel Charles Hapgood led a mere 577 men into the Confederate works and, because of lack of support, suffered an appalling loss of 202 men killed or wounded.[29] Colonel Hapgood commanded the regiment after Cross's death until he was wounded in the arm in June 1864 at Petersburg. He was discharged in the fall of that year. After the war Hapgood was superintendent of the Massachusetts Soldiers Home in Chelsea, Massachusetts, until his death in 1909. He is buried in the Mountain View Cemetery in Shrewsbury, Massachusetts.[30]

The story of the Fifth New Hampshire is the story of soldiers like Private Reuben E. Gilpatric, who enlisted in October 1861 and was discharged, disabled, in January 1864. The young Dover resident had seen all the battles between those times. He was wounded both at Antietam and Gettysburg and survived the war. He is buried in the immaculately kept cemetery in Newington, New Hampshire.[31]

The Fourteenth New Hampshire Regiment was mustered out of the service of the United States on July 8 while onboard a ship that transported them from Savannah, where the regiment had been engaged in garrison duty at Fort Pulaski. Upon their arrival in New Hampshire on July 18, the men were granted a week's furlough. The 565 men of the Fourteenth New Hampshire gathered one week later and were paid off. The strange service of the Fourteenth New Hampshire regiment was over. The Fourteenth had spent twenty-two months of its three-year term on Provost Guard duty in Washington, D.C. Just when the men thought they would never see action, they were thrown headlong and with no military experience into the violent and sanguinary battles of Third Winchester and Cedar Creek. The regiment paid heavily in those two engagements and left many of their comrades buried in the Winchester area. The regiment then went back to guard duty in Georgia until the end of the war.[32]

On July 16, 1865, the First New Hampshire Cavalry reached Concord and was paid off on July 21. The regiment's 532 men had been mustered out near Cloud's Mill, Virginia. Twenty-three men died in battle, and more than one hundred died of disease; over half of the deaths were in Confederate prisons.

Starting the war as part of another state's regiment, the New Hampshire horse-men finally got their own regiment and were all together at the end of the war.[33]

The long, hard road of war was now over for the Sixth New Hampshire as well. Simon Goodell Griffin began the war as a captain in the Second New Hamp-shire and as a brevet major general led his division and old regiment down Pennsylvania Avenue in the Grand Review. His horse was covered with the gar-lands and wreaths offered by young women along the parade route. Griffin was offered a commission in the regular army, but he graciously declined. He re-turned to civilian life and was elected to the New Hampshire Legislature. He became Speaker of the House in 1867 and failed in a bid for Congress in 1871. Griffin became involved in land and railroad deals in Texas but finally retired to his home in Keene, where he remained until his death in 1902.[34] The Sixth New Hampshire was mustered out on July 17, 1865, in Alexandria, Virginia, and headed for New Hampshire two days later. The regiment arrived in Concord on July 23 and was met by Governor Smyth. The regiment turned in its flags, and it, too, was treated to a banquet at the Eagle and Phenix hotels. It took a week before the soldiers were finally paid off and dismissed, but in that time they probably reflected and reminisced about the record of their regiment. The Sixth New Hampshire had participated in twenty-three battles and numerous small skirmishes. The regiment was mauled at Second Bull Run, and it had to leave many of its comrades in graves across the landscape of Virginia.[35]

Phineas P. Bixby had been taken prisoner at the Second Battle of Bull Run but was exchanged in October 1862. He was in command of the Sixth New Hamp-shire after the death of Colonel Henry Pearson at the North Anna in May 1864. Bixby finished the war a brevet colonel and retired to civilian life with the rest of the regiment. He returned to his business in Concord and died in 1877 in that city.[36]

The mustering out for the Seventh New Hampshire Regiment took place July 20 in Goldsboro, North Carolina. The regiment arrived in Concord at noon on August 3 and was met by the veterans of the Fifth New Hampshire. After the ceremony at the State House, the regiment dined at the American House. The remaining 322 men of this regiment also waited a week to be paid off and dis-charged.[37] The Seventh had fought in twenty-two engagements and served in a variety of locations. In the beginning the regiment languished on guard duty at Fort Jefferson in the Dry Tortugas but then fought at the sanguinary battle of Fort Wagner, where the regiment lost heavily in officers and men. In February 1864 the Seventh went on the expedition to Florida and fought in the misman-aged battle at Olustee, again suffering heavy losses. The regiment served the remainder of 1864 in Virginia, fighting at Deep Bottom, Bermuda Hundred, and Petersburg. The Seventh was present at the Battle of Fort Fisher in North Caro-lina and finished its service in that state. When the regiment returned to New

Hampshire, only one officer in its ranks had departed with the original regiment three and a half years before. Colonel Haldimand Putnam was killed at Fort Wagner, and Lieutenant Colonel Thomas A. Henderson died at Deep Bottom.

Joseph C. Abbott, who started the war by turning down the colonelcy of the Seventh New Hampshire, finished the war as a brevet brigadier general. After Putnam's death in July 1863, Abbott commanded the regiment until the summer of 1864, when he was promoted to the command of a brigade. After the war Abbott became involved in the lumber business in North Carolina. He entered the political arena in that state and ran successfully for a seat in the United States Senate. Abbott died in 1881 in Wilmington, North Carolina, where the Seventh New Hampshire fought its last battles.[38]

The Third New Hampshire was also mustered out on July 20 in Goldsboro, North Carolina. The regiment arrived in Concord on July 28 with 26 officers and 324 men. The regiment turned in its banners to the governor and was addressed by Adjutant General Head and Brevet Brigadier General Michael T. Donohoe. The Third New Hampshire had participated in over thirty battles and had shared its fortunes with the Fourth New Hampshire and partially with the Seventh New Hampshire.[39] The Third was roughly handled in its first engagement with the Confederates at Secessionville in June 1862, but it was at Drewry's Bluff that the regiment suffered the most casualties. During its history, the regiment was commanded by five different men and was present at Fort Wagner, Olustee, Deep Bottom, and Fort Fisher. The first colonel of the Third New Hampshire, Colonel Enoch Quimby Fellows resigned in June 1862. Succeeding commanders of the regiment were John Henry Jackson, wounded at Fort Wagner; John Bedel, captured at Fort Wagner; Josiah I. Plimpton, killed at Deep Run; and James F. Randlett, wounded at Drewry's Bluff.[40]

Two soldiers of the Third New Hampshire who deserve special mention are Daniel Eldredge and Elbridge J. Copp. Eldredge finished the war as a lieutenant and later became the official historian of the regiment. He authored his exhaustive history of the Third New Hampshire in 1893, and his journal is at the New Hampshire Historical Society in Concord. Adjutant Copp returned to his home in Nashua after the war and authored the highly informative *Reminiscences of the War of the Rebellion* in 1911.

The men of the Fourth New Hampshire were mustered out in Raleigh, North Carolina, on August 23, 1865. The regiment started for home, and when it reached Manchester, it was treated to a respectful celebration. Only 144 soldiers from the regiment were on hand for the turning in of the flags, because fifty of its members were sick in the hospital. The men were paid off in the first week of September 1865, and the Fourth New Hampshire passed out of existence.[41]

The first person to command the Fourth New Hampshire, Thomas J. Whipple died and was buried in Laconia in 1889. After serving in the First New

Hampshire, Whipple commanded the Fourth and was an inspiration to the men of the Twelfth New Hampshire from his native Belknap County. Colonel Louis Bell was killed at Fort Fisher and is buried in Chester, New Hampshire. The highly opinionated George F. Towle finished the war as an assistant inspector general and retired to New Castle. He died in 1900 and is buried in the Harmony Grove Cemetery in Portsmouth, near his father George W. Towle of the Tenth New Hampshire, who died in 1887.[42]

The Eighth New Hampshire Regiment was mustered out in two parts. Approximately 150 men of the regiment whose enlistments ran out in the end of 1864 were mustered out in January 1865. The remainder, known as the Veteran Battalion, was sent to Vicksburg and mustered out there on October 28, 1865. The small group of ten officers and 180 men arrived home on November 7, 1865, in Concord. They were paid off and discharged two days later.[43] Many of the soldiers of the Eighth New Hampshire considered their regiment the "forgotten regiment" because they served so far away from the eastern theater and the perception that, beyond the regimental level, they had been poorly used and led. The failure of the Red River campaign under Banks and the unsanitary camps are two reasons given for the regiment's poor mortality percentage. Ninety-nine men in the regiment were killed in battle, and 232 succumbed to disease. Despite these dreadful losses, the Eighth New Hampshire was not included in Fox's *Regimental Losses in the American Civil War*. In Mather Cleveland's *New Hampshire Fights the Civil War*, the author aptly points out, "A soldier who dies of disease in service is just as dead as one who dies of gunshot wounds."[44]

The regiment with the longest term of service was the Second New Hampshire, kept in service long after all the other New Hampshire regiments had been mustered out. The Second finally joined the other regiments on December 19, 1865, at City Point, Virginia. The regiment had been mustered in on June 10, 1861, and was on hand for the First Battle of Bull Run where it suffered twelve deaths. The regiment was roughly handled at the Second Battle of Bull Run, but it was at Gettysburg that it suffered the most casualties. The Second New Hampshire arrived home two days before Christmas, and, on Christmas Day 1865, the largest parade ever seen in Concord took place. A throng of people accompanied the men of the Second New Hampshire to the ceremony at the State House. Governors Smyth and Joseph Albee Gilmore were on hand, and Colonel Walter Harriman addressed the men.[45]

Colonel Gilman Marston of the Second New Hampshire finished the war as a brigadier general, served one more term in Congress, and returned to his law practice in Exeter. The colonel of the first three-year New Hampshire regiment died in 1890 and is buried in Exeter.[46]

The Second New Hampshire was paid off on December 26 and became the last New Hampshire regiment to be discharged. Thus ended the term of service for all the volunteer regiments from New Hampshire. All that was left after that were the scars, stories, and memories of the scores of battles and skirmishes fought for freedom and preservation of the Union.

Two women who deserve mention are Harriet Patience Dame and Sarah Low. Dame, although she nursed and tended to soldiers from other regiments, will always be remembered for her association with the Second New Hampshire. After the war Dame held a clerical position with the United States Treasury and was a yearly visitor at postwar reunions. She worked at the Treasury for twenty-eight years until she became an invalid in 1895. Dame died in 1900 in Concord. Governor Frank Rollins led a large funeral procession to the cemetery. The next year the state legislature appropriated money to have a portrait of Dame painted. When it was completed, it became the first painting of a woman to hang in the New Hampshire State House.[47]

Sarah Low returned home to Dover in August 1865 and died in December 1913. She was the granddaughter of William Hale and the last member of the Hale family to live in the Lafayette House, which is now the Saint Thomas Episcopal Church Parish House. Senator John Parker Hale wrote to Sarah's mother that at a breakfast in Washington, Governor Morrill of New Hampshire praised Low, "Think of it, a young Lady who you see at once is educated and refined, having position, friends, home and parlor which she adorned, coming here to look after, and take care of those poor fellows, of whom she knows nothing except they are sick and suffering. If I ever go to heaven may I be in her ward."[48]

A variety of small organizations raised in the state performed garrison duty. Captain Israel B. Littlefield of Dover commanded the Strafford Guard that was assigned the duty of guarding Fort Constitution in Portsmouth, New Hampshire, for sixty days. The National Guards, which was commanded by Captain James O. Chandler, performed the same duty. The Martin Guards, Lafayette Artillery, as well as a host of volunteers, took a turn at guarding New Hampshire's fort in New Castle. Because the soil of New Hampshire never came under attack, there were no battle casualties among these groups.[49]

Telling the story of New Hampshire men in the United States Navy and Marines, beyond biographical sketches, is difficult, because no state records were kept regarding their participation in the war. During the war, 366 soldiers from New Hampshire were in the marine corps. A postwar estimate of New Hampshire men in the navy is given as 3,526, but a modern estimate that takes into account desertions and removal of dubious names from the register places the number closer to 1,200. The most accurate number that could be found using local sources was that 120 men joined the navy from Dover, and 248 were from Portsmouth. Of those numbers, nine men were killed in action, and fifty died of disease.[50]

When taking into account the variety of numbers given from the end of the war to the present day regarding New Hampshire's participation in the war, it is important not to forget those men living in New Hampshire border towns, such as, Cornish, Nashua, or Milton, who served in regiments from neighboring states. The estimated number of men who served in this way is 2,122.[51]

Total participation of New Hampshire troops was 32,486. The total number deaths from battle and disease stands at 4,840; of those, 1,934 died in battle or from their wounds received in battle. New Hampshire men who died in Confederate prisons was 242. The total number of desertions was 4,260.[52] The *Civil War Book of Lists* shows 33,937 people, or roughly ten percent of the population of the state, participated in some fashion in the war. This source gives 4,882 as the total number of deaths of New Hampshire soldiers and sailors. Modern New Hampshire historian Mather Cleveland sets the number of New Hampshire men lost a bit higher at 5,012, and the overall participation lower at 28,000.[53] Statistics for each regiment can be found in the regimental histories of those units. The Third, Fifth, and Twelfth New Hampshire regiments all sustained more battle deaths than deaths from disease; the Sixteenth New Hampshire had no battle deaths, but deaths from disease accounted for nearly 25 percent of the regiment's losses.[54]

Twenty-eight soldiers and sailors from the state of New Hampshire were awarded the Medal of Honor, including two lieutenant colonels, five privates, and two quartermasters. Eleven sergeants received the coveted Medal of Valor. Men from the Ninth New Hampshire received the most medals at five, and there were seven New Hampshire regiments whose men received none. Seven New Hampshire sailors, including two born in Ireland and one in Scotland, were given the nation's highest honor. Manchester, Portsmouth, and Nashua were each represented by three medal recipients. Nineteen medals were bestowed on soldiers for their actions in a battle or campaign in Virginia; nine of these were for the Richmond-Petersburg area alone. Fredericksburg and Spotsylvania each generated two medal recipients, and two medals were given for action in Louisiana.[55]

The war debt of the state went from $30,000 in 1861 to $1,825,000 in 1863. By the end of the war, that figure had risen to $13,000,000 or about one-tenth of New Hampshire's total assessed value. What accounted for most of this expense was the exorbitant bounties paid out by many of the towns in their losing efforts to fill their quotas after 1863. The first-ever income tax was levied against the residents of New Hampshire, but it was still not enough to stave off the staggering inflation that hit the state. By the end of the war, flour was nearly $20.00 per barrel, kerosene was $1.50 per gallon (the same as in 2003), cornmeal was $4.25 a bag, and a pair of men's boots was $8.00—astronomical sums. People of the state were hopeful that the United States government would help with the crushing debt that New Hampshire had to bear for her part in preserving the Union. Such hopes were misplaced. New Hampshire was reimbursed but for only $900,000. The remainder of the state's debt would be assumed by the towns, and it would be years before the state's debt was paid off.[56]

The State of New Hampshire had four governors during the war years. Ichabod Goodwin was elected just before the war began. In April 1861 he met the crisis in an able fashion and made arrangements with the banks of New Hampshire to prepare the state's first fighting units. Nathaniel Springer Berry was governor when the majority of three-year regiments and other organizations were raised. He was present to witness the excitement and surge of patriotism in the mass of New Hampshire men who volunteered for the war in 1861 and 1862. Joseph Albee Gilmore was New Hampshire's third wartime governor and came to office just as the draft crisis was breaking out, not only in New Hampshire but also across the North. He, too, competently dealt with the crisis of the draft, thrust so unfairly upon a small state that had already scoured its hills and valleys for able-bodied men. Governor Gilmore presided over a state that was becoming rapidly discouraged with the war when the casualty lists began pouring in from the violent and bloody battles of the spring of 1864. The peace movement gained ground in the state and elsewhere. New Hampshire's last governor of the war actually took office two months after the war, but he is included because he was left with the task of healing the state's battered economy. Frederick Smyth had to find a way to deal with the massive war debt and with the rampant inflation that was straining every New Hampshire family to its limits.[57] In his message to the New Hampshire legislature on June 7, 1866, Smyth reviewed the state's finances and addressed the problem of war debt. It was his suggestion that whatever reimbursements paid by the federal government be directly passed to the towns to alleviate their debts. Smyth presided over the state when the remains of the proud and once-large regiments returned home. He was on hand for many of the heartbreaking ceremonies when the diminished regiments turned in their tattered battle flags. Many have said that the transition from civilian to soldier was not nearly so hard as going back to their lives as civilians. The sweetness of coming home was turned slightly bitter when it was discovered that perhaps twenty and as many as forty of the young men they had left home with would not return.

On the subject of those who had been wounded or disabled during the war, Smyth said, "Some provision should be made by the State for the support of those who were entirely disabled in the service, or have since become so by reason of wounds or exposure, beyond the amount paid by the General Government."[58]

Smyth finished his address with a comment on the flags that the regiments returned. The comment is rather lengthy but is included in its entirety as a plea to today's New Hampshire legislators to take steps to preserve an important part of New Hampshire history. An ad hoc, volunteer, or unfunded committee can never be expected to shoulder such a burden. The preservation must be done with reverence and respect by the state that sent these men to fight and die for the cause of freedom.

Battle Flags
On the return of peace, with its new responsibilities, those emblems of American nationality under which our soldiers fought their way to victory, and beneath whose folds they died, that our country might live, have come back to us, the Regimental Flags of New Hampshire have all been gathered together—the memorials of the valor and devotion of her sons. What a tale they could tell of heroic patriotism, of patience and courage, of agony and distress. Silent witnesses of that strife which ended in glory for the republic, they come now to remind us of our duty as citizens of that country, for which our dearest blood has been shed. They call upon us to be true to those great principles of humanity, which made all men equal on the battlefields of freedom. They call upon us to be devoted to those great doctrines of free government which can alone elevate mankind to the standard of a Christian commonwealth. They call upon us to remember the great free rallying cry of the war, now that the tempting and enervating hours of peace are upon us. They lessons which they teach us may never be forgotten, and as they are assigned each its honorable place in our Capitol, may their presence warm our hearts to their highest endeavors, and stimulate us to the unflinching performance of the high duty which yet lies before us.[59]

Throughout the current volume, a special emphasis was placed on giving the location of the burial sites of those New Hampshire soldiers who fell in battle or having survived the war found their final resting places at home or other locations. Many New Hampshire towns and cities do an outstanding job in the care and preservation of the cemeteries where New Hampshire soldiers are buried. Unfortunately, there are also cemeteries in the state that have not been properly maintained. Memorial Day comes and goes, but cemeteries need to be cared for year-round in order to properly respect the memory and deeds of the soldiers of New Hampshire. Time inevitably draws its veil over the past. We are inclined to forget history and the important events that happened as the years turn to decades, and the decades turn to centuries. History then becomes nothing but remote events and dates shrouded in the mists of time. The graves are still there, even though many people of the current generation are incapable or unwilling to appreciate the lives of the occupants of those graves. The same sun rose and fell, the people lived and loved, had colorful or bland lives, just as we do today. What sets them apart is that they passed through a harrowing trial that has thankfully never been repeated in this country's history.

Corporal Henry Ellis of Lebanon, New Hampshire, served in the Thirty-third Massachusetts Infantry and was wounded at the Battle of Bentonville on March 21, 1865 and died from his wounds. But in 1863, he provided probably the best summary of why soldiers of both North and South fought in the war: "I am getting tired of war. I want to have it fought out, and the clash of arms to cease on all sides. But I ask not for this until right and justice prevails. Father and Mother, you think that you know something of this war and what the soldiers have to endure, but I can tell you that you have not seen anything. Perhaps you may say that I am discouraged, but I say no, not a bit of it. I fully considered all things before I left and my mind is just the same now as it was then. I came out for my country's good and I hope that when I return, that I may have the assurance in my own brest that I have done my duty."[60]

The men who served from the Granite State performed heroically on every battlefield, regardless of the long periods of demoralization because of the frequent changing of army commanders and the subsequent defeat of those commanders. The enormous sacrifices and deprivations that had to be endured by the New Hampshire soldier can be read about in the pages of this book. The American Civil War is the fulcrum on which rests all of American history. Everything that came before it was a preparation for the crisis, and everything that came after was in some way influenced by it.

A debt is owed to all the men and women of the State of New Hampshire who served in the war. It is for us to cut through the mists and veils of time that make people indifferent. As long as books are printed and reflections are cast to those days long ago, the deeds of these people will be remembered.

NOTES

Introduction

1. Squires, *Granite State,* 320–21.
2. Ibid., 227; G. W. Smith, 276–77. Smith details the austere lifestyle of the New Hampshire subsistence farmer in the nineteenth century.
3. G. W. Smith, 276–77.
4. Squires, *Granite State,* 321.
5. American Revolution Bicentennial Administration, 16; United States Department of State, 27.
6. Boatner, 326.
7. W. A. Wallace, 275–87.
8. McClintock, *History,* 583–84.
9. American Revolution Bicentennial Administration, 16–18.
10. Squires, *Granite State,* 211; *"To Restore Our Glorious Union,"* 3.
11. Squires, *Granite State,* 212.
12. Ibid., 211; Hayes, 7.
13. Emerson, 2:984.
14. Stackpole, 3:257; Squires, *Granite State,* 213.
15. R. S. Wallace, chap. 1:19, chap. 2:6.
16. Squires, *Granite State,* 213.
17. Ibid., 214.
18. R. S. Wallace, chap. 2:8.
19. Somers, 140–41.
20. Squires, *Granite State,* 217.
21. Ibid., 218; R. S. Wallace, chap. 2:9.
22. Squires, *Granite State,* 217–18; Sewell, 147–48.
23. Stackpole, 3:62.
24. Gara, 37–39; Squires, *Granite State,* 218.
25. Squires, *Granite State,* 219.
26. F. Pierce; United States GPO, 103–9.
27. United States GPO, 103–9.
28. United States GPO, 103–9.
29. Gara, 48–49.
30. R. S. Wallace, chap. 1:23–26; Squires, *Granite State,* 362.
31. Gara, 45, 97.
32. Ibid., 88–96, 130–133; Squires, *Granite State,* 364; Nevins, *Ordeal,* 109–13.
33. Squires, *Granite State,* 288.
34. Stackpole, 3:156–57.
35. *New Hampshire Patriot and State Gazette,* July 18, 1855, 2.
36. Stackpole, 3:160.
37. Squires, *Granite State,* 376.
38. Noon, 111.
39. Noon, front flap.
40. Merrill, 135–37; Lanzendorf, 72, 125, 184, 202.
41. Noon, front flap.
42. Merrill, 138; Noon, front flap.
43. Squires, *Granite State,* 375.
44. Klein; H. McFarland, 253–54.
45. Nevins, *Ordeal of the World,* 517.
46. Stamp, 139; McClintock, *History of New Hampshire,* 607.
47. R. S. Wallace, chap. 2:12.
48. Sewell, 179–81.

49. Squires, *Granite State,* 365–66; R. S. Wallace, chap. 1:35.
50. Squires, *Granite State,* 366.
51. Nevins, 184–86.
52. Page, 28–29; W. A. Wallace, 35.
53. Page, 30, 36; Squires, *Granite State,* 367–68.
54. Page, 60–61.
55. Squires, *Granite State,* 368.
56. Ibid., 369–70.
57. Emerson, 3:311.
58. Squires, *Granite State,* 371.

CHAPTER 1. New Hampshire Responds to the National Crisis

1. Robinson, 23.
2. Ibid., 24.
3. Ibid., 30–31.
4. McClintock, *History, History,* 613
5. Speech of the Honorable Mason W. Tappan of New Hampshire on February 5, 1861, Courtesy of Dartmouth College Library, 2.
6. Ibid.
7. Ibid., 6.
8. Ibid., 7.
9. Robert Sobol, 3:962–63.
10. Winslow III, 16–17.
11. Ibid., 122–23.
12. Long, 32, 35, 38.
13. Russell, Jon,, 185–86.
14. Long, 51–52.
15. Nashua History Committee, 124.
16. Ibid.
17. Long, 54.
18. Nashua History Committee, 124.
19. Long, 56–57.
20. Copp, 11–12.
21. Abbott, 67, 53.
22. Sewell, 191.
23. Abbott, 55.
24. Waite, *New Hampshire,* 37.
25. Ibid., 50.
26. Potter, 379.
27. Dow, 302.
28. *Portsmouth (New Hampshire) Chronicle,* April 18, 1861.
29. Waite, *New Hampshire,* 52–55; Vol. 1, 1.
30. Nason, 5.
31. Ibid., 222.
32. Hoehling, 21, 70.
33. Ibid., 72–77; Haydon, 163–66.
34. Nashua History Committee, 127.
35. Ibid.
36. Waite, *Claremont's,* 21.
37. Nashua History Committee, 127.
38. Catalfo Jr., 310; Thomas, *History of Fremont,* 422.
39. Scales, 217.
40. Ayling, 1.
41. Abbott, 110–11; Scott Lanzendorf, 184.
42. Sewell, 192.
43. Portsmouth Atheneum, 5; *New Hampshire and the Civil War,* 1:1.
44. Haynes, 3–4.
45. Ayling, 1; Natt Head, xiv.
46. Caleb Dodge to brother, May 6, 1861, Caleb Dodge Papers.
47. Caleb Dodge Papers.
48. Hoehling, 86.
49. Keene History Committee, 109.
50. Waite, 103.
51. Portsmouth Atheneum, 5.
52. Thomas, 1.
53. Thomas Leaver to mother, May 9, 1861, Thomas Leaver Papers.
54. Charles E. Jewett to brother, May 11, 1861, Charles E. Jewett Papers Milne Special Collections and Archives Department, University of New Hampshire Library, Durham, N.H.
55. General Order #16, Order of the Day, Camp Constitution, May 19, 1861.
56. Winslow, 83.
57. Livermore, 20; *History of Carroll County,* 174. For excellent descriptions of New Hampshire uniforms

and others see *Rebels and Yankees,* 234.

58. Abbott, 112–13.
59. Ibid., 113.
60. McFarland, 232.
61. Waite, 67.
62. Nashua History Committee, 128.
63. Nashua History Committee, 123.
64. Brigadier General J. K. F. Mansfield to Colonel Mason Tappan, May 30, 1861.
65. Waite, 103; Nason, 7.
66. Waite, 116–17; Faust, 476; Lanzendorf, 125.
67. Struthers, ed., 149; Waite, 306–7.
68. Hoehling, 88–89.
69. Ibid., 94
70. Ibid., 91–98
71. Robert Sobol, 3:963; Stackpole, 4:79.
72. See also Squires, 1–2.
73. L. Bell to Mollie, June 7, 1861, Louis Bell Papers, Milne Special Collections and Archives Department, University of New Hampshire Library, Durham, N.H.
74. Waite, *New Hampshire,* 69–70; Faust, 720.
75. Abbott, 138.
76. Waite, *New Hampshire,* 71–72.
77. L. Bell to Mollie, June 20, 1861, Louis Bell Papers.
78. Waite, *New Hampshire,* 72–73.
79. Abbott, 138.
80. Waite, *New Hampshire,* 78–79.
81. Thomas B. Leaver to mother, June 9, 1861, Thomas B. Leaver Papers.
82. Thomas B. Leaver to sister, June 17, 1861, Thomas B. Leaver Papers.
83. Martin A. Haynes, 7–8.
84. Charles E. Jewett to brother, June 16, 1861, Charles E. Jewett Papers, MC123, Milne Special Collections and Archives Department, University of New Hampshire Library, Durham, N.H.

85. Haynes, 11–15; Waite, *New Hampshire,* 129–34; Head, 422.
86. Charles E. Jewett to brother, June 26, 1861, Charles E. Jewett Papers, Milne Special Collections and Archives Department, University of New Hampshire Library, Durham, N.H.
87. Haynes, 17.
88. Enoch G. Adams to mother and brother, June 26, 1861, Enoch G. Adams Papers, Milne Special Collections and Archives Department, University of New Hampshire Library, Durham, N.H.
89. Haynes, 18; Longver, n.p.
90. Haynes, 18.
91. John L. Putnam to Haldimand S. Putnam, June 21, 1861, Putnam Papers.
92. Waite, *New Hampshire,* 85; Head, 150.
93. Waite, *New Hampshire,* 80.
94. Matthew E. Thomas, 422–23.
95. Colonel Charles Stone to Colonel Mason Tappan, July 9, 1861, *1st New Hampshire Volunteers General Order Book.*
96. Waite, *New Hampshire,* 82; Major General Patterson to all commands, July 11, 1861, *1st New Hampshire Volunteers General Order Book.*
97. Waite, *New Hampshire,* 82–84.
98. Livermore, *Days and Events,* 17.
99. Waite, *New Hampshire,* 135; Charles E. Jewett to brother, July 20, 1861, Charles E. Jewett Papers, Milne Special Collections and Archives Department, University of New Hampshire Library, Durham, N.H.
100. Waite, *New Hampshire,* 135.
101. Head, 424–26; Griffin, 2.
102. Griffin, 2; Donovan, 240.
103. Waite, 136; Griffin, 4.
104. Davis, *Battle at Bull Run,* 192.
105. Griffin, 4.

106. Waite, *New Hampshire,* 136; Haynes, 39.
107. Foster, 50, 51.
108. McClintock, *Granite Monthly New Hampshire Magazine* 1 (1888): 344.
109. Charles E. Jewett to brother, July 29 and July 28, 1861, Charles E. Jewett Papers, Milne Special Collections and Archives Department, University of New Hampshire Library, Durham, N.H.
110. Enoch G. Adams to mother, August 4, 1861, Enoch G. Adams Papers, Milne Special Collections and Archives Department, University of New Hampshire Library, Durham, N.H.
111. Haynes, 39.
112. Haynes, 42–43.
113. Long, 103.
114. Head, 419.
115. Head, 419–20.
116. Abbott, 172–74; Livermore, 22.
117. Marvel, *First New Hampshire Battery,* 2–5.
118. Eldredge, *Third New Hampshire,* 15.
119. Waite, *New Hampshire,* 169.
120. Ayling, 117; Eldredge, journal, August 2, 1861, 3.
121. Waite, *New Hampshire,* 215.
122. Ibid., 402.
123. Merrill, 726; Lanzendorf, 72.
124. Towle, journal, July 1861, 23.
125. Towle, journal, July 23, 1861, 27.
126. Eldredge, journal, 10.
127. Copp, 18.
128. Eldredge, *Third New Hampshire,* 22.
129. Hutchinson, *History of the Fourth,* 25–26.
130. Ibid.
131. Towle, journal, September 27, 1861, 31.
132. Marvel, *First,* 4.
133. Ayling, 964.
134. Child, 5–6.
135. Long, 122–23.

136. Towle, journal, October 3, 1861, 33.
137. Thomas, *History of Fremont,* 436–37.
138. Towle, journal, October 12, 1861, 35.
139. Ibid., 37.
140. Child, 5–6.
141. Waite, *New Hampshire,* 297.
142. Ibid., 306–7.
143. Marvel, *First,* 6–7.
144. Savas, 3.
145. Ibid.
146. Eldredge, *Third New Hampshire,* 48–50.
147. Hutchinson, 58–59.
148. Hutchinson, 39–42.
149. Towle, journal, October 29, 1861, 41.
150. Towle, journal, October 31, 1861, 41.
151. Stephen J. Wentworth to parents, November 4, 1861.
152. Towle, journal, October 31, 1861, 41.
153. Stephen J. Wentworth to Parents, November 4, 1861.
154. Hutchinson, 42; Towle, journal, November 2, 1861, 45; Eldredge, *Third New Hampshire,* 48–50.
155. Towle, journal, November 3–4, 1861, 45.
156. Savas, 3, 5.
157. Towle, journal, November 5, 1861, 45.
158. Savas, 4–5.
159. Stephen J. Wentworth to parents, November 9, 1861.
160. Towle, journal, November 7, 1861, 47.
161. Eldredge, *Third New Hampshire,* 64.
162. Savas, 7.
163. Towle, journal, November 7, 1861, 47.
164. Stephen J. Wentworth to parents, November 9, 1861.
165. Wentworth; Towle, 47–48.
166. Stephen J. Wentworth to parents, November 9, 1861; Faust, 226.
167. Towle, 48.
168. Waite, *New Hampshire,* 231.

169. Ibid., 297; Child, 30.
170. Stephen J. Wentworth to brother, December 2, 1861.
171. Waite, *New Hampshire,* 338.
172. Ibid., 345–47; Natt Head, xiv.
173. Calvin Shedd to wife, December 5, 1861, Calvin Shedd Papers, Archives and Special Collections University of Miami Library, www.library.miami .edu/archives/shedd/62feb09.html (accessed February 18, 2001); Ayling, 392.
174. Towle, journal, December 7, 1861, 57.
175. Ibid.
176. Waite, 365.
177. Winslow, 85, 87.
178. Jackman and Hadley, 10–13.
179. Samuel E. Douglass to father, December 31, 1861, Samuel E. Douglass Papers.
180. S. J. Wentworth to brother, December 24, 1861.
181. Cheney to brother, December 19, 1861.
182. Charles E. Jewett to brother, December 30, 1861.
183. Long, 152–53.

CHAPTER 2. New Hampshire to the Front

1. Wilkinson, diary, January 1, 1862; Ayling, 202.
2. Charles E. Jewett to his brother, January 1, 1862.
3. Waite, *New Hampshire,* 347; Young to his son Hamilton, January 17, 1862.
4. Caleb Dodge to sister, January 6, 1862. Dodge had been a private in the First New Hampshire Regiment.
5. Griffin, 6.
6. Waite, *New Hampshire,* 315.
7. Head, 627–28; Waite, *New Hampshire,* 372; Hunt, 163. Thirty-five-year-old Hawkes Fearing Jr. began

the Civil War as the lieutenant colonel of the Fourth Massachusetts Infantry. In September 1861, he was commissioned colonel of the Eighth New Hampshire regiment and despite receiving a leg wound in April 1863 at Fort Bisland, Louisiana, stayed with the regiment until the end of the war. After the war Fearing was active in the Massachusetts Legislature and was the librarian of the Hingham Public Library.

8. Styple, 71.
9. Child, 21; Ayling, 266.
10. Little, 35–36.
11. Head, 609.
12. Caleb Dodge to brother, March 15, 1862.
13. Ibid., 628–29.
14. Cleveland, 71.
15. Head, 512.
16. Shedd to parents, March 2, 1862.
17. Towle, journal, March 3, 1862, 67; Head, 513; Ayling, 197.
18. Head, 577–78; Hunt, 161; Griffin, 6.
19. Jackman and Hadley, 38.
20. Albert Gove to Alvin Gove.
21. Towle, journal, 75.
22. Head, 429–30.
23. Stone, 224.
24. Eldredge, journal, 86.
25. Head, 477.
26. Ibid., 540; Child, 48–49.
27. Long and Long, 191.
28. E. G. Adams to home, April 4, 1862.
29. Child, 51.
30. E. G. Adams to mother, April 14, 1862.
31. Long and Long, 198–99.
32. Hastings, 106.
33. E. G. Adams to mother, April 18, 1862.
34. Hoehling, 132–35.
35. C. A. Stevens, 41; Ayling, 968.
36. Stanyan, 64.

37. Perkins, 66–67.
38. Caleb Dodge to sister, April 20, 1862.
39. Shedd to wife, April 25, 1862.
40. Ibid.
41. Ayling, 382.
42. Waite, *New Hampshire,* 191; United States War Department, 14:2, 336.
43. E. G. Adams to home, April 27, 1862.
44. E. G. Adams to home, May 2, 1862.
45. Haynes, 81.
46. E. G. Adams to home, May 10, 1862; Ayling, 29.
47. Long and Long, 206–7.
48. Haynes, 74–82.
49. Child, 57.
50. Livermore, *Days and Events,* 63.
51. Young to son, May 28, 1862.
52. Long and Long, 218–19; Boatner, 272–73; Child, 82.
53. Livermore, *Days and Events,* 65.
54. Ibid., 66–67.
55. Faust, 668.
56. Livermore, *Days and Events,* 68; Conn, 62.
57. Styple, 101; Child, 85.
58. Livermore, *Days and Events,* 68–69.
59. C. D. Chase, 202.
60. Ayling, 222.
61. Livermore, *Days and Events,* 69–70.
62. Boatner, 272; Faust, 668.
63. Gilman Griffin to Albert H. Taft, June 4, 1862, Albert H. Taft Papers.
64. Taft, papers; Ayling, 503.
65. Young to wife, June 6, 1862.
66. Bedel, 522.
67. Faust, 664; Eldredge, *Third New Hampshire,* 173.
68. Bedel, 522.
69. McCaslin, 119.
70. Ibid.
71. Bedel, 523.
72. Ibid.
73. Eldredge, *Third New Hampshire,* 173.
74. Ayling, 109.
75. Bedel, 523.
76. Copp, 143.
77. McCaslin, 147.
78. Ibid; Copp, 147.
79. Head, 483.
80. Ibid.
81. Eldredge, journal, 150.
82. Faust, 664.
83. Waite, *New Hampshire,* 191; Hunt, 166; Ayling, 138. John Henry Jackson, the inspector of the Boston Custom's House before the war, had served as a captain in the Ninth U.S. Infantry during the Mexican War. Jackson, a resident of Portsmouth, joined the Third New Hampshire in August 1861 as its lieutenant colonel.
84. Charles E. Jewett to brother and sister, June 19, 1862.
85. Captain Samuel Sayles to Enoch George Adams, June 19, 1862, E. G. Adams Papers.
86. Boatner, 603; Faust, 541.
87. Haynes, 93–98.
88. Haynes, 99.
89. Ibid., 100–101.
90. Ayling, 98, 209.
91. Born in Portsmouth, New Hampshire in 1822, Fitz-John Porter was the son of Captain John Porter, the commander of the Portsmouth Navy Yard. Fitz-John was also the cousin of Admiral David D. Porter and Commodore William Porter and attended Phillips Exeter Academy in nearby Exeter and then West Point. Wounded and twice brevetted for gallantry in the Mexican War, Porter went on to be an artillery instructor at West Point. Porter became a brigadier general in August 1861 and became chief of staff of the Department of Pennsylvania (Faust, 594–95; Boatner, 661).
92. Faust, 594–95; Boatner, 661.
93. Ibid.

94. Haynes, 299–301. Harriet Patience Dame was born in Concord in January 1815.
95. Ibid.
96. Ibid.
97. Ibid.
98. Towle, journal, June 25, 1862.
99. Faust, 376; Towle, journal, July 3, 1862.
100. Wilkinson, diary, June 25, 1862.
101. Long and Long, 234.

CHAPTER 3. Into "a furnace of strife"
1. Head, 671; Waite, *New Hampshire,* 396.
2. Long and Long, 236.
3. Waite, *New Hampshire,* 404; Hunt, 164.
4. Livermore, *Days and Events,* 102.
5. Ibid., 103.
6. Haynes, 118.
7. Copp, 149–50.
8. Nulty, 71.
9. Towle, journal, July 6, 1862.
10. Silber and Sievens, 90–91.
11. Ayling, 122.
12. Silber and Sievens, 63–64.
13. Ayling, 341.
14. Thurston to father, July 18, 1862.
15. Ayling, 340.
16. Wilkinson, diary, July 17, 1862.
17. Cleveland, 75.
18. J. H. McFarland to Reverend James Barbour, July 25, 1862.
19. Sayles to Ellen Jane Tolman, February 19, 1863.
20. Long and Long, 247.
21. Ibid., 246.
22. McDaniel to sister, August 7, 1862.
23. Faust, 450, 829; Davis, *Breckenridge,* 323.
24. Ayling, 435; Longver, n.p.
25. Michael T. Donohoe was born in Lowell in 1838 and educated there and at the College of the Holy Cross

in Worcester, Massachusetts. The beginning of the war found "Mike" Donohoe deeply involved in business and the Irish community in Manchester.
26. Head, 701–2; Waite, *New Hampshire,* 427–29.
27. Cogswell, 7, 634.
28. Ibid., 23–24. Walter Harriman was born in 1817 into a family of seven brothers and two sisters. He studied theology at the age of twenty-three and became a Universalist minister in Warner. In 1849 Harriman's interest turned from religion to politics, and he was elected the state representative from Warner for one term. Harriman successfully ran for a state senator seat in 1859 and with the advent of the war offered his services to the state.
29. Ibid., 28–29.
30. Hastings, 140.
31. Ayling, 980.
32. Hastings, 144.
33. Boatner, 102.
34. Haynes, 122–23.
35. Long and Long, 250; Jackman and Hadley, 73–76.
36. Eldredge, *Third New Hampshire,* 198–206.
37. Taft, diary, August 25, 1862.
38. Taft, diary, August 29, 1862.
39. Moulton, diary, August 27, 1862.
40. Boatner, 102–3.
41. Hennessy, 555–60. This source gives the Order of Battle and the specific brigades, divisions, and corps that had New Hampshire units.
42. Ayling, 973, 977, 978.
43. Hastings, 146.
44. Boatner, 104.
45. Haynes, 128–37; Hennessy, 250.
46. Sergeant Hugh R. Richardson to the father of Charles E. Jewett,

September 16, 1862, Charles E. Jewett Papers.

47. Ayling, 79.
48. Haynes, 134–35.
49. Jackman and Hadley, 79–86; Hennessy, 262.
50. Jackman and Hadley, 82.
51. J. Smith to sister, September 6, 1862.
52. Hennessy, 264–65.
53. Jackman and Hadley, 84.
54. *Names and Records,* 18–19.
55. Cheney to brother, September 5, 1862.
56. Ibid.
57. Griffin, 8.
58. Ibid.
59. Jackman and Hadley, 90.
60. Haynes, 131–32; Ayling, 92.
61. Jackman and Hadley, 91; Ayling, 339.
62. Haynes, 127.
63. Faust, 94.
64. Ayling, 971, 985.
65. Boatner, 105.
66. Long and Long, 259.
67. J. Smith to sister, September 6, 1862.
68. Sears, *George B. McClellan,* 260–62.
69. Long and Long, 259–61.
70. Cleveland, 94.
71. John Henry Chandler to mother, September 3, 1862.
72. Head, 763; Bartlett, 12, 749.
73. Bartlett, 9–10; Waite, *New Hampshire,* 469–70. Joseph Hayden Potter, who was born in Concord in 1821, received his early education in Portsmouth and an appointment to West Point, graduating in 1843. Wounded in the Mexican War, Potter was brevetted first lieutenant for gallant and meritorious service. At the outbreak of the Civil War, Potter was forty-one years old and commanded the regiment at Fort Niagara.
74. Waite, *New Hampshire,* 483–84; Head, 782. Aaron Fletcher Stevens had been an active lawyer and legis-

lator before the war. Born in 1819, Stevens was a partner in a successful law firm in Nashua and a member of the Whig Convention held in Baltimore in 1852.
75. Head, 811–12; Waite, *New Hampshire,* 502–3. Robert Wilson was born in September 1811 and graduated from Amherst College in Massachusetts in 1832. Wilson had extensive militia experience and was given the command of the Keene Light Infantry in 1847.
76. Hadley, 118.
77. Marvel, *First New Hampshire Battery,* 20.
78. Templeton to brother, September 13, 1862.
79. J. L. Chase to father, September 14, 1862.
80. *Portsmouth Journal,* September 13, 1862, 2:7.
81. Bailey, 38, 60.
82. Lord, 77.
83. Lord, 83; Ayling, 486–87.
84. Lord, 71–77.
85. Templeton to brother, September 13, 1862.
86. Marvel, *First,* 20.
87. Ibid.
88. Conn, 66. Dr. William Child was born in Bath in 1834 and received his medical degree from Dartmouth in 1857. He was mustered into the Fifth New Hampshire in August 1862.
89. M. Sawyer, B. Sawyer, and T. Sawyer, 31.
90. Ibid., 33.
91. Luvaas, *United States Army War College Guide to the Battle of Antietam,* 123.
92. Cheney to sister, September 10, 1862.
93. Luvaas, *United States Army War College Guide to the Battle of Antietam,* 126.

94. Cheney to sister, September 10, 1862.
95. Taft, diary, September 16–17, 1862.
96. Cleveland, 29–30.
97. Luvaas, *United States Army War College Guide to the Battle of Antietam,* 202; Cleveland, 30.
98. Livermore, *Days and Events,* 135.
99. Holden, 48.
100. Ibid., 49.
101. Livermore, *Days and Events,* 141.
102. Holden, 49.
103. Ayling, 234, 257; Holden, 49.
104. Luvaas, *United States Army War College Guide to the Battle of Antietam,* 221–22, 291.
105. Bailey, 121, 126.
106. Tucker, 87.
107. Ibid., 93–94.
108. Ibid., 98.
109. Jackman and Hadley, 104.
110. Ibid.
111. Bailey, 124, 139; Lord, 106.
112. Lord, 111.
113. Jackman and Hadley, 107.
114. Ibid., 108–9.
115. Lord, 126; Ayling, 484.
116. Head, 674.
117. Cheney to sister, September 10, 1862; Marvel, *First,* 21.
118. M. Sawyer, B. Sawyer, and T. Sawyer, 33.
119. Northam Colonist Historical Society, n.p.
120. A. F. Pierce to brother, September 21, 1862.
121. Head, 702.
122. Ibid., 703.
123. Bartlett, 21–22.
124. Ibid., 23–26.

CHAPTER 4. Frozen Hell at Fredericksburg

1. Neal, diary, September 29, 1862.
2. Ibid.
3. George H. Chandler to Kate, October 3, 1862. George Henry Chandler Papers, Tuck.
4. Ibid.
5. Long and Long, 272–73.
6. Head, 835.
7. Hunt, 166–67; Waite, *New Hampshire,* 519–20. Colonel John W. Kingman was born in Barrington, New Hampshire, in 1821, attended Philips Exeter Academy, and graduated in 1843 from Harvard Law School. Kingman was fortunate to study law with Daniel Webster in Boston before opening his own practice in Cincinnati, Ohio. After the war Kingman served as associate judge of the Wyoming Territory Supreme Court until 1873. He returned home to run several successful paper and oatmeal mills and died in 1903. He is buried in the Pine Hill Cemetery in Dover, New Hampshire.
8. Johnson, diary, October 7, 1862.
9. Waite, *New Hampshire,* 519.
10. Jenks to wife, October 3, 1862.
11. J. L. Chase to brother, October 3, 1862.
12. Hadley, 119.
13. Thomas, *History of Fremont,* 437.
14. A. F. Pierce to brother, October 10, 1862.
15. M. Sawyer, B. Sawyer, and T. Sawyer, 45–47.
16. Neal, diary, October 13, 1862.
17. J. F. Wentworth to sister, October 13, 1862.
18. Shedd to wife, October 12, 1862.
19. Hutchinson, *History of the Fourth,* 3:246–53.
20. Towle, journal, October 22, 1862.
21. Hutchinson, *History of the Fourth,* 251.
22. Towle, journal, October 22, 1862.
23. Keeter, 8.
24. Eldredge, *Third New Hampshire,* 222.

25. Head, 514–15; McCaslin, 121; Eldredge, *Third New Hampshire*, 225.

26. Keeter, 10.

27. Waite, *Claremont*, 84.

28. Neal, diary, October 30, 1862.

29. Stanyan, 140–44; Ayling, 431, 451.

30. Ayling, 790; Cleveland, 80–81.

31. Cleveland, 80; Hunt, 173. Colonel James Pike held a Doctor of Divinity degree and was a Methodist minister. Born on November 10, 1818, in Salisbury, Massachusetts, Pike resided for most of his life in South Newmarket (Newfields), New Hampshire. He attended Wesleyan University in Middletown, Connecticut, and was a New Hampshire congressman from 1855 to 1859. After the war Pike went back to a quiet life in Newfields as a minister and died in 1895. He is buried in the Locust Grove Cemetery in Newfields, near many of the New Hampshire men who preceded him.

32. Horace H. Adams to William, November 2, 1862.

33. J. L. Chase to mother, November 4, 1862.

34. Knight, journal, November 6, 1862.

35. J. L. Chase to mother, November 9, 1862.

36. Hadley, 121.

37. Young to wife, November 9, 1862.

38. Putnam to father, November 25, 1862, Tuck.

39. Head, 835–36.

40. Johnson, diary, November 20, 1862.

41. Little, 168. Not only was Little the official historian of the Seventh New Hampshire but was also one of the twelve people from New Hampshire to receive a Congressional Medal of Honor.

42. Templeton to parents, November 12, 1862.

43. Taft, diary, November 16–19, 1862.

44. Hadley, 122.

45. Hunt, 164–65; Waite, *New Hampshire*, 396. Colonel Enoch Quimby Fellows, who served on the New Hampshire Legislature after the war, died in 1897 and is buried in Grove Cemetery in Center Sandwich, New Hampshire.

46. Cleveland, 81.

47. J. L. Chase to sister, November 22, 1862. Chase's comment is ironic because although Burnside had little trouble taking Fredericksburg, his forces were cut to pieces by the massive amount of Confederate artillery on Marye's Heights behind Fredericksburg.

48. Thomas, *History of Fremont*, 438.

49. Knight, journal, November 27, 1862.

50. J. L Chase to brother, November 29, 1862.

51. Hadley, 123.

52. Waite, *New Hampshire*, 521.

53. A. F. Pierce to brother, December 7, 1862; Ayling, 680.

54. Livermore, *Days and Events*, 159–60.

55. J. L. Chase to brother, December 8, 1862.

56. Shedd to wife, December 11, 1862.

57. Templeton to sister, December 11, 1862.

58. Taft, diary, December 11, 1862.

59. Luvaas and Nelson, 122–23.

60. Musgrove, *Autobiography of Captain Richard W. Musgrove*, 48.

61. Ibid.

62. Taft, diary, December 12, 1862.

63. Templeton to sister, December 12, 1862.

64. J. L. Chase to parents, December 12, 1862.

65. Marvel, *First*, 24; O'Reilly, *Battle of Fredericksburg*, map 1. Illustrated by John Dove, this is probably the finest

map set of the Battle of Fredericksburg to date.

66. Marvel, *First*, 24.

67. Cheney to brother and sister, January 2, 1863.

68. O'Reilly, *Battle of Fredericksburg*,
map 1.

69. C. Smith, 52–53.

70. Holden, 57.

71. Ibid., 59.

72. Livermore, *Days and Events*, 177.

73. Holden, 81.

74. Ibid., 80.

75. O'Reilly, *Battle of Fredericksburg*,
map 2.

76. Paige, 32.

77. Ayling, 579.

78. Paige, 33.

79. Templeton to brother and sister,
December 14, 1862.

80. Paige, 35.

81. Hadley, 129–30.

82. Templeton to brother and sister,
December 14, 1862.

83. Paige, 36.

84. Cleveland, 96.

85. Hadley, 132–33.

86. Taft, diary, December 13, 1862.

87. Knight to friends, December 15,
1862.

88. Jackman and Hadley, 127; Ayling,
307.

89. Knight to friends, December 15, 1862.

90. Head, 676–77; Cleveland, 96.

91. Marvel, *First*, 24.

92. Knight to friends, December 15,
1862; Ayling, 317.

93. C. Smith, 67.

94. Luvaas and Nelson, 317; O'Reilly,
Battle of Fredericksburg, map 4.

95. Stevens to Gov. Nathaniel Berry,
December 22, 1862.

96. Ibid.

97. Julian to unknown, December 26,
1862.

98. Stevens to Gov. Nathaniel Berry,
December 22, 1862.

99. O'Reilly, *Fredericksburg Campaign*,
421.

100. *OR* (*The War of the Rebellion: A
Compilation of the Official Records
. . .*, hereafter *OR*), 337.

101. *OR*, 336.

102. Cleveland, 119.

103. Ibid., 96

104. Nason, 16.

105. J. L. Chase to parents, December 15,
1862.

106. Musgrove, *Autobiography of Captain
Richard W. Musgrove*, 51.

107. George Henry Chandler, December
18, 1862.

108. M. Sawyer, B. Sawyer, and T. Sawyer,
71–72.

109. Low to mother, December 22, 1862.

110. Griffin, 12; Jackman and Hadley,
123–24.

111. Cleveland, 96.

112. Joseph Willey to parents, December
21, 1862.

113. J. L. Chase to parents, December 15,
1862.

114. Cleveland, 173.

115. M. Sawyer, B. Sawyer, and T. Sawyer,
77.

116. George Henry Chandler to mother,
December 25, 1862.

117. Johnson, diary, December 17, 1862.

118. Ibid., December 21, 1862; Ayling,
425, 444.

119. Ibid., December 24, 1862.

120. O'Reilly, 452.

121. Ayling, 1132; Marvel, *Alabama and
the Kearsarge*, 98.

122. Long and Long, 300; J. L. Chase to
brother, December 27, 1862.

123. Lord, 247.

124. Bean, 103–4.

125. J. L. Chase to brother, December 29,
1862.

CHAPTER 5. "We poured a deadly fire into their ranks"

1. Long and Long, 306–7.
2. J. L. Chase to parents, January 18, 1863.
3. Thomas, *History of Fremont,* 440.
4. Cleveland, 79.
5. Silber and Sievens, 77–78.
6. Waite, *New Hampshire,* 535–36.
7. Ibid., 536–37.
8. Jacob F. Chandler to home, January 6, 1863.
9. Johnson to home, January 4, 1863.
10. Caleb Dodge to sister, January 10, 1863.
11. Johnson to home, January 4, 1863; Ayling, 753; Longver, Charles G. Perkins entry, n.p.
12. Johnson, diary, January 14, 1863; Ayling, 749.
13. Long and Long, 312–13; Gilliss, 458.
14. J. L. Chase to father, January 29, 1863.
15. Templeton to friends, January 31, 1863.
16. E. G. Adams to mother, January 26, 1863.
17. J. L. Chase to father, January 29, 1863.
18. Long and Long, 315.
19. Hopkins, 164; Ayling, 220.
20. J. L. Chase to father, January 29, 1863.
21. Howes to wife, January 29, 1863.
22. M. Sawyer, B. Sawyer, and T. Sawyer, 91.
23. J. L. Chase to mother, February 8, 1863.
24. Mason to home, February 11, 1863.
25. O. F. Rumrill to nephew, February 14, 1863. O. F. Rumrill Letters.
26. "Mascomy," 38.
27. J. L. Chase to brother, February 19, 1863.
28. Reull Willey to parents, February 21, 1863.
29. Mason to home, February 24, 1863. Mason refers to the dissatisfaction of the men of the Twelfth New Hampshire over the naming of Potter as colonel and not Thomas J. Whipple.
30. Putnam to father, February 21, 1863, Tuck.
31. Putnam to father, February 23, 1863.
32. Long and Long, 325.
33. Randall to Obadiah F. Rumrill, uncle, March 9, 1863. Randall uses the old Middle English adverb *lief* here, which means "willingly" or "might as well be now as later."
34. Albert T. Austin to mother, March 3, 1863; Ayling, 767.
35. Reull Willey to wife, March 4, 1863; Ayling, 543.
36. J. L. Chase to mother, March 1863, letter 23.
37. Templeton to sister, March 3, 1863.
38. Squires, *Granite State,* 399. Born on June 10, 1811, in Weston, Vermont, Joseph Albree Gilmore attended school there. Moving to Concord, New Hampshire, he later became superintendent of the Concord Railroad. After a short time as a Whig, Gilmore became a Republican and was elected to the state senate, becoming its president in 1859.
39. Sobol, 3:964; Squires, *Granite State,* 399.
40. Head, 444.
41. Albert McDaniel to sister, April 3, 1863, John McDaniel Papers.
42. Boatner, 817.
43. Foye to brother, April 5, 1863; Ayling, 668.
44. Horace H. Adams to William, April 5, 1863; Ayling, 531, 541, 551.
45. J. L. Chase to parents, April 2, 1863.
46. Lieutenant Colonel Joseph Abbott to Colonel Haldimand S. Putnam, April 1, 1863, H. S. Putnam Papers, Tuck.

47. Miller, 252; Sifakis, 182.
48. Long and Long, 335–36.
49. Colonel Louis Bell to wife, April 8, 1862.
50. Head, 516–17.
51. Putnam to father, April 11, 1863, Rauner.
52. Shedd to unknown, undated (probably late April 1863).
53. Mason to friends, April 11, 1863.
54. C. Hoyt to sister, April 10, 1863.
55. Winters, 225; Ayling, 455.
56. "Mascomy," April 5, 1863.
57. Templeton to friend, April 26, 1863.
58. J. F. Wentworth to sister, April 20, 1863.
59. Livermore, *Days and Events,* 188.
60. Head, 561.
61. Gilliss, 465.
62. Marvel, *First,* 25.
63. Ibid.
64. Head, 561; Livermore, *Days and Events,* 189.
65. Holden, 83–85.
66. Musgrove, *Autobiography,* 66.
67. Livermore, *Days and Events,* 196.
68. Musgrove, *Autobiography,* 66.
69. Child, 180.
70. M. Sawyer, B. Sawyer, and T. Sawyer, 85.
71. M. Sawyer, B. Sawyer, and T. Sawyer, 86.
72. Livermore, *Days and Events,* 202.
73. Musgrove, *Autobiography,* 67.
74. Boatner, 137–38.
75. Musgrove, *Autobiography,* 68; Head, 766–67.
76. Head, 767; Bartlett, 81–83.
77. Musgrove, *Autobiography,* 68.
78. Head, 767.
79. Musgrove, *Autobiography,* 68.
80. Bartlett, 480, 502; Fisher, 7.
81. Musgrove, *Autobiography,* 68–69.
82. Fisher, 10.
83. Waite, *New Hampshire,* 469–70.

84. Bartlett, 86.
85. Cleveland, 36–37; Sears, *Chancellorsville,* 341.
86. Marvel, *First,* 25.
87. Cheney to sister, May 9, 1863.
88. Holden, 86.
89. Cleveland, 36.
90. Holden, 89.
91. Boatner, 140.
92. Gilliss, 465.
93. Boatner, 817.
94. Reull Willey to wife, April 17, 1863.
95. Head, 787.
96. Howes to wife, May 5, 1863; Ayling, 661; Head, 787.
97. Lieutenant Nathaniel Coffin to family of John H. Foye, May 6, 1863, Solomon Dodge Papers, 1991–44M; Longver, Foye entry, n.p.
98. M. Sawyer, B. Sawyer, and T. Sawyer, 117.
99. Obear, 32–35
100. M. Sawyer, B. Sawyer, and T. Sawyer, 121–22.
101. J. L. Chase to mother, May 20, 1863.
102. Wilkinson, diary, May 13, 1863.
103. Holden, 139–40.
104. Ayling, 291; Waite, *New Hampshire,* 311–12.
105. Boatner, 663; Faust, 596.
106. Head, 641; Cleveland, 84.
107. Boatner, 663; Faust, 596–97.
108. Head, 641–43; Cleveland, 84–85.
109. Boatner, 663.

CHAPTER 6. "We are all going into Wagner like a flock of sheep"

1. Long and Long, 360–61.
2. Mason to home, June 1, 1863.
3. Holden, 141–42.
4. Head, 770; Luvaas, *United States Army War College Guide to the Battle of Gettysburg,* 218.
5. Head, 563; Luvaas, *United States Army War College Guide to the Battle*

of Gettysburg, 218.

6. Stackpole, 4:87.

7. Boatner, 616; Head, 641–43.

8. Head, 642–43; Stanyan, 459.

9. Stanyan, 459.

10. George Henry Chandler to mother, June 14, 1863.

11. E. G. Adams to wife, June 18, 1863.

12. Hadley, 156; Long and Long, 369.

13. Long and Long, 371–72.

14. Templeton to home, June 27, 1863.

15. M. Sawyer, B. Sawyer, and T. Sawyer, 135–36.

16. J. L. Chase, undated (probably end of June 1863).

17. Marvel, *First,* 27.

18. Ibid.

19. Marvel, *First,* 27–28.

20. Haynes, 167; Desjardin, map 3. This excellent map set was produced with the help of Wayne Motts, Scott Hartwig, Harry Pfanz, Timothy Smith, Gerald Bennet, and Charles Fennell.

21. Haynes, 168–69.

22. Ibid., 172; Ayling, 33; Longver, Thomas Bignall entry, n.p.

23. Haynes, 172; Ayling, 58.

24. Luvaas, *United States Army War College Guide to the Battle of Gettysburg,* 121–22.

25. Haynes, 176.

26. Ibid., 177–78.

27. Ibid., 180–81; Luvaas, *United States Army War College Guide to the Battle of Gettysburg,* 122.

28. Haynes, 172.

29. Ibid., 170–84.

30. Cleveland, 37; Head, 447.

31. Head, 770; Musgrove, *Autobiography,* 87; Desjardin, map 3.

32. Musgrove, *Autobiography,* 88, Bartlett, 122; Luvaas, *United States Army War College Guide to the Battle of Gettysburg,* 125–26.

33. Bartlett, 124; Luvaas, *United States Army War College Guide to the Battle of Gettysburg,* 126–27; Musgrove, *Days and Events,* 88.

34. Head, 770; Bartlett, 125; Musgrove, *Days and Events,* 88; Ayling, 621, 640.

35. Head, 771; Bartlett, 125; Musgrove, *Days and Events,* 88; Ayling, 611, 626, 628, 635.

36. Musgrove, *Days and Events,* 94–95; Ayling, 616–19.

37. Bartlett, 672.

38. Ibid., 496–97.

39. Carroll, 102–3.

40. Cleveland, 37.

41. Bartlett, 143.

42. Aunt "C. T." to Lizzie, June 30, 1863, Christopher Hoyt Papers.

43. Livermore, *Days and Events,* 247.

44. Jordan, 91.

45. Luvaas, *United States Army War College Guide to the Battle of Antietam,* 116, 217.

46. Livermore, *Days and Events,* 250; Pfanz, 273.

47. Pfanz, 273; Ayling, 260.

48. Cleveland, 37; Child, 208.

49. Ayling, 213, 274; Longver, Allen and Trickey entries, n.p.

50. Ayling, 973–74.

51. Marvel, *First,* 28–29.

52. Ibid., 29.

53. Cheney to brother, July 22, 1863.

54. Boatner, 339; Cleveland, 37. Cleveland lists 745 men present for duty from the three infantry regiments. The number of New Hampshire men is around 950 when the three New Hampshire sharpshooter companies and the First New Hampshire Light Battery are factored in.

55. Haynes, 188–89.

56. M. Sawyer, B. Sawyer, and T. Sawyer, 139.

57. George Henry Chandler to mother, July 2, 1863; Long and Long, 378–79.

58. Long and Long, 379.

59. H. McFarland, 253–54.

60. Templeton to brother, August 23, 1863.

61. E. G. Adams to mother, July 11, 1863.

62. McCaslin, 159.

63. Savas, 8–9.

64. A. H. C. Jewett, 36–37.

65. Ibid., 37.

66. Hutchinson, 281.

67. Wilkinson, diary, July 10, 1863.

68. Copp, 229–30.

69. Ibid., 230.

70. Ibid., 230, 233–35.

71. Head, 488.

72. Chaitin, 120; Head, 488.

73. Towle, journal, July 11, 1863.

74. Putnam to father, July 10, 1863, Rauner.

75. Bedel, 527; Cleveland, 58.

76. Chaitin, 125.

77. Cleveland, 57–58; Copp, 239.

78. Towle, journal, July 18, 1863.

79. Eldredge, journal, July 17, 1863.

80. Towles, journal, July 18, 1863.

81. Eldredge, journal, July 17, 1863.

82. Copp, 239.

83. Eldredge, journal, July 18, 1863; McCaslin, 160; Copp, 240.

84. Little, 119.

85. Chaitin, 125.

86. Eldredge, journal, July 18, 1863.

87. Bedel, 527.

88. McCaslin, 160.

89. Bedel, 528; Ayling, 104.

90. Bedel, 528; Copp, 242; Boatner, 301.

91. Eldredge, journal, July 18, 1863.

92. Chaitin, 127; Copp, 243; Bedel, 528.

93. Eldredge, journal, July 18, 1863.

94. Cleveland, 58; Bedel, 528.

95. Little, 122; from a sketch of Lieutenant Henry W. Baker in Coffin, "History of Boseawen," *Granite Monthly,* 208.

96. Little, 121.

97. Baker, 208; Little, 123.

98. Head, 617; Baker; 208; Little, 124–25.

99. Little, 125–26; Chaitin, 127.

100. Worcester, 231–32; Little, 126.

101. Cleveland, 58–59.

102. Little, 171–72.

103. *Boston Globe,* "With Gould Shaw at His Burial," September 1, 1911.

104. Long and Long, 387–88; Chaitin, 128–29.

105. W. L. Foster, 5.

106. Foster, *Conscription in New Hampshire,* 9; *Portsmouth (New Hampshire) Chronicle,* July 17, 1863.

107. Foster, 11–17.

108. Winslow, 183–88.

109. Ibid., 186.

110. C. Hoyt to home, July 27, 1863.

111. Horace H. Adams to William, July 23, 1863.

112. Cleveland, 38–40.

113. Ibid., 98.

114. Ibid.

115. J. L. Chase to Sarah, July 28, 1863.

116. Griffin, 15.

117. Cleveland, 98.

118. Thompson, 171–85.

119. Horace H. Adams to friend William, July 11, 1863.

120. Thompson, 177.

121. Perkins, 116–19.

CHAPTER 7. "Our force was at work throwing grape and canister"

1. J. L. Chase to brother, August 1863.

2. Harris to father, August 13, 1863.

3. George Henry Chandler to mother, August 13, 1863.

4. Wilkinson, journal, August 17, 1863.

5. Towle, journal, August 18, 1863.

6. Wilkinson, journal, August 19, 1863.

7. Caleb Dodge to sister, August 7, 1863.
8. Cleveland, 85–86.
9. Lyford, 1:506–7.
10. Ibid.
11. *Belknap Gazette,* August 22, 1863.
12. Sauers, 115–27. John B. Bachelder was born in Gilmanton, New Hampshire, in 1825 and attended school locally and in Pembroke. In the 1850s, he taught many subjects, including penmanship, at a small military school in Pennsylvania and received a colonelcy in a Pennsylvania militia regiment. Bachelder returned to New Hampshire and married Elizabeth Barber Stevens of Nottingham, a niece of General Benjamin Butler, who had been born in nearby Deerfield. Bachelder made his living by teaching and painting in Manchester and traveled around New England painting landscapes. He, his wife, and their daughter are buried in Nottingham, New Hampshire, just off Stevens Hill Road.
13. *Belknap Gazette.*
14. Stackpole, 4:91.
15. Towle, journal, September 6, 1863.
16. Ibid.
17. Ibid.
18. Wilkinson, journal, September 7, 1863.
19. Towle, journal, September 7, 1863.
20. Eldredge, *Third New Hampshire,* 363–67; Towle, September 7, 1863; Ayling, 1224.
21. Savas, 14–16.
22. "Confederate Commerce Destroyer Alabama Sunk," *Boston Globe,* June 19, 1914.
23. George Henry Chandler to mother, September 13, 1863.
24. Cleveland, 101.
25. J. L. Chase to parents, October 1, 1863.
26. Head, 742.
27. Templeton to home, October 31, 1863.
28. Low to home, November 3, 1863.
29. Northam Colonist Historical Society, n.p.
30. J. L. Chase to brother, November 1, 1863.
31. Thomas, *History of Fremont,* 441.
32. *Boston Globe* scrapbook, November 13, 1863; Head, 743.
33. Paige, 82.
34. J. L. Chase to sister, November 14, 1863.
35. "When Longstreet Besieged Burnside in Knoxville," *Boston Globe,* November 17, 1863.
36. Paige, 83.
37. "When Longstreet Besieged Burnside in Knoxville," *Boston Globe,* November 17, 1863.
38. Head, 743–44.
39. Templeton to home, November 20, 1863.
40. Jones to uncle, November 23, 1863.
41. Templeton to home, November 22, 1863; Long and Long, 439.
42. Templeton to home, November 23, 1863.
43. Long and Long, 436–38.
44. Templeton to home, November 26, 1863.
45. M. Sawyer, B. Sawyer, and T. Sawyer, 189.
46. Templeton to home, November 28, 1863.
47. J. L. Chase to parents, December 6, 1863.
48. Boatner, 297.
49. J. L. Chase, letter, December 6, 1863.
50. Templeton to home, November 28, 1863.
51. Boatner, 297.
52. J. L. Chase to parents, December 1863.

53. Templeton to home, November 28, 1863.
54. Templeton to home, November 29, 1863.
55. J. L. Chase to parents, December 6, 1863.
56. Faust, 278.
57. E. Douglass to wife, February 15, 1864; Ayling, 474.
58. Boatner, 298; Ayling, 593; Head, 740.
59. Mason to mother, November 13, 1863.
60. Towle, journal, December 2, 1863; Copp, 297–98.
61. Copp, 297–98.
62. Cleveland, 87.
63. Marvel, *Alabama and the Kearsarge,* 207.

CHAPTER 8. "He did all in his power to rally his command"

1. Towle, journal, January 1, 1864.
2. Wilkinson, journal, January 12, 1864.
3. Horace H. Adams to brother, January 4, 1864.
4. Eldredge, journal, February 16, 1864.
5. Little, 208.
6. Nulty, 69–72.
7. Ferry, 8.
8. Little, 209; *Seventh New Hampshire Infantry.*
9. Little, 210–12.
10. *Manchester Mirror* correspondent, *Boston Journal,* March 4, 1864. Letters compiled by Thomas Hayes, http://extlab1.entnem.ufl.edu/olustee /letters/7thnh.html (January 19, 2001).
11. Little, 216.
12. "Battle of Olustee."
13. Ferry, 44–45.
14. Hawley.
15. J. C. Abbott.
16. Marvel, "Stampede at Olustee," 46.

17. *Manchester Mirror* correspondent, *Boston Journal,* March 4, 1864.
18. Ferry, 47.
19. Boatner, 608; Cleveland, 62; Marvel, *Andersonville,* 47.
20. Nulty, 207.
21. Cleveland, 62.
22. Eldredge, journal, April 29, 1864.
23. Worcester, 233–34; Ayling, 369; Longver, Lieutenant Charles H. Farley entry, n.p.
24. *Letters of James Flynn.*
25. Little, 35; *Letters of James Flynn.*
26. *List of the Union Soldiers Burial at Andersonville,* 28.
27. Little, 5.
28. Towle, journal, February 24, 1864.
29. Young to wife, February 22, 1864.
30. Northam Colonist Historical Society, n.p.
31. Ibid.
32. Hutchinson, *Roster,* 3:309.
33. Ibid.
34. Wilkinson, diary, February 21 to 22, 1864.
35. Hutchinson, *History,* 309–10.
36. Towle, journal, February 28, 1864.
37. Cleveland, 61; Eldredge, journal, February 28, 1864.
38. Towle, journal, March 4, 1864.
39. Head, 492–93.
40. *Rochester Courier,* March 25, 1864.
41. Ibid., March 18, 1864.
42. Ibid., March 25, 1864.
43. Horace H. Adams to brother, March 3, 1864.
44. Head, 875; Waite, *Claremont's,* 217–18.
45. Cleveland, 160.
46. Ibid., 160–61.
47. Ayling, 1089–92.
48. Young to wife, March 19, 1864.
49. Haynes, 212–13.
50. J. W. Adams, 10.
51. Haynes, 212–13.

52. *Rochester Courier,* April 1, 1864.
53. Boatner, 352–53; Faust, 320; Long and Long, 480.
54. Waite, *New Hampshire,* 156.
55. Haynes, 215–16.
56. J. W. Adams, 13–14.
57. Osborn, diary, April 16, 1864; Eldredge, *Third New Hampshire,* 848.
58. Boatner, 685.
59. Cleveland, 88.
60. Head, 648; Ayling, 432.
61. Boatner, 686; Ayling, 433.
62. Cleveland, 89.
63. J. F. Chandler to home, April 18, 1864.
64. Boatner, 42.
65. J. F. Chandler to home, April 18, 1864.
66. Northam Colonist Historical Society, n.p.
67. Towle, journal, April 18, 1864.
68. Ibid., April 21 and 30, 1864.
69. Cleveland, 63.
70. Eldredge, journal, April 29, 1864.
71. *Rochester Courier,* April 29, 1864.
72. Cleveland, 63; Robertson, 256–57.
73. Sergeant Paul Whipple to Sophia Dodge, April 23, 1864, Caleb Dodge Papers.
74. Ayling, 366.
75. J. L. Chase to brother, April 26, 1864.
76. Cheney to sister, April 28, 1864.
77. Ayling, 898.

CHAPTER 9. "Our regiment had the toughest time"

1. George Henry Chandler to brother, April 30, 1864.
2. George Henry Chandler to brother, May 3, 1864.
3. Ayling, 201. The Gillmore Medal, created by Major General Quincy Gillmore, was awarded for gallant and meritorious service in operations during the Charleston campaign.
4. S. J. Wentworth to mother, May 2, 1864.

5. Marvel, *First,* 32.
6. Long and Long, 492; "Orders Issued to Various Commanders to Move Forward," *Boston Globe,* May 3, 1864.
7. Marvel, *First,* 32.
8. Cogswell, 337–38; Boatner, 921.
9. Boatner, 924.
10. Hastings, 203.
11. Ibid.
12. Ayling, 977–78.
13. Templeton to parents, May 6, 1864.
14. Ibid.
15. Hadley, 170.
16. Ibid.
17. Cogswell, 348.
18. Head, 749; Cogswell, 353; Ayling, 564, 569.
19. Head, 595, 687–88; Jackman and Hadley, 218–25.
20. Marvel, *First,* 32–33.
21. Boatner, 925.
22. Marvel, *First,* 33.
23. Cram to parents, May 7, 1864.
24. Hastings, 202.
25. John W. Chase to sister, May 12, 1864. J. Lewis Chase letters.
26. Boatner, 786; Rhea, 76.
27. Hanson, diary, May 9, 1864.
28. Rhea, 110.
29. Marvel, *First,* 33.
30. Templeton to brother, May 10, 1864.
31. Hanson, diary, May 10, 1864.
32. Marvel, *First,* 33.
33. Ibid.; Ayling, 898.
34. Cogswell, 362.
35. Rhea, 183–84.
36. Hanson, diary, May 11, 1864.
37. Horace H. Adams to brother, May 11, 1864.
38. S J. Wentworth to mother, May 11, 1864.
39. Horace H. Adams to brother, May 11, 1864.
40. Thompson, 268; Robertson, *Back Door to Richmond,* 115.

41. Robertson, 257–59.
42. Boatner, 785–87.
43. Jackman and Hadley, 240–41; Ayling, 292, 302.
44. Cogswell, 364; Jackman and Hadley, 241–42; Lord, 371–72.
45. Cogswell, 364.
46. Lord, 372.
47. Hastings, 204.
48. Ibid., 374–75; Ayling, 465, 503, 508; Cleveland, 101.
49. George H. Chandler to brother, May 13, 1864.
50. George H. Chandler to mother, May 17, 1864; Ayling, 468.
51. Cogswell, 365, 511.
52. C. A. Stevens, 427; New Hampshire Antiquarian Society.
53. Cleveland, 101; Cogswell, 366; Jackman and Hadley, 262.
54. *Civil War Book of Lists,* 96; Rhea, 311–12.
55. Copp, 371–72.
56. Robertson, 147–48.
57. Copp, 374.
58. Osborn, diary, May 13, 1864.
59. Eldredge, journal, 146.
60. Copp, 377.
61. Ibid., 382.
62. Eldredge, journal, 146–49.
63. Little, 249–50.
64. Eldredge, journal, 158; Ayling, 107.
65. Hutchinson, *History,* 322.
66. Ibid., 323.
67. Hastings, 204.
68. Hutchinson, *History,* 322–23; Towle, journal, May 16, 1864.
69. Robertson, 184; Hutchinson, *History,* 324–25.
70. Hutchinson, *Roster,* 40.
71. Haynes, 225–26.
72. J. W. Adams, 17–19.
73. Haynes, 227; Head, 774; Cleveland, 63–64.
74. Head, 721, 791.
75. Cleveland, 63–64.
76. Faust, 228; Livermore, *Numbers and Losses,* 113.
77. Thompson, 321–22.
78. Ricker to mother, May 17, 1864; Ayling, 638.
79. Hastings, 209; Ayling, 596.
80. S. J. Wentworth to mother, May 21, 1864.
81. Ayling, 160, 197.
82. Hutchinson, *Roster,* 3:329–30.
83. Long and Long, 507.
84. Hastings, 211.
85. Ayling, 977.
86. Hastings, 211.
87. Young to wife, May 26, 1864.
88. Cram to parents, May 28, 1864.
89. Stearns, letter, May 31, 1864.
90. Ayling, 502.

CHAPTER 10. "My horror and indignation were great"

1. Faust, 149; Ayling, 512.
2. Faust, 150; Boatner, 163; Furgurson, 268.
3. Head, 722, 792.
4. Faust, 150.
5. Ibid.; Boatner, 163.
6. Head, 722.
7. Paige, 120.
8. Ibid., 121.
9. *Rochester Courier,* June 10, 1864.
10. Furgurson, 134–35.
11. Boatner, 163.
12. Furgurson, 261–76.
13. Boatner, 163; Faust, 150.
14. Child, 256–57.
15. Livermore, *Days and Events,* 351–52.
16. Ibid., 352.
17. Ibid.
18. Waite, *New Hampshire,* 288–89.
19. Marvel, *First,* 34.
20. Head, 722–23.
21. Goodale, diary, June 3, 1864.
22. Ayling, 530.

23. Head, 792.
24. Boatner, 164; Haynes, 235–36.
25. Haynes, 237–38.
26. Ibid., 237; Ayling, 52, 85: Longver, William H. Smith entry, n.p.
27. Haynes, 239.
28. Bartlett, 203.
29. Ibid., 207.
30. Ibid., 203.
31. Ibid., 204–5.
32. Musgrove, *Autobiography*, 144.
33. Head, 751–52.
34. Paige, 123.
35. Cogswell, 237.
36. Head, 752.
37. Musgrove, *Autobiography*, 142.
38. Furgurson, 279.
39. Howes to wife, June 6, 1864.
40. Northam Colonist Historical Society, n.p.
41. Conn, 229.
42. Thomas, *Civil War Happenings*, 9.
43. Head, 649; *Rochester Courier*, June 10, 1864; Stanyan, 459–60; Longver, George S. Cobbs entry, n.p.
44. Head, 649.
45. *Rochester Courier*, June 10, 1864.
46. Copp, 404.
47. Eldredge, journal, June 8, 1864; Copp, 405.
48. Ayling, 127.
49. Copp, 405.
50. Towle, journal, June 10, 1864.
51. Ibid., June 14, 1864.
52. Musgrove, *Autobiography*, 144.
53. Child, 255–56.
54. Cleveland, 64; Little, 267–71.
55. Eldredge, journal, 198.
56. Little, 268.
57. Eldredge, journal, 199.
58. Ibid., 202.
59. Cleveland, 64.
60. Ibid., 125–26; Thompson, 384–85.
61. Cleveland, 126.
62. Thompson, 402–3.
63. Catalfo, 322–23.
64. Ibid.
65. Cleveland, 126.
66. *Holyoke Transcript*, July 30, 1864.
67. Winslow, 243–44; *Boston Globe* scrapbook, "Battle of the Kearsarge and Alabama."
68. M. Hoyt.
69. Ibid.
70. Long and Long, 525–26.
71. Cleveland, 160; Long and Long, 527.
72. Head, 894–96.
73. S. Dodge to sister, July 2, 1864.
74. Hutchinson, *History*, 341.
75. Silber and Sievens, 48.
76. Horace H. Adams to brother, July 6, 1864.
77. Bixby, July 20, 1864.
78. Waite, *New Hampshire*, 311–14.
79. Musgrove, *Autobiography*, 145.
80. Long and Long, 535–36.
81. M. Sawyer, B. Sawyer, and T. Sawyer, 243.
82. J. L. Chase to brother, July 1864.
83. Long and Long, 535–36.
84. Hadley, 182–83.
85. Ibid., 184.
86. Waite, *New Hampshire*, 451; Longver, Walter Harriman entry, n.p.

CHAPTER 11. "They seemed to be all about us"

1. Squires, *Granite State*, 380; Long and Long, 541; Head, 869.
2. Boatner, 775–76; Horace H. Adams to brother, July 25, 1864.
3. Hastings, 239.
4. Cleveland, 107–9; Boatner, 647–49.
5. Cleveland, 109–10.
6. Ibid., 110–11; Kinard, 42–44.
7. Hanson, diary, July 28, 1864.
8. Ibid., July 29, 1864.
9. Boatner, 648; Cleveland, 111; Kinard, 48.
10. Hanson, diary, July 30, 1864.

11. Cleveland, 109–11; Jackman and Hadley, 312; Lord, 533; Cogswell, 115.
12. Kinard, 51; Jackman and Hadley, 315.
13. Head, 601; Ayling, 297.
14. Head, 696; Lord, 499, 512; Ayling, 508.
15. Cleveland, 107–8.
16. Lord, 496–97.
17. Ibid., 510–11.
18. Head, 696; Cleveland, 115.
19. Head, 752.
20. Childs, 11.
21. Ibid., 10; Ayling, 590, 595.
22. Cogswell, 419.
23. Hutchinson, *History,* 347–53.
24. Head, 527–28.
25. Boatner, 649; Cleveland, 112–15.
26. J. L. Chase to brother, August 1, 1864.
27. Louis Bell to wife, August 4, 1864, Tuck.
28. *Rochester Courier,* August 5, 1864.
29. Boatner, 558.
30. Perkins, 146.
31. Faust, 254; Long and Long, 551–52.
32. Perkins, 146.
33. Faust, 504; Boatner, 558.
34. Ayling, 1154.
35. Boatner, 230; Head, 499–500.
36. Boatner, 231; Little, 291.
37. Copp, 442.
38. Eldredge, journal, August 16, 1864.
39. Ibid.
40. Copp, 448.
41. Head, 501.
42. Copp, 460–61.
43. Eldredge, journal, August 16, 1864.
44. Cleveland, 65.
45. Ibid., 65; Little, 293.
46. Cleveland, 65; Waite, *New Hampshire,* 339.
47. Head, 528.
48. Ibid., 529, Ayling, 177.
49. Boatner, 231; Cleveland, 65; Head, 529.
50. Cleveland, 66.
51. Long and Long, 557.
52. Ayling, 554, 891.
53. C. Hoyt to brother and sister, August 25, 1864.
54. Ayling, 712.
55. Long and Long, 563.
56. *Farmers' Cabinet,* September 1, 1864; Ayling, 416.
57. *Farmers' Cabinet,* September 1, 1864; Conn, 387.
58. Long and Long, 565.
59. Hunt, 177–78.
60. Jenks to wife, September 10, 1864.
61. Head, 819.
62. Boatner, 937–39; Faust, 835; Head, 818.
63. Buffum, 204.
64. Ibid., 204–18; Cleveland, 141–42; Boatner, 937–38.
65. Livermore, *History of the Eighteenth New Hampshire,* 18; Cleveland, 149–50.
66. Ibid.
67. Head, 529, 602, 697, 726, 753, 799.
68. Ibid., 726.
69. Boatner, 588.
70. Cleveland, 128–29.
71. Boatner, 588–89; Head, 726–27; Thompson, 459.
72. Head, 798–99; Thompson, 460–62.
73. Thompson, 463; Head, 727; Cleveland, 128.
74. Ayling, 520.
75. Head, 727.
76. Ibid., 727–28; Thompson, 480–82; Cleveland, 129.
77. United States War Department, 42:254.
78. Cleveland, 66.
79. Towle, journal, September 29, 1864.
80. Boatner, 660; Cleveland, 104.
81. Cleveland, 104.

82. Cogswell, 429; Head, 753; Cleveland, 104.
83. Charles P. Chamberlin Papers.
84. Ayling, 602.

CHAPTER 12. "God only knows what is in store for me"

1. Jenks to wife, October 1, 1864.
2. R. D. Sawyer, 205.
3. Jacob F. Chandler, November 12, 1864.
4. Little, 308; Ayling, 362, 372.
5. Eldredge, *Third New Hampshire*, 541–46; Ayling, 152.
6. Head, 821–22.
7. Buffum, 275, 293.
8. Faust, 121; Boatner, 132.
9. Buffum, 274; Wert, 314.
10. Buffum, 278; Head, 822.
11. Head, 821–22.
12. Ibid., 823; Boatner, 134.
13. Head, 823.
14. Cleveland, 143; Longver, John Henry Jenks entry, n.p.; Ayling, 713.
15. Head, 825; Ayling, 723; *Portsmouth Journal*, August 4, 1866, 2.
16. Cleveland, 145.
17. Horace H. Adams to brother, September 4, 1864.
18. Cleveland, 129; Long and Long, 589.
19. Cleveland, 130.
20. Head, 728; Cleveland, 130.
21. Thompson, 501.
22. Cleveland, 130.
23. Ayling, 517; Longver, Horace H. Adams.
24. Cleveland, 130.
25. Ibid.
26. Stackpole, 4:95.
27. Ibid., 4:96.
28. Prescott.
29. Long and Long, 594.
30. Pillsbury, 2:548; Thomas, *Civil War Happenings*, 14–15.

31. Long and Long, 594; Pillsbury, 548; Cleveland, 44, 91.
32. Cleveland, 67.
33. Lonn, 128–30, 234.
34. Head, 406.
35. Ibid., 406; Hutchinson, *Roster*, 176–77.
36. Harriman, 399.
37. Eldredge, *Third New Hampshire*, 1033–34; Osborn, diary, December 27, 1864.
38. Lonn, 207.
39. Thompson, 518. Men in the Ninth New Hampshire managed to scrape together enough Confederate money that they could buy some potatoes, onions, and beef for their Christmas that was spent in a Confederate prison camp. See Lord, 600.
40. Long and Long, 614.
41. Ibid., 615; Boatner, 292–93.
42. S. Dodge to sister, December 27, 1864.

CHAPTER 13. "They looked like living skeletons"

1. Downs, diary, January 3, 1865.
2. Ibid., January 22, 1865.
3. Boatner, 293–94; Long and Long, 623; Faust, 273.
4. Eldredge, 578 and map opposite 592.
5. Boatner, 293.
6. Ibid., 293; Eldredge, *Third New Hampshire*, 601; Cleveland, 67–68.
7. Boatner, 293–94.
8. Gragg, 172.
9. Ibid., 195.
10. Cleveland, 68.
11. Gragg, 196.
12. Ibid., 197–98.
13. Cleveland, 68; Gragg, 264.
14. Gragg, 198.
15. Ibid., 204; Boatner, 294; Cleveland, 68.

16. Boatner, 294.
17. Towle, journal, January 16, 1865.
18. Eldredge, *Third New Hampshire*, 624; Cleveland, 294.
19. *List of the Union Soldiers Buried at Andersonville*, 28. For the numbers on New Hampshire prisoner-of-war casualties, see also Head, 406; Stackpole, 4:53; and Cleveland, 181.
20. *List of the Union Soldiers Buried at Andersonville*, 28.
21. Chadwick, 7.
22. Denney, 339–40.
23. *Portsmouth Journal*, March 25, 1865, 2; J. Foster, 51, 67.
24. See entries in Longver for Hall, Flint, and Whidden, n.p. Hall in the Third New Hampshire and Flint in the Fourth New Hampshire have incorrect information in Ayling's *Register*.
25. Livermore, *History of the Eighteenth New Hampshire*, 46–48.
26. Bartlett, 261–62.
27. Eldredge, *Third New Hampshire*, 630–31.
28. Ayling, 906.
29. Ibid., 912.
30. Gideon Gilman, February 26, 1865.
31. Edmund K. Brown to wife, February 25, 1865; Ayling, 293.
32. Long and Long, 644, 652, 654.
33. Towle, journal, March 3, 1865.
34. Cleveland, 47.
35. *Portsmouth Journal*, March 4, 1865.
36. Sobol, 965.
37. Long and Long, 647.
38. Boatner, 61.
39. Towle, journal, March 20, 1865.
40. Boatner, 298–99.
41. Ibid., 298–99; Ayling, 282.
42. Livermore, *Days and Events*, 52–53.
43. F. P. Harriman, 146–47.
44. Livermore, *Days and Events*, 53–54.
45. Chadwick, 11–13.

46. Boatner, 282–83; Head, 571.

CHAPTER 14. "Soldiers scarred by many a battle . . . wept aloud"

1. Boston newspaper scrapbook, April 3, 1865; Cleveland, 132. Cleveland states, "It seems unquestionable that the 13th New Hampshire was the first organized body of Union troops to enter Richmond after the evacuation."
2. Boatner, 22; Faust, 20.
3. Cleveland, 47–48.
4. Child, 300–303.
5. J. L. Chase to parents, April 10, 1865.
6. Copp, 505–6.
7. Sewell, 221–22; Sifakis, 274.
8. M. Sawyer, B. Sawyer, and T. Sawyer, 339–42.
9. Eldredge, journal, April 15, 1865.
10. Squires, *Granite State*, 392.
11. Eldredge, journal, April 15, 1865.
12. Lincoln's funeral observance broadside.
13. *"To Restore Our Glorious Union,"* 31–32.
14. Thomas, *Civil War Happenings*, 16–17.
15. Northam Colonist Historical Society, n.p.
16. Young to wife, April 20, 1865.
17. S. Dodge to sister, April 22, 1865.
18. Hadley, 210.
19. Cleveland, 146.
20. Cleveland, 146–47.
21. Copp, 513–21. Copp gives a memorable and vivid description of the Grand Review.
22. Young to wife, May 24, 1865.
23. Cogswell, 453–54.
24. Child, 308.

CHAPTER 15. Bringing the Boys Home

1. Cleveland, 178–79.

2. Ibid., 179.
3. Hastings, 290.
4. Head, 949–50; Ayling, 977, 982.
5. Ayling, 980.
6. Cogswell, 454–58.
7. Ibid., 455.
8. Ibid., 458.
9. Pillsbury, 552.
10. Cogswell, J. Lewis Chase entry in roster, n.p.; Snow, 139–45; *Exeter News-Letter,* January 25, 1884.
11. Cogswell, 238.
12. Ayling, 899; Marvel, *First,* 35.
13. Ayling, 898–99.
14. Lord, 559; Head, 699–700.
15. Waite, *New Hampshire,* 406; Lord, 740–43; Longver, Herbert B. Titus entry, n.p.
16. Lord, 676–77; Longver, George H. Chandler, n.p.
17. Cleveland, 153–54; Ayling, 808.
18. Cleveland, 133; Head, 729.
19. Bartlett, 315; Thompson, 609.
20. Waite, 427–28; Copp, 292.
21. Bartlett, 477.
22. Ibid., 480; Fisher, 6–7.
23. Bartlett, 509–10.
24. Waite, 483–86; Longver, Aaron F. Stevens entry, n.p.
25. M. Sawyer, B. Sawyer, and T. Sawyer, 365.
26. Ibid., 366.
27. Child, 113; Hunt, 169; Longver, Thomas L. Livermore entry, n.p.; Livermore, *Days and Events,* 73.
28. Ayling, 282; Cleveland, 48–49.
29. Child, 256–57; Cleveland, 49.
30. Hunt, 165–66; Child, 318.
31. Ayling, 235; Longver, Reuben E. Gilpatric entry, n.p.
32. Buffum, 360–61; Cleveland, 147–48.
33. Cleveland, 161; Head, 909.
34. Jackman and Hadley, 257–65,

367–68.
35. Jackman and Hadley, 370–73.
36. Jackman and Hadley, 375–76; Longver; Bixby.
37. Little, 428.
38. Head, 607–26; Waite, 348–52.
39. Eldredge, *Third New Hampshire,* 673; Cleveland, 69.
40. Head, 473–507.
41. Cleveland, 69; Head, 534–35.
42. Waite, *New Hampshire,* 223–25, 228–29; J. Foster, 21, 65; Longver, Thomas J. Whipple, George F. Towle, and George W. Towle entries, n.p.
43. Cleveland, 91–92; Head, 651.
44. Cleveland, 92.
45. Head, 466–67; Ayling, 98.
46. Waite, *New Hampshire,* 166–21; Haynes, 72 (roster).
47. Cleveland, 44–45; Haynes, 302.
48. Northam Colonist Historical Society, n.p.
49. Ayling, 986–98.
50. Cleveland, 181.
51. Ayling, 1088. Men from New Hampshire served in other regiments: 1,158 in Massachusetts regiments, 258 in Maine, 237 in Vermont, 79 in Rhode Island, and the remainder spread out across the rest of the Union.
52. Stackpole, 5:53.
53. *Civil War Book of Lists,* 22, 94; Cleveland, 181.
54. Ayling, 152, 282, 649, 790.
55. "New Hampshire Civil War Medal of Honor Heroes."
56. Pillsbury, 547; Squires, *Granite State,* 393–94.
57. Sobol, 962–65.
58. Smyth, 41.
59. Ibid., 42–43.
60. Carroll, 105.

BIBLIOGRAPHY

Abbreviations

Milne   Milne Special Collections and Archives Department, University of New Hamp-
            shire Library, Durham, N.H.
Rauner   Rauner Special Collections Library, Dartmouth College, Hanover, N.H.
Tuck   Tuck Library Special Collections, New Hampshire Historical Society (NHHS),

Unpublished Papers, Letters, Journals, and Manuscripts

Enoch George Adams Papers. MC56, Milne
Horace H. Adams Letters. Private collection
Albert T. Austin Papers. 1993, 011M2, Tuck
Louis Bell Papers. Manuscript. Box 3, Tuck, and MC165, Milne
Phineas P. Bixby Diary. 1913, 2, Tuck
Boston Globe newspaper scrapbooks. Fifty Years Ago Today Series. 6 vols. Author's per-
    sonal collection
Edmund K. Brown. Transcript. Edmund K. Brown Letters, Ossipee Historical Society,
    Ossipee, N.H.
George H. Caverly Papers. 1992, 039, Tuck
Charles P. Chamberlin Letters.1988, 38M, Tuck
Jacob F. Chandler Letters. Transcript. Private collection
John Henry Chandler Papers. 1987, 8, Tuck
J. Lewis Chase Letters. Private collection
Thomas C. Cheney Papers. MC173, Milne
John E. Cram Letters. Private collection
Caleb Dodge Papers. 1989, 055M, Tuck
Solomon Dodge Papers. 1972, 63M, Tuck
Elisha Douglass Papers. 1988, 14M, Tuck
Samuel E. Douglass Papers. 1988, 14M, Tuck
John R. Downs Papers. 1982, 34M, Tuck
Daniel Eldredge Journal. 1948, 3, Tuck
First New Hampshire Volunteers General Order Book. 1970, 15, Tuck

John Harrison Foye Papers. 1991, 044M, Tuck

Camp Constitution General Order #6. Order of the Day. May 19, 1861. Thayer Cummings Library and Archives, Strawbery Banke, Portsmouth, N.H.

Gideon Gilman Letters. Transcript. Ossipee Historical Society

Silas T. Goodale Papers. 1981, 22M, Tuck

Alvin A. Gove Papers. MS17, Milne

Griffin, Simon Goodell. *Civil War Recollections*. 001842, Rauner

Howard M. Hanson Papers. MS19, Milne

Myron W. Harris Letter. 1980, 29M, Tuck

David W. Hill Papers. MC157, Milne

James S. Howes Papers. 1982, 48M, Tuck

Christopher Hoyt Papers. 1961, 13M, Tuck

Israel Hoyt Letter. Private collection

Martin Hoyt. "Naval Engagement between U.S.S. Kearsarge and the Confederate Steamer Alabama. . . ." Langdon Public Library, Newington, New Hampshire

John Henry Jenks Papers. MC111, Milne

Charles E. Jewett Papers. MC 123, Milne

Jonathan Huntington Johnson Papers. Tuck

Martin Jones Papers. Alton Historical Society, Alton, N.H.

George Naylor Julian Papers. MC161, Milne

Harlan Pope Knight Journal. Nelson Historical Society, Nelson, N.H.

Thomas B. Leaver Papers. Tuck

Lincoln Funeral Observance. Broadside. Concord Public Library. Special Collections

Sarah Low Letters. Tuck

William P. Mason Papers. MS165, Milne

John McDaniel Papers. 1991, 055M, Tuck

James H. McFarland. Letter. Sullivan Historical Society, Sullivan, N.H.

Charles W. Moulton Diary and Papers. MS175, Milne

Ransom Merritt Neal Diary. New Hampshire State Library, Concord, N.H.

New Hampshire Antiquarian Society. "The Hopkinton Boys." Vertical files. New Hampshire Antiquarian Society

Alphonso Osborn Diary. Peterborough Historical Society, Peterborough, N.H.

Alonzo F. Pierce Papers. 1981, 116M, Tuck

Benjamin F. Prescott. "Copperhead" Broadside. private collection

Haldimand S. Putnam Papers. 1992, 041, Tuck, and Rauner

Oran E. Randall Letters. Chesterfield Historical Society, Chesterfield, N.H.

Ephraim W. Ricker Letters. Private collection

Samuel P. Sayles. Letter. Sullivan Historical Society, Sullivan, N.H.

Calvin Shedd Papers. Archives and Special Collections, Otto G. Richter Library. University of Miami. www.library.miami.edu/archives/shedd/62feb09.html and www.library.miami.edu/archives/shedd/62mar02.html (accessed January 18, 2001)

Jonathan Smith Letters. Peterborough Historical Society, Peterborough, N.H.

Albert B. Stearns Papers. 1983, 05M, Tuck

Aaron Stevens Papers. 1990, 170M, Tuck

Albert Taft Papers. Nelson Historical Society

Mason W. Tappan. Speech to Congress. "The Union as It Is and the Constitution as Our Fathers Made It." February 5, 1861, Rauner

Willard J. Templeton Letters. New Hampshire State Library, Concord, N.H.

Albion P. Thurston Papers. Ossipee Historical Society, Ossipee, N.H.

George F. Towle Journal and Papers. 1980, 15, Tuck

Joseph F. Wentworth Letters. Moultonborough Public Library

Stephen J. Wentworth Letters. Civil War Roundtable of New Hampshire Library, Epping, New Hampshire

Samuel Wilkinson Diary and Papers. MS166, Milne

Joseph Willey Letters. New Durham Public Library

Reull Willey Letters. New Durham Public Library

Andrew H. Young Letters. Dover Public Library

BOOKS, ARTICLES, AND INTERNET SOURCES

Abbott, Joseph C. "Report of Colonel Joseph C. Abbott Seventh New Hampshire Volunteer Infantry, on the Engagement at Olustee, Florida." http://battleofolustee.org/reports.abbott.html (accessed January 19, 2008).

Abbott, Stephen G. *The First Regiment New Hampshire Volunteers in the Great Rebellion.* Keene, N.H.: Sentinel, 1890.

Adams, John Wesley. *A Civil War Chaplain's Story.* Wells: Book Barn, 1995.

American Revolution Bicentennial Administration. *The Underground Railroad in New England.* Washington, D.C.: American Revolution Bicentennial Administration, 1975.

Ayling, Augustus D. *Revised Register of the Soldiers and Sailors of New Hampshire in the War of the Rebellion 1861–1866.* Concord, N.H.: Ira C. Evans, 1895.

Bailey, Ronald. *The Bloodiest Day: The Battle of Antietam.* Alexandria: Time-Life, 1984.

Bartlett, Asa W. *History of the Twelfth Regiment New Hampshire Volunteers in the War of the Rebellion.* Concord, N.H.: Ira C. Evans, 1897.

"Battle of Olustee: A Capsule History." http://battleofolustee.org/reports.abbott.html (accessed January 19, 2008).

Bean, W. G. *Stonewall's Man: Sandie Pendleton.* Chapel Hill, N.C., 1959.

Bedel, John. "Historical Sketch of the Third Regiment New Hampshire Volunteers." *Granite Monthly* 3 (1880).

Belknap Gazette. Letter from "Joe" to editor. August 22, 1863. http://belknapcountynh.accessgenealogy.com/custom3.html (accessed August 16, 2003).

Bemis, Charles A. *History of the Town of Marlborough, Cheshire County, New Hampshire.* Boston: George H. Ellis, 1881.

Boatner, Mark M., III. *The Civil War Dictionary.* New York: David McKay, 1988.

Brown, Craig. "Hopkinton in the Civil War." *Antiquarian Update* (Spring/Summer 1997).

Bryant, Elias. *The Diary of Elias A. Bryant of Francestown, New Hampshire.* Concord, N.H.: Rumford, n.d.

Buffum, F. H. *A Memorial of the Great Rebellion: Being a History of the Fourteenth Regiment New Hampshire Volunteers.* Boston: Franklin, 1882.

Carroll, Roger. *Lebanon 1761–1994: The Evolution of a Resilient New Hampshire City.* West Kennebunk, Maine: Phoenix, 1994.

Catalfo, Alfred, Jr. *The History of the Town of Rollinsford, New Hampshire 1623–1973.* Somersworth, N.H.: New Hampshire Printers, 1973.

Chadwick, Hale. *Sketch of "Ours" and Reminiscences.* Penacook: n.p., 1910.

Chaitin, Peter. *The Coastal War.* Alexandria: Time-Life, 1984.

Chase, Carolyn D. *Our Yesterdays: The Story of Brookfield, New Hampshire.* Brookfield, N.H.: Queen's Bay, 1999.

Child, William. *A History of the Fifth Regiment New Hampshire Volunteers in the American Civil War 1861–1865.* Bristol, N.H.: Musgrove, 1893.

Civil War Book of Lists, The. Conshohocken: Combined, 1993.

Cleveland, Mather. *New Hampshire Fights the Civil War.* New London: Self-published, 1969.

Coffin's History of Boscawen. "The N. H. Seventh at Fort Wagner." *Granite Monthly* 2 (1879).

Cogswell, Leander W. *A History of the Eleventh New Hampshire Regiment Volunteer Infantry in the Rebellion War 1861–1865.* Concord, N.H.: Ira C. Evans, 1897.

Conn, Granville P. *History of the New Hampshire Surgeons in the War of the Rebellion.* Concord: Ira C. Evans, 1906.

Copp, Elbridge J. *Reminiscences of the War of the Rebellion.* Nashua: Telegraph, 1911.

Davis, William C. *Battle at Bull Run.* Baton Rouge: Louisiana State University Press, 1977.

———. *Breckenridge: Statesman, Soldier, Symbol.* Baton Rouge: Louisiana State University Press, 1974.

Denney, Robert E. *Civil War Prisons and Escapes.* New York: Sterling, 1993.

Desjardin, Thomas A. *The Battlefield at Gettysburg.* Gettysburg: Friends of the National Park at Gettysburg, 1998.

Donovan, D. *History of the Town of Lyndeborough, New Hampshire 1735–1905.* Salem, Mass.: Higginson Book, 1997.

Dow, Joseph. *History of the Town of Hampton, New Hampshire.* Salem, N.H.: Salem, 1893.

Dunham, Chester Forest. *The Attitude of the Northern Clergy toward the South 1860–1865.* Toledo, Ohio: Gray, 1942.

Eldredge, Daniel. *The Third New Hampshire and All about It.* Boston: Stillings, 1893.

———. *How the Flag of the Eleventh New Hampshire Regiment Was Saved at Petersburg.* N.p.: 11th New Hampshire Flag Committee, New Hampshire State Library Archive, n.d.

Emerson, Edwin. *A History of the Nineteenth Century Year-by-Year.* 3 vols. New York: Collier and Son, 1901.

Faust, Patricia L., ed. *Historical Times Illustrated Encyclopedia of the Civil War.* New York: Harper and Row, 1986.

Ferry, Richard J. "The Battle of Olustee or Ocean Pond, February 20, 1864." *Blue and Gray Magazine* (February/March 1986): 8.

Fisher, Albert V. *History of Alton Part III from 1840.* Alton, N.H.: Self-published, 1973.

Foster, Joseph. *The Soldiers' Memorial.* Portsmouth, N.H.: Self-published, 1923.

Foster, William L. *The Conscription in New Hampshire.* Concord, N.H.: Fogg, Hadley, 1863.

Freeman, Douglas Southall. *Lee's Dispatches.* Baton Rouge: Louisiana State University Press, 1957.

Furgurson, Ernest B. *Not War but Murder: Cold Harbor 1864.* New York: Knopf, 2000.

Gara, Larry. *The Presidency of Franklin Pierce.* Lawrence: University Press of Kansas, 1991.

Gifford, William H. *Colebrook: A Place Up Back of New Hampshire.* Colebrook, N.H.: Sentinel, 1993.

Gilliss, J. M. *Astronomical and Meteorological Observations Made at the United States Naval Observatory during the Year 1863.* Washington, D.C.: GPO, 1865.

Gragg, Rod. *Confederate Goliath.* New York: HarperCollins, 1991.

Hadley, Amos. *The Life of Walter Harriman.* Boston: Houghton Mifflin, 1888.

Harriman, Frank P. "A Night in the Eighteenth New Hampshire Volunteers." *Granite Monthly* 5 (1882): 146–47.

Harriman, Walter. *The History of Warner, New Hampshire, for One Hundred and Forty-four Years from 1735 to 1879.* 1879. Repr., n.p., Somersworth, 1975.

Hastings, William H. *Letters from a Sharpshooter: The Civil War Letters of Private William B. Greene, Company G, Second United States Sharpshooters (Berdan's) Army of the Potomac 1861–1865.* Belleville, Wisc.: Historic, 1993.

Hawley, Joseph R. "Report of Colonel Joseph R. Hawley. Forty-eighth Connecticut Volunteer Infantry, Commanding Hawley's Brigade on the Engagement at Olustee, Florida." http://extlab.entnem.ufl.edu/olustee/reports/hawley_report.html (accessed January 19, 2001).

Haydon, F. Stansbury. *Military Ballooning during the Early Civil War.* Baltimore: Johns Hopkins University Press, 1941.

Hayes, John L. *A Reminiscence of the Free-Soil Movement in New Hampshire 1845.* Cambridge, Mass.: J. Wilson and Son, 1885.

Haynes, Martin A. *A History of the Second Regiment New Hampshire Volunteer Infantry in the War of the Rebellion.* Lakeport, N.H.: Republican Press Association, 1896.

Head, Natt. *Report of the Adjutant-General of the State of New Hampshire.* Concord, N.H.: George E. Jenks, State Printer, 1866.

Hennessy, John J. *Return to Bull Run: The Campaign and Battle of Second Manassas.* New York: Simon and Schuster, 1993.

Henney, Nella. *The Early Days of Eaton, New Hampshire.* Eaton, N.H.: Town of Eaton, 1967.

Hoehling, Mary. *Thaddeus Lowe: America's One-Man Air Corps.* Chicago: Kingston House, 1958.

Holden, Walter. *Stand Firm and Fire Low: The Civil War Writings of Colonel Edward E. Cross.* Hanover, N.H.: University Press of New England, 2003.

Hopkins, Doris. *Greenfield, New Hampshire: Story of a Town 1791–1976.* Milford, N.H.: Wallace, 1977.

Hunt, Roger D. *Colonels in Blue: Union Army Colonels of the Civil War, the New England States.* Atglen, Penn.: Schiffer, 2001.

Hutchinson, John G. *History of the Fourth Regiment New Hampshire Volunteers: What It Was, Where It Went, What It Accomplished.* Manchester, N.H.: John B. Clarke, 1913.

———. *Roster—Fourth Regiment New Hampshire Volunteers.* Manchester, N.H.: John B. Clarke, 1896.

Jackman, Lyman, and Amos Hadley. *History of the Sixth New Hampshire Regiment in the War for the Union.* Concord, N.H.: Republican Press Association, 1891.

Jewett, Albert H. C. *A Boy Goes to War.* Bloomington, Ill.: Grace Jewett Austin, 1944.

Jordan, David M. *Winfield Scott Hancock: A Soldier's Life.* Bloomington: Indiana University Press, 1996.

Keene History Committee. *Upper Ashuelot: A History of Keene, New Hampshire.* Keene, N.H.: City of Keene, 1968.

Keeter, Raleigh F. *The Battle's Breath of Hell and David C. Hayes.* Schenectady, N.Y.: Self-published, 1990.

Kent, Charles N. *History of the Seventeenth Regiment New Hampshire Volunteer Infantry 1862–1863.* Concord, N.H.: Rumford, 1898.

Kinard, Jeff. *The Battle of the Crater.* Abilene, Tex.: McWhiney Foundation, 1998.

Kingston Improvement and Historical Society. *History of Kingston, New Hampshire 1694–1969.* Kingston, N.H.: Kingston Improvement and Historical Society, n.d.

Klein, Philip S. *Franklin Pierce.* www.grolier.com (accessed February 2, 2002).

Lanzendorf, Scott. *New Hampshire Militia Officers: 1820–1850: Division, Brigade and Regimental Field and Staff Officers.* Bowie, Md.: Heritage, 1995.

The Letters of James Flynn 7th New Hampshire. http://battleofolustee.org/letters/flynn .html (accessed January 19, 2008).

List of the Union Soldier Burials at Andersonville, Copied from the Official Record in the Surgeon's Office at Andersonville, A. New York: Tribune, 1866.

Little, Henry F. W. *The Seventh Regiment New Hampshire Volunteers in the War of the Rebellion.* Concord, N.H.: Ira C. Evans, 1896.

Livermore, Thomas L. *Days and Events 1860–1866.* Boston: Houghton Mifflin, 1920.

———. *History of the Eighteenth New Hampshire Volunteers 1864–1865.* Boston: Fort Hill, 1904.

———. *Numbers and Losses in the Civil War in America 1861–1865.* Carlisle, Penn.: John Kallman, 1996.

Long, E. B., and Barbara Long. *The Civil War Day by Day: An Almanac 1861–1865.* New York: DaCapo, 1971.

Longver, Phyllis O. *New Hampshire Civil War Death and Burial Locations.* Bowie, Md.: Heritage, 2000.

Lonn, Ella. *Desertion during the Civil War.* Lincoln: University of Nebraska Press, 1998.

Lord, Edward O. *History of the Ninth Regiment New Hampshire Volunteers in the War of the Rebellion.* Concord, N.H.: Republican Press Association, 1895.

Luvaas, Jay. *The United States Army War College Guide to the Battle of Antietam: The Maryland Campaign of 1862.* New York: Harper and Row, 1987.

———. *The United States Army War College Guide to the Battle of Gettysburg.* New York: Harper and Row, 1986.

Luvaas, Jay, and Harold W. Nelson. *The United States Army War College Guide to the Battles of Chancellorsville and Fredericksburg.* New York: Harper and Row, 1988.

Lyford, James. *History of Concord, New Hampshire.* Concord, N.H.: Rumford, 1903.

Marvel, William. *The Alabama and the Kearsarge: The Sailor's Civil War.* Chapel Hill: University of North Carolina Press, 1996.

———. *The First New Hampshire Battery, 1861–1865.* South Conway, N.H.: Lost Cemetery, 1985.

———. "Stampede at Olustee." *Blue and Gray Magazine* February/March 1986.

"Mascomy" [pseud.]. "Letters from the Sixteenth Regiment." *People Journal* (1862 and 1863), Tuck.

McCaslin, Richard B. *Portraits of Conflict: A Photographic History of South Carolina in the Civil War*. Fayetteville: University of Arkansas Press, 1994.

McClintock, John N. *Granite Monthly* 1 (1880); 3 (1888). Periodical bound as *Granite Monthly New Hampshire Magazine*. Concord, N.H. John N. McClintock and the Republican Press Association, 1880–88.

———. *History of New Hampshire*. Boston: Russell, 1889.

McFarland, Henry. *Sixty Years in Concord and Elsewhere*. Concord, N.H.: McFarland, 1899.

McGregor, Charles. *History of the Fifteenth Regiment New Hampshire Volunteers 1862–1863*. Concord, N.H.: Ira C. Evans, 1900.

Merrill, Georgia Drew, ed. *History of Carroll County, New Hampshire*. Boston: Fergusson, 1889.

Miller, David. *The Illustrated Dictionary of Uniforms, Weapons, and Equipment of the Civil War*. London: Salamander, 2001.

Musgrove, Richard W. *Autobiography of Captain Richard W. Musgrove*. Concord, N.H.: Mary D. Musgrove, 1921.

———. *History of Bristol, New Hampshire*. Concord, N.H.: Musgrove, 1904.

Names and Records of All the Members Who Served in the First New Hampshire Battery of Light Artillery during the Late Rebellion from September 26, 1861 to June 15, 1865. Manchester, N.H.: Budget Job Reprint, 1891.

Nashua History Committee. *The Nashua Experience: History in the Making 1673–1978*. Canaan, N.H.: Phoenix, 1978.

Nason, Elias. *A Brief Record of Events in Exeter during the Year, 1861–1862*. Exeter, N.H.: Samuel Hall, 1862.

Nevins, Allan. *Ordeal of the Union: A House Dividing*. Vol. 2. New York: Scribner's Sons, 1947.

———. *The War for the Union: War Becomes Revolution 1862–1863*. New York: Scribner's Sons, 1960.

"New Hampshire Civil War Medal of Honor Heroes." http://www.homeofheroes .com/moh/states/nh.html (accessed January 19, 2001).

New Hampshire Historical Society. *Historical New Hampshire* (Spring/Summer 1999).

Noon, Jack. *Muster Days at Muster Field Farm: New Hampshire's Muster Day Tradition 1787–1850*. Bowie, Md.: Heritage, 1995.

Northam Colonist Historical Society. *Sarah Low: Dover's Civil War Nurse*. Dover, N.H.: Northam Colonist Historical Society, 1962.

Nulty, William H. *Confederate Florida*. Tuscaloosa: University of Alabama Press, 1990.

Obear, Lydia Anne. *New Ipswich in the War of the Rebellion: What Its Men and Women Did*. Worcester, Mass.: C. P. Goddard, 1898.

O'Reilly, Francis A. *Battle of Fredericksburg*. Fort Washington, Penn.: Eastern National, 2001.

———. *The Fredericksburg Campaign*. Baton Rouge: Louisiana State University Press, 2003.

Page, Elwin L. *Abraham Lincoln in New Hampshire.* Boston: Houghton Mifflin, 1929.

Paige, Charles C. *Story of the Experiences of Charles C. Paige in the Civil War of 1861–5.* Franklin, N.H.: Journal-Transcript, 1911.

Perkins, George Hamilton. *Letters of Geo. Hamilton Perkins, U.S.N.* Concord, N.H.: Rumford, 1901.

Pfanz, Harry W. *Gettysburg: The Second Day.* Chapel Hill: University of North Carolina Press, 1987.

Pierce, Franklin. Inaugural address. United States Inaugural Addresses. 1989. http://www.bartleby.com/124/pres29. html (accessed February 1, 2002).

Pillsbury, Hobart. *New Hampshire Resources, Attractions, and Its People: A History.* Vol. 2. New York: Lewis Historical, 1886.

Potter, C. E. *Military History of New Hampshire.* Baltimore: Genealogical, 1972.

Renda, Lex. *Running on the Record: Civil War Era Politics in New Hampshire.* Charlottesville: University Press of Virginia, 1997.

Rhea, Gordon C. *The Battles for Spotsylvania Court House and the Road to Yellow Tavern, May 7–12, 1864.* Baton Rouge: Louisiana State University Press, 1997.

Robertson, William Glenn. *Back Door to Richmond: The Bermuda Hundred Campaign April–June 1864.* Baton Rouge: Louisiana State University Press, 1987.

Robinson, H. L. *History of Pittsfield, New Hampshire in the War of the Rebellion.* Pittsfield, N.H.: Republican Press Association, 1893.

Roche, James. *The Life of John Boyle O'Reilly.* New York: Cassell, 1891.

Russell, Jon, ed. *The Complete Book of Inaugural Addresses of the Presidents of the United States from George Washington to George W. Bush, 1789 to 2001.* Lincoln, Neb., 2001.

Sauers, Richard Allen. "John B. Batchelder: Government Historian of the Battle of Gettysburg." *Gettysburg Magazine* (July 1990).

Savas, Theodore P., ed. *Charleston: Battles and Seacoast Operations in South Carolina.* Regimental Studies, vol. 5, no. 2. *Civil War Regiments.* Campbell, Calif.: Regimental Studies, 1996.

Sawyer, Merrill, Betty Sawyer, and Timothy Sawyer. *Letters from a Civil War Surgeon: The Letters of Dr. William Child of the Fifth New Hampshire Volunteers.* Solon, Maine: Polar Bear, 2001.

Sawyer, Roland D. *The History of Kensington, New Hampshire 1663–1945.* Farmington, Maine: Knowlton and McCreary, 1946.

Scales, John. *History of Dover, New Hampshire.* Manchester, N.H.: City Councils, 1923.

Sears, Stephen W. *Chancellorsville.* Boston: Houghton Mifflin, 1996.

———. *George B. McClellan: The Young Napoleon.* New York: Tichnor and Fields, 1988.

"Seventh New Hampshire Infantry." http://battleofolustee.org/7t_nh_inf.htm (accessed January 19, 2008).

Sewell, Richard H. *John P. Hale and the Politics of Abolition.* Cambridge: Harvard University Press, 1965.

Sifakis, Stewart. *Who Was Who in the Civil War.* New York: Facts on File, 1988.

Silber, Nina, and Mary Beth Sievens. *Yankee Correspondence: Civil War Letters between New England Soldiers and the Home Front.* Charlottesville: University Press of Virginia, 1996.

Smith, Carl. *Fredericksburg 1862.* Oxford, U.K.: Osprey Military, 1999.

Smith, George Winston. *Life in the North during the Civil War: A Source History.* Albuquerque: University of New Mexico, 1966.

Smyth, Frederick. *Message of His Excellency, Frederick Smyth, Governor of the State of New Hampshire, to the Two Branches of the Legislature, June Session, 1866.* Concord, N.H.: George E. Jenks, 1866.

Snow, Edward Rowe. *Storms and Shipwrecks of New England.* Boston: Yankee, 1943.

Sobol, Robert. *Biographical Dictionary of the Governors of the United States 1789–1978.* Westport, Conn.: Meckler, 1978.

Somers, A. N. *History of Lancaster, New Hampshire.* Concord, N.H.: Rumford, 1898.

Squires, James Duane. *The Contribution of New Hampshire Governors to the Civil War, 1861–1865.* Concord, N.H.: New Hampshire Civil War Centennial Commission, 1963.

———. *The Granite State of the United States: A History of New Hampshire from 1623 to the Present.* Vol. 1. vols. New York: American Historical, 1956.

Stackpole, Everett S. *History of New Hampshire.* 5 vols. New York: American Historical Society, 1916.

Stamp, Kenneth. *America in 1857: A Nation on the Brink.* New York: Oxford, 1990.

Stanyan, John M. *A History of the Eighth Regiment of New Hampshire Volunteers.* Concord: Ira C. Evans, 1892.

Stevens, C. A. *Berdan's United States Sharpshooters in the Army of the Potomac 1861–1865.* St. Paul, Minn.: Price-McGill, 1892.

Stilwell, Lewis D. *New Hampshire and the Civil War.* Concord, N.H.: New Hampshire Civil War Centennial Commission, 1963.

Stone, Melvin Ticknor. *Historic Sketch of the Town of Troy, New Hampshire and Her Inhabitants 1764–1897.* Bowie, Md.: Heritage, 1999.

Struthers, Parke Hardy, ed. *A History of Nelson, New Hampshire 1767–1967.* Keene, N.H.: Sentinel Printing, 1968.

Styple, William B., ed. *Writing and Fighting the Civil War: Soldier Correspondence to the New York Sunday Mercury.* Kearny, N.J.: Bell Grove, 2000.

Thomas, Matthew E. *Civil War Happenings in Rockingham County, New Hampshire, 1861–1865.* Fremont, N.H.: New England Historical Research Associates, 1993.

———. *History of Fremont, New Hampshire: Old Poplin, an Independent New England Republic 1764–1997.* Fremont, N.H.: Town of Fremont, 1998.

Thompson, S. Millett. *The Thirteenth Regiment of New Hampshire Volunteer Infantry in the War of the Rebellion 1861–1865.* Boston: Houghton Mifflin, 1888.

"To Restore Our Glorious Union": Portsmouth and the Civil War. Portsmouth, N.H.: Portsmouth Athenaeum, 2000.

Townsend, Luther Tracy. *History of the Sixteenth Regiment New Hampshire Volunteers.* Washington, D.C.: Norman T. Elliott, 1897.

Tucker, Philip Thomas. *Burnside's Bridge.* Mechanicsburg, Penn.: Stackpole, 2000.

United States Department of State. *Sixth Census or Enumeration of the Inhabitants of the United States as Corrected at the Department of State in 1840.* Washington, D.C.: State Department, 1841.

United States Government Printing Office. *Inaugural Addresses of the Presidents of the United States from George Washington, 1789 to Richard Milhous Nixon, 1973.* Washington, D.C.: GPO, 1974.

United States War Department. *The War of the Rebellion: A Compilation of the Official Records of the Union and Confederate Armies.* Series 1. Vol. 14. Washington, D.C.: 1880–1901. 130 vols.

Waite, Otis F. R. *Claremont's War History: April 1861–April 1865.* Concord, N.H.: McFarland and Jenks, 1868.

———. *New Hampshire in the Great Rebellion.* Claremont: Tracy, Chase, 1870.

Wallace, R. Stuart. *Conscience of a Northern Man: The Story of Amos Tuck.* Exeter, N.H.: Amos Tuck Society, 1998.

Wallace, William A. *The History of Canaan, New Hampshire.* Concord, N.H.: Rumford, 1910.

Wert, Jeffry D. *From Winchester to Cedar Creek: The Shenandoah Campaign of 1864.* Mechanicsburg, Penn.: Stackpole, 1997.

Winslow, Richard E., III. *Constructing Munitions of War: The Portsmouth Navy Yard Confronts the Confederacy 1861–1865.* Portsmouth: Peter E. Randall, 1995.

Winters, John D. *The Civil War in Louisiana:* Baton Rouge: Louisiana State University Press, 1963.

Worcester, Samuel T. *History of the Town of Hollis, New Hampshire.* Boston: Williams, 1879.

INDEX

ABOUT THE AUTHOR

DUANE E. SHAFFER is a cofounder of the Civil War Round Table of New Hampshire and past secretary of the New Hampshire Monuments and Memorials Commission. A library director in the state of New Hampshire for twenty years, he is currently head of collection development for the Sanibel Public Library in Sanibel, Florida.